REFLECTIVE PRACTICE IN GEOGRAPHY TEACHING

REFLECTIVE PRACTICE IN GEOGRAPHY TEACHING

EDITED BY
ASHLEY KENT

Paul Chapman Publishing

First published 2000

Paul Chapman Publishing Ltd
A SAGE Publications Company
6 Bonhill Street
London EC2A 4PU

SAGE Publications Inc
2455 Teller Road
Thousand Oaks, California 91320

SAGE Publications India Pvt Ltd
32, M-Block Market
Greater Kailash - I
New Delhi 110 048

British Library Cataloguing in Publication data

A catalogue record for this book is available from the British Library

ISBN 0 7619 6981 0
ISBN 0 7619 6982 9 (PBK)

Library of Congress catalog record available

Typeset by Anneset, Weston-super-Mare, Somerset
Printed in Great Britain by Cromwell Press, Trowbridge, Wiltshire

Contents

Preface

This book is unashamedly directed at the experienced teacher of geography in secondary (high) schools. It attempts to be novel, refreshing, informative and challenging, but above all to encourage reflection by experienced practitioners. It is intended to be both a constructive support and basis for continuing professional development (INSET) in and beyond school and a resource helping to develop critical and reflective qualities associated with a higher degree, particularly at MA level.

Its origins lie with the well established MA Geography in Education course at the Institute of Education University of London. That course's objectives could well be the objectives of this volume:

- to introduce and encourage a critical understanding of the literature and concepts of geography education;
- to help stimulate interest and enjoyment so that teachers continue with personal and professional development beyond the course (book);
- to contribute to the development of autonomous, reflectively thinking individuals, capable of taking a leading role in education, most often but not always in geography education;
- to provide professionally relevant knowledge, understanding, skills and values.

Traditionally that MA course has only been available to those able to attend regular sessions at the Institute. This volume widens access to the essence of that course to those living at a distance. For instance, it will support those students who engage in the Institute's MA in its distance learning mode (to be available from 2001 onwards).

The authors are 'friends' of the Institute in a wide sense. In other words they are either present or former members of staff and students or have some professional link with the Institute.

It does seem to this writer that given that the National Curriculum in England and Wales has settled down there is a real opportunity for teachers of geography to exercise professional judgement and autonomy and boost the quality and popularity of geography taught in schools. It is the modest hope of this editor that this book will help to achieve those objectives. Much is contextualised within the English system but it is felt that geography educators in the English-speaking world will be able to benefit from themes of wide-ranging currency and applicability.

Dr Ashley Kent
London, April
2000

The contributors

David Balderstone is a Lecturer in Geography Education and PGCE Subject Leader for Geography at the Institute of Education, University of London. He taught geography for 13 years at a large comprehensive school in Bedfordshire, where he was also a Senior Teacher and Head of Geography. He is a co-author of *Learning to Teach Geography in the Secondary School* and a number of school geography textbooks. His research interests are in pedagogy in geography education, assessment and raising student achievement in geography.

Nicola Bright teaches at Putney High School for Girls. She has taught for nine years in a variety of schools in and around London. She completed her MA in Geography Education at the Institute of Education, University of London in 1999. The title of her dissertation was 'The implementation of a curricular development: thinking skills in geography'. Having also been involved in a SCITT scheme, she is interested in the way that new experiences affect professional development.

Shaun Brown is Head of Geography at Forest School, Walthamstow, having previously taught at Elliott School, Putney and The Judd School, Tonbridge. Presently, he is completing an MA in Geography Education at the Institute of Education, University of London, and has taken a particular interest in the divide between geography in schools and universities.

Charlie Carpenter has taught for a number of years in two London comprehensive schools. A former Head of Year and subsequently Head of Humanities, he is now an Advanced Skills Teacher. His particular interest lies in developing the use of ICT in the geography curriculum. He is currently working with a group of schools in Australia on the development of a virtual classroom link. He is also at present conducting a research programme into underachievement among boys.

Joanne Clark is a secondary level geography teacher specialising in A-level and concentrating on sixth form issues. In 1999 she successfully completed her MA in Geography Education at the Institute of Education, University of London. Her dissertation title was 'A study to review progress in the renaissance of geographical education in the USA. She is now working in the USA on geography education, textbook and resource development.

Rod Gerber is Professor and Dean of the Faculty of Education, Health and Professional Studies at the University of New England, Armidale, Australia. Rod is currently Chair of the IGU's Commission on Geographical Education and a member of the Australian National Committee for Geography. He is co-editor of the journal *International Research in Geographical and Environmental Education.* Rod has written widely in the field of geographical education both for teachers and school students. He has lectured at a wide range of international conferences on geographical education.

Andrew S. Goudie is Professor at the School of Geography, University of Oxford. Andrew is a geomorphologist who has worked extensively in deserts, and has interests in climatic change, human impact, weathering and aeolian landforms.

Norman Graves has taught in grammar, technical and comprehensive schools. He was also Lecturer in Education at the University of Liverpool; Senior Lecturer, Reader and Professor at the Institute of Education, University of London; chairman of the IGU Commission on Geographical Education 1972–80; and President of the Geographical Association 1978–79. He is the author of such books as *Geography in Education, Curriculum Planning in Geography* and *The Education Crisis.* He was editor and contributor to the UNESCO *Geography Source Book on Geography Teaching* and *New Movements in the Teaching of Geography.*

Alan Hudson is a Research Fellow in International Political Economy at the Open University where he is looking at issues of global governance, specifically the role of non-governmental organisations and international institutions. Alan is a political economist who worked at the Department of Geography at the University of Cambridge for four years before moving to the Open University in 2000. He has published articles about globalisation, sovereignty, borders and offshore finance in journals such as the *Review of International Political Economy, Political Geography* and *Geopolitics.*

Peter Jackson is Professor of Human Geography at the Department of Geography, University of Sheffield. His research focuses on the relationship between consumption and identity and on the geographies of race and racism. Recent projects include an ESRC-funded study of the production, content and readership of men's lifestyle magazines and a study of commodity culture and South Asian transnationality. His publications include *Maps of Meaning* (Routledge, 1992), *Constructions of Race, Place and Nation* (UCL Press, 1993) and *Shopping, Place and Identity* (Routledge, 1998).

Stephanie Jackson is currently a Research Officer for two European projects and the Earth Science Technology Centre (ESTC) tutor at the Institute of Education, University of London. Both research projects involve innovative uses of ICT in geography classrooms across Europe. She is interested in ICT and geography education, and is currently working on a PhD within this area of research. Her particular interest is the use of the Internet for on-line cooperative learning.

Ashley Kent is Reader in Education and Head of Geography and the Education, Environment and Economy Group at the Institute of Education, University of London. Having taught in secondary schools he became Associate Director of the Geography 16–19 Project. He is a long-standing member of the Geographical Association and was President in 1996–97. He is an active member of the International Geographical Union Commission on Geography Education. He has written widely on geographical education.

Sheila King is Director of Training Partnerships at the Institute of Education, University of London since 1992. Prior to this she taught geography in a variety of schools and was head of humanities in one of the largest secondary schools in west London. Sheila is also a practising OFSTED inspector. She has particular interests in the use of ICT in geography teaching, in classroom observation and in thinking skills. Sheila has written at an academic level and also school textbooks *BBC Bitesize* and *Geography to 14*.

David Lambert is a Reader in Education at the Institute of Education, University of London. David was a comprehensive school teacher for twelve years before embarking on his present career at the Institute of Education. He is involved in initial teacher education and training and currently leads the Geography in Education Masters degree course. He has written widely on curriculum, pedagogy and assessment in geography education. He has co-authored, with David Balderstone, *Learning to Teach Geography* and with David Lines, *Understanding Assessment.*

Ian Langrish is Head of Geography at Tiffin School for Boys, Kingston upon Thames. Ian is currently in his seventeenth year of secondary teaching, and has led his departmental team for the last thirteen years. He has been regularly involved in the Geography PGCE in partnership with the Institute of Education, University of London. Particular professional interest areas include developing able pupils to achieve their maximum potential; A-level fieldwork; urban planning and change in urban environments; and the rural–urban fringe.

David Leat is Senior Lecturer in Education and PGCE Geography Tutor at the Department of Education, University of Newcastle-upon-Tyne. David is coordinator of the Thinking Through Geography Group, an alliance of geography teachers and HE staff involved in research, curriculum development and initial and in-service training. He is also a part of the Thinking Skills Research Group at Newcastle University which works in partnership with local primary and secondary schools in researching and implementing Teaching Thinking across the curriculum.

Adrian McDonald is Professor at the School of Geography, University of Leeds. Adrian was the first graduate in Ecological Science from the University of Edinburgh in 1969. He thereafter worked on risk management and moved into Geography in the early 1970s. Adrian McDonald's main interests are in environmental management with a particular interest in the management of natural resources – water, forests, energy and wild-lands – and has been a consultant in both the UK and abroad to a variety of agencies, companies and governments.

Paul Machon is Senior Director of Studies at Wyggeston and Queen Elizabeth I College, Leicester. Paul has been teaching for some thirty years, in a number of subject areas but particularly in Geography, Politics and Sociology. The boundaries and common ground between disciplines is of interest to him. Research interests include the Holocaust, housing policy and post-16 educational issues. He has written in these and other areas, including the place of citizenship in the social sciences, including geography.

Julian Mayes is joint convener of the Environment, Resources and Geographical Studies degree programmes at the University of Surrey Roehampton in south-west London (formerly Roehampton Institute London). His research interests include the geography of recent and future climatic change in Europe – particularly within the British Isles and the Maltese Islands and the implications of these changes for the study of geography. He is co-editor of a 1997 Routledge text, *Regional Climates of the British Isles*.

John Morgan is a Lecturer in Geography Education at the Institute of Education, University of London and taught geography and politics in schools and colleges in London from 1988 to 1998. He completed his PhD on 'Postmodernism and School Geography' in 1998. He is currently working on a Leverhulme Trust funded project on developments in geography and education. His research interests include social and cultural geography, critical pedagogy, the geographies of young people and the politics of the curriculum.

Brendan Murphy is a teacher of Geography and Coordinator for Personal and Social Education at the Chislehurst and Sidcup Grammar School, Sidcup, Kent. Brendan has taught geography and history at Chislehurst and Sidcup Grammar School for the past ten years, having previously taught geography at schools in Liverpool and Lancashire. He has recently researched the values underlying geography textbooks at GCSE for his MA at the Institute of Education, University of London.

Eleanor Rawling is Professional Subject Officer (Geography) with the Qualifications and Curriculum Authority (QCA) London. During 1999–2000, she was also a Leverhulme Research Fellow and Honorary Research Associate at the University of Oxford, examining the politics and practicalities of recent curriculum change in geography. Eleanor was President of the Geographical Association in 1991–92 and chair of the Council of British Geography in 1993–95, and was awarded an MBE for services to geographical education in 1995.

Margaret Roberts is a Senior Lecturer in the Department of Educational Studies at the University of Sheffield. She is responsible for coordinating the geography PGCE course, and through her PGCE work with students and mentors she is involved with classroom practice. Her research interests include the interpretation of the geography National Curriculum in schools, 'geographical enquiry' and language and learning.

Maggie Smith is Senior Lecturer in Education at the University of the West of England where she teaches on the PGCE course. Her current research interests include environmental education at primary and secondary level, and the primary–secondary and secondary–tertiary interfaces in education. She has contributed to a number of publications including, most recently, the GA Guidance Series and support material for beginning and experienced teachers in the humanities.

Derek Spooner is Senior Lecturer in the Department of Geography at the University of Hull, where he was formerly Head of Department. He has been Visiting Professor at the Universities of Maryland and West Virginia. For six years he was Editor of *Geography*, the journal of the Geographical Association, of which he is President in the year 2000–1. He is also the author of numerous publications on the geographies of mining, energy and regional economic development.

Joseph P. Stoltman is Professor of Geography at Western Michigan University in Kalamazoo. He has served as Chair and as a full member of the Commission on Geographical Education of the International Geographical Union (IGU), and is president elect of the Social Sciences Education Consortium (SSEC). He has received the George J. Miller Award for Outstanding Service from the National Council for Geographic Education (NCGE). He is a graduate of the Central Washington University, the University of Chicago and the University of Georgia.

Helen Walkington is a Lecturer in Geography Education at the University of Reading. Prior to this she taught Geography in a rural secondary school in Zimbabwe with Voluntary Service Overseas (VSO). Her current research interest concerns the teaching strategies which contribute to participatory, collaborative learning. This interest has been focused more recently upon Geography Education and Global Citizenship Education practice in primary schools and collaborative fieldwork in higher education.

Deryn M. Watson is Professor of Information Technologies and Education, School of Education, King's College, University of London. After teaching Geography in London schools, Deryn was involved during the 1980s in the research and development of computer-assisted learning materials in the humanities and languages. Her current research and lecturing interests include issues which influence the take-up and use of IT in schools, institutional policies and practices for IT, and teachers' responses to innovation and change through IT.

Geraldene Wharton is a Lecturer in Physical Geography and Environmental Science at Queen Mary, University of London. Her research interests are in flood estimation and river management. She has served as Secretary of the Geography Section of the British Association for the Advancement of Science (1994–98) and represented the BA on the Council of British Geography. In 1999 she was elected onto the Council of the RGS (with IBG) as Honorary Secretary, Education Division

Michael Williams is Emeritus Professor and formerly Dean of the Faculty of Education and Health Studies and Head of the Department of Education at the University of Wales Swansea. He has directed research and evaluation projects in geographical education, in-service teacher training and lifelong learning. His most recent edited books are *Geographical and Environmental Education: The Role of Research* (Cassell, 1996) and, with Daniella Tilbury, *Teaching and Learning Geography* (Routledge, 1997). He is Visiting Professorial Fellow at the Institute of Education.

Peter Wood is Professor and Head of the Department of Geography, University College London. Peter is a specialist on contemporary business service change and its implications for the restructuring of British and European regions. As well as a wide range of teaching experience in human and economic geography, he has been Schools Admissions Tutor in Geography. He has contributed to textbooks on economic geography and London, and written on curriculum innovation in higher education.

Part One

Progress in Geography: Changing Viewpoints

Geography teachers are faced by a real challenge in trying to keep up to date with an ever burgeoning, and some would say confusing, research frontier in academic geography. As academics become ever more specialised in the face of the research and publishing imperative, so teachers are in danger of becoming ever more distant from the latest philosophical perspectives and specific research findings.

Eight chapters can only give a flavour of some of the latest academic developments and inevitably give a partial picture. However, by inviting two eminent geographers (Goudie and Jackson) to write an overview of their particular broad branches of the subject, there is an attempt at balance between the general and the specific. Authors in this section are a mixture of more and less experienced academics. They were asked to communicate their own area of research interest and expertise and were not expected to pursue the geography education implications of their work.

Chapter 1

Trends in physical geography

Andrew S. Goudie

INTRODUCTION

Many of my generation, and those on either side of it, were brought up on a limited range of physical geography textbooks. Of these probably the most used text in Britain was F.J. Monkhouse's *The Principles of Physical Geography*. Its first edition appeared in 1954 and thereafter it was used intensively for the next quarter of a century, with an eighth edition appearing in 1975. To gain an idea of just how substantially physical geography has changed in the last few decades, it is instructive to revisit Monkhouse, to see how he approached his subject and to analyse those issues he felt were important and those which were largely ignored. Given that his brief was 'somewhat utilitarian', namely 'to cover those aspects of geography which fall into the syllabus laid down by various examining bodies', this analysis will also give a more general view of the practice of physical geography at that time.

First of all, in spite of its title, there is really no discussion of the principles that underlie physical geography and of what physical geography aims to do. Secondly, there is very little concern with theory, very little attempt to relate ideas to individuals, very little airing of controversy and no concern with intellectual constructs like models. Thirdly, it is very strong on description and on classification. Fourthly, with the exception of some of its discussion of climate, there is no concern with systems or with such phenomena as biogeochemical or nutrient cycles. Fifthly, the work is largely unconcerned with ecological approaches and so there is very little attempt at integrating the different components of physical geography. Sixthly, the work is almost entirely qualitative, and it contains not one scientific formula. Seventhly, it is extraordinarily weak (to the extent of ignoring them altogether) on hydrological and drainage basin processes. Eighthly, it was written a decade before the development of plate tectonics as a unifying paradigm for the earth sciences, and so it lacks this approach. Ninethly, there is remarkably little on environmental change, whether natural (for example, glacial and interglacial cycles, neoglaciations, ENSO events) or human induced. Tenthly, humans rear their heads but seldom, and so there is scant concern with hazards, resources, environmental management or the application of physical geography to solving 'real-world' problems.

The modern genre of physical geography texts is extraordinarily different from Monkhouse, not least because most of them seek to insert the word 'environment' squarely into their titles, probably in part in the reasonable expectation that this may help to inflate the size of royalty cheques, but also because they have a direct interest in environmental links with humans (see, for example, H. de Blij and P.O. Muller, 1995, *Physical Geography of the Global Environment*; C. Park, 1997, *The Environment: Principles and Applications* and D. Briggs, P. Smithson, K. Addison and K. Atkinson, 1997, *Fundamentals of the Physical Environment*). Let us consider some of the main characteristics of Physical Geography as it is practised in the last decade of the past millennium.

THE NEW TRENDS

An attempt to review trends in physical geography was made in the mid-1980s by Gregory (1985). He identified five main themes as developing between 1950 and 1970: quantification; chronological studies with an emphasis on the Quaternary; process studies; studies that recognised the importance of human activities; and the systems approach. For the period from 1970 to 1980 he identified two further trends: a concern with time, incorporating such issues as thresholds, complex responses and the like; and an increasing tendency towards the application of physical geographical research to solving environmental problems. Additionally, for the 1980s he drew attention to the burgeoning role of remote sensing and information technology.

In this chapter I select a series of themes for particular attention: the human impact, natural environmental change, the development of new techniques, the application of physical geography and the integration of its various elements and their linkage to social forces. That is not to imply, however, that some of the other themes identified by Gregory have not continued to be highly important and influential. So, for example, most physical geographers employ quantitative methods, develop models, think in a systems framework and undertake detailed studies of processes. Indeed, in the last few years there have been a remarkably large number of fundamental studies of, for example, hillslope hydrology (Anderson and Brooks, 1996) aeolian processes (Cooke et al., 1993), and solute movements (Trudgill, 1995).

THE HUMAN IMPACT

Earlier generations of physical geographers often sought to avoid areas that were tainted with human activity and to seek natural and undisturbed areas in which to undertake their research. Since that time, there has been a growing awareness that such pristine areas are increasingly atypical of the world as a whole, and that the impacts that humans are having on the earth's surface deserve study in their own right. Indeed, there are those who feel that as the subject that straddles the human–environment ecotone, geography should actively be concerned with the human impact, its history and its management. Many of the great issues facing the world today are susceptible to geographical treatment, including acid deposition (Battarbee et al., 1988), forest decline (Innes, 1992), biodiversity loss, desertification (Thomas and Middleton, 1994), deforestation (Williams, 1989), wetland loss (Maltby, 1986), salinity problems (Goudie and Viles, 1997) and global climate change. Equally, there is a growing interest in environmental history (Simmons, 1996; Grove, 1997) and in appropriate means for managing environmental change (see, for example, Unwin and Owen, 1997), including sea-level rise and beach erosion (Bird, 1996). Some of the most powerful studies in physical geography *sensu lato* are those that look at long-term landscape change in the context of human history, as, for example, the studies of heavily impacted landscapes in Northern Nigeria (Mortimore, 1989) and East Africa (Tiffen et al., 1994), and those studies that seek to establish the relative importance of human actions and natural processes in causing environmental changes such as gully initiation (Wells, 1993).

NATURAL ENVIRONMENTAL CHANGE

It is remarkable, but partly uncoincidental, that at the same time that scientists have been concerned with anthropogenic impacts on the environment, they have also become increasingly aware of the frequency, magnitude and consequences of natural environmental changes at a whole range of timescales from relatively short-lived events like ENSO phenomena, to events at the decade and century scales (e.g. Grove, 1988 on the Little Ice Age), to the major fluctuations of the Holocene (Roberts, 1998) and the Younger Dryas (Anderson, 1997), to the cyclic events of the Pleistocene and the longer-term causes of the Cainozoic climate decline. Much of the reason for this concern arises from the development in the last four decades of new technologies for dating and for environmental reconstruction, including the coring of the ocean floors, lakes and ice sheets (Lowe and Walker, 1997; Goudie and Stokes, in press). We now know that all environments, including the humid tropics (Thomas, 1994) and the dead hearts of deserts have been affected by climatic change, and those climatic changes can be of very abrupt onset. It is no longer possible to see most components of the environment as being in equilibrium with some supposedly stable present-day climate. The likelihood is otherwise.

Equally, since the 1960s global tectonics have become a central concern in the earth sciences and from that has arisen a whole series of major research themes that include not only the development and global pattern of such phenomena as earthquakes, volcanoes and mountain ranges (Summerfield, 1991) but also the development of more meso-scale features such as erosion surfaces, escarpments on passive margins, atolls and deltas. It is no longer possible to explain the development of the British landscape without reference to the opening of the North Atlantic, the igneous activity of the early Tertiary, the rifting and subsidence of the North Sea and its margins and even the collision of the African and Eurasian plates. The study of neotectonics is fertile ground for understanding many geomorphological phenomena. However, global tectonics are also fundamental to understanding long-term climatic evolution, particularly because of the uplift of the Himalayas, Tibetan Plateau and the Western Cordillera of the Americas (Ruddiman, 1997), and major patterns in biogeography (Whitmore, 1987).

TECHNIQUES

Physical geographers now have a technical armoury that gives them powers they never had a few decades ago.

1. *Surveying*. Surveying has been revolutionised by new ground survey methods including Differential (Kinematic) Global Positioning Systems based on satellite

signals, and by electronic distance measurers and total stations. At a very local scale surfaces can be surveyed using digital cameras, videography and laser techniques.

2. *Mapping*. The availability of remote sensing images from satellites has revolutionised our ability to map and monitor a very wide range of phenomena at increasingly better resolution over huge areas of the earth and other planets.
3. *Spatial data handling*. One of the most trumpeted and adopted of the new technologies is the use of Geographical Information Systems (GIS) for handling and overlaying spatial data-sets.
4. *Computational power*. Increasing computational power enables the analysis of enormous data-sets and the running of complex models, including Global Circulation Models (GCMs).
5. *Environmental monitoring*. Data-loggers enable the collection and storage of large amounts of environmental data from a range of instruments (e.g. anemometers, sand traps, flow gauges, temperature and humidity sensors). These have, for example, transformed our knowledge of sand and wind flow over sand dunes and our knowledge of weathering cycles in the field.
6. *Environmental reconstruction*. Our ability to establish long-term environmental history has transformed studies of the Quaternary era. Coring of lakes, swamps, peats, ice caps and the oceans is being increasingly productive for identifying changes in climate, the human impact and atmospheric chemistry, scanning electron microscopy has enabled a better characterisation of sediment origins, and a whole range of biological and chemical techniques (e.g. the study of diatoms, ostacodes and isotopic signatures) has provided fundamental information on environmental change.
7. *Dating technology*. The battery of dating techniques that has developed for dating environmental changes has enabled long, high resolution chronologies to be established, enabling interregional correlations. Some of the new techniques (e.g. optical dating) enable new materials (e.g. dune sand) to be dated.
8. *High precision chemical, physical and mineralogical instrumentation*. Physical geographers have benefited from the availability of increasingly automated analytical techniques for accurate analysis of trace amounts of material (e.g. ion chromatography, laser granulometry, mineral magnetics, impulse excitation testing of rock elasticity, X-ray flourescence, atomic absorption spectrophotometry, etc.).

While some might argue that it is dangerous to be technique led, the fact remains that without many of the techniques listed above, many of the most exciting aspects of physical geography and environmental science could not have emerged.

THE APPLICATION AND UTILITY OF PHYSICAL GEOGRAPHY

Physical geography has great potential for application to solving specific environmental issues and for contributing to sustainable environmental management. Considerable progress has been made in this endeavour over the last two decades, especially in geomorphology (Jones, 1980; Cooke and Doornkamp, 1992).

A consideration of the role of the applied geomorphologist, just one type of applied physical geographer, demonstrates some of the skills we possess. Applied geomorphologists undertake the following sorts of tasks (Goudie, 1993):

1. mapping landforms, and describing what they are like;
2. using landforms as indicators of other distributions (such as soils);
3. identifying change through (a) monitoring and (b) historical analysis;
4. analysing the causes of change and hazards;
5. predicting what could happen when humans intervene in systems accidentally or deliberately;
6. deciding what to do to prevent or control the undesirable consequences of such changes.

In the first instance, the applied geomorphologist will attempt to map the distribution of phenomena that have been identified. Both the identification and the mapping are skills, and they depend heavily on having 'an eye for country'. So, for example, if a road is to be built through a desert area, a map of landforms will help to determine the best alignment (e.g. the avoidance of shifting sand dunes, areas prone to flash floods and locations where salt weathering may be extremely detrimental to a road's foundations). It will also help in determining suitable materials for the construction of the road – for certain landforms, especially depositional ones, may be composed of materials with particularly desirable or undesirable properties. Thus landforms can both be resources and hazards. Indeed, the general description of a particular terrain type may provide the engineer with some important information. For example, an alluvial fan is a depositional surface across which streams are prone to wander, where there may be alternations of cutting and filling, and where the cause of deposition is often a mudflow charged with coarse debris and possessing considerable transportational power when confronted with a human-made structure. All these characteristics – instability, cut and fill, coarse debris and the activities of mass movements – need to be considered if an alluvial-fan environment is to be safely and successfully exploited.

Secondly, the applied geomorphologist may use the fact that certain types of landform are especially distinctive on air photos to map the distribution of other phenomena that are less easily determined but are closely related in their distribution to the presence of more distinct forms. For example, using the principle of the catena concept, the mapping of particular slope forms may enable a soil map to be produced which can then be checked by field sampling and modified where necessary.

In addition to mapping, the applied geomorphologist is concerned with processes, changes and hazards. It is important to know, for example, the rates at which geomorphological changes are taking place, how quickly a sand dune is encroaching on an irrigation canal, how much the sea level is changing in a flood-prone low-lying sabkha area, and whether a landslide near the side of a new dam is active or relict. The use of cartographic sources, historical records and air photos may help in this endeavour, as will the instrumentation and direct monitoring of such processes. The increasing concern of geomorphology with process study over the last few decades has enabled an increasingly important contribution to be made in the field.

Fourthly, having identified the changes taking place in the landscape and the environment, it is necessary to be aware of the causes of these changes. As already discussed, the causes of change are complex, involving many human and natural factors, and there are difficulties in establishing cause-and-effect relationships. In order to take the appropriate action to ameliorate the threat of any particular change, it is vital that the real cause or causes of change are identified.

Fifthly, if the decision is made to intervene in the environment to remove or reduce the threat, then it is important to recognise that the intervention itself may have all sorts of repercussions through the environment. For example, as engineers have learnt to their cost, you cannot stop erosion at one point by the simple expedient of building a groyne. Each engineering scheme needs to be seen in the context of not only the individual location, but also the wider area. In many countries all major construction schemes have to be preceded by an environmental impact statement or assessment, in which all the possible ramifications of a particular design are considered before construction can proceed. The physical geographer is able to appreciate the complex interactions within the environment at a variety of scales and so can assist in this task.

Environmental management has become a major field in other branches of physical geography (O'Riordan, 1995), including the use of water resources (Beaumont, 1988), water pollution (Burt et al., 1993) and coastal management (Viles and Spencer, 1995).

INTEGRATION

Although, in common with much science, physical geography has displayed an increasing tendency towards reductionism and specialisation, it has, paradoxically, also displayed an increasing tendency to try and integrate its different components. This may partly be because of the deliberate adoption of systems linking, which by its very nature focuses on interrelationships, or it may be partly a result of an increasing concern with ecology and environment, or it may be because of a realisation that many of the most interesting intellectual developments occur when, for example, earth scientists and life scientists get together, or geomorphologists and biogeographers (e.g. Viles, 1988; Thornes, 1990).

Perhaps a major reason for the tendency towards integration has been the resurgence of biogeography, which for too long, with climatology, was one of the less vibrant parts of the discipline. This is in part reflected in the success of a new journal, *The Journal of Biogeography* (started in 1974), but is also seen in broad-ranging texts that attempt to give an integrated view of landscape types as diverse as ocean islands (Nunn, 1994), caves (Gillieson, 1996) and rainforests (Millington et al., 1995), and also of whole continents (e.g. Adams et al., 1996). Exciting new developments are taking place in our understanding of environments like savannas through an increasing concern with forces such as fire (natural and human), herbivores, soil nutrient status and soil hydrology, and a long history of human land use practices (see, for example, Fairhead and Leach, 1997).

In recent years, physical geographers have made many contributions to the study of hazards (e.g. Jones, 1993; Smith, 1992) and disasters (Alexander, 1993) and in some cases this has also brought them to consider societal issues (see, for example, Chester, 1993) at the same time as they consider geomorphological, hydrological or climatic events.

CONCLUSION

Although this chapter has stressed the changes that have taken place in physical geography in recent decades, there are some aspects of physical geography that have not been mentioned but which continue to be important. One of these is a concern with landscape, for although many contemporary geomorphologists, hydrologists and biogeographers are more interested in, say, processes of solute movement in organic soils on slopes than they are in the tangible shape of the earth's surface and in the way in which landscapes have evolved, landscapes are one of the greatest gifts to human kind and deserve study as tangible objects. Landscapes also have the capability to stimulate interest in the environment and to provide an area where human and physical geographers can produce a coherent story.

Likewise, although for many physical geographers the temporal and spatial scales of investigation have tended to move to the short term and the local, there has since the mid-1960s been an extraordinary growth in interest in global tectonics, the implications of which both for geomorphology and biogeography are profound, and in the significance of long-term climatic change.

REFERENCES

Adams, W., Goudie, A.S. and Orme, A.R. (1996) *The Physical Geography of Africa*. Oxford: Oxford University Press.

Alexander, D. (1993) *Natural Disasters*. London: UCL Press.

Anderson, D. (1997) 'Younger Dryas research and its implications for understanding abrupt climatic change', *Progress in Physical Geography*, vol. 21, no. 1, pp. 230–49.

Anderson, M.G. and Brooks, S.M. (eds) (1996) *Advances in Hillslope Processes*. Chichester: Wiley.

Battarbee, R. et al. (1988) *Lake Acidification in the United Kingdom, 1800–1986*. London: Ensis.

Beaumont, P. (1988) *Environmental Management and Development in Drylands*. London: Routledge.

Bird, E.C.F. (1996) *Beach Management*. Chichester: Wiley.

Briggs, D., Smithson, P., Addison, K. and Atkinson K. (1997) *Fundamentals of the Physical Environment*. London: Routledge.

Burt, T.P., Heathwaite, L. and Trudgill, S.T. (eds) (1993) *Nitrates: Processes, Patterns and Control*. Chichester: Wiley.

Chester, D. (1993) *Volcanoes and Society*. London: Arnold.

Cooke, R.U. and Doornkamp, J.C. (1992) *Geomorphology in Environmental Management*, 2nd edn. Oxford: Oxford University Press.

Cooke, R.U., Warren, A. and Goudie, A. (1993) *Desert Geomorphology*. London: UCL Press.

de Blij, H. and Muller, P.O. (1995) *Physical Geography of the Global Environment*. New York: Wiley.

Fairhead, J. and Leach, M. (1997) *Misreading the African Landscape*. Cambridge: Cambridge University Press.

Gillieson, D. (1996) *Caves*. Oxford: Blackwell.

Goudie, A.S. (1993) 'Human influence in geomorphology', *Geomorphology*, vol. 7, pp. 37–59.

Goudie, A.S and Stokes, S. (in press) *Quaternary Environmental Change*. Oxford: Oxford University Press.

Goudie, A.S. and Viles, H. (1997) *Salt Weathering Hazards*. Chichester: Wiley.

Gregory, K.J. (1985) *The Nature of Physical Geography*. London: Arnold.

Grove, J.M. (1988) *The Little Ice Age*. London: Routledge.

Grove, J.M. (1997) 'The century time-scale', in Driver, T.S. and Chapman, G.P. (eds), *Time-scales and Environmental Change*. London: Routledge, 39–87.

Innes, J. (1992) 'Forest decline', *Progress in Physical Geography*, vol. 16, pp. 1–64.

Jones, D.K.C. (1980) 'British applied geomorphology: an appraisal', *Zeitschift für Geomorphologie NF, Supplementband*, vol. 36, pp. 48–73.

Jones, D.K.C. (ed.) (1993) 'Environmental hazards: the challenge of change, *Geography*, vol. 78, pp. 161–98.

Lowe, J. and Walker, M. (1997) *Reconstructing Quaternary Environments*, 2nd edn. Harlow: Longman .

Maltby, G. (1986) *Waterlogged Wealth: Why Waste the World's Wet Places*. London: IIED.

Millington, A.C., Thompson, R.D. and Reading, A.J. (1995) *Humid Tropical Environments*. Oxford: Blackwell.

Monkhouse, F.J. (1954) *Principles of Physical Geography*. London: Hodder & Stoughton.

Mortimore, M. (1989) *Adapting to Drought: Farmers, Famines and Desertification in West Africa*. Cambridge: Cambridge University Press.

Nunn, P.D. (1994) *Oceanic Islands*. Oxford: Blackwell.

O'Riordan, T. (ed.) (1995) *Environmental Science for Environmental Management*. Harlow: Longman Scientific and Technical.

Park, C. (1997) *The Environment: Principles and Application*. London: Routledge.

Roberts, N. (1998) *The Holocene*, 2nd edn. Oxford: Blackwell.

Ruddiman, W.F. (1997) *Tectonic Uplift and Climate Change*. New York: Wiley.

Simmons, I. (1996) *Changing the Face of the Earth: Culture, Environment, History*, 2nd edn. Oxford: Blackwell.

Smith, K. (1992) *Environmental Hazards: Assessing Risk and Reducing Disaster*. London: Routledge.

Summerfield, M. (1991) *Global Geomorphology*. Harlow: Longman.

Thomas, D.S.G. and Middleton, N.J. (1994) *Desertification: Exploding the Myth*. Chichester: Wiley.

Thomas, M.F. (1994) *Geomorphology in the Tropics*. Chichester: Wiley.

Thornes, J. (ed.) (1990) *Vegetation and Erosion*. Chichester: Wiley.

Tiffen, M., Mortimore, M. and Gichuki, F. (1994) *More People, Less Erosion*. Chichester: Wiley.

Trudgill, S. (ed.) (1995) *Solute Modelling in Catchment Systems*. Chichester: Wiley.

Unwin, T. and Owen, L. (1997) *Environmental Management: Readings and Case Studies*. Oxford: Blackwell.

Viles, H.A. (ed.) (1988) *Biogeomorphology*. Oxford: Blackwell.

Viles, H.A. and Spencer, T. (1995) *Coastal Problems*. London: Arnold.

Wells, N.A. (1993) 'The initiation and growth of gullies in Madagascar: are humans to blame?, *Geomorphology*, vol. 8, pp. 1–46

Whitmore, T.C. (1987) *Biogeographical Evolution of the Malay Archipelago*. Oxford: Clarendon Press and London: Plenum.

Williams, M. (1989) *Americans and Their Forests: A Historical Geography*. Cambridge: Cambridge University Press.

Chapter 2

Ecosystems and their management

Adrian McDonald

INTRODUCTION

Ecology, the study of interrelationships within and between the biotic and abiotic components of the natural environment, has moved from the biological arena and is now central to Geography. Scale, change, movement, development and space, all fundamentally geographical keys, lie at the heart of modern ecology. The abiotic is the non-living components of the natural system (soil, rock, water, etc.); the biotic is the living parts of the natural system (animals, plants, microbes, etc.). Such assemblages of living and non-living components are termed ecosystems or ecological systems and exist at a variety of scales. Examples of small-scale systems could be the parasites on the skin of a large animal, a pond or a single tree. On a larger scale whole forests, moors or mountain systems can be considered ecosystems. Large systems can always be subdivided. A large lake, for example, will have a surface photic environment, an aphotic system on the lakebed and a coastal system at the land–water interface. Small systems build up to large systems and eventually are limited by the size of the planet to form the biosphere. The very largest system, the earth, has been deemed to have the properties of a living individual (the Gaia theory).

All identifications of ecosystems having set spatial boundaries are fallacious. Almost all ecosystems have linkages to other systems. Such linkages may not be direct but may link through several other systems. Nor are the connections immediate. There may be considerable transfer times. But few if any systems are completely independent. Bacterial colonies associated with the heat and elements released from seabed volcanic vents may be one of the more independent ecosystems.

However, this chapter of this book is intended to provide a focus on the key characteristics of some geographical systems, so instead of dwelling further on definitions, let us consider the key questions that face ecosystem analysts and managers. There are perhaps two key questions:

- What is natural?
- What is the future?

When there is a proposal to establish an area of forest in, say, North Yorkshire or Scotland, objectors point to the moorland and claim that this is the true and original land cover. It may be the true land cover, that is the cover that has evolved over thousands of years under the influence of mankind. But it is most certainly not the original land cover that until a thousand years ago was dominated by forests. A case could be made for the argument that the forest to be established is a closer approximation to the original land cover than the moorland. Of course both arguments are somewhat pointless. The modern monoculture, even-aged, forest of Norway spruce, sitka spruce, larch, etc. is a far cry from the intimate mixtures of age and species in the pre-existing forests of rowan, Scots pine, oak, alder. Neither the moor nor the modern forest are 'natural'. So the question becomes a little more fundamental: is mankind natural? Are ecosystems modified by man natural or can that title be reserved only for areas untouched by this (successful?) species?

It may seem a useful simplifying option to leave out the influence of man in our arguments and calculations. In doing so, however, we limit ourselves to backcasting, the consideration of how things were. This might be interesting in allowing us to determine how things might be in the future in the absence of mankind but is it useful? Is the influence of mankind going to vanish? To manage ecosystems we need to have visions of the future. That future includes the influence of people and their cities, transport systems, agricultural and hunting systems, etc.

ECOSYSTEM STRUCTURES

Ecosystems have general structures common across a variety of scales and locations. A very common and elementary view of structure is through the energy flows in the system. This has been somewhat confused by a variety of terminologies – Table 2.1 presents and simplifies these usages.

Table 2.1 Some approaches and terminologies used in capturing ecosystem structure

Hierarchy	*Functional*	*Energy source*	*Activity*
Primary	Producer	Phototrophic	Plant
Secondary	Consumer	Chemotrophic	Herbivore
Tertiary	Decomposer		Carnivore

The simplest and most widely accepted ecosystem structure is defined through energy flows. These are called *feeding* or *trophic structures*. There are two fundamental energy sources: light or chemicals. The ecosystems that rely on light as a driving force are absolutely the most important and widespread. Chemotrophic systems are infrequent and small-scale but do exist.

The first capture of energy from light is made by the 'plants' that may range from bacteria to trees. All these organisms require to use some of the captured energy in order to survive and only the net energy capture (net photosynthesis) is seen as growth in the plant community. Plants become the feed stock for the next group of organisms, the herbivores, which in turn provide the energy input for the predators. There may be several levels of predator ending with a 'top carnivore' (see Figure 2.1). A clearly changed perspective today is the proposal to reintroduce a variety of top carnivores including some perceived as a danger to people. For example, wild pigs and beaver

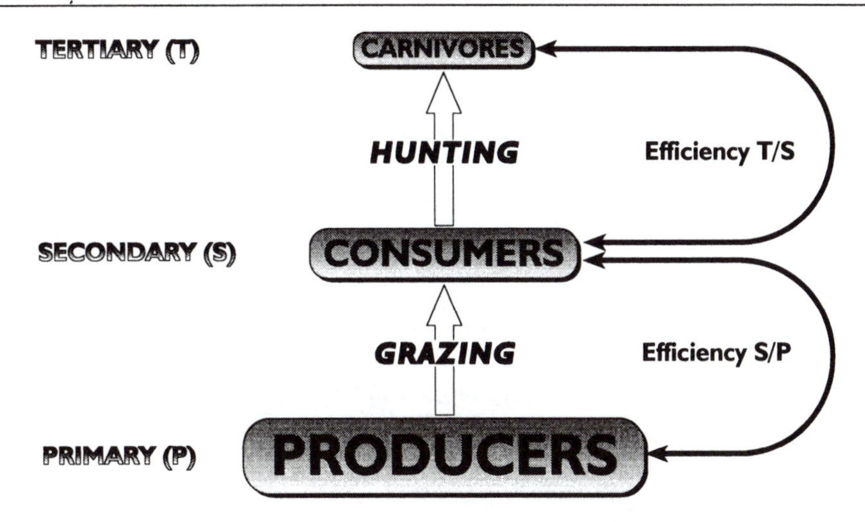

Figure 2.1 The energy pyramid.

are in the course of reintroduction to the UK while wolf reintroduction is at least on the agenda for discussion, a clear change in what is deemed to be politically and publicly acceptable.

At each level the amount of stored energy declines and so it is commonly represented as a trophic pyramid having the greatest biomass and energy asset at the producer/primary/plant level and successively smaller energy holdings at subsequent levels. Since each trophic level requires energy for self-maintenance and since not all components of the energy in one level is consumed or consumable by the next level, the transfer is always incomplete and the measure of this limited energy transfer is called the ecological efficiency of the transfer between trophic levels. Between 1 per cent and 10 per cent is the typical range of such efficiencies. Thus to move just two levels in the pyramid would reduce the energy asset to between 1 per cent and one hundredth of 1 per cent of that initially captured (net) from the sun. The outcome is that a very limited number of carnivore 'layers' can be supported. In conservation and ecological management terms the top carnivores are thus very susceptible to perturbations in the primary energy structure.

Concepts of ecological efficiency and of trophic levels refer not to generalisations of ecology but to typologies. It is effectively a functionally based typology of species groups. If the flow of energy for a particular ecosystem is identified and routed through named species the resulting diagram is called a food chain. An example for a UK upland is shown in Figure 2.2

Such food chains have relevance for management in indicating possible issues and conflicts. For example, where no carnivore exists the population of herbivores will expand until other control mechanisms intervene to control the population. In the course of this the plant population could be greatly damaged by overgrazing. There could be an excess of erosion. The quality of the herbivores could decline due to competition for food at key times. Density of herbivores could cause disease transmission problems or behavioural problems in the population. A large population could invade adjacent areas damaging alternative land uses. Food chains are often a simplification of

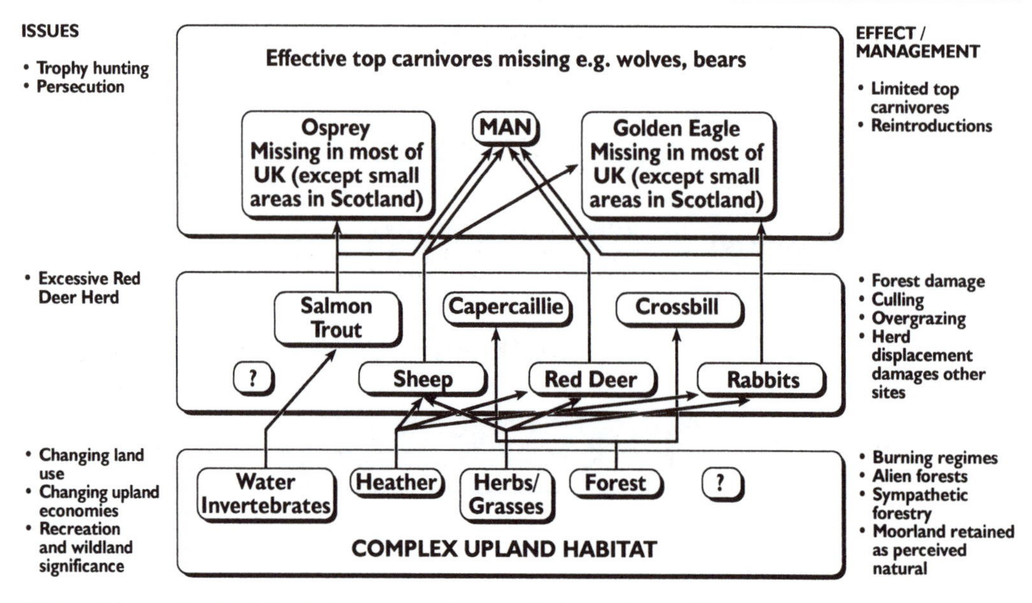

Figure 2.2 Individual food chains for an upland site and possible management issues.

the trophic relationships in an ecosystem. When a more comprehensive linkage diagram is developed the ensuing complexity has been recognised in the term *food web*.

Ecosystems, then, have structure in which energy is stored and through which energy passes with measurable 'efficiency'. In a similar manner nutrients are passed through the ecosystem. Ecosystems are therefore not static but dynamic. The ability of the primary building blocks of ecosystems, the photsynthesisers, to operate depends upon the availability of light, warmth, nutrients and water. Usually only one of these factors limits the rate of growth of the producers and this is referred to as the limiting factor. Ecosystems can effectively be self-limiting. There are two main avenues through which the limitation takes effect: (a) through the storing of nutrient in the biomass; or (b) through the adaptation of the habitat by the existing species making it unsuitable for seedlings. Let us consider each through an example.

Canada is one of the great forest countries in the world today. A belt of forest some 5000 km long and up to 1500 km deep crosses the country. This forest is, however, much more varied than might at first be thought. At the West Coast of Vancouver Island in British Columbia the type of forest found is temperate rainforest. This is a special forest. Its coastal position, allied to ocean currents gives a relatively warm, extremely wet, climate. The trees grow to great heights and indeed outstrip the tropical rainforest. Warmth and water are not the limiting factors, nor, given the height of the canopy, is light. Nutrient limits growth. All the available nutrients are locked in the above-ground biomass of the trees. When, infrequently, senescence or storm causes a tree to fall light enters the forest floor but seedlings do not succeed because of the lack of nutrient. Regrowth is delayed until the surface of the fallen tree starts to decompose and release nutrient. Saplings grow not on the ground but along the line of the (nearly) 100 metre fallen tree. Because the tree provides both the nutrient and the micro-habitat for the new saplings it is often termed a 'parent' or 'mother' tree. The old trunk will eventually disappear (to the untutored eye) but the line of new trees that arises has, on occasions, been taken as evidence of the hand of man rather than a perfectly natural straight line! There is again a serious change in viewpoint here. Even-age monoculture forest is being replaced by mixed age patchwork forest. This is happening because forest regulations have limited the clear-cut size but this is occurring through pressure from groups who believe that small-scale is automatically best. So the change here is that, right or wrong, pressure groups will often prevail and adaptation rather than confrontation is needed in ecosystem management.

Particular species are adapted to particular conditions. Perhaps that is putting an overly positive and widespread spin on the relation between species success and habitat. Often it is simply the case that one species can tolerate circumstances better than the normal competitor species. In ponds and small shallow lakes a period of sedimentation my have to take place before the initial floating aquatic vegetation gives way to rooted aquatics. Such rooted aquatics serve to trap debris and accelerate the process of deposition. As the water shallows and a layer of thicker 'soil' develops species tolerant of saturated conditions, such as willow, emerge and may start to shade out some of the rooted aquatics, but the additional water use by the trees and the additional litter and wind-borne trapped debris will further modify ground conditions to the point where the willow cannot regenerate and a species more adapted to drier conditions will dominate. Effectively the species has adapted the habitat away from conditions in which its progeny can survive. The question arises then: where will it end? Or is there an end point? This we will deal with in the following section.

Thus far we have presented ecosystems as a structured unidirectional set of stores with flows of energy and nutrient. It has also been predominantly a biological argument. If that were the case the earth's environment would be short-lived or ill-developed. At all levels of the ecosystem the material that does not pass to the 'higher' trophic level does not (cannot) simply vanish. It is processed through a further link in the ecological chain, the *decomposer system*. The decomposer system, or web to reflect its complexity (and the term web was applied here long before being used as a food chain related term), operates to reduce the complex organic molecules of life back to the simpler nutrients needed to continue growth (see Figure 2.3). The decomposer system then creates a recycling of material within the ecosystem. The recycled nutrient is held not in a biological store but in the abiotic components of the environment – the soil or the water body, depending on the ecosystem in question. At this stage nutrient will respond to abiotic stimulae. Thus, for example, autumn rains raising water tables in the uplands will remove, in solution, the microbiologically broken products of humic acids. This will be visible as colour in the waters and as trihalomethanes following chlorination in water treatment works. So our arguments cannot remain solely biological and must recognise the impact of and impact on people.

Science is biased. Our work is dominated by interest in species akin to ourselves or to those species we see and admire. Thus the plants, mammals and birds of the world have been over-represented in ecological importance. The importance of the decomposer system cannot be overemphasised and consists of 'grazers' and 'predators' of a richness and diversity undoubtedly the equal of the more traditional image of the ecosystem. Simplified decomposer systems work for the benefit of people in, for example, sewage treatment.

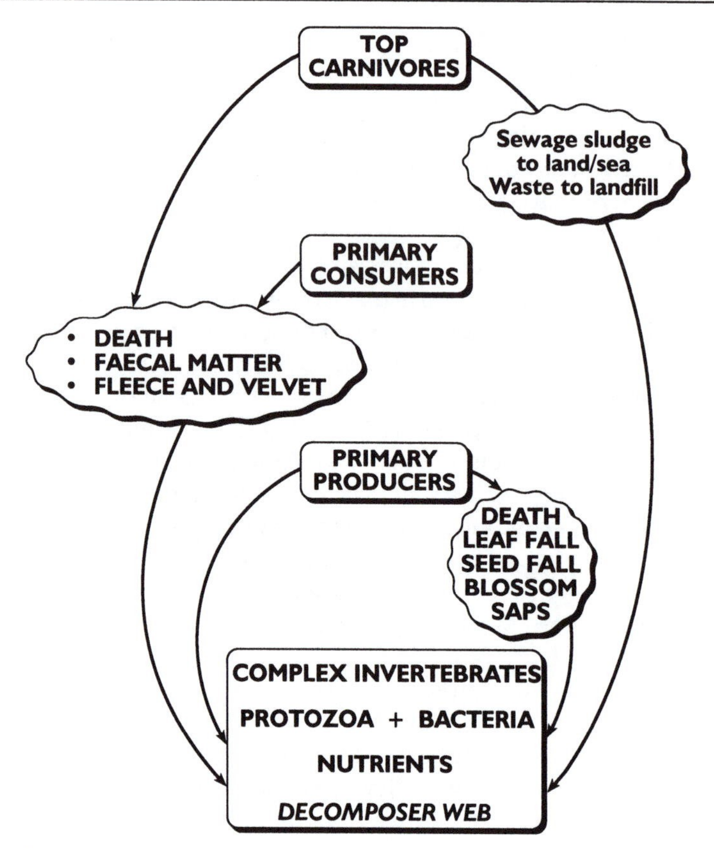

Figure 2.3 Flows of energy from various trophic levels to the decomposer system.

ECOSYSTEM DEVELOPMENT, CHANGE, SUCCESSION AND TYPES OF CLIMAX

The type of ecosystem development outlined at the end of the last section is called *succession*. Over the life of the succession a number of different vegetation communities develop, peak and die. Each stage in the succession is called a sere. So a succession is a collection of seres. In theory a sere that does not change will eventually develop. This final sere is called a climax community.

The early ecologists were mainly plant ecologists. They were much exercised by the theory that eventually there would be a vegetation community that would develop as a reflection of climate conditions in each part of the world. That type of community they termed a *climatic climax*. Climatic climax vegetation was, for a time, afforded particular values of stability, of rightness, of appropriateness. A number of other types of climax community were identified where other characteristics of the site were deemed to limit the development of the 'proper' climatic climax. Fire, soils and people were all held to alter the climax as are identified in Figure 2.4.

Today we recognise that climate changes over relatively short periods, certainly within the lifetime of a succession in many situations, so there is no clear end point to the succession. Rather there is a general slowing of the rate of change followed by a movement between end types depending on the climate conditions at that time. In

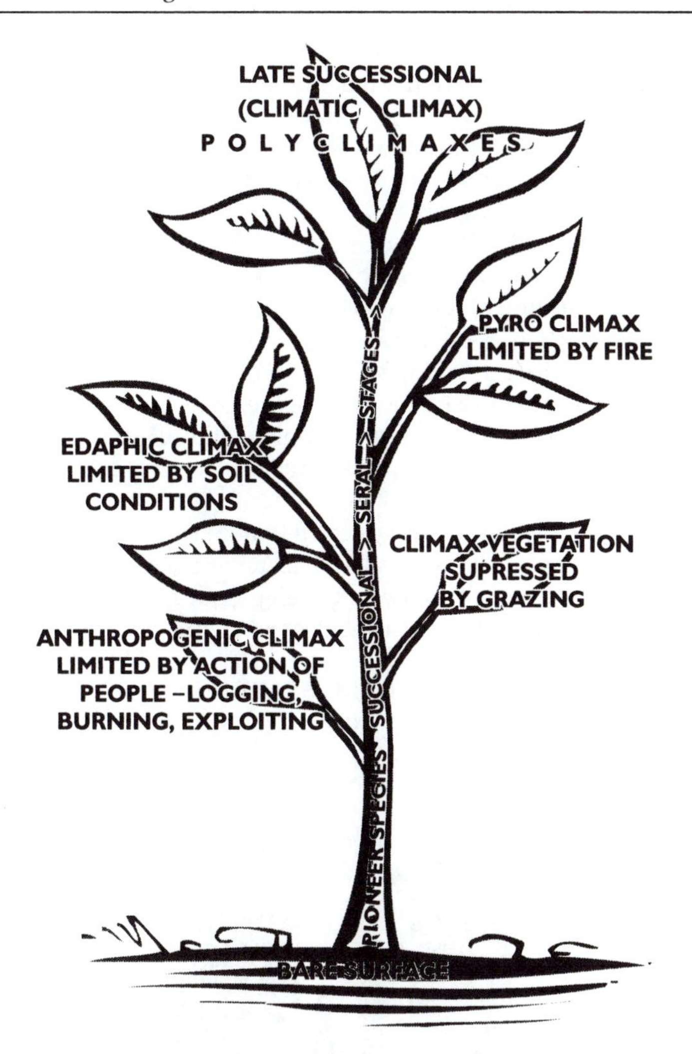

Figure 2.4 Some factors modifying ecosystem development and the alternative climaxes.

terms of ecosystem management there has in the past been a danger that the correct management objective has been to hold an ecosystem to the 'prevailing' characteristics even if the prevailing conditions have changed. Today managers recognise that the ecosystem is a dynamic entity that has to be managed with that characteristic in mind.

RESILIENCE AND TOLERANCE

Every species has a range of conditions within which it can survive. There are many such conditions, for example temperature, humidity, windspeed, soil depth, predator density. The range in theory is almost certainly greater than the range in the natural environment when, at the extremes of the theoretical range, the competitive ability of the organism will be affected. Thus, although some fish may be able to survive lower dissolved oxygen (DO) concentrations, their impaired mobility will reduce their ability both to catch food and escape predation. Thus in the real environment the species will not survive in a stressed habitat even if the conditions are not beyond the theoretical survivable limits. Therefore in setting limits with a view to protecting a species the ecological manager must be aware of the need to treat laboratory information circumspectly. Further, the loading on a species is both cumulative and interactive. Thus lowered pH and reduced DO may operate cumulatively.

In ecological terms, however, the tolerance of a species must be differentiated from ecosystem tolerance. For argument let us consider the Machair grass/herb cover of the raised beaches in the western isles of Scotland: a community may lose the bulk of some species under some conditions but the Machair will survive. In contrast, a simple ecosystem or a monoculture is at risk of a single extreme event, be that drought, wind or pest. One has to think only of the loss of complete elm plantations through Dutch elm disease. Figure 2.5 illustrates the difference between species tolerance and ecosystem tolerance for a simple system.

In broad terms the more diverse an ecosystem the more resilient it will be to external perturbations. Therefore a diverse ecosystem will have a greater longevity. Greater longevity allows complexity and diversity to develop and diversity leads to resilience (see Figure 2.6). Of course this argument is both general and inaccurate in some cases.

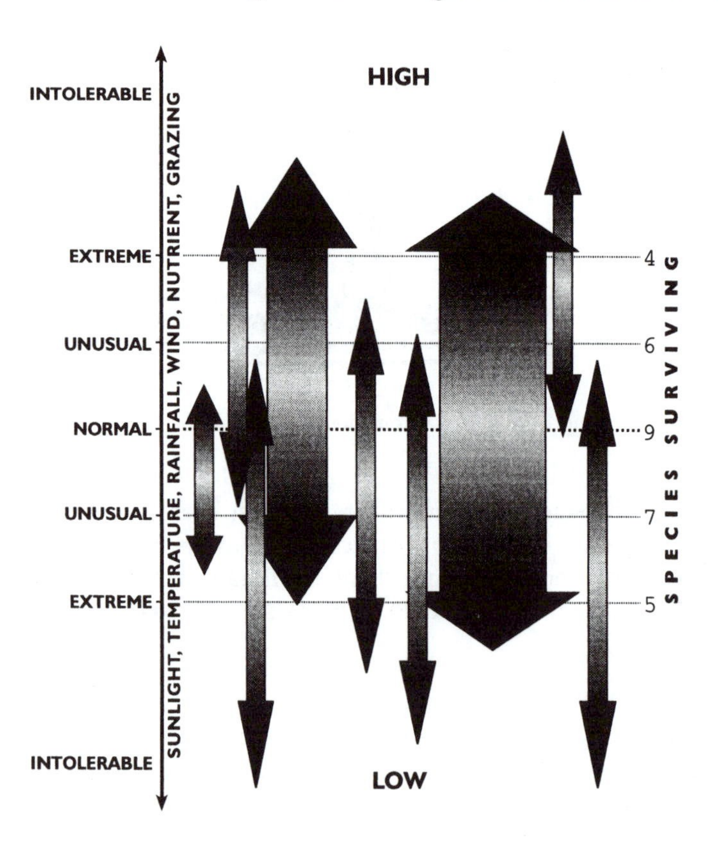

Figure 2.5 Species and ecosystem tolerance.

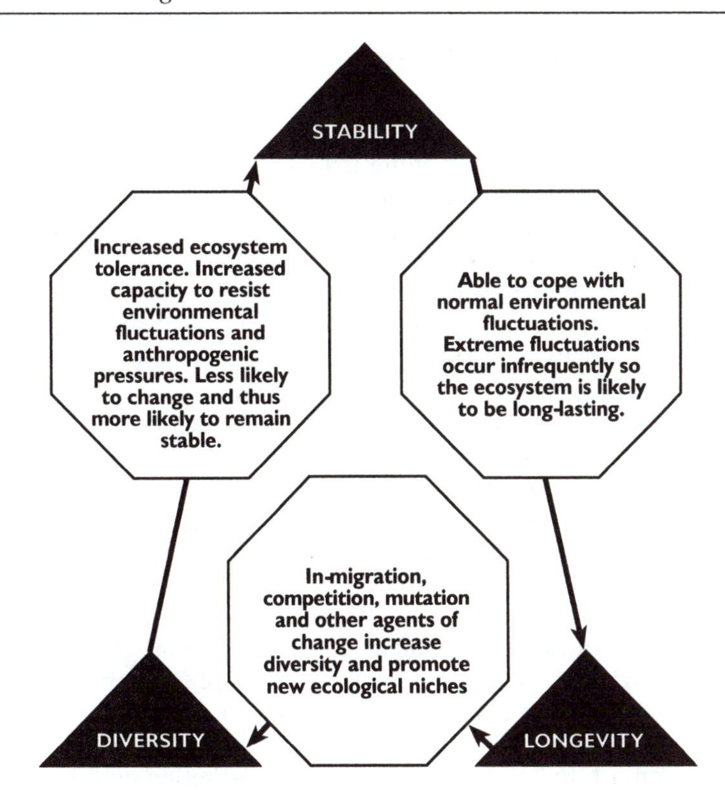

Figure 2.6 The longevity, stability, diversity triangle.

Certainly there are examples of ecosystems that become less diverse and simpler as they mature.

DIVERSITY AND BIODIVERSITY

Diversity is a term that has arisen at several points in this chapter. A similar word, biodiversity, has become much more commonly used since the UNCED affirmed the importance of Bruntland proposals on sustainable development. So what is diversity and how does it differ from biodiversity?

A diverse ecosystem is one that is varied, having many species. In theory because each of these species has a different tolerance to perturbation the diverse ecosystem is robust and long-lasting as outlined above. However, there is a flaw. The definition of species is man-made so some types of system in which people have been interested can be apparently more diverse than those in which science has developed little interest, information, classification or speciation. Further, is an ecosystem consisting of a number of very similar species more diverse than a system of a smaller number of very different species? Yes by definition but no by logic.

Species-based diversity (species diversity) then would more usefully be applied if additional information (biodiversity) was available on:

- richness – total number of species;
- evenness – relative abundance;
- abundance – most abundant species.

Diversity, however, can reflect much more than simple species information. Over the last half-century we have grown to understand more about the genetic structures which form the blueprints for life. More recently still we have embarked upon the identification, characterisation, classification and cataloguing of genes. This work is most advanced in the human genome programme but is advancing for the other species. Thus we are almost in a position to embark on the assessment of genetic diversity, the total variety of genetic material in an ecosystem. In aggregate this represents the potential of the ecosystem to change in the face of adversity (see below).

Ecosystems consist of a number of habitats, each habitat capable of supporting a particular group of animals and plants. Thus the greater the diversity of habitats, the greater the variety of species and genetic material supported by the system. Habitat diversity thus allows a measure of diversity even in the absence of more refined and resource-demanding species or genetic assessments. The downside is the lack of a precise definition of habitat and the difficulty of identifying and describing differences in habitats. At one time a habitat related to the type of environment used by (an animal) species. Today we recognise that a habitat has a conservation and ecological value in its own right although this complicates rather than simplifies habitat characterisation. In reality animals occupy a variety of habitats and their habitat needs change over time. Occupance of different habitats may be at a variety of intensities and durations. So the current approach to habitat characterisation (definition and description) which underplays the significance of animals is wise. The focus today is often on habitat 'fitness for purpose' and the physical linkages between habitat fragments needed to ensure that the whole has greater value than the sum of the parts.

Species, their habitats, their occupance of habitats and their ecological significance change over time. Change takes place due to:

- mutation;
- natural selection;
- migration;
- genetic drift;
- niche development;
- succession.

Some of these attributes are changing rapidly as the impact of humans on the environment grows. Our underground infrastructure offers new communication routes. Cities and their wastes offer better opportunities for, say, foxes and bears than do their natural habitats. Our transportation systems allow the spread of species in areas not hitherto occupied and unlikely to be occupied rapidly under natural circumstances. There are also intentional introductions and the escape of captive animals. Thus in the UK there are large natural populations of mink and marsupials. Such new introductions can displace the natural population by being better competitors as in the case of the grey squirrel displacing the red squirrel, or may carry an exotic parasite or virus to which the indigenous species has no or little resistance as in the case of the American crayfish displacing native freshwater crayfish in the UK.

In the discussion above we have alluded to native and indigenous species as if each species has a right to occupy certain areas. Again we are looking at ecology through the lens of science which is a recent development. To a great extent we accept the status quo as correct and only recently have we grown to appreciate that change is as much the norm as the static. Species can be local or worldwide and can be characterised as shown in Table 2.2. How then do we characterise a species like the coyote that has expanded its occupance from the American Southwest to almost all of continental North America including the Canadian Islands (presumably on iceflows, floating log islands and on ships!) in little more than a generation? Thus the reader might view this as exotic but the reader's children may classify, rightly, it as cosmopolitan.

Table 2.2 Species spatial characteristics

Title	*Distribution*
Endemic	From the locale
Exotic	From elsewhere, new to the area
Cosmopolitan	Wide-ranging but discontinuous
Ubiquitous	Found everywhere

MAURITIUS: EXTINCTION AND RECOVERY

Background and ecological pressures

Mauritius is a small, isolated, volcanic island 20° south of the equator. It has a natural forest cover much differentiated by the strong altitudinal differences on the island. It is only 45 kilometres by 65 kilometres, is hundreds of kilometres from the nearest, even smaller, islands, nearly a thousand kilometres from significant land masses and nearly 2000 kilometres from the nearest continent, Africa. Its key characteristic is therefore isolation.

For much of its history Mauritius was unoccupied. Mauritius was first discovered by the Arabs and was known to the Portuguese but was first utilised and settled by the Dutch as a staging post for the East India sea routes. It was claimed by the French in 1715 and by the British a century later. For the European colonial nations it acted as a staging post and a strategic holding.

Let us consider some of the pressures that have developed on the island's ecosystems as these nations used and developed the natural resources (see also Figure 2.7), and thereafter consider some of the actions taken to reduce the resultant damage and to restore the island's ecosystems.

- Mauritius first came to attention when the Dutch developed commercial sea routes to the East Indies. Such journeys by sail were of long duration and Mauritius was used as a watering station and as a place to provision with wild fruit and meat. The dodo, a flightless bird, was the first casualty being too easy to catch for meat. The expression 'dead as a dodo' has certainly focused the minds of Mauritian authorities on the reputation of the island as the home of extinction! Doubtless some trees were removed for ships' spars etc. as the need arose.

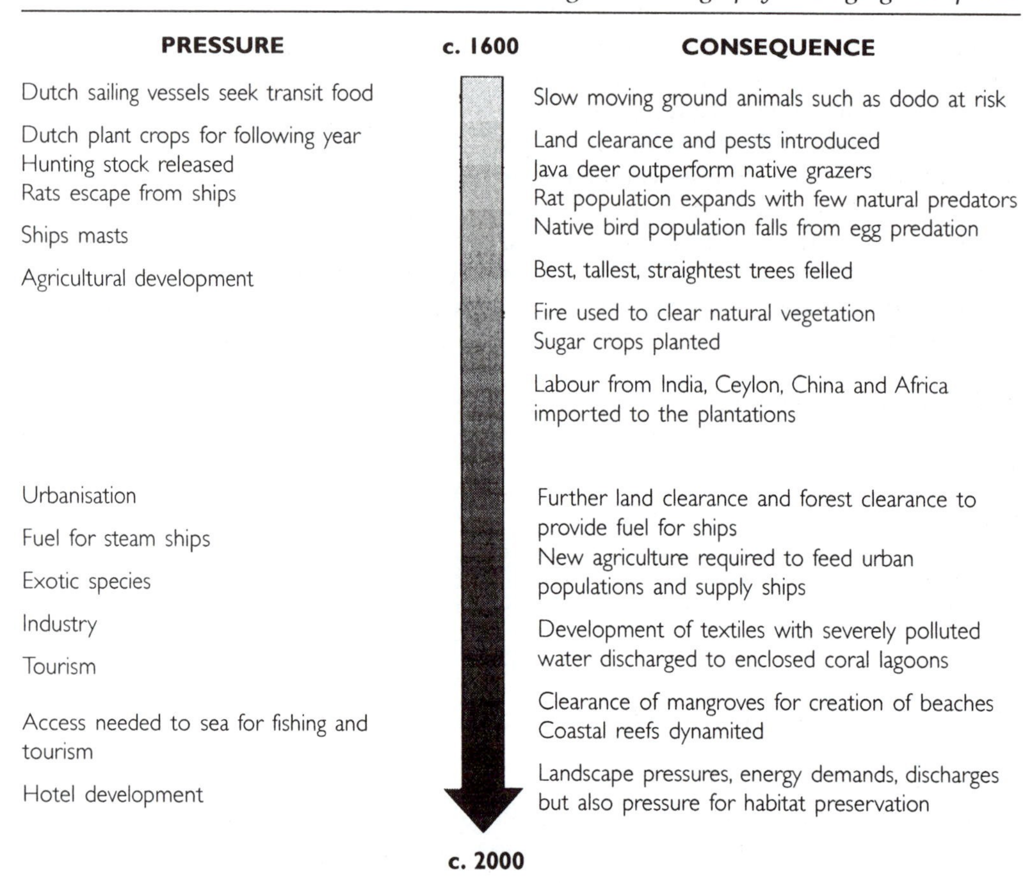

Figure 2.7 Sources of ecosystem pressure and ecological consequences in Mauritius.

- Releases of exotic species into this environment took place over many years both deliberately and accidentally. Pigs, goats, deer and sundry livestock were introduced to provide a meat supply for passing ships. Some of these introductions were for wild harvesting and others for farming. Some land was cleared for the farming operations. Both plant and animal introductions competed with the natural stock. Rats from the ships escaped onto land and quickly expanded in numbers. The mongoose was introduced to try to control rat numbers. Differences in sleeping patterns ensured that the mongoose had little effect on the rats but preyed on the natural populations.
- As colonial interests expanded plantations of sugar cane were established to mark the land holding and improvement and to justify the possession economically. Extensive land clearance, irrigation, drainage and burning were a necessary part of this plantation agriculture. With agriculture came labourers to tend the fields and Mauritius became highly populated and urbanised. Significant additional cropping took place to provide food for the growing population. Some, indeed most, of the crops were exotic to Mauritius and some, such as the guava, escaped to thrive in the natural environment.

- When sail gave way to steam, forests were exploited to provide bunker fuel for the ships. As forests were cleared there was some, although insufficient, replanting, often in exotic pine species.
- Many of the influences above continued after independence in 1966. In this period in Mauritius as elsewhere pesticides were introduced to agriculture, particularly to disease-prone monoculture plantation crops. Such early pesticides were capable of biomagnification. In addition tourism became an important source of revenue. Coastal mangroves were removed to allow access to beaches. Dune systems were disrupted to provide hotel sites and the coral reef that surrounds the whole island at distances from 11 km to a remarkably close 300 metres, were breached to allow access for sport fishing and yachting.
- Improved and mechanised plantation agriculture reduced the number of jobs in this sector and the textile industry expanded to use this plentiful supply of labour. Dyehouse effluents, insufficiently treated, are discharged to sea but in reality are discharged to a reef-trapped lagoon of limited flow and dispersion capacity.

Actions and remediation

In common with many sites Mauritius has a large number of ecological problems but because of the sensitive and special characteristics of the island, environmental problems here are of great concern. Here we deal only with one example involving three species, all close to extinction having very small populations: the echo parakeet (15 individuals), the Mauritian kestrel (5 individuals) and the pink pigeon (about 15 individuals). The kestrel numbers declined due to pesticides used for malaria control largely in the proposed tourist areas. The pesticides, concentrated by biomagnification, in the food chain ended with the kestrel and affected the fecundity of the population. Loss of habitat was the main problem for both the pigeon and the parakeet but predation of eggs and adults by wild cats, monkeys, mongooses and rats are also thought to have been a major cause of decline.

Any management programme that seeks to remedy species decline problems has to address two fundamental and very different issues, namely (a) the eradication of the original problems that caused the initial decline; and (b) the re-establishment of the population. In some cases the latter will happen as a consequence of the former but in extreme situations, where literally a handful of individuals remains (two pairs of kestrels in this case), the death of just two individuals might be all that lies between the current situation and extinction and therefore active strategies are needed to help a population re-establish.

The indigenous vegetation of Mauritius is little more than a few remnants. Agriculture and urbanisation has displaced all natural cover. Even in the national parks exotic species such as guava invade whenever the natural vegetation fails due to, say, cyclone or landslide. Indigenous species are often unable to compete in the face of grazing by Java deer (another introduction for hunting). The park authorities have now established conservation management areas (CMAs) where the natural vegetation is protected. Deer fencing plus boulder bases (to stop wild pigs undermining and eventually destroying the fences) protects the area from grazing. Inside the CMA exotic species are weeded out to encourage the natural vegetation. This hand weeding is expensive and requires labouring staff to be trained to recognise natural and exotic vegetation. The national park has established labelled botanical walks which, while of interest to the visitor, are primarily to help train their own staff in the recognition of plants to be promoted in the CMAs. Unnatural animal predators are controlled. All the exotic competitor species would be culled in an optimal management programme. Rats can be removed by poisoning (although there is a frightening rat population that has grown without any predator control over the last 200 years). Mongooses are trapped and removed. Wildcats can in principle be trapped and removed but are in practice extremely difficult to trap being careful, intelligent and suspicious (although this might be an overly anthropomorphic interpretation). Monkeys are all susceptible to 'culling' by trapping, poisoning or shooting but enjoy a form of quasi protection through public opinion that rails against any programme to control these 'charming' creatures. (In fact these creatures are far from charming and are a major conservation problem and become a real physical danger to tourists if titbits are not forthcoming.) By these actions the park authorities establish areas (islands or refuges might be more meaningful terms) of natural vegetation with nearer natural predation levels.

Breeding a new natural population to occupy these areas is difficult and involves the solution to a variety of problems. Captive for their own protection, the animals are given considerable help in the breeding programme that in Mauritius is centred on the Gerald Durrell Centre. The first problem is genetic stress due to the very small residual genepool and the unavoidable inbreeding. Where there are zoo populations, some additions to the gene pool can be found; thus, in the case of the kestrel, individuals from Jersey Zoo aided the captive breeding genepool. (However, the population of the echo parakeet continues to show signs of genetic distress.) The second problem relates to expertise. All animals are inexpert with new situations and have to learn from experience or demonstration. Sadly these learning options are not available to the very small residual populations. Eggs may have to be incubated artificially (as in the case of the pink pigeon for which artificial eggs are provided until day 13 when the natural egg is returned) or by foster parents (by another parakeet species in this case). The third problem is the transition from a captive population to a free population. The young birds bred and fed in captivity have to be trained to survive in the wild, albeit a carefully modified 'wild' since the CMAs are small patches in a much larger and more competitive environment. The initial releases were the most difficult. The birds are allowed a week or two in large cages on the release sites in the heart of the national park to acclimatise to the new conditions and adapt to noise etc. There then follows a period of foodless days in which, at the end of each day, the birds are released but return shortly to the cages for evening food. The release time is increased slowly and additional and supplementary feeding is provided in the natural environment. Cage feed availability is slowly reduced. Park staff and Mauritius Wildlife Foundation staff who remain permanently on site carefully monitor the programme. Subsequent releases have been easier since there is an existing population to attract new young birds from the cages and to provide examples.

It is possible to bring back a species from the brink of extinction. The five individuals of the kestrel (two pairs) now number 55 and appear to be establishing territories outside the original release areas. But such a success in ecological management requires political commitment in the establishment of the parks, vision by park managers, international expertise in a variety of disciplines and public education about the actions that have to be taken to support island ecology in the face of an influx of highly competitive exotic species.

SUMMARY

Our changing viewpoints in relation to ecology and ecological management are summarised below but caution is advised. A biologist would see very different changes of perspective in the same material – the interpretation is discipline-specific.

- Unrecognised 40 years ago, ecology is central to geography.
- Ecological boundaries are fuzzy both spatially and conceptually.
- People cannot be excluded from ecology.
- Change is the norm; a static endpoint is unlikely.
- Modelling will remain a tool that allows a vision of such changing futures.
- Active intervention is often needed to manage ecosystems.
- Programmes of public education are needed to support active intervention.
- Bias must be recognised in science and in pressure groups.
- Habitat must be seen as a functional entity not as representative.
- Ecological restoration must be addressed.

ACKNOWLEDGEMENTS

I am grateful for the time, expertise and enthusiasm of Paul Moollee, the manager of the Black River National Park; Regis Kwet Min Lam Shaung Yuen, responsible for many aspects of the captive breeding programme in the national parks of Mauritius; and Catherine Murray and Malcolm Nicols (who volunteered for months and stayed for years) of the Mauritius Wildlife Foundation who contribute to the release programme in the national park.

REFERENCES

Bedford, K.H. and Richter, B.D. (1999) 'Conservation of biodiversity in a world of use', *Conservation Biology*, vol. 13, no. 6, pp. 1246–56.

Fagan, W.F., Cantrell, R.S. and Cosner, C. (1999) 'How habitat edges change species interactions', *American Naturalist*, vol. 153, no. 2, pp. 165–82.

He, H.S. and Mladenoff, D.J. (1999) 'Spatially explicit and stochastic simulation of forest landscape, fire disturbance and succession', *Ecology*, vol. 80, no. 1, pp. 81–99.

Kindler, J. (1998) 'Linking ecology and development objectives: tradeoffs and imperatives', *Ecological Applications*, vol. 8, no. 3, pp. 591–600.

Tanner, J.T. (1975) 'The stability and intrinsic growth rates of prey and predator populations', *Ecology*, vol. 56, pp. 853–67.

Trombulak, S.C. and Frissell, C.A. (2000) 'Review of the ecological effects of road on terrestrial and aquatic communities', *Conservation Biology*, vol. 14, no. 1 pp. 18–30.

Williams, J.E. (2000) 'The biodiversity crisis and adaptation to climate change: a case study from Australia's forests', *Environmental Monitoring and Assessment*, vol. 61, no. 1, pp. 65–74.

Chapter 3

New developments in managing river environments

Geraldene Wharton

INTRODUCTION AND BACKGROUND

This chapter is based on seminar papers given at the Institute of Education, University of London as part of the Progress in Geography: Changing Viewpoints module for the MA Geography in Education. The changing nature of physical geography over the last century is briefly considered as a context for a more detailed examination of the changes in one area of applied physical geography, the management of river systems. The central role that physical geographers, mainly geomorphologists, have played in changing, first, ideas and, second, actual working practices in river management, is highlighted. There have been some dramatic advances since the early 1970s and new ideas and practices continue to develop as more information becomes available about the nature and functioning of river environments. One particularly exciting new area is the development of ideas and approaches for restoring river systems which have been adversely affected by hard engineering schemes.

THE (CHANGING) NATURE OF PHYSICAL GEOGRAPHY

In 1985 K.J. Gregory published *The Nature of Physical Geography* which provided a survey of physical geography and could be treated as a companion text to R.J. Johnston's (1983) *Geography and Geographers: Anglo-American Human Geography since 1945*, although Gregory's book began with the period 1851–1950. Arguably, physical geography has not been so obviously affected by several paradigms and a brief insight into its changing nature can be provided by considering some of the key chapters in *The Nature of Physical Geography* (see Table 3.1) The themes of 'Conservation and Environment' and of applied research ('Advancing Application') are particularly relevant to any discussion of developments in river management.

While the conservation movement is generally thought to have started with a book by George Perkins Marsh (1864) *Man and Nature*, this concern for conservation and environment seems to have had little effect on physical geography until the twentieth century. In part two of his book, 'Themes for two decades 1950–1970', Gregory (1985) argues that a more environmental physical geography came from three trends: a revival of interest in human activity; a greater focus in physical geography research upon the magnitude of the human impact; and hazard research that was facilitating closer links

Table 3.1 The (changing) nature of physical geography

I	A century for a foundation 1851–1950
	Evolution
	Exploration and Survey
	Conservation and Environment
	Positivism (Scientific Method)
	W.M. Davis
II	Themes for Two Decades 1950–1970
	Measurement Mounting
	Chronology Continuing
	Processes Prevailing
	The Advent of Man (Environmental Physical Geography)
III	Trends in Ten Years 1970–1980
	Time for Change
	Advancing Application (Applied Physical Geography)

Source: Gregory (1985) pp. v–vi.

between human and physical geography. These trends can be identified in river management research with investigations initially focusing on quantifying and understanding the impacts of river engineering and flood hazards prior to much greater interest in revised methods of management and the challenges of river restoration.

In the final section of *The Nature of Physical Geography* ('Trends in Ten Years 1970–1980'), Gregory (1985) highlights the development of applied physical geography. He describes how physical geographers have shown a considerable reticence in becoming involved in applications of their research and a reluctance to propose a single solution for a particular problem, perhaps because a geographer's training focuses attention towards all the factors influencing a particular situation. Briggs set out the challenge of applied research in 1981 in the editorial of the first issue of the journal *Applied Geography*: 'The applied geographer needs to be brave. He needs to commit himself before he knows all the answers. He needs to be prepared to make public mistakes. But he must be prepared to learn from them.'

In the field of river management, geomorphologists, ecologists, hydrologists and others have had to act with best available knowledge and techniques. The critical point is encouraging the wide dissemination of results from successful and unsuccessful schemes alike; greater lessons may be learned from failures.

HISTORY AND EXTENT OF RIVER CHANNELISATION

Rivers and their floodplains have arguably been the most exploited of all natural environments because of their wide-ranging and fundamental resources and to facilitate this development and sustain the exploitation of resources, river channels have been directly modified in a variety of ways. Methods used to alter river channels by engineering for the purposes of flood control, drainage improvement, reduction of bank erosion, maintenance of navigation or reduction for highway construction are referred to as 'river channelisation' (Brookes, 1988).

River channelisation is not a recent practice, however. River channels have been directly modified for thousands of years: in the sixth millennium BC, Mesopotamia and Egypt practised flood control and manipulated water to sustain settled agriculture; around 2000 years BC the Emperor Yu in China ordered the control of rivers in the interests of land reclamation; by 600 BC flood banks had been constructed along the Yellow River, China; and in Britain, the Romans constructed embankments to protect low-lying marsh areas in the Fens and the Somerset Levels.

Although river channelisation is extensive in many countries throughout the world, the highest density of channelised streams tends to be found in developed countries with high population densities and intensive farming. In England and Wales channelisation works were undertaken on a total of 8500 km of main rivers in the period 1930 to 1980 and a further 35 500 km of main river channel had been subjected to maintenance activities such as weed cutting and dredging during the same period (Brookes, 1988). In the lowland countries of Western Europe, such as Denmark, the Netherlands and northern Belgium, there has been even more extensive river channelisation. In Denmark, for example, 98 per cent of all rivers and streams have been straightened resulting in a density of modified watercourses of 0.09 km km^{-2}. This compares with a density of 0.06 km km^{-2} in England and Wales (Brookes, Gregory and Dawson, 1983) and 0.003 km km^{-2} in the USA (Leopold, 1977). Denmark thus has a density of channelised rivers 15 times greater than England and Wales and 300 times greater than the USA (Brookes, 1987).

CONTROVERSY OVER THE IMPACTS OF CHANNELISATION

Despite its long history, the problems surrounding channelisation only came to the fore in the late 1960s and early 1970s, particularly in the USA. Bauer and East (1970) described it as an 'insidious cancer' which contradicts many of the basic principles of water management. And Martin Heuvelmans in his book entitled *The River Killers*, published in 1974, called for the abolition of the US Corps of Engineers because they had 'systematically ruined the nation's rivers'. Table 3.2 lists some publications which reflect the degree of public concern emerging in the 1960s and 1970s in the USA over the detrimental environmental consequences of river channelisation. A Committee on Government Operations of the House of Representatives reported in 1973 that:

> A common thread running through the Subcommittee's hearings, correspondence, and subsequent studies was not that channelisation, per se, was evil, but rather that inadequate consideration was being given to the adverse environmental effects of channelisation. Indeed, there is considerable evidence that little was known about the effects and, even more disturbing, little was done to ascertain them.
>
> (Committee on Government Operations, 1973, reported in Brookes, 1988, p. 21)

One of the outcomes of this 1973 report was that a larger-scale programme of studies was initiated throughout the USA to investigate the instream impacts of river engineering, and river channelisation became a topic of research for geomorphologists (such as Ed Keller and Luna Leopold) and ecologists at various universities.

Since the early 1970s controversy surrounding the effects of conventional engineering practices has extended from the USA to other countries, particularly in Europe, and

Table 3.2 Articles describing the controversy surrounding channelisation*

Title of article	*Area*	*Source*
'Our ruined rivers'	Georgia	Bagby (1969)
'The gravediggers'	USA	Bauer and East (1970)
'Crisis on our rivers'	USA	Miller and Simmons,1970)
'The stream that used to be'	Montana	Seaburg (1971)
'The River Killers'	USA	Heuvelmans (1974)
'How to kill a river by "improving" it	–	Whistleblower (1974)
'Channelization: short cut to nowhere'	Virginia	Corning (1975)

*All references are given in full in Brookes (1988).
Source: Brookes (1988).

this has been followed by efforts to elucidate the effects and implement alternative designs which attempt to 'work with Nature rather than against it', following McHarg's (1969) 'Design with Nature' school of thought, Leopold's (1977) plea for a 'reverence for rivers'; and Keller's (1975) 'search for a better way'.

TRADITIONAL RIVER ENGINEERING

Traditional ideas and methods

A fundamental aim in the traditional approach adopted by engineers was that river control was to be achieved by methods of river training and taming. The methods were designed to tame flooding and restrain all forms of river channel adjustment. In the pursuit of river control, a large number of 'hard' river engineering techniques have been employed, although many channelisation schemes are described as comprehensive or composite because more than one technique is used. The four main methods are: resectioning, embanking, straightening or realignment, and lining river channels with non-vegetative materials (see Brookes, 1988, and Wharton, 2000, for further details).

Resectioning involves enlarging rivers by widening and/or deepening them so that flood flows are contained and water flows through the channel at a lower and safer level. The trapezoidal cross-section (sloping channel sides and a flat river bed) is the most commonly engineered form for unlined earth channels. If a rectangular channel is excavated the whole channel must be lined in a rigid material like concrete to ensure stability. Rectangular channels are commonly constructed in urban areas. River channels may also be deepened to lower the water table in the adjacent flood plain as part of a land drainage operation. Land drainage has been widespread in many developed countries to facilitate the intensification of agricultural production, usually from summer grazing to cereal production.

Embankments, also known as levees, flood banks and stop banks, are built to increase the capacity of the river and prevent flood flows spreading out onto the floodplain. Embankments are key components of the flood control systems along many of the world's most important rivers. In the US, embankments have been built along the Mississippi, Missouri and Sacramento rivers to protect the major towns and cities that have become established on the wide floodplains. There are also over 1000 km of embankments alongside the Nile, 1400 km alongside the Red River in Vietnam and 700 km along the Yellow River in China.

The construction of embankments is one of the structural measures proposed in the Flood Action Plan for Bangladesh (*Horizon*, 1994; see also Brammer, 1990). The basic plan includes proposals to:

- narrow the width of the Brahmaputra river to about 4 km (its width currently ranges from 5 to 14 km);
- turn the multi-streamed channel into two channels by closing some waterways; and
- construct levees along all the major rivers (about 8000 km of embankments).

Opinion is divided as to whether a structural flood defence project of such magnitude is technically possible and economically viable. It is estimated that the works would take over 100 years to complete and would cost 10 billion US dollars. When finished, the annual maintenance costs could be higher than the country's GDP.

Straightening a channel reduces flooding in the engineered river section by improving the ease with which water flows through the river reach. The straightened reach has a steeper slope which increases water velocities allowing discharges to flow through the engineered reach at a lower level. Straightening can be achieved by meander cut-off programmes such as those used on the Greenville Reach in the Lower Mississippi (Winkley, 1982).

To protect against erosion, river channels have traditionally been lined with concrete or steel sheeting, or their banks have been reinforced with quarried stone, also known as rip rap, or they have been protected by rock-filled wire mattresses called gabions.

Impacts of 'hard' river engineering

A fundamental problem of traditional river engineering is that structural flood defences encourage floodplain development but even the most sophisticated and extensive channelisation schemes cannot guarantee complete protection against flooding and its associated channel form adjustments. This is because it is physically impossible to control the very rare high magnitude flood events. A further problem is that 'hard' river engineering has led to many unexpected and undesirable river channel changes. Although the physical impacts of channelisation are many and varied, a typical response is for erosion to be triggered in both the channelised section and the downstream reach because the powerful flood flows are contained within the engineered channel. For example, channel straightening, resectioning and lining along reaches of the Santa Cruz River, Arizona, have resulted in bank erosion and channel widening immediately downstream of the channelised section. Similarly, along the River Trannon in Wales, straightening increased the velocity and erosive capacity of the channel which cut through the reinforced channel banks (Newson, 1986), and without remedial action the Trannon would have returned to its original meandering course.

The many morphological impacts of channelisation not only require extensive and costly maintenance but may even exacerbate flooding. For example, the levees along the Mississippi have been blamed by some for increasing the flood levels in the 1993 flood because they ponded up the flood waters, although these claims have not been proven. Certainly, channelisation has been shown to result in earlier and larger flood peaks in the unmodified downstream reaches of many rivers which increases the flood risk in these areas. And there are additional concerns that structural flood defences give a false sense of security to floodplain occupants.

Of further cause for concern are the biological impacts of channelisation schemes. Study after study has shown how channelisation can affect a large number of water quality variables including total suspended sediment, velocity, temperature, turbidity, colour, conductance, pH and dissolved oxygen. For example, on the River Wylye, near Salisbury, Wiltshire, 514 tonnes of sediment were released to downstream reaches of the river as a result of realignment works over a period of 15 working days. Sediment loads were 40 times greater than normal (Brookes, 1988). And during dredging on the Yellow Creek, north-east Mississippi, mean values of specific conductance, turbidity, colour, chemical oxygen demand, total alkalinity, hardness, ammonia, phosphorus, sulphate, iron, lead and manganese were recorded at levels between 50 and 100 per cent greater than normal (Shields and Sanders, 1986). The observed water quality changes were related to the increased input and the changed nature of the sediments.

These water quality changes are superimposed on the extreme physical disturbance caused by river engineering and can result in serious damage to stream ecosystems. Typically, this results in reductions in species numbers and species diversity because of the loss of habitat diversity which channelisation causes. Aquatic macrophytes (river plants), invertebrates, fish, amphibians, birds and mammals are all adversely affected. Most research, however, has focused on the impacts of river engineering on fish populations. Resectioning of the North Carolina Coastal Plain streams, USA, provides a very typical example of the impact of river engineering. The channelisation reduced stream cover and increased water temperatures, and a 75 per cent reduction in the number of game fish was recorded. Recovery only occurred after 15 years with no maintenance activities taking place during that time (Brookes, 1988, pp. 123–5).

NEW IDEAS AND APPROACHES IN RIVER CHANNEL MANAGEMENT

So what are the alternatives to traditional 'hard' river engineering? Many river environments are so intensively developed that continued management is necessary and we are certainly not in a position to return all the world's rivers to an entirely natural state. One way forward which has been advocated and is gradually being implemented is an approach which embodies the principle of McHarg's 'Design with Nature' school of thought. Leopold (1977) argued that revised construction procedures and new river designs offered a means of achieving a 'reverence for rivers' and the possibility of alleviating the problems of flooding and erosion in ways that minimise the environmental impact. The adoption of 'softer' approaches has also emerged from the realisation that structural flood control measures will never totally eliminate the flood risk. Despite increased expenditure on structural flood defences in the developed world, the cost of flood damage continues to rise. With more environmentally friendly designs and practices there is also the prospect of reducing the long-term costs of flood management by avoiding the expensive remedial and maintenance operations often associated with traditional river channelisation.

Research by geomorphologists over the last three decades has changed the way we view river systems (see Knighton, 1998) and has demonstrated a number of important river attributes that must be central to river management strategies. First, rivers are dynamic systems whose variables are closely interlinked. If one aspect of the channel is altered, such as channel width, this will result in changes to the water velocity and the amount and type of sediment transported by the river. Furthermore, high energy streams in upland areas can respond very rapidly to any changes, including imposed engineering structures. Brookes (1987) discovered that high energy streams in Denmark had an ability to restore their natural meandering planform following straightening. Second, some channel features are more adjustable and sensitive to change than others. Rivers can adjust their width and depth dimensions very quickly, for example, and rapid cross-sectional changes can thus take place downstream of engineered reaches. Third, straight channels are uncommon in nature whereas meandering channels are frequently the equilibrium channel form. Natural channel patterns reflect an adjustment to the prevailing catchment characteristics and if we attempt to control channel pattern and put the river in a straitjacket of channel reinforcements, there will be knock-on effects. Fourthly, because each section of river is part of a channel network, impacts can be transmitted far beyond the modified reach throughout the river system in both upstream and downstream directions and therefore have far-reaching consequences. And finally, river fauna and flora depend on habitat diversity which is determined by morphological diversity (pools and riffles, overhanging river banks and a range of sediment sizes on the channel bed, for example). To retain ecological diversity river designs must therefore be physically diverse (Wharton, 2000, p. 61).

Alternative designs and mitigation procedures thus advocate managing rivers based on an understanding of river channel processes to alleviate the adverse impacts of river flooding and erosion while minimising environmental degradation. The two key objectives of the new approach are to work with nature and to manage rivers in an integrated and holistic way so that river channels are not divorced from the processes and characteristics of their catchments. A number of new designs and practices have emerged recently (see for example RSPB, NRA and RSNC, 1994; Brookes and Shields, 1996) and the following are just a few examples to illustrate some of these 'softer' approaches to river channel management.

Alternative river designs and river restoration

Natural river channel designs emulate the geomorphology and ecology of natural, stable rivers. It is now acknowledged that well-designed meandering channels are more stable, provide a greater variety of flow conditions and aquatic habitat diversity, and are aesthetically more pleasing that artificially straightened channels. Although they are more expensive to construct than straight channels, due to the greater excavation costs of dredging an asymmetric channel, the environmental benefits and reduced maintenance costs may offset increased construction costs over the life of the scheme. In the design of a stable meandering channel, the existing natural meander geometry and slope should be used as a guide. Similarly, flexible two-stage flood channels, as used on the River Roding, Essex, have proved to be an effective design for alleviating floods on some rivers with fewer adverse impacts on the river environment than conventional methods of channel enlargement. In the two-stage design, the aim is to preserve the original channel which continues to carry the normal range of river flows. A larger channel is excavated around the existing natural channel to conduct the larger flood flows. The 'flexible' design, whereby the excavated area alternates from bank to bank, helps to avoid damage to sensitive river habitats and improves the morphological and habitat diversity of the river, as well as its appearance.

For some channelised rivers there is the opportunity to 'restore' them to a more natural form. The process of restoration is often one of river enhancement or rehabilitation as it is rarely possible or even desirable to return a river exactly to its pre-channelisation conditions. Thus, some formerly straightened rivers are now having their 'bends' put back in again. For example, the River Wandse in Hamburg-Rahlstedt, Germany, has been restored to a meandering channel along with its riparian vegetation as have many straightened rivers in Denmark (e.g. the River Brede) and Sweden (e.g. the Stensbaek stream).

Pools and riffles should also be retained in natural river designs whenever possible to maintain habitat diversity and promote channel stability. Within sizeable river projects, unaltered areas, such as deep pools, should be preserved to serve as biological refugia. Channel substrate and vegetation should also be left in place whenever possible because this is critical for the river fauna. Alternatively, the original substrate and vegetation can be stockpiled and reinstated after excavation has been completed (see Brookes, 1988, pp. 217–21).

In 1990 the UK River Restoration Project (RRP) was born out of a series of discussions between enthusiastic professionals at a conference entitled 'The Conservation and Management of Rivers'. The group expanded to bring together an even broader range of expertise and experience in conservation, geomorphology, engineering and biology, the aim being to focus on the practical application of restoration techniques to reverse the damage done in the past. The restoration research was undertaken at three demonstration sites: the River Cole on the Oxfordshire/Wiltshire border to the north of Swindon; the River Skerne, near Darlington; and the River Brede in Denmark (Holmes and Nielsen, 1998). The three demonstration projects had a total budget of £500 000 from the EU LIFE Fund and were a joint venture between Sonderjyllands Amt and the National Environmental Research Institute in Denmark and seven organisations in the UK. The main partners in the UK were English Nature, the Environment Agency, the Countryside Commission, the National Trust, Darlington Borough Council and Northumbrian Water Ltd, led by the non-profit-making River Restoration Project Ltd. The EU LIFE demonstration projects have been significant in highlighting the need for river restoration and showcasing some of the possible approaches to practical restoration.

In 1998 the RRP came to an end although post-project monitoring continues at the demonstration sites. A new River Restoration Centre (RRC) was formed on 1 April 1998 with a website (http://www.qest.demon.co.uk/rrc/rrc.htm). The RRC is a non-profit-making organisation and will assemble and manage a UK database and information network, detailing river restoration schemes and techniques, which will allow impartial advice to be offered to practitioners and scientists involved in river restoration. It is also a founder member of the European Centre for River Restoration (ECRR).

Bio-engineering techniques

Vegetation is of fundamental importance to the new approaches in river management. Most commonly we think of the role of tree roots in binding and strengthening river banks particularly if the roots penetrate to the toe region of the bank. However, many types of vegetation are now being used for a range of purposes throughout the whole river environment. Thus, aquatic plants can be used in the channel to stabilise the river bed and promote a range of habitats whereas shrubs and softwood trees provide protection against bank erosion and a variety of riparian habitats.

The benefit of using woody material, compared with 'hard' defences such as rock, concrete or steel, is that the woody material creates 'natural' habitats for river bank plant species to establish themselves. The use of channel and bankside vegetation also provides food for the river fauna and, by acting as a buffer zone, reduces the amount of harmful nitrogenous fertilisers entering the river from adjoining agricultural areas (Petersen, Petersen and Lacoursiere, 1992). Often natural vegetation must be used in conjunction with man-made materials so that the latter can provide protection until the vegetation becomes properly established. For example, immediately downstream of Clifton Hampden Lock on the River Thames in Oxfordshire, bank repair and long-term protection works were carried out in 1988 using a combination of geotextile and emergent planting. Now the reeds are so well established that they completely screen the geotextile materials and they promote the accretion of river sediments which further stabilises the previously eroding banks (RSPB, NRA and RSNC, 1994, p. 361).

River corridors or streamways

A third major recommendation in the new approach to river management is the use of river corridors or streamways whose design is based on an acceptance that 'rivers are meant to flood and must have room to move'. The approach recommends allowing rivers to meander across part of the floodplain in a wide 'corridor' or streamway, ideally three times as wide as its lowest channel. Gardiner and Cole (1992, p. 398) have argued that the minimum river corridor is the 'area of land required for the river to achieve a natural meandering course with associated riparian habitats'. Defining a river corridor in urban areas is more difficult but it may still be beneficial to designate an ideal corridor even in situations where the floodplain is completely developed. One reason is to draw attention to the potential flood hazard of the floodplain development, and a second is so that future development will be obliged to recognise the restoration of the river corridor as a conservation principle. Within the USA, communities must adopt a regulatory floodway to be eligible for the National Flood Insurance Program and developments within the floodway that increase the height of the 100-year flood over one foot are prohibited (Brookes, Baker and Redmond, 1996).

There are numerous benefits to be achieved by promoting river corridors and returning the floodplain to a natural water storage system. Perhaps the most important benefits of river corridors are: first, they provide an environmentally acceptable way of managing floods and river channel change which avoids modifying the existing channel; secondly, they conserve wetland habitats and preserve the morphological and biological characteristics of the channel; and thirdly, they will help to retain open land protected by Green Belt or other designations. Thus, river corridors may be particularly advantageous in environmentally sensitive areas and areas where flood protection of farmland or buildings by expensive structural engineering methods is uneconomic. An important question for society, however, is whether the 'loss' of land which river corridors entail is a price worth paying for more environmentally acceptable flood management.

CONCLUSIONS

Since Luna Leopold (1977) wrote of the need for a 'reverence for rivers' a more sustainable and environmentally sensitive approach has emerged with improved decision-making, river designs and working practices. This more 'reverent' approach has its origins in concerns over the impacts of traditional engineering and in changed viewpoints about how rivers should be managed. Table 3.3 contrasts some of the old ideas and working practices with the new(er) ones. The challenge ahead is to try to reconcile the often conflicting pressures of nature conservation and various land use activities with management of floods and river channel changes. This may be an attainable goal if the basic principles of sound river management can be followed:

- Work with nature not against it and emulate nature in river channel designs.
- Adopt river designs and working practices that are known to have the least impact on the environment.
- Always apply the principles of sustainable development.
- Adopt integrated, catchment-wide planning.
- Employ a detailed appraisal process and consult widely, considering all environmental issues alongside the engineering and economic objectives.
- Always carry out post-project appraisal so that knowledge about the impacts of river management continues to grow.

Table 3.3 Changing viewpoints and working practices in river management

Old ideas/practices	*New ideas/practices*
River taming	Work with nature
Confine rivers	Create river corridors (and recognise that rivers are meant to flood and must have room to move)
Straighten rivers	Retain meanders and morphological diversity
Construct embankments	Design flexible two-stage flood channels
Bank protection using rip rap, gabions or concrete	Use vegetation to protect river banks; vegetation also provides shade and food and creates a diverse habitat
Solutions through a structural civil engineering approach	Solutions through an interdisciplinary and holistic approach with rivers considered an integral part of the catchment

REFERENCES

Bauer, E.A. and East, B. (1970) 'The gravediggers', *Outdoor Life*, July (see Brookes, 1988).

Brammer, M. (1990) 'Floods in Bangladesh: geographical background to the 1987 and 1988 floods', *Geographical Journal*, vol. 156, no. 1, pp. 12–22.

Brookes, A. (1987) 'The distribution and management of channelised streams in Denmark', *Regulated Rivers*, vol. 1, pp. 3–16.

Brookes, A. (1988) *Channelized Rivers: Perspectives for Environmental Management*. Chichester: Wiley.

Brookes, A. and Shields, F.D. Jr (eds) (1996) *River Channel Restoration, Guiding Principles for Sustainable Projects*. Chichester: Wiley.

Brookes, A., Baker, J. and Redmond, C. (1996) 'Floodplain restoration and riparian zone management', in Brookes, A. and Shields, F.D. Jr (eds), *River Channel Restoration, Guiding Principles for Sustainable Projects*. Chichester: Wiley, pp. 201–29.

Brookes, A., Gregory, K.J. and Dawson, F.H. (1983) 'An assessment of river channelisation in England and Wales', *Science of the Total Environment*, vol. 27, pp. 97–112.

Gardiner, J.L. and Cole, L. (1992) 'Catchment planning: the way forward for river protection in the UK', in Boon, P.J., Calow, P. and Petts, G.E. (eds), *River Conservation and Management*. Chichester: Wiley, pp. 321–35.

Gregory, K.J. (1985) *The Nature of Physical Geography*. London: Edward Arnold.

Heuvelmans, M. (1974) *The River Killers*. Harrisburg, PA: Stackpole Books (see Brookes, 1988).

Holmes, N.T.H. and Nielsen, M.B. (1998) 'Restoration of the rivers Brede, Cole and Skerne: a joint Danish and British EU-LIFE demonstration project, I – setting up and delivery of the project'. *Aquatic Conservation: Marine & Freshwater Ecosystems*, vol. 8, pp. 185–96.

Horizon (1994) 'After the Flood', (programme transmitted on 18 April).

Johnston, R.J. (1983) *Geography and Geographers: Anglo-American Human Geography Since 1945*, 2nd edn. London: Edward Arnold.

Keller, E.A. (1975) 'Channelisation: a search for a better way', *Geology*, vol. 3, pp. 246–8.

Knighton, D. (1998) *Fluvial Forms and Processes, A New Perspective*. London: Edward Arnold.

Leopold, L.B. (1977) 'A reverence for rivers', *Geology*, vol. 5, pp. 429–30.

McHarg, I.L. (1969) *Design with Nature*. Garden City, NY: Doubleday.

Marsh, G.P. (1864) *Man and Nature or Physical Geography as Modified by Human Action*. New York: Charles Scribner (see Gregory, 1985).

Newson, M.D. (1986) 'River basin engineering – fluvial geomorphology', *Journal of the Institution of Water Engineers and Scientists*, vol. 40, pp. 307–24.

Petersen, R.C., Petersen, L.B.-M. and Lacoursiere, J. (1992) 'A building-block model for stream restoration', in Boon, P.J., Calow, P. and Petts, G.E. (eds), *River Conservation and Management*. Chichester: Wiley, pp. 293–309.

RSPB, NRA and RSNC (1994) *The New Rivers and Wildlife Handbook*. Royal Society for the Protection of Birds, Sandy, Bedfordshire.

Shields, F.D. and Sanders, T.G. (1986) 'Water quality effects of excavation and diversion', *Journal of Environmental Engineering, American Society of Civil Engineers*, vol. 112, pp. 211–28.

Wharton, G. (2000) *Managing River Environments*. Cambridge: Cambridge University Press.

Winkley, B.R. (1982) 'Response of the Lower Mississippi to river training and realignment', in Hey, R.D., Bathurst, J.C. and Thorne, C.R. (eds), *Gravel-bed Rivers*. Chichester: Wiley, pp. 652–81.

Chapter 4

Changing perspectives on changing climates

Julian Mayes

INTRODUCTION

> Planet Earth is intrinsically dynamic, and humans, for their very survival, must be dynamic too, moving, changing and evolving. Stability is never an option.
>
> (Moore, Chaloner and Stott, 1996, p. vii)

With the emergence of global warming onto the world's political, social and economic agendas, climatic information and data have been subject to unprecedented scrutiny. Climatic change straddles the physical and human sciences and the contentiousness of our responses to it is heightened when apparently conflicting perspectives are presented. Two questions are fundamental to these arguments: is climate changing? and (if it is), how is it changing? This chapter will start by addressing these questions. Scenarios of future climates will be appraised and a variety of response strategies will be evaluated. This will highlight the challenges of communicating scientific uncertainties to the public and to political decision-makers alike and in encouraging a greater public understanding of environmental change.

IS CLIMATE CHANGING?

Climate has always changed. For the first hundred years or so of instrumental observations (to about 1900) global climate appeared to be relatively stable over the relatively small part of the world that had climate observing sites (Hulme, 1994; Lamb, 1995). The phenomenon of global warming can only be quantified satisfactorily if data is collected on a global basis. Figure 4.1 shows the widely accepted 'official' data-set of sea and land surface temperature compiled by the Climatic Research Unit at the University of East Anglia[1] and the Hadley Centre of the Meteorological Office.[2] This is an amalgam of over 8000 sea surface temperature measurements by shipping and buoys together with over 1000 land temperature observations from conventional climatological stations (Jones, 1994; Parker, Horton and Gordon, 1998). The data are then expressed in terms of a regular grid spacing to give an even geographical coverage. These observations are expressed as anomalies from average temperatures for 1961–90, revealing a warming of about 0.6° C over the last 90 years. The cooling from around 1940 to around 1970 is widely believed to be due to natural variability, largely in the Northern Hemisphere.

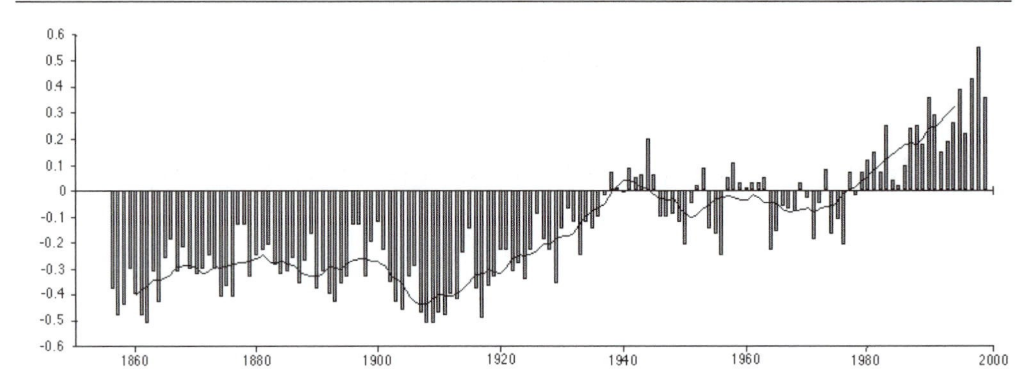

Figure 4.1 Global surface temperature changes, 1856–1999.

Past temperature changes have been analysed in detail by the Intergovernmental Panel on Climate Change (Houghton et al., 1996; Houghton, 1997). This chapter will aim to distil the key findings and compare these with alternative interpretations.

Figure 4.1 shows that many years since the mid-1980s have broken the record for the warmest year on record. Each of the 10 warmest years on record has occurred since 1982. The warmest year on record (so far) was 1998 with a global average temperature 0.55 °C above the 1961–90 average. The next warmest years were as recently as 1997 (+0.43 °C) and 1995 (+0.38 °C) while 1999 and 1990 were equal fourth warmest (+0.36). Provisional data indicate that 1999 was the warmest year in Central England since records began in 1659. However, as the public has become used to the notion of global warming, has the alarmist element in the media coverage of this issue provoked a degree of scepticism? An alternative perspective is provided by satellite measurements of atmospheric temperature (see Table 4.1) and this has aroused considerable debate because it does appear to portray a different perspective.

Table 4.1. Trends in global temperature (in °C/decade) from satellite, radiosonde and surface observations

Source	*Rate of warming*
Land and sea surface temperature data	+0.17
Satellite data (lower troposphere)	–0.05
Satellite data (revised for orbital changes)	+0.07
Radiosonde data	+0.10

*Note that a concentration of warming at the surface is consistent with a strengthening greenhouse effect – the satellite data represent changes at an average altitude of 3.5 km above the surface, similar to the radiosonde data.

Sources: Nicholls et al. (1996); Wentz and Schabel (1998).

CAN WE BELIEVE THE DATA?

The discrepancy between the two sources of data has been used by some commentators[3] as a reason for discrediting the conventional record. However, the two data-sets do not measure the same variable – the satellite data refers to the temperature above the earth's surface, above the zone in which we live (Burroughs, 1997). The satellite data is only available for a relatively short period – 1979 to present. Initial explanations of the downward trend cited the short-term effects of El Niño and volcanic events; removal of these showed a slight 'real' warming trend (Nicholls et al., 1996). However, a gradual change in the orbiting height of the satellites has been subsequently discovered (Wentz and Schabel, 1998) which is now believed to distort the consistency of the satellite data.

Sceptics have pointed out that warming may have been caused by urbanisation.[3] However, the urban heating effect is small in comparison with the changes in temperature that we experience from one year to the next and have been acknowledged by means of adjustments (albeit estimates) to the original data (Jones et al., 1994).

Conventional observations are rarely continuous and the creation of a long temperature record involves the amalgamation of observations from adjacent observation points. There are also adjustments that have to be made to sea temperature data obtained from ships, allowing for such factors as the way in which a water sample was obtained. Until the mid-twentieth century this was usually by means of lowering a bucket into the water and recent research has even considered the effect of the material the bucket was constructed of (Nicholls et al., 1996). However, perhaps the most common uncertainty is that of gaps in the geographical data network, especially the early part of the record in the nineteenth century.

EVIDENCE FROM THE NATURAL ENVIRONMENT

The natural environment can respond in a variety of ways to temperature changes and can thus be compared with conventional temperature observations. Many species of plants and animals are sensitive to small temperature changes and this ecological check on climatic observations is becoming more useful as evidence is gathered of continuing responses of plant and animal distribution to warming. For example, changes in the distribution of several bird and butterfly species in the British Isles have been attributed to recent warming (McNally et al., 1997). There is also evidence of a lengthening growing season in the Northern Hemisphere since the 1980s (Myneni et al., 1997).

A longer-term perspective is provided by records of changing ice and snow cover. Snow cover in the Northern Hemisphere has declined by 10 per cent between the mid-1970s and the mid-1990s (Nicholls et al., 1996). However, all is not quite what it seems. In Norway, local glacier expansion is actually consistent with warming because warmer winters have provided a greater source of snowfall because of a higher frequency of westerly winds.

EVIDENCE FOR THE ENHANCED GREENHOUSE EFFECT

The influence of the greenhouse effect on temperature has been well understood for about 100 years. This is a natural phenomenon caused by the absorption of some of the infra-red radiation emitted by the surface of the earth into the atmosphere. This can be likened to a partial barrier to outgoing radiation, restricting the loss of heat to space. It is most clearly illustrated by the relative warmth of cloudy nights – clouds consist of a common (but highly variable) greenhouse gas, water vapour. The changing contribution of the greenhouse gases to earth surface temperature is shown in Figure 4.2. These gases remain in the atmosphere for many years (even centuries) and are therefore evenly mixed throughout the world – it is a genuinely global issue.

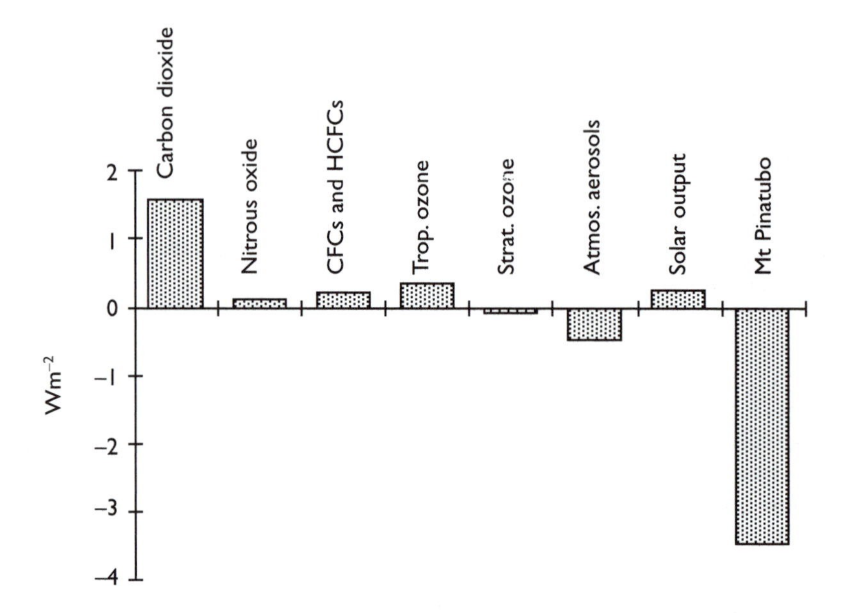

Figure 4.2 Changes in the strength of greenhouse gases from roughly 1850 to the late twentieth century (expressed as radiation in Watts per square metre). The cooling effect of additional atmospheric aerosol loading is shown together with the warming effect of increased solar output. For comparison, the short-term cooling effect of the eruption of the Mt Pinatubo volcanic eruption in the Philippines (June 1991) is also shown.

HOW DOES CLIMATE CHANGE?

Climate can change on a variety of timescales and for a variety of reasons. The main causes are:

- long-term natural variability of cycles in the shape of the earth's orbit around the sun – in particular, the Milankovitch cycles;
- variability in the output of the sun associated with differing numbers of sunspots in accordance with cycles of 11 and 76 years;
- changes in the amount of solar radiation being absorbed at the earth's surface. This can be due to land-cover changes (which affect the reflectivity or albedo of the surface) or by changes in the clarity of the atmosphere (due to dust and other pollutants in the atmosphere, notably from volcanic eruptions);
- variations in the atmospheric circulation – the strength and direction of the winds. Global airflow is dominated by a westerly airstream above the surface (the upper westerlies). These are driven by equator to pole (and smaller scale) temperature contrasts. Thus, if global warming changes the pattern of temperatures, the degree of dominance of westerly winds is likely to be affected. The period since the late

1980s has witnessed an abrupt increase in the vigour of the mid-latitude westerlies (Mayes and Wheeler, 1997), the reason for widespread changes in rainfall across much of Europe and for the increased snowfall on the Norwegian Alps cited above;
- changes in the proportion of outgoing radiation absorbed in the earth's atmosphere, i.e. the greenhouse effect. The strength of the greenhouse effect changes in accordance with the concentrations of greenhouse gases. All major greenhouse gases have increased in concentration since the start of the Industrial Revolution: carbon dioxide by 30 per cent, methane by 145 per cent and nitrous oxide by 15 per cent. This is largely due to pollution derived from human activity, though the rate of removal of greenhouse gases is determined by the characteristics of the natural environment. This is, in turn, influenced by changes in land-cover (initiated by changes in agricultural practice, for example) and by changing rates of biological activity in the oceans, both sources of continuing uncertainty.

A vigorous debate has developed between those who attribute recent warming to the strengthening greenhouse effect and those who attribute it to changes in solar activity. In particular, two new perspectives on solar activity have been advanced:

- the output of the sun (and hence global temperature) is higher when the 11-year solar cycle becomes shorter than average (Calder, 1997; Chambers 1998);
- a suggested link between solar output, the emission of cosmic rays from the sun, global cloud amount and earth surface temperature (Calder, 1997). Unfortunately, it is difficult to implicate changing cloud amount as a major factor in recent warming – it is one of the more constant aspects of the climate system and few significant changes have been apparent at the global scale.

CAN WE IDENTIFY THE CAUSE(S) OF RECENT WARMING?

While it is easy to list the causes of climatic change, it is difficult to disentangle the causes of particular changes in temperature at particular times. Human-induced effects on climate will be superimposed on the background 'noise' of short-term natural climatic variability.

The pattern of the warming above the surface of the earth can give us a clue to its cause. If warming is caused only by an increase in the concentrations of greenhouse gases, the heating effect should be concentrated in the lower part of the atmosphere. Acting in the absence of increased solar radiation, the greenhouse effect can only influence the distribution of heat. Air is warmed from below – by radiation from the earth's surface. A stronger greenhouse effect traps more of this warming in the lower part of the atmosphere (the first few kilometres above the surface) where the atmosphere – and therefore the greenhouse gases – is at greatest density. The upper atmosphere therefore cools down – less heat is escaping from the earth to warm the upper troposphere (around 10–12 km) and the stratosphere (12–14 km upwards). Observations from satellites are capable of detecting changes at these different heights in the atmosphere and these do indeed show this 'signature' of a strengthened greenhouse effect. Although ozone depletion is an additional factor promoting cooling in the stratosphere, it should be noted that it does not promote warming at the surface, as is often believed.

The rate of warming that appears to have taken place over the last 100 years (see

Figure 4.1) is believed to be at the limit of what could happen from natural variations alone (Hulme, 1994). In view of the rapid and unprecedented rise in greenhouse gases at the same time, it is possible to understand why most climate scientists are convinced that this is the main cause (or one of the main causes) of the warming. Sceptics say that this cannot be proven, but it is difficult to attribute such changes to the greenhouse effect with complete certainty. Others point to evidence for sharp temperature changes at the end of the last glacial (for example, Chambers, 1998), although direct comparison would be misleading unless we also consider the climate sensitivity of the modern world.

HOW FAST IS TEMPERATURE PROJECTED TO RISE?

Projections of future temperature are updated by increasingly sophisticated climate models. Until the late 1980s most models were so-called equilibrium models – i.e. they gave a projection of temperatures not for a specific date but for when global temperatures have come into equilibrium with a doubling of CO_2. This will take place many decades after the actual doubling of CO_2 due to the time taken for the oceans to warm up. Most models produced in the 1990s are transient models – they give an indication of the rate of warming, i.e. they attempt to take account of the rate at which the oceans will warm. The best estimate of warming according to the IPCC is one of 2 °C between 1990 and 2100 (Kattenberg et al., 1996, and Figure 4.3). This is lower than the figure the IPCC quoted in 1990 due to refinements in models. However, this represents a faster rate of warming than any experienced over the last 10 000 years

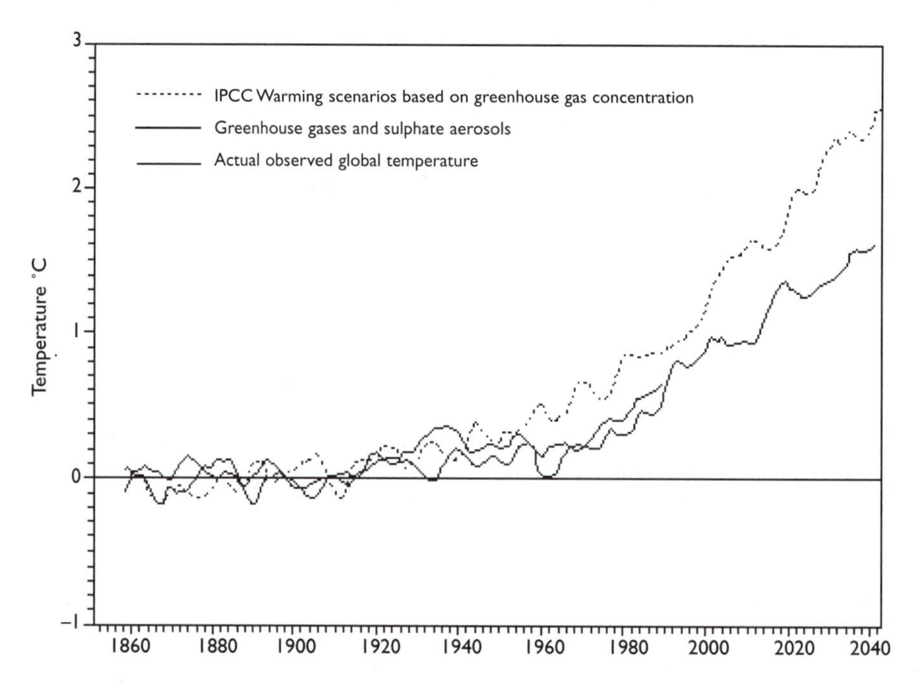

Figure 4.3 The IPCC scenario of rising global temperature, 1856 to 2040 (adapted from Kattenberg et al., 1996).

and a quadrupling of the warming rate of the last 100 years. Furthermore, it also represents only about 50–90 per cent of the 'equilibrium' warming that we would have committed ourselves to. This means that even if concentrations of greenhouse gases stabilise by 2100, warming would continue for several decades to follow as the oceans and coastal areas 'catch up' with the warming experienced elsewhere. Sea level is expected to rise by 50 cm by 2100, though the range of variation between low sensitivity and high sensitivity is from 15 cm to 90 cm (Warrick et al., 1996).

Significant warming is expected to initiate two important feedback mechanisms:

- *Ice-albedo feedback.* Areas of ice and snow are able to reflect a large proportion of the incoming solar radiation (up to 90 per cent) – they are therefore said to have a high albedo or surface reflectivity. Large areas of ice or snow help to keep the earth's surface cool. If significant melting takes place over coming decades, the open water or land areas that will take the place of ice will absorb a larger proportion of the radiation from the sun and thus contribute to further warming – a positive feedback.
- *Cloud-albedo feedback.* Warming is expected to change the frequency of different cloud types. High cloud – cirrus – has a high albedo and thus has a warming effect on the atmosphere whereas low cloud – for example, cumulus – has a lower albedo and thus a cooling effect. The balance between the frequency of these cloud types will influence future warming rates.

One important negative feedback to have emerged in the 1990s is the cooling effect of sulphate aerosol particles that can go on to develop acid rain. Sulphate aerosols produce a shading effect on solar radiation and thus lead to a cooling. They differ from greenhouse gases also because they are washed out of the atmosphere in a matter of days and thus do not have time to disperse evenly around the world. If we continue to tackle the emissions from burning sulphur-rich coal we will reduce this cooling effect as well as fight acid rain. We might then realise that this cooling effect, which is believed to amount to several °C in Europe at times, may have been masking a still larger greenhouse warming. This is an example of a real conflict between measures introduced to tackle different environmental problems.

COMPARISON OF FUTURE SCENARIOS WITH RECENT CLIMATIC EVENTS – REGIONAL CHANGES

The climate system can be likened to a set of delicately linked webs in which a disturbance in one area is transferred to others in sequence. Three regional climatic anomalies are reviewed and possible links to global warming are evaluated.

El Niño events

El Niño is a periodic extensive warming of the upper layers of the tropical South Pacific lasting for up to a year or more. This phenomenon triggers interaction with the atmosphere in many different parts of the world. These events are caused by the entry of warm ocean currents to the coast of South America which induces a lowering of atmospheric pressure here and a counterbalancing increase on the Australasian side of the ocean. These air pressure changes weaken the trade winds that normally blow across the Pacific (towards Australasia), reinforcing the above average sea temperatures as the upwelling of cold water is discouraged. The resulting warm pool of water imparts a great deal of energy into the atmosphere. Temperatures may reach 5 °C above normal in the severest episodes.

One of the strongest El Niño events in recorded history developed through 1997, a contributary factor to the warmth of that year (Parker, Horton and Gordon, 1998). This event was also notable because it came so soon after the protracted El Niño of 1990–95 and provoked two responses in the climate system:

- Drought in Indonesia contributed to the severity of the smoke haze resulting from widespread and uncontrolled forest fires in Indonesia and adjacent countries (Jim, 1999). El Niño-related drought also intensified across much of Africa and the southern States of the USA.
- Severe flooding and mudslides in California in the first weeks of 1998. This event was well forecast due to known associations between El Niño events and the location of the jet-stream across North America, the focal point for heavy rains and storms.

The North Atlantic 'conveyor'

A less publicised oceanic influence on weather concerns the movement of water in the North Atlantic. The mildness of Western Europe in winter is associated with the north-eastward flow of the Gulf Stream and the North Atlantic Drift, driven by the sinkage of water further north. This is highly sensitive to the density of the water, which is itself determined by the proportion of fresh water here. Incursions of fresh water reduce the density of the surface water and discourage the sinking that drives the current (Pickering and Owen, 1997). This creates ideal conditions for a negative feedback to warming in this region – warming will increase the runoff of fresh water into the North Atlantic (in the form of melt-water), leading to a possible regional cooling effect. This could be why the North Atlantic region was one of the last parts of the world to experience the recent rise in temperature.

Changes in mid-latitude temperature and precipitation patterns

Geographical patterns of temperature and precipitation over Europe are controlled by the North Atlantic Oscillation Index (NAOI). This is said to be in a positive mode when the difference in air pressure between the Azores high pressure and the Icelandic low pressure is greater than normal, resulting in an invigorated westerly airstream across Europe. Weak pressure contrasts (and hence weaker, less dominant westerly winds) represent the negative mode. In the positive phase, maritime winter mildness (and coolness in summer) extends further east into Europe and rainfall becomes more strongly concentrated in north-west Europe while high pressure maintains dry conditions over the Mediterranean. This condition was remarkably dominant in winters from the late 1980s to the mid-1990s (see Figure 4.4), encouraging a larger number of deep low pressure systems and wetter, stormier winters. For example, between December 1994 and June 1995 parts of Spain and neighbouring countries had less than half average rainfall, while northern Europe was exceptionally wet. These rainfall anomalies were abruptly reversed by the following winter (1995–96) when the NAOI changed from its highest to its lowest value on record (see also Hulme, 2000).

In summer, the area of low summer rainfall extends northwards from the sub-tropics across the Mediterranean region. Hot summers see a further northward expansion of

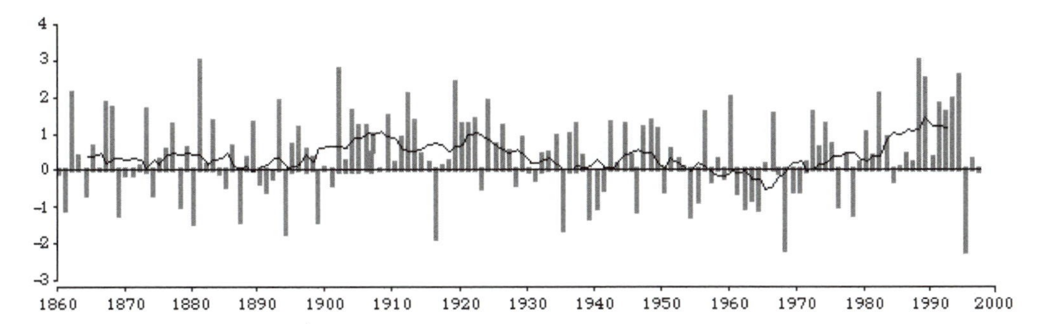

Figure 4.4 The North Atlantic Oscillation Index. This shows the air pressure difference between Iceland and the Azores for the winter months. The negative values are indicative of a weakened westerly airstream (note the mid-twentieth century decline) and positive values show an invigorated flow pattern. Note the abrupt change to positive values in the 1980s and early 1990s followed by sharp inter-annual fluctuations.

this area of dryness. The probability of experiencing a summer as warm as that of 1976 or 1995 increases dramatically for a given change in mean summer temperature (Burroughs, 1997). Hulme (1996) has estimated that if summer temperatures increase by about 1.5 to 2 °C by the 2050s, the probability of such an 'extreme' summer would change from 0.013 (as in 1961–90) to 0.33.

Changes in rainfall across the British Isles have increased the north-west/south-east climatic contrast since the 1970s (Mayes and Wheeler, 1997, and Figure 4.5). This change, which is consistent with the positive phase of the NAOI, is the most inconvenient possible change in view of the availability of regional water resources across the country. The droughts of 1988–92 and 1995–97 were most severe in south-eastern Britain where water resources are usually scarcest (Marsh and Turton, 1996). Across England and Wales as a whole, the 24 months ending spring 1997 and the 30 months to October 1997 were both the driest on records which began in 1697. The year 1996 was the driest since 1921 in England. This enhancement of the north-west/south-east moisture availability contrast is consistent with results of some transient climate models (Kattenberg et al., 1996), though more recent models give more equivocal evidence (see, for example, Hulme, 2000).

Lack of moisture is going to be compounded in a warmer environment by increased evapotranspiration, reducing soil moisture levels for a given rainfall amount. Surface runoff in South East England is already highly sensitive to variations in precipitation and temperature in summer. Combined with the sharpened NW/SE climatic gradient, this is a problem that poses major challenges for future water planning.

RESPONSES TO GLOBAL WARMING

Should we respond? How should we respond? Who should respond?

If we accept that global warming poses a threat to our social and economic well-being, together with our health and that of natural environments, we need to identify the causes. Human-induced warming is amenable to treatment – we would need to reverse some of the changes in energy consumption that we have instigated over the last 50

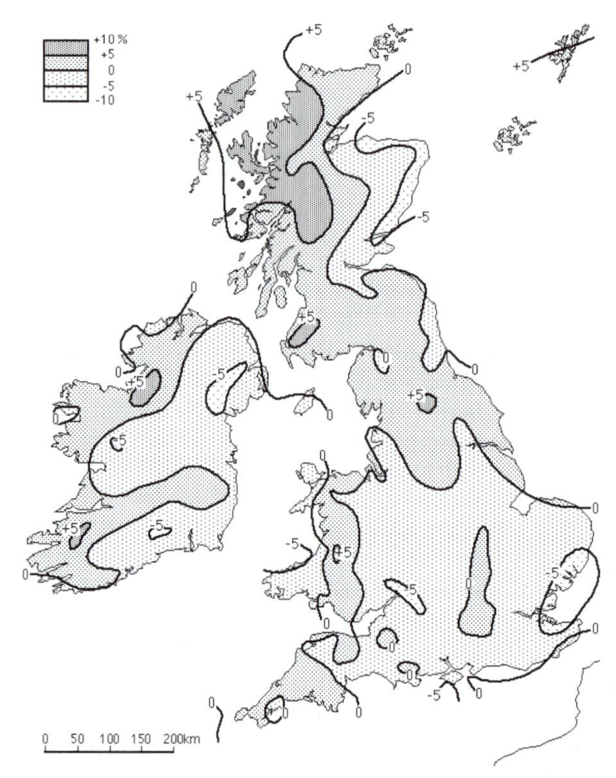

Figure 4.5 Percentage change in annual precipitation in the British Isles, 1941–70 to 1961–90 (adapted from Mayes and Wheeler, 1997)

years. This identifies how we should respond – sources of greenhouse gases can be identified. The issue of who should respond is more difficult. To address the problem effectively we should all act – individuals have the power to determine the changes in energy consumption and energy efficiency we need to achieve. The debate then becomes enmeshed in political issues such as commitment to affordable energy pricing on welfare grounds and the resulting policy conflict can lead to a delay in the political responses to the problem (Schneider, 1996). Much interest has recently been shown in 'no regrets' policies, which would be worthwhile in their own right on grounds other than the (possibly contentious) issue of controlling future climate. An example is energy conservation, an integral part of sustainable development (Jepta and Munasinghe, 1998).

Limitation or adaptation?

These two responses relate to how quickly action can be taken. The aim of limitation is to limit the increase in concentrations of greenhouse gases by changing energy use so that the projected increases do not come fully to fruition. How feasible is this? The main challenge here is the time lag between a change to the emissions of a greenhouse gas and the effect this may have on overall global concentrations. The gases emitted today will still be contributing to the greenhouse effect at the end of the twenty-first century. In the words of the Secretary-General of the World Meteorological Organisation: 'The inertia of the climate system means that we may have to live with the consequences of past actions for many years to come and if change is inevitable, learn to adapt to it' (Obasi, 1998, p. 3). This is why effective limitation of the problem depends upon acting on emissions well in advance of the time when we want to stabilise the greenhouse effect itself. Adaptation implies acceptance of living with the consequences of a stronger greenhouse effect and the likely changes in climate that this will bring. It highlights our use of the earth and its resources in a changing climate, a reminder that environmental change is an ongoing, inevitable process and one that humankind needs to come to terms with (Moore, Chaloner and Stott, 1996).

Informing the policy-makers

Climatologists have established a new global dialogue with others and with policy-makers. The main conferences that have achieved this aim have included the following:

- *The Toronto Conference on the Changing Global Environment 1988.* This called for a 50 per cent cut in CO_2 emissions by 2100 in order to stabilise the overall concentration of greenhouse gases.
- *The United Nations 'Earth Summit' at Rio 1992.* The Framework Convention on Climate Change was agreed which has the goal of stabilising emissions to 1990 levels by 2000 in developed countries. The aim was to slow warming to a rate that would allow ecosystems to adapt naturally, minimising losses to either food production or economic development.
- As follow-ups to Rio, conferences in Berlin in 1995 and Kyoto in 1997 have established a goal of cutting emissions by only around 5 per cent by 2008–12 and have started to address the issue of the global distribution of cutbacks between developed and developing countries.

CONCLUSIONS

The rapidly accumulating evidence for climatic change in the 1980s and 1990s has been matched by an unprecedented public and media debate about the issues and the possible responses. A wide variety of explanations and perspectives have emerged. Contrasting viewpoints regarding the magnitude, causes and consequences of global warming highlight the importance of protecting and enhancing the monitoring of global weather and climate. The complexity of understanding climate change is that it is often multi-causal and the degree to which we can attribute global warming to the enhanced greenhouse effect remains a key challenge.

Local and regional climatic trends often diverge from the global average, creating fertile ground for contradictory interpretations. A current priority in climate research is the greater understanding of regional climatic events such as El Niño, the North Atlantic Oscillation and the movement of large-scale ocean currents. The extent to which these phenomena will be influenced by global warming is still uncertain.

A central issue is the way in which a response to global warming will be motivated. It may be that responses are generated less by abstract-sounding global statistics than by our direct experience of local climatic events and hazards. Reactions may be provoked if the response of the climate system to greenhouse gas forcing is non-linear

– that is, if weather patterns change abruptly instead of evolving steadily to some new state. To achieve a balanced perspective we need to evaluate the contribution (and consistency) of these short-term local events to the mosaic of longer-term global changes and their (as yet) more subtle effects.

NOTES

1. The Climatic Research Unit, University of East Anglia: http://www.cru.uea.ac.uk/
2. The Hadley Centre for Climate Prediction and Research, Meteorological Office: http://www.met-office.gov.uk/sec5/sec5pg1.html
3. John Daly's website, Tasmania: http://www.vision.net.au/%7Edaly

REFERENCES

Burroughs, W.J. (1997) *Does the Weather Really Matter? The Social Implications of Climatic Change*. Cambridge: Cambridge University Press.

Calder, N. (1997) *The Manic Sun*. Northamptonshire: Pilkington Press.

Chambers, F. (1998) 'Global warming: new perspectives from palaeoecology and solar science', *Geography*, vol. 83, no. 3, pp. 266–77.

Houghton, J. (1997) *Global Warming – The Complete Briefing*, 2nd edn. Cambridge, Cambridge University Press.

Houghton, J.T., Meira Filho, L.G., Callander, B.A., Harris, N., Kattenberg, A. and Maskill, K. (1996) *Climate Change 1995: The Science of Climate Change*. Cambridge: Cambridge University Press.

Hulme, M. (1994) 'Historic records and recent climatic change', in Roberts, N. (ed.), *The Changing Global Environment*. Oxford: Blackwell.

Hulme, M. (1996) *The 1996 CCIRG Scenario of Changing Climate and Sea-Level for the UK*, Technical Note No. 7. Norwich: Climatic Research Unit.

Hulme, M. (2000) 'Climatic change', in Gardiner, V. and Matthews, S.H. (eds), *The Changing Geography of the United Kingdom*, 3rd edn. London: Routledge.

Jepta, C.J. and Munasinghe, M. (1998) *Climate Change Policy*. Cambridge: Cambridge University Press.

Jim, C.Y. (1999) 'The forest fires in Indonesia 1997–98: possible causes and pervasive consequences', *Geography*, vol. 83, no. 3, pp. 251–60.

Jones, P.D. (1994) 'Hemispheric surface air temperature variations: a reanalysis and an update to 1993', *Journal of Climatology*, vol. 7, pp. 794–802.

Kattenberg, A., Giurgi, F., Grassl, H., Meehl, G.A., Mitchell, J.F.B., Stouffer, R.J., Tokioka, T., Weaver, A.J. and Wigley, T.M.L. (1996) Climate models – projections of future climates, in Houghton, J.T. et al. (eds), *Climate Change 1995: The Science of Climate Change*. Cambridge: Cambridge University Press.

Lamb, H.H. (1995) *Climate History and the Modern World*. London: Routledge.

McNally, S., Crowards, T., Cannell, M.G.R. and Sparks, T.H. (1997) 'The natural environment', in Palutikof, J.P., Subak, S. and Agnew, M.D. (eds), *Economic Impacts of the Hot Summer and Unusually Warm Year of 1995*. London: Department of the Environment/Norwich: University of East Anglia.

Marsh, T.T.J. and Turton, P.S. (1996) 'The 1995 drought: a water resources perspective', *Weather*, vol. 51, no. 2, pp. 46–53.

Mayes, J.C. and Wheeler, D.A. (1997) 'Regional perspectives on climatic variability and change', in Wheeler, D.A. and Mayes, J.C. (eds), *Regional Climates of the British Isles*. London: Routledge.

Moore, P.D., Chaloner, B. and Stott, P. (1996) *Global Environmental Change*. Oxford: Blackwell.

Myneni, R.B., Keeling, C.D., Tucker, C.J. Asrar, G. and Nemani, R.R. (1997) 'Increased plant growth in the northern high latitudes from 1981 to 1991, *Nature*, vol. 386, pp. 698–702.

Nicholls, N., Gruza, G.V., Jouzel, J., Karl, T.R., Ogallo, L.A. and Parker, D.E. (1996) 'Observed climate variability and change', in Houghton, J.T. et al. (eds), *Climate Change 1995: The Science of Climate Change*. Cambridge: Cambridge University Press.

Obasi, G.O.P. (1998) 'Foreword', *World Climate News*, no. 13, p. 3.

Parker, D.E., Horton, E.B. and Gordon, M. (1998) 'Global and regional climate in 1997', *Weather*, vol. 53, no. 6, pp. 166–75.

Pickering, K.T. and Owen, L.A. (1997) *An Introduction to Global Environmental Issues*, 2nd edn. London: Routledge.

Schneider, S. (1996) *Laboratory Earth – The Planetary Gamble We Cannot Afford to Lose*. London: Weidenfeld & Nicholson.

Warrick, R.A., Le Provost, C., Meier, M.F., Oerlemans, J. and Woodworth, P.L. (1996) 'Sea level rise', in Houghton, J.T. et al. (eds), *Climate Change 1995: The Science of Climate Change*. Cambridge: Cambridge University Press.

Wentz, F.J. and Schabel, M. (1998) 'Effects of orbital decay on satellite-derived lower-tropospheric temperature trends', *Nature*, vol. 394, p. 661.

Chapter 5

New directions in human geography

Peter Jackson

INTRODUCTION

These are exciting times for human geography as the discipline is experiencing a period of rapid change, reflecting dramatic shifts in the world about us (Philo, 1991). The work of leading human geographers, such as David Harvey and Doreen Massey, is generating considerable interest beyond the discipline's boundaries in politics, sociology and especially in cultural studies. Geographical concepts of space and place, boundaries and borders, centres and margins have increasing currency among a range of social sciences. Once dominated by questions of temporality (or change over time), the social sciences are now increasingly aware of the significance of space (Gregory and Urry, 1985). Like sociology in the 1960s, human geography became fashionable during the 1980s and 1990s. The popularity of geography at university level increased dramatically as undergraduate and postgraduate numbers soared (Richards and Wrigley, 1996). New journals emerged like *Ecumene: A Journal of Environment, Culture, Meaning* (launched in 1994), *Gender, Place and Culture* (1994) and *Space and Polity* (1997) carrying on the vanguard role of earlier journals like *Antipode* (founded in 1969) and *Society and Space* (1983). While this burst of activity reflects a variety of institutional pressures to 'publish or perish' (most notably the Higher Education Funding Council's periodic Research Assessment Exercises), it also signals a genuine release of energy and intellectual excitement as narrow disciplinary boundaries have been transcended and new movements (including feminism and postcolonial studies) have taken researchers off in new directions, revealing the limitations of previous approaches and transforming the very nature of human geography.

While these are all welcome developments for many human geographers – opening up new spaces, new debates and new alliances – they are perceived by some as a threat to the 'core' of the discipline, with its traditional interest in human–environment relations, to understanding the evolving meanings of landscape and place, and to sustaining the vital links between human and physical geography. For such critics, the new directions outlined above are blind alleys at worst, diversions at best. In Ron Cooke's presidential address to the Institute of British Geographers in 1992, for example, several disciplinary 'imperatives' were identified, all subsumed within the core belief that understanding environmental change and managing the environment were at the heart of the discipline. Similarly, for David Stoddart, 'reclaiming the high ground' meant refocusing the discipline on issues such as flood plain management in Bangladesh, with a disdain bordering on contempt for other fields of research. Apparently fictitious studies of the distribution of fast food restaurants in Tel Aviv and geographical influences in the Canadian cinema were taken as examples of excessively narrow or trivial research topics. Ironically, however, one could make the case that it is in precisely such areas that the discipline has developed most rapidly and most productively since Stoddart's (1986) paper. Though not on precisely the topics that Stoddart satirised, recent work in human geography has seen path-breaking contributions to the study of 'culinary culture' and the geographies of consumption (Cook and Crang, 1996; Bell and Valentine, 1997) as well as compelling new research on media representations, environmental meaning and the social construction of nature (Burgess, 1990; Harrison and Burgess, 1994).

Rather than continue in this polemical vein, however, the rest of this chapter will attempt to provide a critical appraisal of the recent changes taking place in human geography from the perspective of someone who broadly welcomes these changes.

GEOGRAPHIES OF DIFFERENCE

Like most of the other social sciences, human geography experienced a 'cultural turn' during the last few years, signalled by a 'crisis of representation' in which the traditional belief in 'objective' knowledge has given way to more sceptical and critical understandings of the relationship between power and knowledge. David Livingstone's retelling of Geography's history, for example, rejects the 'conventional and comfortable image of science as the disinterested and objective pursuit of knowledge' (1992, p. 1) in favour of a thoroughly subjectivist account, emphasising the selective, provisional, contested and negotiated nature of geographical knowledge. Debates about our positionality as social scientists, about our authority to represent other people and places, have become increasingly commonplace as the inevitably 'situated' nature of geographical knowledge has been (somewhat reluctantly) acknowledged.

Numerous political and intellectual currents came together to force this acknowledgement of the partiality of geographical knowledge. Feminist theory was crucial in revealing the masculinist nature of 'objective' scientific knowledge, combined with psycho-analytic theory to challenge taken-for-granted theories of a fixed or 'essentialist' self (Rose, 1993; Pile and Thrift, 1995). Post-colonial theory was no less vital in demonstrating how 'Western' identities and concepts of the self have been forged through sometimes bloody encounters with 'non-Western' (colonial) others. Edward Said's study of *Orientalism* (1978) is the key text here, revealing how British and French imperialists constructed 'the Orient' as a place of romance, exotic beings, haunting memories and landscapes, and remarkable experiences. According to Said, 'East' and 'West' are mutually constituted: 'The two geographical entities support and reflect each other' (1978, p. 5). Nor are these references to geography coincidental. Said drew on the work of the French geographer Gaston Bachelard to describe Orientalism as an 'imaginative geography' or 'textual universe'. In his later work, too, Said writes of the 'overlapping territories' and 'intertwined histories' through which the crossovers between culture and imperialism can be understood, describing his project as 'a kind of geographical inquiry into historical experience' (1993, p. 6).

Besides feminism and post-colonial theory, the other main influence on recent developments in human geography has been the impact of cultural studies. Drawing on literary and cultural critics like Raymond Williams and Stuart Hall, this strand of work has insisted on the plurality of cultures and the multiple landscapes with which those cultures are associated. Often caricatured as a 'new' cultural geography, such an approach defined its agenda as 'contemporary as well as historical (but always contextual and theoretically-informed); social as well as spatial (but not confined exclusively to narrowly-defined landscape issues); urban as well as rural; and interested in the contingent nature of culture, in dominant ideologies and in forms of resistance to them' (Cosgrove and Jackson, 1987, p. 95).

Though such definitions have been the subject of sometimes heated debate (reviewed in Kong, 1997), there have been wholesale changes in the nature of human geography, including the dramatic growth of interest in various forms of difference, encompassing geographies of gender (McDowell and Sharp, 1997; WGSG, 1997), race (Bonnett, 1996), sexuality (Bell and Valentine, 1995) and disability (Imrie, 1996). Rather than approaching these issues as involving fixed and stable identities, a simple product of biology or nature, there has been a growing recognition of the social construction of human difference, rooted in the complexities of history and politics. Identities are also now defined in the plural, rather than assuming that every individual has only a singular and invariable 'identity': 'No one today is purely one thing. Labels like Indian, or woman, or Muslim, or American are no more than starting-points, which if followed into actual experience for only a moment are quickly left behind' (Said, 1993, p. 407). Moreover, once such differences are shown to be geographically and historically variable, rather than timeless or universal, it is clear that they are subject to change, becoming the focus of new political alliances and social movements.

Associated with the growth of interest in geographies of difference has been an insistence on the embodied nature of human identities. Inspired by Adrienne Rich's (1984) essay on the politics of location, which describes the body as 'the geography closest in', geographers have written on contracepted and pregnant bodies, able-bodied and disabled bodies, racialised and sexualised bodies. Geographers might, however, also take note of Rich's insistence on examining the more subjective level of personal experience, as suggested by the following observation:

> Perhaps we need a moratorium on saying 'the body'. For it's also possible to abstract 'the' body. When I write 'the body,' I see nothing in particular. To write 'my body' plunges me into lived experience, particularity: I see scars, disfigurements, discolorations, damages, losses, as well as what pleases me. Bones well nourished from the placenta; teeth of a middle-class person seen by the dentist twice a year from childhood. White skin, marked and scarred by three pregnancies, an elected sterilisation, progressive arthritis, four joint operations, calcium deposits, no rapes, no abortions, long hours at a typewriter – my own, not in a typing pool – and so forth. To say 'the body' lifts me away from what has given me a primary perspective. To say 'my body' reduces the temptation to grandiose assertions.
>
> (Ibid., reprinted in 1986, p. 215)

Geographers have often been 'squeamish' about personalising their accounts in this way, especially on topics as 'intimate' as sex and sexuality (Bell, 1994). There has, however, been a welcome shift from focusing exclusively on Other identities, associated with marginalised or 'minority' groups, to include a critical engagement with 'dominant' constructions of masculinity, heterosexuality and 'whiteness' (see, for example, Jackson, 1991; Valentine, 1993; Jackson, 1998). This has involved a recognition that all identities are situationally specific and built up through negotiation, in relation to a network of socially significant 'others'.

Similarly, at a wider scale, there has been an insistence on the 'hybrid' character of modern cultures, as processes of displacement and diaspora have become common characteristics of most if not all contemporary societies. Here, geographers are following their anthropological colleagues in tracing the transnational migration of people and the associated flows of commodities and information. Rather than seeing such developments as a simple process of 'globalisation', however, they are increasingly understood as a reflection of the relational connections between 'the local' and 'the global' (Mitchell, 1997). Understanding the nature of transnationality is therefore high on the agenda for geographical research in the new millennium.

DIFFERENT GEOGRAPHIES

While geography at school-level has been dominated by a concern with maintaining standards and resisting the forces of homogenisation that were implicit in the imposition of a National Curriculum, at university-level human geography has been characterised by a diversity that has often been characterised in terms of fragmentation. As I have argued elsewhere (Jackson, 1996), it is possible to see these changes in a more positive light. The blurring of boundaries between 'economic' and 'cultural' geography, for example, has been extremely productive whether one is concerned with understanding the workplace geographies of production (Peck, 1996; duGay, 1996; McDowell, 1997) or with the 'domestic' world of consumption (Mackay, 1997; Miller et al., 1998).

As these examples suggest, it is now widely recognised that the separation of 'production' from 'consumption' (and the identification of the former with 'the economic' and the latter with 'the cultural') is an unhelpful distinction. On the 'consumption' side, increasing attention has been paid to the skilled work that often goes unrecognised in the production of retail landscapes and in the highly gendered social relations of domestic consumption. On the 'production' side, a new retail geography is emerging which focuses on the restructuring of retail capital, the regulation of retail markets and the geographies of consumption sites, spaces and chains (Wrigley and Lowe, 1996). Besides their long-standing interest in the conventional retail environments of the high street and the shopping mall, geographers have also begun to investigate the 'alternative' consumption spaces of car boot sales, factory outlets and charity shops (Gregson and Crewe, 1994). Geographical research on this 'second cycle' of exchange is beginning to reveal a complex social world involving relations of reciprocity and exchange, performance and possession. As with anthropological research on consumption, it soon becomes clear that what constitutes a 'bargain' or what is represented as 'thrift' involve moral as well as economic notions of value, often embedded in highly gendered notions about the family and the social and spatial constitution of domestic life.

Far from being an isolated and momentary act of purchase, these studies emphasise the need to understand consumption as a process that goes on well beyond the point of sale, involving a complex network that extends back into the social relations of production and forward into successive cycles of use and reuse. It also suggests the need to understand the active role of consumers in shaping the 'landscape of consumption' rather than seeing them as passive dupes or hapless victims. Geographers have also begun to demonstrate the benefits of tracing particular commodity chains from production to consumption, collapsing the distinction between 'the global' and 'the local' as even the most globalised commodities are creatively reworked in local contexts of consumption (Jackson, 1999). For, as Doreen Massey's (1994) work amply demonstrates, a 'local' sense of place is no longer constituted within narrowly bounded neighbourhoods but involves extensive networks of social relations that extend far across space through the porous boundaries of 'community', linking places at a variety of scales from the neighbourhood to the nation (and beyond).

It goes without saying that the changes taking place in human geography have not occurred in an intellectual vacuum but reflect wider changes in Western industrial society. This is most clearly seen in the transition from Fordist to post-Fordist modes of production, signalled by the dramatic shift from manufacturing to service-sector employment. In Sheffield, for example, employment in the steel industry collapsed during the 1980s, followed by a growth of service-sector employment in banking, insurance and related fields. Sheffield now also boasts one of the largest shopping centres in Europe (Meadowhall) and a thriving Cultural Industries Quarter (housing the Showroom Cinema, the National Centre for Popular Music, the Red Tape (music) Studios, a photographic gallery and a video post-production facility). Associated changes in technology and the introduction of more 'flexible' work practices have not been of equal benefit to everyone, with the rise of short-term contracts and part-time employment leading to a 'feminisation' of the workforce. These changes have been accompanied (in some cases led) by new forms of urban governance, described by David Harvey (1989a) as a shift from managerialism to entrepreneurialism. Development corporations, public–private partnerships and new agencies such as the lottery-funded Millennium Commission all now play a significant role in influencing the future shape of the built environment.

Harder to characterise are the complex cultural changes that have accompanied the shift to more 'flexible' modes of production. Many observers have attempted to understand these changes as a transition from modernism to postmodernism, with most such studies (in geography at least) focusing on architecture and urban form. At least two contrasting readings of postmodern urbanism are available. Based on research in Vancouver, David Ley (1987) provides an upbeat reading of postmodernism as involving the 're-enchantment' of the urban environment, characterised by sensitive urban place-making and a return to vernacular styles at a human scale. By contrast, David Harvey's (1989b) reading of the postmodern city, based on examples from Baltimore to Los Angeles, is much more pessimistic, involving the erosion of local cultures through processes of commodification and globalisation. Festival marketplaces, spectacular shopping malls and other forms of 'heroic consumption' are taken by Harvey as evidence of a 'voodoo economics' where a world of surface gloss and glitz barely conceals the underlying poverty and exploitation, and private affluence triumphs amid public squalor. For Harvey, postmodernism is little more than the cultural clothing of late capitalism. These studies and the debates that surround them suggest that there can be no simple elision between the shifts from Fordism to post-Fordism, from production to consumption, and from modernism to postmodernism, however tempting it might be to make such an inference.

CONCLUSION

This chapter has attempted to identify a range of new directions being taken within human geography, particularly within the UK. Many of these ideas and approaches have yet to make any significant impact on geography teaching in schools and colleges. For some observers, these changes threaten a unitary view of geography as the integrated (human/physical/environmental) study of place. For others (myself included) they represent an expansion of our intellectual horizons and an opportunity to contribute to the wider understanding of society, including the chance to shape that wider world in a 'progressive' manner (through a more adequate recognition of the cultures of difference that are highlighted in the first part of this chapter).

While this chapter has focused on new directions in human geography, physical geography is not immune from similar changes. Recent work on the social construction of nature, including studies of the human and non-human aspects of environmental change, provides one exciting avenue for future research on the 'natural' environment. To cite just one example, David Harvey's study of *Justice, Nature and the Geography of Difference* (1996) encompasses many of the changes highlighted in this chapter. It includes a concern for social and environmental justice, a commitment to (re)establishing certain foundational concepts for understanding space, time, place and nature, and a (re)emphasis on the political significance of socially constructed categories of 'otherness' and 'difference'. Harvey brings together a range of issues that are rarely treated in such a comprehensive and coherent way by other social scientists. Such an ability to establish connections remains one of the key components of a truly human geography. For, as Edward Said concludes in his monumental study of *Culture and Imperialism*: 'Survival in fact is about the connections between things' (1993, p. 408). These are indeed exciting times for human geography, as a recognition of the geographies of difference begins to call forth different kinds of geography.

REFERENCES

Bell, D. (1994) 'Erotic topographies', *Area*, vol. 26, pp. 96–100.

Bell, D. and Valentine, G. (eds) (1995) *Mapping Desire: Geographies of Sexualities*. London: Routledge.

Bell, D. and Valentine, G. (1997) *Consuming Geographies: You Are Where You Eat*. London: Routledge.

Bonnett, A. (1996) 'Constructions of "race", place and discipline: geographies of "racial" identity and racism', *Ethnic and Racial Studies*, vol. 19, pp. 864–83.

Burgess, J. (1990) 'The production and consumption of environmental meanings in the mass media: a research agenda for the 1990s', *Transactions, Institute of British Geographers*, vol. 15, pp. 139–61

Cook, I. and Crang, P. (1996) 'The world on a plate: culinary culture, displacement and geographical knowledges', *Journal of Material Culture*, vol. 1, pp. 131–53.

Cooke, R.U. (1992) 'Common ground, shared inheritance: research imperatives for environmental geography', *Transactions, Institute of British Geographers*, vol. 17, pp. 131–51.

Cosgrove, D. and Jackson, P. (1987) 'New directions in cultural geography', *Area*, vol. 19, pp. 95–101.
duGay, P. (1996) *Consumption and Identity at Work*. London: Sage.
Gregory, D. and Urry, J. (eds) (1985) *Social Relations and Spatial Structures*. London: Macmillan.
Gregson, N. and Crewe, L. (1994) 'Beyond the high street and the mall: car boot fairs and the new geographies of consumption in the 1990s', *Area*, vol. 26, pp. 261–7.
Harrison, C.M. and Burgess, J. (1994) 'Social constructions of nature', *Transactions, Institute of British Geographers*, vol. 19, pp. 291–310.
Harvey, D. (1989a) 'From managerialism to entrepreneurialism: the transformation in urban governance in late capitalism', *Geografiska Annaler*, vol. 71B, pp. 3–17.
Harvey, D. (1989b) *The Condition of Postmodernity*. Oxford: Blackwell.
Harvey, D. (1996) *Justice, Nature and the Geography of Difference*. Oxford: Blackwell.
Imrie, R. (1996) *Disability and the City*. London: Paul Chapman.
Jackson, P. (1991) 'The cultural politics of masculinity: towards a social geography', *Transactions, Institute of British Geographers*, vol. 16, pp. 199–213.
Jackson, P. (1996) 'Only connect: approaches to human geography', in E.M. Rawling and R.A. Daugherty (eds.) *Geography into the Twenty-First Century*. Chichester: Wiley, pp. 77–94.
Jackson, P. (1998) 'Constructions of "whiteness" in the geographical imagination, *Area*, vol. 30, pp. 99–106.
Jackson, P. (1999) 'Commodity cultures: the traffic in things', *Transactions, Institute of British Geographers*, vol. 24, pp. 95–108.
Kong, L.L.L. (1997) 'A "new" cultural geography?' *Scottish Geographical Magazine*, vol. 113, pp. 177–85.
Ley, D. (1987) 'Styles of the times: liberal and neo-conservative landscapes in inner Vancouver', *Journal of Historical Geography*, vol. 13, pp. 40–56.
Livingstone, D. (1992) *The Geographical Tradition*. Oxford: Blackwell.
Mackay, H. (ed.) (1997) *Consumption and Everyday Life*. London: Sage.
Massey, D. (1994) *Space, Place and Gender*. Cambridge: Polity.
McDowell, L. (1997) *Capital Culture: Gender at Work in the City*. Oxford: Blackwell.
McDowell, L. and Sharp, J. (eds) (1997) *Space, Gender, Knowledge*. London: Arnold.
Miller, D., Jackson, P., Thrift, N., Holbrook, B. and Rowlands, M. (1998) *Shopping, Place and Identity*. London: Routledge.
Mitchell, K. (1997) 'Transnational discourse: bringing geography back in', *Antipode*, vol. 29, pp. 101–14.
Peck, J. (1996) *Workplace: The Social Regulation of Labor Markets*. New York: Guilford.
Philo, C. (ed.) (1991) *New Words, New Worlds*. Institute of British Geographers: Social and Cultural Geography Study Group.
Pile, S. and Thrift, N. (eds) (1995) *Mapping the Subject*. London: Routledge.
Rich, A. (1984) 'The politics of location', reprinted (1986) in *Blood, Bread, and Poetry*. New York, W.W. Norton, pp. 210–31.
Richards, K. and Wrigley, N. (1996) 'Geography in the United Kingdom 1992–1996', *Geographical Journal*, vol. 162, pp. 41–62.
Rose, G. (1993) *Feminism and Geography*. Cambridge: Polity.
Said, E.W. (1978) *Orientalism*. New York: Pantheon.
Said, E.W. (1993) *Culture and Imperialism*. London: Chatto & Windus.
Stoddart, D.R. (1996) 'To claim the high ground: geography for the end of the century', *Transactions, Institute of British Geographers*, vol. 12, pp. 327–36.
Valentine, G. (1993) '(Hetero)sexing space: lesbian perceptions and experiences of everyday spaces', *Environment and Planning D: Society and Space*, vol. 11, pp. 395–413.
WGSG (Women and Geography Study Group) (1997) *Feminist Geographies*. Harlow: Longman.
Wrigley, N. and Lowe, M. (eds) (1996) *Retailing, Consumption and Capital*. Harlow: Longman.

Chapter 6

Towards a global geopolitical economy

Alan Hudson

INTRODUCTION

This chapter introduces two lively areas of contemporary human geography – economic and political geography – and provides an outline of recent research which seeks to understand processes of globalisation from a geographical perspective.

The chapter begins by introducing economic geography and political geography, identifying key areas of research, and detailing the commonalities in the recent development of these important subdisciplines. In the second part of the chapter I briefly review recent research around the theme of globalisation and cross-border activities and introduce the approach of geopolitical economy, an approach which seeks to understand the changing organisation of power (politics) and wealth (economics) by focusing on their geographies.

ECONOMIC GEOGRAPHY

The development of contemporary economic geography

Economic geography has, over the decades, been one of the most dynamic subdisciplines within human geography. In the late nineteenth century, British economic geography, for better or worse, helped to catalogue the worldwide distribution of resources and in particular the resources available for commercial exploitation throughout the British Empire. In the first half of the twenthieth century, economic geographers concentrated their efforts at the regional level, contributing to rich but undertheorised descriptions of particular regions – the cotton industry in Lancashire, the steel industry around Sheffield, shipbuilding in Clydeside. From the 1960s, with the advent of computers and the desire to become more scientific, economic geographers such as Michael Chisholm, Peter Haggett and David Harvey (in his earlier positivist non-Marxist guise) were at the forefront of the so-called quantitative revolution. During this period economic geographers sought to produce mathematical models to better explain and predict the spatial organisation of economic activity. Variables such as market size, volume of inputs into the manufacturing process and transport costs were combined, producing formal well-defined models, developing a body of work called industrial location theory which had a great influence beyond the subdiscipline.

Despite the beauty of many of these models, by the 1970s criticisms of the quantitative revolution began to appear. David Harvey's conversion to Marxism marked an important development within economic geography as it was increasingly felt that mathematical models sidestepped the all important questions, making unrealistic assumptions about the way the world is – it's not really a flat isotropic plain populated by unflinchingly rational economic actors with perfect information! – and about the relationship between social science and the real world. Economic geographers such as Doreen Massey began to develop a Marxist economic geography which considered the economy as a subset of a capitalist society characterised by great inequalities of power and wealth (Massey, 1984).

Such an approach to economic geography, despite some trenchant criticisms of Marxism, was dominant through the 1980s and still persists, although, in part as a result of the arrival of postmodernism within the social sciences, the agenda has become considerably more eclectic (Lee and Wills, 1997). In a recent exciting development, the other social sciences – sociology, political science, law and even economics – have begun to rediscover the importance of geography to the way the world works. Geography and geographers play increasingly important roles within the social sciences with economic geographers – David Harvey, Doreen Massey, Ed Soja and Michael Storper for instance – taking the lead (Harvey, 1989 and 1996; Massey, 1994; Soja, 1989).

Key themes in contemporary economic geography

We can outline the focus of contemporary economic geography in terms of three aspects of the social and spatial organisation of wealth: production, consumption and circulation. Historically, economic geographers have tended to focus on production, making economic geography all but synonymous with industrial geography. Although the focus has expanded considerably, much of the work within economic geography is still concerned with issues of production. Over the last ten years 'restructuring' has been perhaps the key theme within economic geography as economic geographers have sought to understand the ways in which, and the reasons why, advanced industrial economies have changed over the last twenty or thirty years.

An important model of restructuring, developed in part by economic geographers, sees processes of restructuring as involving a shift from a Fordist regime to a post-Fordist regime in which manufacturing is more flexibly organised and consumers demand greater variety than the 'any colour you like, as long as it's black' option of Fordism (Harvey, 1989). One implication of this model which economic geographers have considered is whether Fordism and post-Fordism have characteristic geographies and spatial divisions of labour (Massey, 1995), with post-Fordism perhaps leading to a new international division of labour in which manufacturing activity is increasingly located in the Third World where labour costs are low and potential profits are high, while research and development takes place in places like Silicon Fen (Cambridge) and Silicon Valley (California) which can attract top-quality scientists and engineers (Dicken, 1998).

Related to this research theme, economic geographers have sought to understand the changing geographies of labour and work within the UK economy (Peck, 1996). Researchers have examined the implications of the decline of manufacturing industry and the rise of service industries, small firms and hi-tech industries (with the Cambridge Science Park providing an important case study), the feminisation of the workforce and the changing roles and geographies of trade union activity (Martin, Sunley and Wills, 1996).

Consumption provides a second main theme within economic geography, with researchers seeking to understand the organisation of shopping and its particular geographies (Wrigley and Lowe, 1996). The themed shopping experience offered by shopping malls such as the MetroCentre (Newcastle), Lakeside (Essex) and Merryhill (Birmingham) has been heavily researched, but geographers have also looked at more marginal sites of consumption such as car boot sales and markets. Rather than looking simply at the practice of shopping, geographers have investigated the geographies of provision – the chains which link distant producers and consumers – and the geographies of usage in which different people in different places use the things they buy in different ways, using exotic foods, art, furnishings, etc. to construct their identities in particular ways.

A third and as yet less significant theme (in terms of volume of research) of contemporary economic geography concerns circulation, the ways in which commodities, money, people, capital, ideas, information and images flow around the world, constructing particular economic geographies. Important research has been conducted on the geographies of money and the ways in which flows of money link distant places and lubricate the wheels of the capitalist economy (Leyshon and Thrift, 1997).

POLITICAL GEOGRAPHY

The development of contemporary political geography

Political geography too has been central to research within human geography for more than a century. As Agnew puts it: 'Political geography concerns the processes involved in creating, and the consequences for human populations of, the uneven distribution of power over the earth's surface' (1997, p. 1). Despite changes in its approach and focus over the decades, such a definition usefully emphasises the central question for political geographers: how does the spatial organisation of power come about and how does it affect the way the social world works?

In the late nineteenth and early twentieth centuries political geography concerned itself with the production of advice for statesmen, about how best to organise their powers. Such a focus is clearly illustrated by the role played by political geographers in the Versailles Peace Conference which redrew the boundaries of Europe following the First World War. Of particular note is Mackinder's Heartland thesis which suggested that the state which controlled Central Europe would maintain its dominance.

In the mid-twentieth century political geography fell into disrepute through its association with German *Geopolitik* and the imperial ambitions of the Nazi regime. Employing environmentally determinist metaphors of the state as an organism which requires space (*Lebensraum*) to expand if it is to survive, and building on the work of Haushofer, *Geopolitik* was arguably instrumental to the simultaneously spatial and political strategies of the Nazis. Such an association left political geography in the doldrums through the 1940s and 1950s, a situation which was not helped by the relative failure of political geographers to usefully develop mathematical models of geopolitical processes during the quantitative revolution of the 1960s.

Political geography began to develop in a more useful direction through the 1970s as political geographers concentrated their efforts around the analysis of intra-state territorial conflicts and externalities – where should hospitals and toxic waste disposal facilities be located, and how might racial conflicts in urban areas be reduced? An important and related sub-theme at this time was electoral geography which sought to describe, explain and perhaps even predict election results from a spatial perspective: what difference did the location of constituency boundaries make?; how important was location as a factor in determining individuals' voting behaviour?

From the 1980s, stimulated by the development of a Marxist economic geography, and crystallised by the establishment of the journal *Political Geography* (quarterly), the subdiscipline moved out of the doldrums and into the mainstream of disciplinary developments. Political geographers began to look beyond the borders of individual states to consider the world system as a whole and the relationships between countries in the rich Northern core and the poor Southern periphery (Taylor, 1993). In recent years, political geography, with its continuing focus on the spatial organisation of power, has positioned itself centrally within contemporary human geography (Agnew, 1997; Allen, 1997).

Key themes in contemporary political geography

Although much of contemporary human geography concerns itself with issues of power and its spatial organisation, there remains a certain distinctiveness to political geography research, which concerns itself with issues of statehood, citizenship, nationalism and new social movements. As the primary geopolitical unit, the state provides the reference point for many political geographers, even for those whose focus is on politics beyond state borders or at sub-state scales.

A first research theme examines the nature of the state and how states were historically made and are currently being transformed under the pressure of new social forces, loosely termed globalisation. Political geographers seek to understand the meanings of citizenship and democracy and their geographical aspects. What rights and obligations does citizenship or membership in the club of a state confer upon individuals, and how can these rights and obligations best be implemented? How has the nature of democratic politics developed over the years and what are its geographies?

A second related theme considers place and the processes through which places are socially and politically constructed as relatively separate and different from other places. Given the centrality of geographical difference to the disciplinary project of geography, such research is of great importance. Interestingly, in this area of research, parallels are often drawn between the construction of individual identity or selfhood, and the construction of places and their characteristics (Keith and Pile, 1993). Places are made by the intersection of many different social processes – class, gender, race – just as an individual's identity may include being a man, being a Northerner, being an academic, being a football supporter and being a violinist.

A third theme investigates the ways in which people feel a sense of belonging to particular places and social groups, especially their nations. Research on nationalism sees such a facet of identity as both a feeling of belonging and an ideology which states can use to develop a national project – 'Cool Britannia' for instance – but which nations can also use to argue and fight for political autonomy from states which exercise power over more than one nation.

A fourth research theme investigates the role of so-called new social movements, which organise around issues such as feminism, environmentalism, gay and lesbian issues, the rights of indigenous tribal groups and anti-nuclearism. Contrasts are drawn between the cross-border geographies of such social movements and the intra-state organisation of traditionally institutionalised politics (Wapner, 1996).

Common to all research within political geography is a concern with the intersection of issues of space and power. How is power organised spatially, and how does the way in which power is spatially organised make a difference to the exercise of power? This, despite the lingering state-centrism of political geography, is what geopolitics is all about.

COMMON TRENDS: SOCIETY, SPACE AND SCALES

Despite their differences, it is possible to identify some similarities and convergence between economic and political geography, both historically and in terms of contemporary research.

Breaking down the (sub)disciplinary walls

Ironically enough, a first similarity and convergence is that it is increasingly difficult to draw clear boundaries around the subdisciplines, to say what is political or economic geography and what isn't. Under the influence of Marxist approaches to social science which see (sub)disciplinary boundaries as artificial and unhelpful divides, and postmodern discourses which muddy the meanings of all concepts, walls between subdisciplines and disciplines are gradually being dismantled.

At the disciplinary level there have been exciting cross-disciplinary developments between human geography and its sister social sciences of economics, politics, sociology, cultural studies, international relations and law. At the subdisciplinary level it is increasingly difficult, and perhaps pretty pointless, to pigeon-hole individual researchers as historical, cultural, economic, political, developmental or environmental geographers.

Relatedly, throughout human geography, including the subdisciplines of economic and political geography, there have been interesting and important moves to develop a more gender-aware approach. Rather than just adding 'women' as another category, researchers have sought to systematically understand the ways in which gender – the roles assigned to, and the parts played by, men and women – makes a difference to the way the world works (Massey, 1994).

Society and space

A second commonality between research in economic and political geography – as well as in other branches of contemporary human geography – concerns the ways in which the relationship between society and space is conceptualised (Gregory and Urry, 1985; Soja, 1989). As human geography focuses on the spatial organisation of social life, the way in which society and space are related to each other is absolutely central to the development of human geography.

At one time – the first part of the twentieth century – the dominant view was that spatial or environmental factors – climate, soils, vegetation – determined what societies were like:

Space/environment → Society

Such an environmental determinism was discredited over the years to the point when, in the quantitative revolution, spatial patterns were seen as just being spread over the social world with little explanation of the processes involved:

Society on Space

Through the 1970s, the pendulum continued to swing, affording greater explanatory weight to social causes, such that spatial outcomes were seen as having social causes, that is capitalist social processes produced capitalist geographies:

Capitalist society → Capitalist space

Over the last fifteen or twenty years, the society–space relationship has been reconceptualised as a two-way street such that social processes do shape spatial patterns, but then these spatial patterns in turn make a difference to the ways in which social processes work. Society is space; space is society; geography matters!

Society ←→ Space

Much research in contemporary human geography seeks to illustrate and explain that geography matters, and, recently, geographers have begun to make considerable and crucial efforts not to just assert that geography matters, but to explain the ways in which geography matters – through features and concepts such as space, place, boundaries, territories, flows, landscapes and scales. This is another commonality between contemporary economic and political geography.

Linking scales

A third area of commonality between economic and political geography, not to mention environmental and physical geography, concerns the ways in which different scales – the local, regional, national and global – relate to each other, and, in fact, what it even means to talk of scales and scale.

Up until at least the 1970s, both economic and political geography tended to focus on processes and patterns at one scale, in many cases the national scale. Nation-states were seen as relatively self-contained social units and as suitable units – with readily available national statistical data – for analysis. However, in the 1970s – with the oil price hikes, the collapse of the Bretton Woods international monetary system and the rise of multinational manufacturing – it was increasingly realised that the fate of national economies was very much influenced by processes operating in other nation-states and across the borders. Similarly, research began to focus on the idea that the way in which a state operates as a political unit is shaped by the ways in which other states operate and how they relate to each other.

Rather than a simplistic conceptualisation of global processes causing local outcomes, or conversely local processes producing global outcomes, economic and political geographers have begun to appreciate that there is a two-way relationship between the global and the local – what some geographers have called 'glocalisation'. Contemporary research examines social processes which operate at a variety of scales, with the key issue now being how different scales are linked up, and more fundamentally, how scales are not given but are socially produced and therefore changeable (Harvey, 1996).

GLOBALISATIONS

The geopolitical economy of globalisations

These three trends which are common to economic and political geography are especially apparent in research concerned with processes of globalisation. Economic and political geography both throw light on processes of globalisation, particularly when their efforts are combined; globalisation is at once a social and a spatial process; and globalisation involves the social production and transformation of scale.

Globalisation refers to processes which increase the scale of social life, and therefore increasingly involve processes which operate across borders at multiple scales. In recent years many commentators – academics, journalists, politicians, activists – have begun to talk about a variety of globalisations (Anderson, Brook and Cochrane, 1995). Prominent examples include: the spread of financial activity across state borders, as seen in the exit of the pound sterling from the European Exchange Rate Mechanism in 1992 and the ongoing East Asian financial crisis; the near-worldwide take-up of a Reaganite/Thatcherite political ideology in the 1980s; the diffusion of American culture worldwide through products such as Coca-Cola, McDonald's, MTV and CNN; the increasingly important role of transnational corporations in the world economy; the development of the Internet, a social space which is relatively placeless; and the globalisation of environmental issues as illustrated through global problems such as the hole in the ozone layer, biodiversity loss and global warming.

So, there are multiple globalisations, some of which seem economic, some political, some cultural and some environmental. However, these multiple globalisations do have a common denominator, a common denominator which is intrinsically geographical. What all these processes of globalisation have in common is that they involve an upward shift in the scale of social life, changes in the meaning and porosity of national boundaries and increases in the volume, velocity and importance of cross-border flows, no matter whether these are flows of money, goods, ideas, images or pollutants. In this way, processes of globalisation lend themselves to geographical analyses. In fact, I would go so far as to say that we cannot understand processes of globalisation unless we understand their geographies.

That said, and in line with the earlier point about society and space shaping each other, it is not enough to simply try to understand the geographies of globalisation without considering the power relations and exchange relations which shape and drive processes of globalisation. Globalisation is a shift in scale; scales are institutions which are socially produced through political and economic processes; so, political economy is likely to prove useful as an approach to understanding globalisation.

Close to human geography in the disciplinary landscape, the approach of International Political Economy tends to examine globalisation in terms of the relationships between states and markets (Strange, 1988). States are seen as the key political players, with markets the key economic players or medium. Globalisation is then conceptualised as markets seeking to escape the restrictions imposed by states. Although this idea of states and markets as separable actors is open to criticism, it does provide an interesting first stab at an understanding of globalisation. With the addition of a geographical imagination – making for a geopolitical economy approach – international political economy provides a useful tool for understanding processes of globalisation.

States and markets, like many other social institutions have distinctive geographies. On the one hand we have states: institutions which set the rules or govern the activities which take place, and the people who live, in a particular territory with fixed borders. On the other hand we have markets: institutions which facilitate the process of exchange between producers and consumers, exchange which pays little attention to borders and will happily cross them. There is therefore a mismatch of scales. States are relatively fixed at the national scale, while markets more easily transcend borders. It is this mismatch or spatial tension which I would argue drives processes of globalisation. Or, at least, this is one useful way of looking at it.

Geopolitics is about boundaries, identities and territories; geoeconomics is about flows and exchanges; geopolitical economy is about flows and exchanges which take place over, and in turn reshape, a landscape of borders and places. Through investigating this reshaping of the regulatory landscape we can begin to understand and explain – and perhaps even shape in fairer and more sustainable directions – processes of globalisation. Geographers working from a geopolitical economy perspective have sought to examine processes of globalisation in terms of their geographies, employing, and further developing, ideas about scales and scaling, places and placing, territories and territoriality, borders and border-crossing, and landscapes and landscaping (Agnew and Corbridge, 1995).

Financial globalisation

Early research into the geopolitical economy of globalisation frequently concerned the paradigmatic case of international finance. Financial globalisation involves financial flows which cross borders and reshape the regulatory landscape, altering the identity of places. One area of geographical research into processes of financial globalisation looks at what are called global cities – places such as London, New York and Tokyo. Potentially, globalisation and the telecommunications technologies which facilitate a spreading out of economic activity could remove the need for concentrated centres of activity in global cities. However, as much of the global cities literature argues, rather than destroying such cities, globalisation changes their role and makes them even more important. A social system which is global in scope gets very complicated and messy, so global cities are increasingly important centres of control, places from which the flows of money, ideas, images, information and people are organised. In this way, globalisation reworks what London, New York and Tokyo are as distinctive places in a globalising economy (Hamnett, 1995; Sassen, 1991).

My own research into offshore financial centres took a similar tack, trying to understand the relationship between places such as the Bahamas, the Cayman Islands, Jersey and Guernsey and processes of financial globalisation (Hudson, 1998). Offshore financial centres are places which offer investors a low-tax high-secrecy place in which to conduct their financial activity. They offer a regulatory environment which is more attractive than the onshore regulatory environment found in larger more tightly regulated countries such as the USA and the UK.

Offshore financial centres developed rapidly from the 1960s as the USA – for domestic political reasons – sought to restrict the flows of dollars across its borders, and to increase the level of regulation in its territory. The Bahamas and Cayman Islands – as separate sovereign territories with clear boundaries – were able to set up their own regulatory environments which were more attractive for financial purposes than the USA. So, large volumes of dollar-denominated banking fled offshore and out of the USA's regulatory space. Sovereignty, the authority to set the rules of the game within a specific geographical territory, provided an excellent resource for these small marginal places to use in their development strategy.

However, somewhat paradoxically, the development of the Bahamas and Cayman Islands as offshore financial centres increased their dependence on processes and events which took place onshore. The USA was annoyed with the offshore financial centres because they facilitated tax evasion and the laundering of money from international crimes, particularly the international drugs trade. The USA retained some control or legislative authority over US banks such as Citibank which had branches in the Bahamas and Cayman, and so was able to exercise some power over the offshore financial centres by working through the transnational banks. In this way, although the offshore financial centres were built upon the principle of sovereignty, they in turn were forced to surrender aspects of their sovereignty.

This is the important point about the development of offshore financial centres. The international political economy had, for three centuries, a particular geography. That is, it was organised in terms of sovereign states and their boundaries. The development of offshore financial centres was a key phase in the dismantling or transformation of sovereignty, a key moment in the reshaping of the regulatory landscape which is globalisation.

Environmental globalisation and non-state actors

Just as financial assets increasingly flow across borders, environmental goods and bads – the impact of efforts to prevent the ozone hole increasing, or pollutants and greenhouse gases – similarly extend across the borders from the places where they originate. So, environmental globalisation also challenges the spatial organisation of the international political economy and its basis in sovereignty (Blowers and Glasbergen, 1996).

When environmental problems are increasingly global in scope it is difficult for individual sovereign states to tackle them. Because of this collective action problem, new institutions – international regimes – with new geographies in which state borders are relatively unimportant have developed. For example, there is an international regime which seeks to coordinate the actions of states in relation to the hole in the ozone layer, and there are developing regimes to tackle global warming and to preserve biodiversity. These international regimes shape and constrain the actions of individual states, transforming the meaning of sovereignty.

Of particular interest are cases when the goals of different international regimes –

and perhaps their geographies – are in conflict. We might think here of the World Trade Organisation (WTO) which governs international trade and the increasing numbers of cases in which the operation and rules of the game of the WTO come into conflict with the desire to protect environmental resources. Although the USA, for instance, might wish to protect dolphins caught off the shores of Mexico, the WTO framework means that the USA is unable to restrict imports of tuna which is caught in ways which kill too many dolphins. The problem is that one country is seeking to extend its values – its prioritisation of dolphin well-being over tuna cheapness and fishermen's livelihoods – beyond its borders. The WTO is built on particular geopolitical assumptions – states as the key actors – which conflict with environmental issues, dolphins for instance, which do not respect international borders.

To cope with the globalisation of economic activity and environmental issues, states and corporations have sought to establish international institutions and new rules of the game to manage globalisation and its resultant value conflicts. Away, but not separate from, the corporate and state power centres, other actors – NGOs, trade unions, religious organisations, consumer groups: broadly termed civil society – also argue that the rules of the game of the global political economy need to be changed, and seek to institutionalise different sets of values. A variety of new non-state actors – Greenpeace, Amnesty International, the Third World Network – have emerged to try and alter the rules of the game of international regimes and to try and mediate between different value systems, reshaping the regulatory landscape in particular ways. Researchers in geography, but more especially in International Political Economy and International Relations have sought to understand the emergence of a wide variety of non-state actors, many of whom are involved in activities which are global in scope and pay little respect to national borders (Princen and Finger, 1994; Wapner, 1996). In fact for some commentators it is the cross-border geography of some non-state actors which gives them their leverage in the international political economy, as they are able to link the local with the global, pressing for issues of local concern to be placed on the global political agenda. In order to understand processes of globalisation it is important to explore their geographies.

CONCLUSION

Economic and political geography continue to be vibrant subdisciplines which can contribute to the understanding of contemporary social and spatial dynamics, particularly when their insights and approaches are combined. In an era when processes of globalisation are increasingly dominant a geopolitical economy approach which considers the geographical dimensions of economic and political processes is an important viewpoint for understanding the way the world works.

REFERENCES

Agnew, J. (1987) *Place and Politics: The Geographical Mediation of State and Society*. Boston: Unwin Hyman.

Agnew, J. (ed.) (1997) *Political Geography: A Reader*. London: Arnold.

Agnew, J. and Corbridge, S. (1995) *Mastering Space: Hegemony, Territory and International Political Economy*. London: Routledge.

Allen, J. (1997) 'Economies of power and space', in Lee, R. and Wills, J. (eds), *Geographies of Economies*. London: Arnold, pp. 59–70.
Anderson, J., Brook, C. and Cochrane, A. (eds) (1995) *A Global World?* Oxford: Open University Press.
Blowers, A. and Glasbergen, P. (eds) (1996) *Environmental Policy in an International Context: Prospects for Environmental Change*. London: Arnold.
Dicken, P. (1998) *Global Shift: The Internationalization of Economic Activity*. London: Paul Chapman.
Gregory, D. and Urry, J. (eds) (1985) *Social Relations and Spatial Structures*. London: Macmillan.
Hamnett, C. (1995) 'Controlling space: global cities', in Allen, J. and Hamnett, C. (eds), *A Shrinking World?* Oxford: Open University Press, pp. 103–42.
Harvey, D. (1989) *The Condition of Postmodernity*. Oxford: Blackwell.
Harvey, D. (1996) *Justice, Nature and the Geography of Difference*. Oxford: Blackwell.
Hudson, A. (1998) 'Reshaping the regulatory landscape: border skirmishes around the Bahamas and Cayman offshore financial centres', *Review of International Political Economy*, vol. 5, pp. 534–64.
Keith, M. and Pile, S. (eds) (1993) *Place and the Politics of Identity*. London: Routledge.
Lee, R. and Wills, J. (eds) (1997) *Geographies of Economies*. London: Arnold.
Leyshon, A. and Thrift, N. (1997) *Money/Space: Geographies of Monetary Transformation*. London: Routledge.
Martin, R., Sunley, P. and Wills, J. (1996) *Union Retreat and the Regions: The Shrinking Landscape of Organised Labour*. London: Jessica Kingsley.
Massey, D. (1984/1995) *Spatial Divisions of Labour: Social Structures and the Geography of Production*. London: Macmillan.
Massey, D. (1994) *Space, Place and Gender*. Cambridge: Polity Press.
Peck, J. (1996) *Workplace: The Social Regulation of Labor Markets*. New York: Guilford.
Princen, T. and Finger, M. (1994) *Environmental NGOs in World Politics: Linking the Local and the Global*. London: Routledge.
Sassen, S. (1991) *The Global City*. Princeton, NJ: Princeton University Press.
Soja, E. (1989) *Postmodern Geographies: Towards a Reassertion of Space in Critical Social Theory*. London: Verso.
Strange, S. (1988) *States and Markets*. London: Pinter.
Taylor, P. (1993) *Political Geography: World-Economy, Nation-State and Locality*. London: Longman.
Wapner, P. (1996) *Environmental Activism and World Civic Politics*. Albany, NY: State University of New York Press.
Wrigley, N. and Lowe, M. (eds) (1996) *Retailing, Consumption and Capital: Towards the New Retail Geography*. Harlow: Longman

Chapter 7

New geographies of energy

Derek Spooner

'Coal is history, Miss Mullins.'

Such was the judgement of the official presiding over the closure of Grimley colliery in *Brassed Off*, one of the hit movies of 1996. Grimley colliery and its brass band were loosely based on Grimethorpe colliery, South Yorkshire, one of many to close in the wake of the UK's 'coal crisis' of 1992. The movie captured brilliantly the mood of bitterness and despair among the miners of Grimethorpe/Grimley, as well as providing a powerful reminder of the rich musical tradition and resilient humour in adversity present in many such communities.

Colliery closure is, of course, hardly a new phenomenon. Nearly thirty years previously, playwright Alan Plater's drama, *Close the Coalhouse Door*, drew attention to many similar themes to those evinced in *Brassed Off* (but in the context of the Northumberland–Durham coalfield), and to earlier phases in the 'rationalisation' of the British coal industry:

WILL: The connection is that this village, and this pit, got rationalisation.
VICAR: How do you mean? The pit got rationalisation?
WILL: I mean, the NCB [National Coal Board] says we've got to rationalise the industry . . . we've got to rationalise Brockenback pit . . .
(Pause)
I mean, they closed the bugger.

(Plater, 1969)

Both *Brassed Off* and *Close the Coalhouse Door* are about the struggle between labour and capital interests in the coal industry, and in the case of *Close the Coalhouse Door* about the dilemmas and disappointments of state ownership. They are recent twists of a story that goes back to the nineteenth-century oppression of labour in the coalfields, and which provided the subject matter for one of the great French novels of that period, Emile Zola's *Germinal* (1885), set in the strife-torn coalfield of northern France (and converted by Claude Berri into a successful movie in 1993). *Germinal* is an emotional epic of human misery, focused around the mine of Le Voreux which closes for a more dramatic reason, destroyed by sabotage after a strike and the shooting of strikers. A century later in Nord-Pas de Calais underground mining has shrunk to little more than a heritage feature.

In the UK the steep decline of the deep-mining industry since the mid-1980s (when the last great miners' strike, frequently recalled by the miners in *Brassed Off*, failed to break the resolve of government to curb the power of the National Union of Mineworkers (NUM)) has produced a new geography of coal mining. In some coalfields mining has virtually ceased; in others opencast mining is now the prevalent form. Major underground mines survive in private ownership at only a handful of sites. The UK produces less than 40 million tonnes per annum, with more than a third of output derived from opencast; this is considerably less than half the total mined during the industry's Indian summer in the late 1970s. Coal imports (sometimes through traditional coal-exporting ports like Hull) are now a major traffic and part of a global coal trade. In 1997 the major sources of UK imports were the USA, Australia, Colombia, South Africa and Canada. The legacy of mineworking in settlement and communication patterns is persistent, but is now slowly being modified in many coalfields, and despoiled landscapes are gradually being restored. But the most dramatic changes are those on which *Brassed Off* and *Close the Coalhouse Door* focused. Today there are 11 000 mine-workers in an industry which 25 years ago employed more than a quarter of a million. The effect of this change has been dramatic for many local and regional economies, and has strongly influenced policies of regional aid at both European and national levels.

There are also new elements in the causes of decline. It is interesting that in *Close the Coalhouse Door* Plater's 'Expert' cited nuclear reactors and natural gas as the problem for coal:

> EXPERT: How many of you know the North Sea?
> JACKIE: The North Sea. Aye, you can see it from Whitley Bay . . .
> EXPERT: And what lies beneath the North Sea, full forty fathoms deep?
> *(Pause)*
> GEORDIE: Bird's Eye cod pieces?
> EXPERT: High speed gas.
> *(A quick kneel).*
> Which we shall suck-up from the sea-bed in great man-made vacuum cleaners and then blow it out over this green and pleasant land as the basis of the technological revolution.
> JACKIE: Natural gas.
> EXPERT: High speed . . . natural gas . . . as you so well put it. Armed only with nuclear reactors and high speed gas the nation shall scale the heights . . .
>
> (Plater, 1969)

Alan Plater was referring here to the replacement of coal-based 'town gas' by natural gas from the North Sea – removing one of coal's major markets. But in the era of *Brassed Off*, natural gas has emerged as formidable competition in a new way, with the 'dash for gas' in electricity generation (Spooner, 1995). Before the privatisation of the UK's electricity industry in 1989 the use of natural gas in power generation was negligible; in less than a decade gas has captured one-third of the market, and if present trends continue will soon overhaul coal as the major fuel used.

The reasons for the 'dash for gas' are bound up with the particular form that privatisation took in the UK and the new market arrangements, but also include the need to reduce coal-burn to meet European pollution reduction targets (especially in relation to acid deposition), a factor that had not emerged at the time of *Close the Coalhouse Door*.

These reflections on the demise of the British coal industry provide a useful entry point for the exploration of new geographies of energy, though it would be misleading to assume from UK experience that coal is no longer a significant player on the world energy scene. Worldwide, coal is far from being 'history'. It is still a huge and growing industry in many countries, and it is backed by powerful lobbies. But the example reminds us that the geography of energy is dynamic, and that it is shaped by a wide array of considerations – economic, political and environmental.

To what extent is it possible in the year 2000 to speak of new geographies of energy? Perhaps we should begin by noting that geographers have not been particularly active in the energy field, and that many of our studies draw us into an interdisciplinary arena in which, for example, economists, political scientists, engineers and physicists play leading roles. However, we might consider the question from two interrelated perspectives. Firstly, has there been a change in the ways in which we, as geographers, think about and study energy, in the concepts that we use and the range of variables that we consider? Secondly, if we look at energy geographies, the subject matter of our studies, are these new or significantly different from those of, say, twenty or thirty years ago? In this chapter I will attempt to look at some of the ways in which our approach to the geography of energy has evolved, and at some of the significant new features 'out there' in the energy world. A neat distinction between these two elements is not possible, however, as changes 'out there' inevitably influence our approach. It must be noted, too, that the chapter concentrates largely on geographies of production rather than consumption, and upon the advanced economies.

FINDING A PLACE FOR ENERGY

Geographers have traditionally been interested in the 'economic geography' of energy production, with a focus upon two elements: the locational pattern of extractive industries (e.g. coal mines, oil wells) and the siting of energy conversion facilities (e.g. oil refineries, power stations). Writers like Manners (1964) approached these questions through an analysis of predominantly economic factors (with transport costs a key consideration); others like Wilson (1968) formulated location theories for mine siting in which the interplay between production costs and transport costs was particularly critical. Hauser's study of the state-owned electricity generating industry in England and Wales (1971) showed that locational questions could not be divorced from an understanding of the electricity system as a whole.

However, there were growing indications that the problems of siting were becoming politicised. In the UK, Owens' study of power stations (1985) showed that proposals for new sites were making increasingly heavy weather of passage through the land-use planning system, with increasing opposition from local communities. The problem of 'finding a place for energy' in the USA was highlighted by Calzonetti (1981). Fears about the potential environmental impacts of large power plants were leading to vociferous and increasingly sophisticated opposition by organised groups able to exploit opportunities in the regulatory system. Calzonetti described the frustration of South California Edison in pursuit of the Kaiparowits coal-fired power project in Southern Utah, where plans first laid in 1961 were finally abandoned in 1976 after a decade of conflict, permit-filing and project revisions, 'beaten to death by the environmental interests' (in the words of a company executive). Nearer home, despite the fact that the sites (allegedly) were not chosen purely on economic grounds, proposals for three new coal mines in the Vale of Belvoir (East Midlands) put forward in 1976 achieved the go-ahead for only one mine (Asfordby) seven years later.

In order to combat this problem some companies and authorities have developed sophisticated site selection techniques, using, for example, sieve mapping and geographical information systems to identify acceptable sites for new energy facilities. However, such rational approaches to site selection do not guarantee success. The system employed by the state of Maryland to identify suitable power plant sites could still not convince local residents to accept a coal-fired plant at Hagerstown (Calzonetti, Sayre and Spooner, 1987).

Such problems are best exemplified by the nuclear power industry, which needs sites both for power stations and radioactive waste disposal. In the UK the former Central Electricity Generating Board (CEGB) developed a set of criteria for power station site selection (including safety factors). Openshaw (1986) concluded that there was still a superabundance of potential sites. However, the UK industry has not developed at a new greenfield location for many years, but appears to have settled for a defensive strategy, extending existing sites where tolerance has increased through receipt of local economic benefits. Stewart and Prichard (1987) in the USA concluded that the acceptability of nuclear waste disposal would be highest where there were existing nuclear facilities or ones that had closed, thus creating local unemployment. After several abortive attempts the UK industry has abandoned searches for new repository sites. Nuclear power has become the ultimate LULU (Locally Unwanted Land Use).

These examples indicate that the siting of energy facilities can no longer be studied only in terms of economic considerations. These still set a framework, but in the advanced economies companies may be forced to settle for sub-optimal locations, or may struggle to develop at all. Siting has become a political as well as an economic problem, and geographers need to take on board an appreciation of power relations, the role of interest groups and different perspectives on decision-making. In western societies community tolerance has fallen. Recent opposition to windfarm siting in the UK indicates that even the renewable energy sector can encounter such problems. Although windfarms have been used as positive marketing images to sell cars and compact discs, some find them an intrusive assault on romantic pastoral visions (Thayer, 1994). Indeed, Thayer points out that people now react strongly to any locally sited technological facility (not just energy facilities), even if they are renewable and benign environmentally.

In the 1980s geographers began to borrow political science concepts to help explain the outcomes of conflict over resource exploitation decisions between different interest groups (e.g. Rees, 1985). Pluralist, elitist and structuralist perspectives competed for attention. In the pluralist interpretation, power is dispersed among different interests (e.g. corporate, trade union, environmentalist) and conflict is resolved openly through cooperation and compromise; decision-making is visible. In the elitist account, some interests, usually corporate, possess resources and access to decision-makers that confer on them superior power, and may exercise power in invisible ways. Elites engage in non-decision-making strategies, which involve suppression of issues and non-participation of groups affected by them. Structuralist (Marxist) interpretations emphasise the fusion of political and class conflict, with the state supporting capital interests. None of these perspectives need be regarded as wholly correct in a particular instance, and each may provide useful insights into the decision-making process. It should be evident from this discussion that energy geography has become political as much as economic geography.

ENERGY AND ENVIRONMENT

Geographers are crucially interested in people–environment relationships and this has strong relevance to energy, where the impact of energy industries upon the environment has become a matter of international concern. Here the emphasis shifts from the causes to the consequences of geographical production patterns. Traditional concerns about air quality and public health arising from the burning of fossil fuels have been joined by worries about, for example, acidification of the environment, rising levels of greenhouse gases (the global warming debate), radioactive releases (either controlled or accidental), oil spills and traffic pollution.

Geographers' interests in, and approach to, the environmental impact of energy facilities has been influenced by the development of Environmental Impact Assessment (EIA) techniques. EIA looks at the impact of individual facilities and their interaction with particular environmental conditions (see Figure 7.1). The timing and scale of the

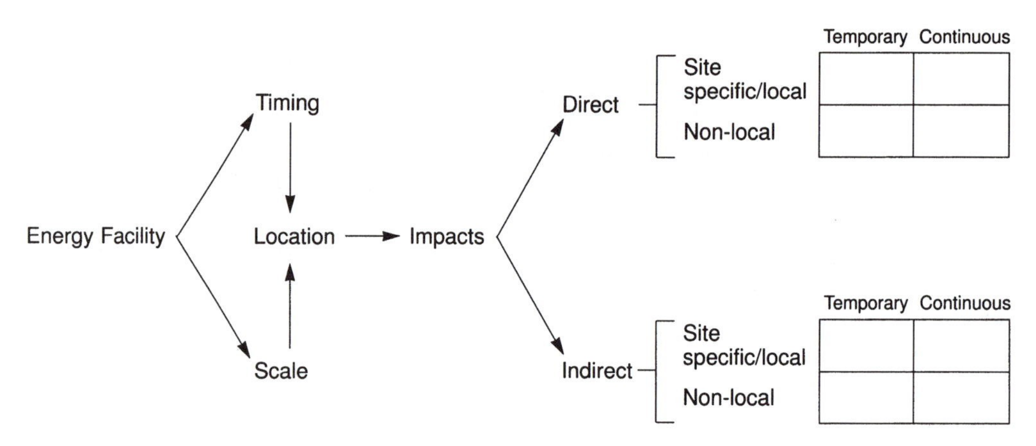

Figure 7.1 The impact of energy facilities.

project provides the context; impacts can be temporary (during construction) or continuous, and can arise directly or indirectly (through ancillary facilities or via the population needed to service the project). Impacts are both physical and socio-economic; the environment is considered in its totality. Impacts, moreover, can be routine, normal and predictable – in other words deliberate, and therefore controllable by design modification, the imposition of limiting conditions or regulation – or accidental, unpredictable and irregular. Nuclear power is a good example of an energy technology where many of the perceived problems focus upon unplanned accidents as opposed to 'normal' impacts (see Figure 7.2).

It must be stressed, however, that all energy technologies present some environmental impact – even the renewables, usually portrayed as environmentally benign. This is more obvious with potentially large-scale structures like tidal barrages

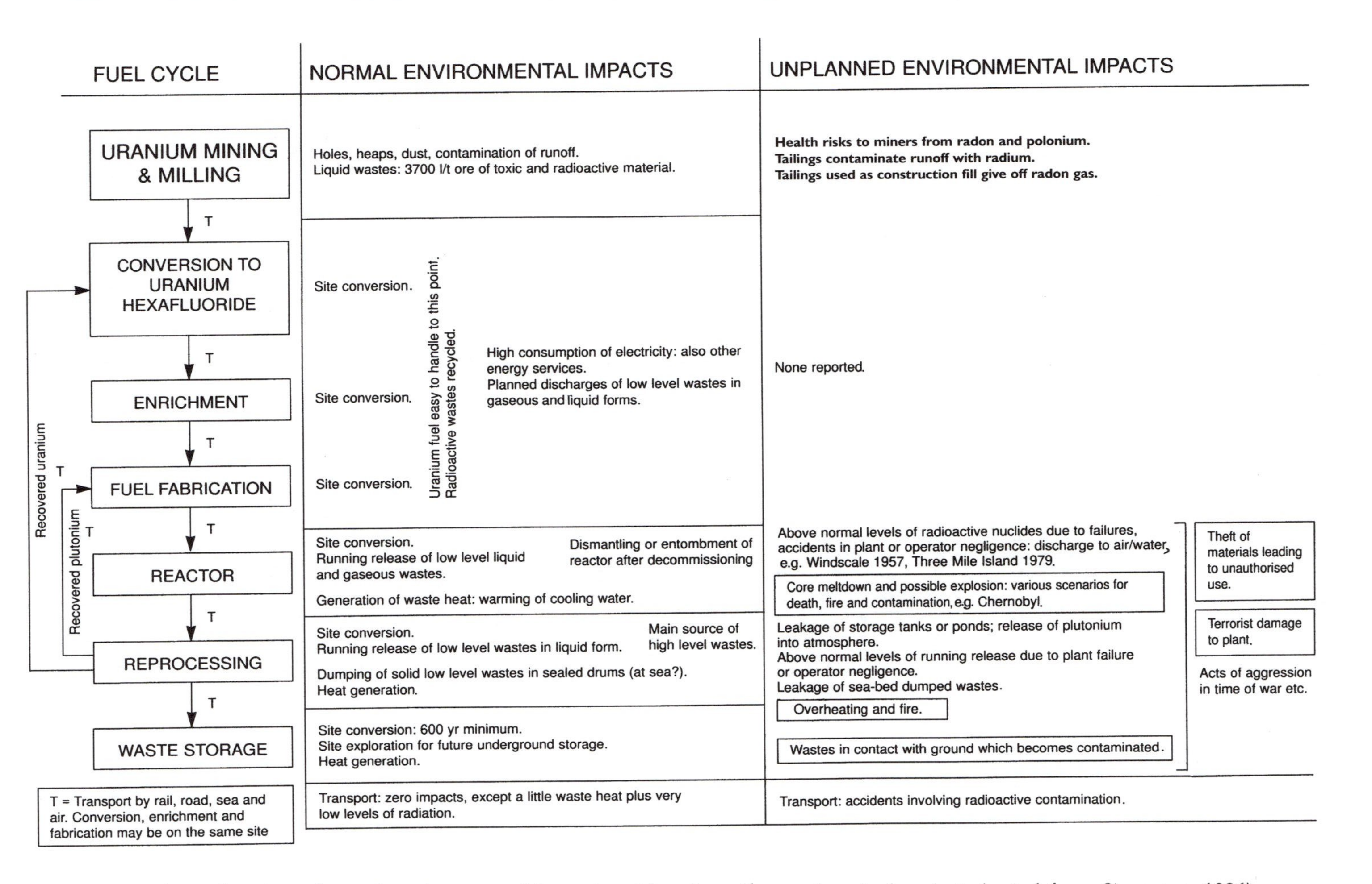

Figure 7.2 Planned and unplanned environmental impacts arising from the nuclear fuel cycle (adapted from Simmons, 1996).

or hydro-electric dams, which induce a complex set of changes both up- and downstream, but for many renewables the most substantial impact is intrusion on the view. But what is particularly important from a geographical standpoint is the scale of area over which impacts are felt. A crude classification between local, regional and global (see Table 7.1) underlines significant differences in this respect between

Table 7.1 The environmental impacts of selected renewable and conventional technologies

Technology	*Local*	*Regional*	*Global*
Renewables			
Onshore wind energy	Noise, visual intrusion electromagnetic interference	None	None
Offshore wind energy	Impeded navigation and fishing rights	None	None
Hydro power	Visual intrusion, ecological impact	None	None
Tidal power	Visual intrusion, ecological impact	Ecological impact	None
Wave energy	Impeded navigation and fishing rights	None	None
Geothermal hot dry rocks	Noise, visual intrusion, water requirements, radon release	None	None
Geothermal aquifers	Visual intrusion	None	None
Photovoltaics	Visual intrusion	None	None
Active solar	Visual intrusion	None	None
Passive solar design	None	None	None
Municipal and general industrial wastes	Particulate and toxic emissions, visual intrusion, fuel transportation	Particulate and toxic emissions, waste disposal	None
Landfill gas	Particulate and toxic emissions, visual intrusion	Particulate and toxic emissions	None
Agricultural and forestry wastes	Particulate emissions, fuel transportation	Particulate emissions	None
Energy crops	Particulate emissions, visual intrusion, fuel transportation	Particulate emissions	None
Conventional			
Coal	Particulate and toxic emissions, visual intrusion, fuel transportation	Particulate and toxic emissions, waste disposal	Carbon dioxide release
Oil	Particulate and toxic emissions, visual intrusion, fuel transportation	Particulate and toxic emissions	Carbon dioxide release
Gas	Particulate and toxic emissions, visual intrusion	Particulate and toxic emissions	Carbon dioxide release
Nuclear	Visual intrusion, accidental leakage of radioactive material	Waste disposal, possible major accident	Possible major accident

renewable and conventional technologies.

However, environmental impact studies go beyond the examination of individual facilities (a mine, a gas well, a tidal barrage). They embrace technology assessment, a macro-view of the impacts arising from the use of technology in the whole set of activities leading to end-use. Increasingly we conceptualise the delivery of energy in terms of chains or cycles. The exploitation of the fossil fuels comprises a chain of linked activities (e.g. mine – preparation plant – railway – power station – transmission line) (see Figure 7.3). Each of these elements can be looked at individually (and they may be separate economic undertakings) and each has particular and specific environmental impacts; technology assessments look at the bigger picture. In the case of nuclear power, there is a cycle, with spent fuel from the nuclear reactor potentially being recycled after reprocessing. Many of the recent problems of the nuclear power industry have stemmed from previous failures to take account of the whole cycle of activities, with reprocessing and waste disposal – the 'back end' of the nuclear cycle – proving the industry's Achilles' heel.

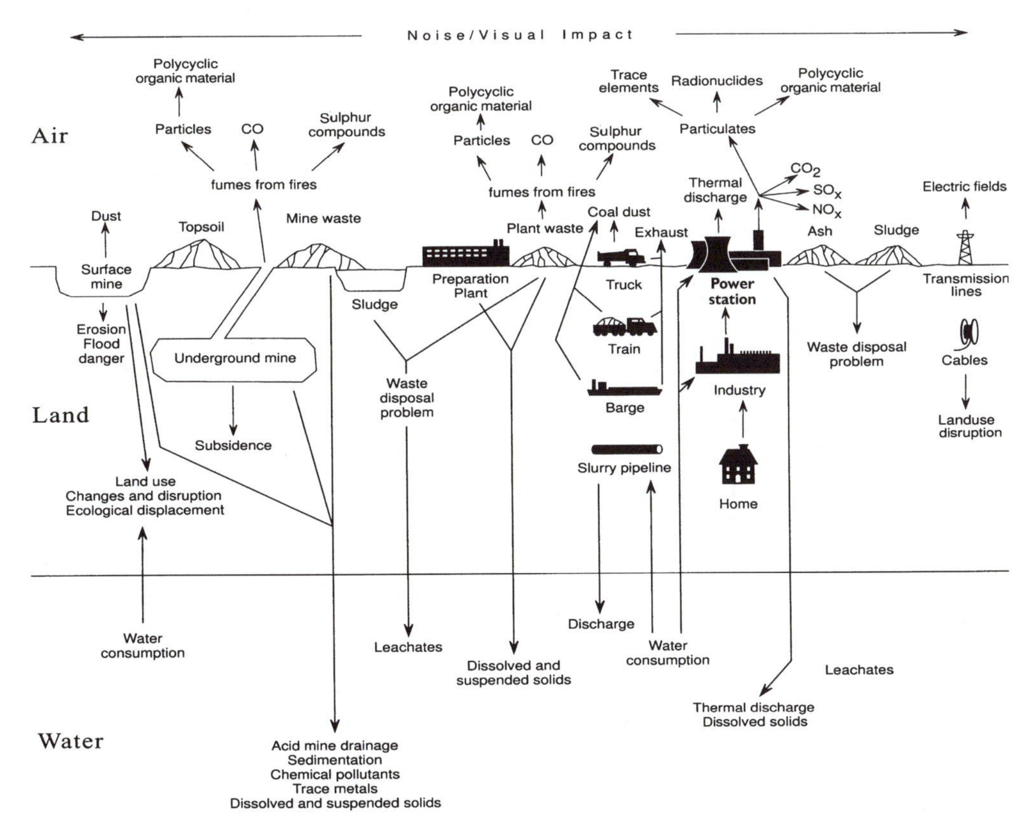

Figure 7.3 Direct impacts on the physical environment arising from the coal chain. NB: Does not include indirect impacts like miners' villages and camps.

ENERGY CRISES AND TRANSITIONS

Geographers have been drawn to another aspect of people–environment relations – the problems of resource use and depletion, and evaluation of the true nature of energy crises. Here they are touching on an issue of great concern in society at large, which has crystallised during the last decade into debates about sustainability.

World history can be interpreted as a series of energy transitions, with civilisation's advances perceived by Smil (1994) as a quest for higher energy use converted into increased food harvests and greater mobilisation of materials. However, Smil rejects 'rigid periodicisation'; there are obvious national and regional differences in the timing of innovation and widespread adoption of new fuels and prime movers (in many parts of rural Asia, Africa and Latin America, for example, reliance on human and animal energy is still the norm). Moreover, energy transitions tend to be evolutionary, often taking place over long periods. Thus draft animals, water power and steam engines coexisted in industrialising Europe for more than a century – one of the enduring images of *Germinal* is the awful death of the horse, Bataille, drowning underground in the wreckage of the sabotaged mine.

The major transition in world history lies between the millennia dominated by animate prime movers and biomass fuels, and the more recent past heavily dependent on fossil fuels. This was broadly a shift from a reliance on renewable to non-renewable resources, though this is a simplification; today water power generates one-fifth of world electricity.

The concept of an energy crisis arising from the depletion and increasing scarcity of hydrocarbons has been much debated since the oil price hikes of 1973–74 and 1979–80; these events seemed to confirm to many that the world was indeed 'running out of resources'. Many took the view that the crises of the 1970s were inevitable because the growth of world oil demand had begun to exceed the growth of world oil production and reserves, and some experts argued the need for another energy transition towards a more sustainable energy future based upon renewable energy. Others have pointed out that the crises of the 1970s were contrived by the Organisation of Petroleum Exporting Countries (OPEC), and therefore reflected geopolitical rather than physical scarcity (Rees, 1990). Many oil economists (and resource optimists) have continued to argue that hydrocarbon resources remain relatively abundant. Some analysts consider that the world may still face shortages of oil, gas and uranium in around forty years, but there are large elements of uncertainty in any such calculations.

These arguments intermesh with those surrounding the impact of fossil fuel consumption on the global environment, and the absorptive capacity of the planetary ecosystem. This problem was highlighted by the influential Brundtland report in 1987, which noted that to bring developing countries' energy use up to the level of industrialised countries by 2025 would require an increase from present consumption levels by a factor of five, and seriously questioned the ability of the planetary ecosystem to withstand this if fossil fuel consumption still predominated (World Commission on Environment and Development, 1987). Brundtland expressed the growing sense of interdependence of a number of problems: 'These are not separate crises: an environmental crisis, a development crisis, an energy crisis. They are all one.' The concept of sustainable development was given a massive endorsement.

The sustainability debate, one might argue, had already surfaced in the 'energy' context in the 1970s in the concept of 'hard and soft energy paths', put forward by the American Amory Lovins (1977). His advocacy of the soft energy path should be seen in the context of the geopolitical conditions of the time. In the United States dependence on oil imports had led to public trauma; President Carter declared the energy crisis to be the moral equivalent of war. Lovins considered that western economies had been relentlessly following a hard path, based upon fossil fuels and nuclear power, dominated by large-scale, low-efficiency, capital-hungry, high-risk production, poorly matched in scale to end-use needs, environmentally damaging and often subject to weak democratic control. Such a path was often backed by aggressive subsidies and state regulation to ensure that economic growth was not held back. 'Technical fixes', often massive in scale, were seen as the potential route around problems, keeping the crisis at bay. Lovins argued that this approach was increasingly unworkable (and we would now say unsustainable), relying as it did on the ransacking of remote and fragile environments, and increasingly intolerable in its side effects. Echoing the 'small is beautiful' philosophy of Schumacher (1973), Lovins advocated the choice of the 'road not taken', a soft path based on an aggregate of small-scale contributions, flexible and (relatively) low technology, matched in scale to end-use needs, based on a different socio-political structure, and emphasising conservation and quality of energy resources. Renewable energy sources and energy efficiency would be key ingredients of this ecologically sound pathway. The approach focuses not on the fuels or electricity themselves but upon the 'energy services' that they provide. Transition to the soft energy path would be achieved by a continuing use of fossil fuels but not nuclear power, which to Lovins exemplified the negative features of the hard path.

The collapse of the world oil price in 1986 deflected interest from the resource depletion problem towards the environmental impact of resource use. Sustainable development, with its focus upon meeting the needs of the present without compromising the future, came to be viewed less as a problem of resource depletion than as an issue of the environment's capacity to absorb emissions from fossil-fuel use. Like Lovins' soft energy path, sustainable development may require more than technical fixes. It presents a range of social and organisational choices – at a minimum conservation, recycling and less consumerism, or, according to more radical 'greens', more dramatic changes involving social, economic and technological decentralisation (Elliott, 1997). However, some technical fixes can be good news. Lovins himself in his most recent study (Weizsacker, Lovins and Lovins, 1997) stresses the potential for efficiency gains in resource use through the application of new technologies (from hypercars to low-energy beef) which revolutionise productivity. This is the so-called Factor Four approach – 'doubling wealth, halving resource use'.

Elliott (1997) attempts to establish a set of criteria to guide the choice of sustainable energy technologies. In his view, these should:

- avoid the use of fuels which will run out;
- improve the efficiency of energy generation and utilisation as an interim measure;
- match energy production and fuel choice to end-use;
- design technology and systems to use energy efficiently;
- minimise local environmental impacts of energy technologies, and trade off those remaining against global environmental impacts;

- avoid extracting more energy from natural flows than the local ecosystem can cope with;
- devise technologies so that human activities stay within the energy limits and carrying capacity of the planet.

This is clearly easier said than done. Moreover, there are still those who challenge the underlying assumptions about the planet's absorptive capacity, in particular with reference to global warming, the key driver in the debate. Carbon dioxide, emitted by power stations and cars, is a greenhouse gas which contributes to global warming; while there may be an emerging consensus on the fact of global warming, there are disagreements about causes and trends, and many scientists remain cautious. Acceptance of the need to adopt the precautionary principle, in advance of full scientific agreement on the dimensions of the problem, would strengthen the case for choosing the paths outlined above.

NEW TECHNOLOGIES, NEW GEOGRAPHIES?

The development of new energy geographies is associated in part with the adoption of new energy technologies. Technological change is a feature of all energy industries, including the 'conventional'. Thus the quest for clean-coal technology is significant in many countries, while new developments in the exploitation of offshore oil and gas reserves continue to alter the dimensions and prospects of the hydrocarbons industries. In the nuclear industry huge sums have been devoted to research and development, although the Fast Breeder Reactor (FBR) programme is in eclipse in most countries, and nuclear fusion still has some way to go before it can be seen as anything more than a long-shot option (Elliott, 1997).

Most interest in the 1990s focuses upon the renewables, which offer escape from the restrictions of finite resource stocks. The use of renewables is not, of course, new. There were 10 000 windmills in nineteenth-century Britain; biomass in the form of firewood has been the main source of fuel for millions of people worldwide (and now presents many poorer countries with their own version of energy crisis); large-scale hydro-electric power generation has become a familiar feature of the energy landscape in many countries. But the oil crisis of the 1970s gave fresh impetus to the quest for modern, economically competitive alternatives to conventional sources.

Renewable energy technologies are based on natural energy flows. A distinction can be made between continuous sources, like solar, wind and wave, available on a continuous basis regardless of human use, and flow resources, like biomass, where availability can be depleted, sustained or increased by human action. Some flow resources may be so badly affected by depletion that natural recovery of the supply fails to take place; these are critical zone resources. Many renewables are used to contribute to electricity supply, but they can be used to provide direct heat. They may, moreover, be supplied on a domestic, non-commercial scale (the traditional situation in many poorer societies).

A current paradox in relation to renewable energy is that interest has remained strong at a time when oil prices have fallen to low levels (comparable in real terms to the pre-1973 crisis period). There may be a number of reasons for this. Physical and technical obstacles are seen as less significant than a decade ago. New concerns about climatic change and sustainability, a loss of faith in nuclear power and perceived benefits to other sectors like farming may be significant. In the UK, government policy has played a key part.

The process by which new energy technologies evolve from invention to widespread adoption may be a lengthy one involving several stages – science-based research, engineering-based development, the construction and demonstration of prototypes, followed by commercial adoption and public and economic acceptability. Costs of production fall as the technology progresses. The process is both technological and socio-political, and government support may be important in helping the infant technology become established. Such support may come through investment in research and development (R & D), or through subsidy and market enablement. The UK presents a good example of both; before electricity privatisation, support was via R & D programmes (notably for wave power, large wind turbines, solar and geothermal power) but success was limited (Mitchell, 1996). Since 1989 much greater success has been achieved through the Non Fossil Fuel Obligation (NFFO), which obliged the regional electricity companies to take 20 per cent of their supply from nuclear and renewable resources, subsidising projects via a contracted premium price for electricity generated, and a levy on electricity bills. The outcome has been the realisation of a large number of small renewable projects.

The final stage of public acceptability can be problematical. Although most surveys of public attitudes to renewable energy show high levels of support, specific proposals for particular places can be viewed very differently (Walker, 1997). There may be a backlash of public opposition. New technologies do not only need to achieve financial viability; they have to achieve planning viability too. In the case of wind power, Garrad (quoted in Grubb and Vigotti, 1997) has put forward a four-stage model, based upon the experience of different countries. In the first, capacity is installed (slowly) as part of R & D efforts, with demonstrations and trial commercialisation by utilities; in the second there is rapid development as private generation is encouraged; thirdly, as incentives are removed, opposition and planning problems increase; finally a mature stage of public and economic acceptability is reached. While the UK may have now reached the third stage, Denmark appears to have already reached the fourth.

The geographical patterns associated with renewable technologies appear to be much more dispersed than the traditional concentrated patterns associated with many other forms of energy production. Distributions reflect both supply and demand factors. Windfarms, small hydro stations and energy from waste and landfill gas plants require the availability of a localised resource, and in the last two cases locations will be determined primarily by earlier decisions over waste disposal sites. In the case of windfarms there is a supply bias towards areas of higher wind speeds, but the detailed distribution reflects a range of other factors. Thus despite abundant possibilities there are as yet few windfarms in Scotland compared to England and Wales; this is explained principally by the later development of government incentives for Scotland.

There are important issues concerned with the way small-scale primary renewable energy electricity sources are integrated into large transmission and distribution systems. It is notable that renewables offer particular advantages in offshore island systems, which in Europe frequently offer good resources (e.g. winds, shorelines, high rainfall, strong sunlight) and suffer from the high costs of conventional supply, either because of the lack of grid connections or because of the higher costs of submarine cables to mainland supplies (Grubb and Vigotti, 1997).

NEW POLICIES, NEW PLAYERS

It should be clear from much of the preceding discussion, that it is very difficult to contemplate geographies of energy without entering the realm of public policy. Because of the central importance of energy supply to the modern economic system, it is inevitable that this should be the case. Although there has been a significant decline in the last thirty years in energy ratios/intensity in the advanced economies (energy ratios measure the relationship between the rates of change in energy consumption and economic growth (GDP)), post-industrial societies remain committed to the development of electricity as the dominant energy source and show few signs of an imminent release from a dependence on the petroleum fuels for transportation. However, energy policy is a relatively recent (post-oil crisis) development in many countries, and the fortunes of the energy sector are also influenced by a range of other government policies, including, for example, macro-economic, fiscal, environmental, transport, industrial and trade policies. At the same time, it might be argued that the international characteristics of many energy markets makes the energy sector notoriously difficult to control by domestic policies. This is a sector of economic activity where globalisation has been present for a long time, and where the influence of the world's largest transnational corporations is huge. In 1992, five of the top 25 non-financial multinationals were oil companies, five were car and truck makers and two were electrical equipment suppliers (Smil, 1994). Energy companies are major agents of globalisation through their trade in fuels, technology transfers and investment flows.

There are four observations that I would like to make about energy policy and its influence on the geographies of energy. Firstly, the oil crises of the 1970s led to much stronger articulation of energy policy in the advanced economies. In France, highly dependent on energy imports, a powerful commitment to nuclear power developed, aided by the strong tradition of central government intervention and state ownership of the electricity industry. Successful implementation of a policy 'toute nucléaire' gives France a much higher dependence on nuclear power than any other major economy. In the UK, policy led to major investment in the state-owned coal industry, including development of the Selby coalfield, and to continuing backing for the nuclear power industry, including approval of massive investment in reprocessing at Windscale (now Sellafield). However, in the USA, the wildly ambitious Project Independence launched by President Nixon in 1973 ('by the end of the decade we will have developed the potential to meet our own energy needs without depending on any foreign energy sources'), and the more balanced National Energy Plan of President Carter, both failed to deliver (Stobaugh and Yergin, 1983). The latter included a crash programme of investment in 'synfuels' (coal-gasification, oil shales), but little of this survived the Reagan administration, with its return to laissez-faire.

Secondly, in the 1980s we see in the UK (and the USA) a strong shift to domestic policies based on the ideology of the free market. In the UK this had major implications for the energy sector, which spearheaded the drive towards privatisation. Gas, electricity and coal passed into the private sector. Successive administrations, led by Prime Ministers Thatcher and Major, blamed the problems and inefficiencies of the energy industries upon state ownership and bureaucracy. Privatisation, particularly of electricity, has produced a very different structure to the market and a wholly new set of players – the new private companies. Many of these are already international in their sphere of operations. But corporate restructuring has not been a once and for all process, as takeovers and mergers have soon altered the new arrangements – thus many of the British companies now have foreign (mainly American) owners. New patterns of investment, like the 'dash for gas' in electricity generation, with their impact on the geography of production, can only be understood by reference to these far-reaching structural changes (Spooner, 1995, 1999).

Thirdly, in Europe we see the growing influence of the European Union in the energy field – a Europeanisation of policy. Effects are felt through competition policy (supporting the free market thrust), and environmental policy (where the Large Combustion Plant Directive has been conspicuous in its influence on the electricity industry, through the need to reduce sulphur dioxide emissions by fuel switching or installing 'scrubbing' equipment) as much as through energy policy per se. Energy policy is directed at market integration, managing external dependency, technology and sustainable development, with an action plan for the promotion of renewable resources.

But, fourthly, the widening of the arena of policy goes beyond Europe. Increased awareness of the global environmental implications of energy production, and the emergence of transboundary pollution as a significant problem, has produced new initiatives in the international community. Actions taken by one state or activities within one set of borders can have a direct impact on other states (often quite distant). Early examples of the tensions that can be produced were the complaints about acid rain from Scandinavia to Britain, Germany to Eastern European neighbours, and Canada to the United States, problems that needed multilateral solutions. Sweden proposed and hosted the 1972 United Nations (UN) Conference on the Human Environment (Stockholm) – an important first step in the new international involvement in large-scale environmental issues, many of them with an energy dimension. More recently the UN Sulphur Protocols and the Framework Convention on Climatic Change (FCCC) (subsequently signed by 155 countries), debated at the Rio Earth Summit in 1992 and at Kyoto in 1997, are significant attempts to control acidification of the environment and the emissions of greenhouse gases. The Kyoto Conference has produced agreed quantified targets for the industrialised countries to reduce their greenhouse gas emissions, though ratification, implementation and enforcement of compliance are problematical. Such gatherings are heavily lobbied by powerful interest groups, many representing the major industries. International non-governmental organisations (NGOs) have grown in number and importance – at the Rio summit there were more than 1400 accredited NGOs, advocating their views (O'Riordan et al., 1998). Such organisations may represent business or the public interest. International politics and relations have become much more complex and the individual nation-state is no longer the sole appropriate unit of analysis in world affairs.

Whether we consider the national or the international scale, the formulation of policy is a process of negotiation among coalitions of institutional actors. At the national scale, for example, these may include political parties, government departments and agencies, private firms, social movement organisations and communities. It is common for these to form two principal coalitions, one adopting a precautionary stance towards problems like acid rain or climate change, the other favouring economic growth, and led by business and the economic and trade ministries.

CONCLUSION

In this chapter I have tried to show that new geographies are evident both in the ways that we think about energy and the tools and concepts that we use, and in the patterns of activity that are evolving 'out there' in the real world. Although conventional fuels still dominate energy markets, the world may be approaching another energy transition, driven as much by environmental problems as by supply-demand imbalances. The relation between energy and environment has become increasingly central in all sorts of ways, and the politics and policy of energy–environment now stand alongside economics as keys to our understanding of energy geography at a variety of scales.

Indeed, scale remains an important organising concept, and the political economy approach to this provided by Taylor (1982) still has much to commend it as a framework for our thinking. Taylor identified three scales as an organising principle – the scale of reality (global), the scale of ideology (national) and the scale of experience (urban/local). The scale of reality for the energy industries is the global scale – the world economy – the fortunes of individual enterprises/industries are bound up with international economic relationships. And as I have tried to demonstrate, much policy relevant to energy has become enmeshed in the global scale too. Although political influence and real power is diffusing from the nation-state to international and domestic policy networks (O'Riordan et al., 1998), the scale of ideology is arguably still the national scale. I see this demonstrated in the case of French nuclear power, or in privatisation and the retreat from coal in the UK. But the scale of experience is local; this is the scale at which the effects of investment and disinvestment decisions are felt in the daily lives of individuals and communities – whether it is the redundant miners of Grimethorpe or the neighbours of a new windfarm, oil refinery or opencast coal mine.

REFERENCES

Calzonetti, F.J. (1981) *Finding a Place for Energy: Siting Coal Conversion Facilities*. Washington, DC: Association of American Geographers.

Calzonetti, F.J., Sayre, G.G. and Spooner, D. (1987) 'A reassessment of site suitability analysis for power plant siting: a Maryland example', *Applied Geography*, vol, 7, no. 3, pp. 223-42.

Elliott, D. (1997) *Energy, Society and Environment*. London: Routledge.

Grubb, M. and Vigotti, R. (1997) *Renewable Energy Strategies for Europe, Volume Two, Electricity Systems and Primary Electricity Sources*. London: Earthscan.

Hauser, D.P. (1971) 'System costs and the location of new generating plants in England and Wales', *Transactions of the Institute of British Geographers*, vol. 54, pp. 101–21.

Lovins, A. (1977) *Soft Energy Paths*. Harmondsworth: Penguin.

Manners, G. (1964) *A Geography of Energy*. London: Hutchinson.

Mitchell, C. (1996) 'Renewable generation – success story?', in Surrey, J. (ed.), *The British Electricity Experiment*. London: Earthscan.

Office of Technology Assessment (1979) *The Direct Use of Coal*. Washington, DC: Congress of the US.
Openshaw, S. (1986) *Nuclear Power: Siting and Safety*. London: RKP.
O'Riordan, T., Cooper, C.L., Jordan, A., Rayner, S., Richards, K.R., Runci, P. and Yoffe, S. (1998) 'Institutional frameworks for political action', in Rayner, S. and Malone, E.L. (eds), *Human Choice and Climate Change, Volume One, The Societal Framework*. Columbus, OH: Battelle.
Owens, S.E. (1985) 'Energy participation and planning: the case of electricity generation in Great Britain', in Calzonetti, F.J. and Solomon, B.D. (eds), *Geographical Dimensions of Energy*. Dordrecht: Reidel.
Plater, A. (1969) *Close the Coalhouse Door*. London: Methuen.
Rees, J. (1990) *Natural Resources: Allocation, Economics and Policy*. London: Methuen.
Schumacher, E.F. (1973) *Small is Beautiful*. London: Blond and Briggs.
Simmons, I.G. (1996) *Changing the Face of the Earth*. Oxford: Blackwell.
Smil, V. (1994) *Energy in World History*. Oxford: Westview.
Spooner, D. (1995) 'The "dash for gas" in electricity generation in the UK', *Geography*, vol. 80, no. 4, pp. 393–406.
Spooner, D. (1999) 'Landscapes of power; the shaping of the UK's new energy geography', *Geography*, vol. 84, no. 1, pp. 66–79.
Stewart, J.C. and Prichard, W.C. (1987) 'Institutional aspects of siting nuclear waste disposal facilities in the United States', in Blowers, A. and Pepper, D. (eds), *Nuclear Power in Crisis*. Beckenham: Croom Helm.
Stobaugh, R. and Yergin, D. (eds) (1983) *Energy Future*, 3rd edn. New York: Vintage.
Taylor, P.J. (1982) 'A materialist framework for political geography', *Transactions of the Institute of British Geographers*, vol. 7, pp. 15–34.
Thayer, R.L. Jr. (1994) *Gray World, Green Heart: Technology, Nature and the Sustainable Landscape*. Chichester: Wiley.
Walker, G. (1997) 'Renewable energy in the UK: the Cinderella sector transformed?', *Geography*, vol. 82, no. 1, pp. 59–74.
Weizsacker, E.U. von, Lovins, A.B. and Lovins, L.H. (1997) *Factor Four: Doubling Wealth – Halving Resource Use*. London: Earthscan.
Wilson, M.G.A. (1968) 'Changing patterns of pit locations on the New South Wales coalfields', *Annals of the Association of American Geographers*, vol. 58, pp. 78–90.
World Commission on Environment and Development (1987) *Our Common Future*. Oxford: OUP.
Zola, E. (1885) *Germinal*, trans. L.W. Hancock (1954). Harmondsworth: Penguin.

Chapter 8

New approaches to the geography of services

Peter Wood

OLD APPROACHES

Geography has a long tradition of service sector analysis. This includes studies of retailing patterns, transportation networks, office locations, port development and trade relations. Their purpose has been primarily to explain geographical distributions of these activities at various scales – local retailing patterns, regional transportation networks and office distributions, and national and international port and trade developments. In principle, the larger the hinterland over which a service can be delivered, the more coarse-grained and uneven is its geographical pattern of provision.

In much discussion of the causes of economic growth and development, however, services have not generally been regarded as capable of leading growth even at relatively local or regional scales. Many rely on predominantly local markets, and are often contrasted with extractive and manufacturing industries which may draw income to their home regions through long-distance trade with other regions and nations. The success of these industries is thus often seen as more 'basic' to regional prosperity. Services are 'intangible' and often require direct contact between provider and recipient. Their distribution therefore generally mirrors that of the consumer population. As a consequence, the most influential theory of service location is Walter Christaller's Central Place Theory. This predicts the optimum pattern of centres required to provide a range of consumer services to a dispersed population that is prepared to travel over only limited distances to purchase them.

Most services provision is thus traditionally regarded as taking place for private consumers within limited urban market hinterlands. Spending on these services depends on income from more basic economic functions within these hinterlands. 'Tradable' goods provide most of the basic income of an area although this may be modified by the activities of public agencies, for example through net taxation or subsidies. Local service employment thus depends largely on the 'multiplier effect' of spending based on outside income.

It has always been recognised, however, that some services do engage in long-distance exchange, and so may perform a basic, income-earning function for their regions. In particular, as we have already seen, ports and other transportation and trade functions support the extended movement of goods, information and capital. The expansion of personal transportation has also extended the role of tourism as a tradable service. Not all services can therefore be relegated to the secondary status assumed in much economic development thinking. Like goods production, they may support uneven regional, and even international economic growth.

As is often the case, exceptions such as these point to more fundamental flaws in conventional approaches to the geography of services. First, by focusing on spatial exchange and geographical patterns of development, they ignore the wider economic relationships in which services are always engaged. These not only serve consumption, but also material production, capital investment, human resource development, goods circulation and information communication. The great diversity of service functions is ignored. Equally, traditional approaches tell us nothing about why services have grown to employ over two-thirds of workers in high-income economies. Even more damagingly, the assumption that services, especially at local and regional scales, primarily depend on local extractive/manufacturing incomes perpetuates in geography the increasingly discredited approach to economic development associated with 'sector theory'.

Sector-based assumptions still pervade theories of economic development, much economic and policy thinking and, we shall see, much economic data collection. They emphasise the distinction between extractive (primary), manufacturing (secondary) and service (tertiary) functions. These supposedly play different roles in supporting the technological basis of economic competitiveness and wealth creation. According to sector theory the material processing sectors are the founts of technological innovation and the prime sources of new products and production processes. They ultimately create the material wealth which supports consumption and the services. Services are not only consumer-oriented, they are also labour intensive and generally lagging in technological development.

This interpretation of economic relations has become increasingly difficult to sustain with the expansion of service employment and output during this century. These trends have been at the expense of the apparently more productive extractive and manufacturing sectors. Over an even longer historical period economies have shifted from dependence on agricultural and mining activities, through a manufacturing-dominated phase from the late eighteenth century, towards a 'tertiarised', service-dominated state today. By the 1970s, one reaction was even to raise the spectre of a 'de-industrialisation' crisis in Europe and the USA. The debate later fortunately moved on to a wider discussion of many aspects of the emergence of a so-called 'post-industrial' society (Allen and Massey, 1988).

The basis of such pessimistic reactions lay in the privileged economic role awarded to material processing by sector-based approaches. They were also reinforced by the use of sector-based employment data. In the UK between 1981 and 1991 total employment hardly changed. Employment in firms which were nominally manufacturers, however, fell by almost one quarter, to 4.5 million, and the services grew by 16 per cent, to over 15.4 million (70 per cent of the total). It therefore appears that jobs in technologically intensive material processing continued to fall, while intangible, labour-intensive, consumer-orientated services expanded. This common impression encompasses many fallacies. The most obvious is that declining manufacturing employment equates with declining output or competitiveness. In fact, as new technology is adopted, the reverse is likely to be true. Then, all services are not the same. Many support the competitiveness of other business functions, including manufacturing. In fact, an element in their growth may simply be the 'outsourcing' of business functions from other firms. Also, some growing services may be more innovative and productive than most manufacturing. The evidence needs to be examined in more detail.

Service growth in the 1980s was also not universal. While the consumer services, catering and recreational activities grew fastest, public administration declined. This was often a result of the 'privatisation' of jobs into the commercial sector, but educational and health services each still grew by one fifth. The greatest service losses were in transportation, including rail, road passenger and sea. Even air transport and telecommunications employment fell, each dominated by technological changes balancing growing demand. The fastest employment growth, however, was in services supporting other businesses. Computer services more than trebled (to 148 000), business services almost doubled (to around 900 000), and financial services grew by over one quarter, to about 1 million.

Direct comparisons with the 1990s are difficult because of classification changes, but Table 8.1 presents more recent trends. As far as practicable, the services are presented as functional groups, reflecting their predominant markets (consumer/business or mixed) and ownership (private/public). Manufacturing was showing some employment recovery, especially in vehicles, engineering and electrical equipment. In contrast, some professional, legal and accountancy services now appeared to be declining. As in manufacturing, new technology and rationalisation was displacing routine work, and some firms may also have been reclassified into other business services. On the other hand, consumer and wholesaling services continued expanding, although with growing proportions of part-time work. The main seat of employment growth, however, was still in the business services, especially computing-related activities, expanding by more than a half over only three years.

These trends therefore indicate several important features of the modern service-based economy. First, private consumer services are thriving, but on the basis of radical changes in scale, technology and types of employment, including the growth of part-time work. Then, public services, especially health, education and social welfare, retain their importance in spite of the attempts to cut them back. Demand evidently remains strong. Thirdly, pressures for rationalisation appear to be affecting traditionally labour-intensive professional and financial services in the 1990s, as they have affected transportation services over a longer period. Fourthly, much of the expertise and advice supporting all these technical and organisational transformations, in manufacturing and services, come from specialist services, most obviously from computing and business consultancy.

Finally, some services have confounded sector-based assumptions by leading improvements in productivity and tradable competitiveness. This may occur in various ways. Retailing, banking or air transportation, for example, sponsor many manufacturing innovations by orchestrating new demands for computer and information systems, interactive communications networks, new forms of construction, or larger and more sophisticated transportation systems. Then, some of today's most radical changes are in service organisation and delivery, creating new forms of retailing, financial and professional services, transportation, media activity or health care.

Table 8.1. Great Britain: employment, 1994–97 (000s)

	June 1994	*June 1997*	*% change*
All employees	21 104	22 232	5.3
Manufacturing	3 789	4 001	5.6
Services	*15 913*	*16 866*	*6.1*
Consumer	*3 845*	*4 134*	*7.5*
Retailing and repair	2 663	2 856	7.2
Hotels and restaurants	1 182	1 278	8.1
Circulation	*2 171*	*2 286*	*5.3*
Transport, storage and communication	1 288	1 305	1.3
Wholesale/dealing	883	981	11.1
Consumer/business professional	*1 655*	*1 735*	*4.8*
Financial intermediaries	944	1 018	7.8
Legal	196	177	–9.7
Accountancy, etc.	151	129	–14.6
Other real estate, renting, etc.	364	411	12.9
Business services	*1 755*	*2 179*	*24.1*
Computer and related	191	295	54.4
Other business services, R & D	1 161	1 491	28.4
Industrial cleaning	403	393	–2.5
Primarily public sector	*6 487*	*6 533*	*0.7*
Public administration and defence	1 372	1 303	–5.0
Education	1 782	1 791	0.5
Health and social work	2 383	2 473	3.8
Other community, social and personal	950	966	1.7

Source: Estimates, *Employment Gazette*, October 1995; *Labour Market Trends*, November 1997.

Manufacturing-based technological change also requires service innovations in business organisation, training and marketing. The reverse is not generally the case, however. Many service innovations do not depend on specific manufacturing technologies. They combine established and new methods in original ways.

In conclusion, successful manufacturing technology today often employs fewer people on the factory floor. But like all modern forms of organisation, it also increasingly requires high quality 'business service' support. Thus, even though the economy is still being monitored in Table 8.1 in terms of manufacturing and service producers, as is commonly the case, in reality these essentially depend upon each other. Interdependence within the economy is much more significant than any distinction between sectors. These are over-simple generalisations perpetuating old-fashioned assumptions about the relative economic roles of service activities.

NEW APPROACHES: SERVICE INTERDEPENDENCE AND DIVERSITY

With services now occupying a large majority of the working population, even economists have begun to suspect that there is more to this than growing consumer demand. Once sector distinctions are discarded, the modern 'service' or 'post-industrial' economy appears no more real than the 'industrial' economy that it has supposedly displaced. Production and consumption of goods and services have always depended on combinations of material processing and service inputs. Modern service growth is no more than the continuing extension of what Adam Smith, over two hundred years ago, described as the 'division of labour' into interrelated specialist activities. Today, services are integral to the economic development and prosperity of any nation or region especially as a source of specialist labour functions and skills.

What has markedly changed in recent decades is the growing 'service intensity' of all goods and services. By this is meant the degree and variety of human expertise required to produce and deliver them. This may seem paradoxical, since there is much talk of the 'capital-intensive' nature of modern economic activity, and of technology displacing work, whether on the factory floor or at the fast food outlet. This view once more reflects the traditional preoccupation with employment in material processing. Where do the skills come from to innovate, design, organise, finance, market, distribute and service today's more sophisticated goods and services? Work today involves less manual production than in the past, but much more service expertise, either within organisations to serve their own needs or brought in from outside service firms. This is as true for successful extractive and manufacturing firms as it is for services.

As in past eras, these developments in the division of expert labour create new problems. Many medium-skilled manual, clerical and managerial jobs are being displaced by automation in manufacturing and services. Much service employment, for example in catering, cleaning, retailing and security services, are unskilled, low-paid, part-time, insecure, undertaken at 'unsocial' hours and offer poor career prospects. One critical consequence of the growing service-intensity of the economy is therefore a polarisation of workforce opportunities between those with more or less expertise, based on education, training or experience. In fact, we still depend on 'manual' labour to undertake many functions, but it is well-rewarded only when associated with specialist expertise, for example associated with a high-technology manufacturing organisation, or in vital construction, repair and maintenance functions.

Service diversity therefore reflects the varied roles of service functions in a complex and interdependent modern economy. Figure 8.1 attempts to represent this by dividing the economy into key 'arenas' of interdependent activities, rather than into separate 'sectors'. Economic relations are not defined primarily from the point of view of goods produced, but of the economic functions required to support key aspects of modern life. These include material production, but also domestic consumption, public service provision and financial capital circulation. Other overlapping, interdependent 'arenas' might be added, for example the 'media' arena, the 'transportation' arena or the 'voluntary sector' arena. The financial services arena is undergoing major changes both in international commercial capital markets and the restructuring of domestic banks and building societies. As we have seen, the public services have resisted attempts to contract their activities or transfer some into private ownership. They remain vital to the quality of life of communities and the incomes of substantial numbers of workers. These cannot be explored in detail here, but the material production and domestic arenas illustrate some general themes about the importance of service relationships.

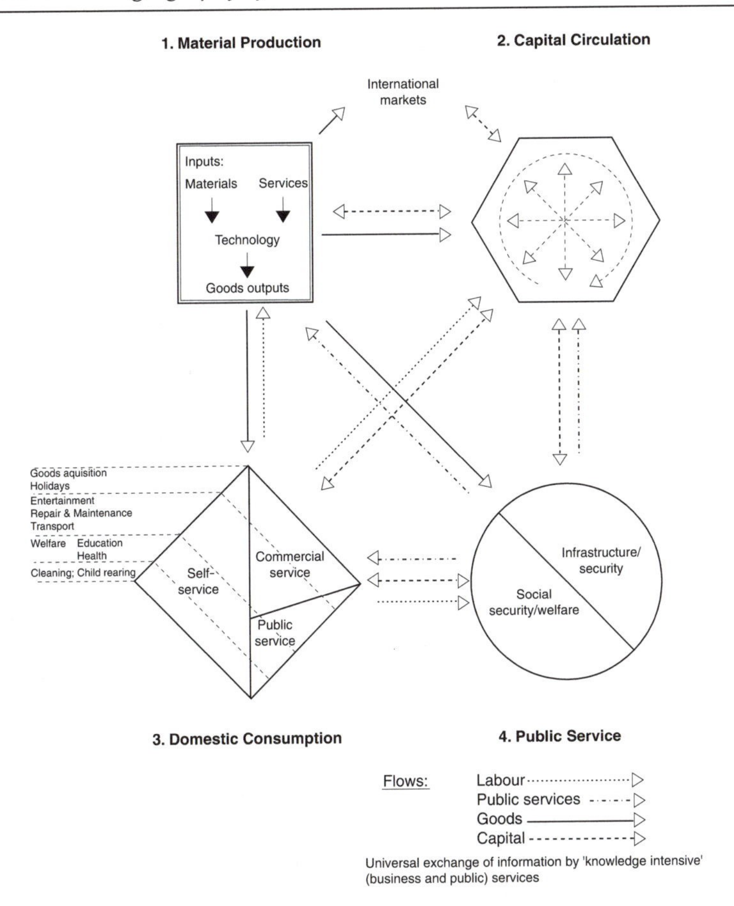

Figure 8.1 Interdependence of four 'arenas' of the economy (from Wood, 1991).

The material production arena

In spite of the declining share of employment in the extractive and manufacturing industries, they remain the basis of technical innovation and much international trade. Competitive manufacturing firms are still a vital component of modern economic development. Within the arena of material production, they must not only sustain their own production and support divisions, but also collaborate with outside firms specialising in complementary material technologies and key support and market-orientated services. Their success also depends on markets in the other arenas, for example communications and computing capacity for the financial services, consumer goods for domestic households, or construction materials for the public services. Dependence also runs the other way: from the financial services, manufacturing requires capital investment and advice; from the domestic arena, consumer spending and a trained workforce. The last, in turn, is founded on high quality education, supported largely by the public sector. This is also still a dominant influence on much transportation and communications infrastructure.

These days, a smaller proportion of employees than in the past is engaged directly in material processing even within manufacturing firms themselves. More staff work on research and development, design, training, financial control, management planning, market research and marketing, distribution and even after-sales service. The costs of actually transforming materials are now only a small fraction of all the resources required to serve modern markets competitively and to invest in future development. It is often commented that the modern 'value added' to raw materials by manufacturing depends more on information-processing than materials-processing. Simply having access to more information, however, may create more problems than it solves. Today, the most pressing need is for specialist 'expertise' to interpret and act on what is often an excess of information. The search for this expertise is the basis for the modern, service-based, 'division of labour'.

As well as the growing dependence of manufacturing on service skills, firms also increasingly depend on specialist outside 'producer' or business services for similar or complementary support. This is why, as we have seen, independent computer, business and financial consultancies have been among the most rapidly growing activities over the past twenty years. These support other service companies and the public sector in addition to manufacturing clients. Sometimes they simply offer experience in the relatively routine management of 'facilities' such as catering, security or building maintenance services. In other cases they may offer international experience of complex technical or organisational change. In all cases they are repositories of the key expertise and experience whose specialist nature and cost mean that clients cannot efficiently provide them for themselves.

The domestic arena

Everyone has experience of the domestic arena. The most basic and universal services, in fact, do not come from either the commercial or the public sector, but from unpaid, 'informal', interpersonal exchanges, mainly in and around the home. They include washing, cleaning, cooking, child care, and DIY repair and maintenance. Traditionally undertaken mainly by women, these activities are often rendered invisible in the analysis of service developments and trends. They are nevertheless the bedrock of everyday consumer service provision, and have a fundamental impact on the uses of other services in the commercial, public and voluntary sectors.

Local patterns of retailing, for example, reflect varying household social, income and age characteristics, influenced by national, often media-driven aspirations (Bromley and Thomas, 1993). Trends in the geography of shopping provision, from the regional centre to the corner shop, have to be understood in this context. Most significantly, domestic household patterns have been transformed by moves towards later child-rearing, an ageing population and especially by expanding female employment, much in the service sector. This has major implications for patterns of child care, the performance of domestic tasks, and accessibility to shopping and other activities such as work and leisure. The markets for many manufactured products, such as vacuum cleaners, washing and washing-up machines or pre-packaged 'convenience foods' are built on these patterns of behaviour, and new forms of domestic 'self-service' (Gershuny, 1977). Further innovations, for example in IT-based shopping, are on the way. There is little evidence, however, that these have increased the amounts of discretionary time available, especially for working women. The growing complexity of domestic activity, including the geographical dispersion of employment and support services, increasingly requires access to car transportation and often domestic help. The latter may come informally from family and friends, from public welfare services or voluntary agencies, for example to help the elderly, or from commercial agencies.

The growing need for domestic support affects the poor more acutely than the rich, and the old in different ways from the young. For example, the extended family and its network of help from relatives has generally been in decline, although less among some social and ethnic groups than others. This partly explains why demand for public sector health care, child support and transportation provision continues to grow, with voluntary agencies sometimes filling the gaps in provision. Private domestic service has also been on the increase for those who can afford it. Figure 8.1 simply illustrates the mix of domestic service provision from different sources. At one extreme, for example, domestic goods come mainly from commercial sources, as does an increasing proportion of modern holiday-making. Many people, of course, also engage in 'self-provision' holidays. In contrast, basic health and education, including child rearing, is dominated by informal domestic conditions. Public and private services are mutually adapted to this basic provision. In between, for example in entertainment, transportation or repair and maintenance, we rely on different mixes of self-service, commercial and public sources, reflecting, for example, age, income, taste and the quality of local provision.

Modern approaches to the diversity of service functions therefore not only emphasise that commercial services may actually lead economic change and competitive success. They also recognise their interdependence with trends in public, voluntary and informal, including domestic provision. Services exist to provide for the needs of individuals, businesses and public agencies. Formal provision and employment combine with the support both people and organisations provide for themselves, in farms, factories, offices and, most fundamentally, in households.

NEW APPROACHES: SERVICES AND REGIONAL DEVELOPMENT

The new geography of services has a triple significance for understanding processes of regional growth and prosperity. First, service support for regional manufacturing, and for other local service activities, can no longer be regarded as a secondary, dependent economic function. Because of the importance of high quality expertise, service quality may enhance the competitiveness of other activities, and a region's attractiveness to investment from outside. There are distinct differences in the UK between the quality of `business and financial services' in the South East and other regions. These service markets are dominated by large client organisations, but they also affect the support environment for small–medium companies. They reinforce the South East's cumulative economic advantage alongside its high proportions of large company headquarters, high technology and research activities, international financial services and key government functions, all adding to high levels of consumer spending (Allen, 1992).

Secondly, the development even of consumer services is significant for regional economic development (Williams, 1997). These include tourism, sports developments, universities, regional shopping centres, major exhibition facilities, and popular and 'elite' cultural activities, especially associated with the music industry. Most directly, they retain spending and employment locally which might otherwise go outside.

Williams argues that this may be as important for local economies as attracting income through exports. In rural areas, for example, local services help retain the benefits of earnings from farming, tourism and other business development. Improved consumer and recreational services also boost local construction and other public activities, although they may also displace traditional retailing or local public facilities.

The attractiveness of cities for further investment nowadays also depends on a range of modern consumption activities. This may also help retain the quality workforce needed to draw in high-income office and manufacturing functions. Such changes of image have been particularly important for industrial cities such as Birmingham, Cardiff, Glasgow, Leeds, Manchester, Newcastle and Sheffield. As the range and quality of consumption services grows, therefore, cities and regions need to encourage their development as much as investment in tradable manufacturing and services.

Growing service 'tradability'

Finally, perhaps the most significant formal service sector changes in recent decades have been the growing 'tradability' of many functions. Just as port and trading activities earned income from distant places in the past, so many other services today no longer have to be near their markets to thrive. As a consequence, more services can be delivered from a few national centres, even to international markets, and these may form part of the competitive basis of their home regions in their own right.

The basis of this expanding geography of service interaction is summarised in Figure 8.2 for international service transactions, although similar influences are changing service relationships between regions within countries. Service delivery requires some form of interaction between provider and user. Over extended distances this may most obviously occur as a result of one moving to the other. The growth of service tradability reflects the increasing ease with which this can be done, often combining various means. First, the service user may move internationally to the provider ('Type 2' movement), most commonly as a tourist or, for example, when

Movement of user (temporary)	Movement of provider: Low	Movement of provider: High — Temporary	Movement of provider: High — Permanent
Low	**Type 1** Wholesale banking Wholesale insurance Telecommunications	**Type 3** Road transport Business services Airlines Construction	**Type 4** Retail banking Retail insurance Business services Distribution
High	**Type 2** Hotels Distribution Tourism		

Figure 8.2 Summary of international service transactions.

business travellers attend international business or cultural events, seeking out luxury or specialist retailing.

Conversely, the service provider may move to the user. Again, transportation developments have increasingly enabled service staff to travel abroad to serve clients ('Type 3' exchange). These include lorry drivers delivering goods, airline staff, specialist engineers, architects or designers, consultants or other expert managerial or technical personnel. One consequence is that, although service organisations are still predominantly small, some larger companies are increasingly internationally dominant. These service corporations thus invest in national and multinational branch networks. They include hotel chains, fast food purveyors, food retailers, banks and insurance companies, accountants, consultancies, engineers and architects, facilities management and property companies. The services of international government and aid agencies are similarly delivered around the globe. These may move staff temporarily, of course, but also often support the longer-term migration, or the international secondment of key managers and technical experts ('Type 4' exchanges).

Perhaps most remarkably, modern communications technology enables specialist business, financial, communications and even public service agencies instantaneous access to national and international contacts and markets. Neither their clients nor their own staff have to move or set up branches to export their skills ('Type 1' exchanges). Global communications enable access to both routine data and specialist expertise from almost anywhere. This rapid growth of international service exchange by a variety of modes is still not adequately measured by conventional trade statistics. The extent and economic significance of expertise exchange thus remain paradoxically among the least understood facets of the modern information economy.

There remain important barriers to service exchange, especially in international markets, even within Europe. Some of these are linguistic and cultural, making it difficult to translate services designed for one country into the needs of another. These are unlikely to disappear in the foreseeable future. Other barriers, however, are based in regulations and laws often designed to protect consumers, for example in the financial services. Some of these measures are matters of habit and tradition, and simply protect inefficient local suppliers from more efficient outsiders. The European airline industry is often cited as an example. The consumer may thus suffer significantly higher costs and/or lower quality of service. These barriers are being attacked by international negotiations and agreements, including those supporting the emergence of the European Single Market. The strong traditional national 'protection' of many services suggests that any future liberalisation will have significant effects on patterns of service provision. This has already been evident in the financial services since the mid-1980s, and may extend, for example, to transportation, the media, business services and the professions.

Long-distance service trade may also have important regional effects. Growing reliance on nationally and especially internationally traded services may become the basis of growing inequality between core and peripheral regions. Already the South East of England is a service-dominated, export-orientated region, increasingly economically divorced from other parts of the UK. This is reflected in cycles of property costs, inflationary pressures and patterns of consumer spending (Allen, 1992). These developments provide a more powerful basis for future regional inequality in the UK than any extractive or manufacturing developments. Although services have been dominated by urban locations in the past, there is also evidence of decentralisation, especially of relatively routine functions, driven by high operating costs in the cities and supported by ease of telecommunications. In Britain, the beneficiaries will nevertheless probably remain largely in the south outside London.

CONCLUSIONS: SERVICES AND THE TEACHING OF GEOGRAPHY

The simple certainties of sector theory – the clear distinction between extractive, manufacturing and service divisions in the economy – may have been convenient in the past, but simply do not reflect modern economic realities. Perhaps even more significantly, they are largely irrelevant to the common experience of modern work. Most employment today, including that offered by manufacturing firms, primarily requires service skills, whether intellectual, interpersonal or manual, often in combination. The teaching of geography needs therefore to explore the range of such skills required and available in different places, and their essential interdependence across regions and nations.

To illustrate from three well-known cases. First, successful car production, for example, requires a complex assembly system of technically sophisticated components on a continental or even global scale. Its planning, design, implementation and delivery to wide markets depends on the coordination of a vast array of service skills. These must control the core assembly process, which is increasingly carried out by computers and robots, as well as the labour-intensive workshops across the world where many components originate. Secondly, global financial services are concentrated into a relatively few locations, dominated by New York, Tokyo and London. As a production system, this depends on a range of highly specialised service skills, and the particular ways they are assembled in such places and communicated around the world. Finally, the out-of-town supermarket has revolutionised retailing in the past twenty years. Many young people get part-time jobs there, shelf-stacking or on check-outs. Many will take up retail management careers. How is the uninterrupted stream of goods from farms and factories around the world sustained? How is local, national and international expertise critical to the process? What benefits or otherwise accrue to the local community? These are the types of 'service-informed' questions that need to be addressed by modern economic geography (Marshall and Wood, 1995).

The quality and experience of the workforce, and their application through successful private and public institutions, is the basis of local and regional economic fortunes. Such skills may contribute directly or indirectly to the prosperity of local communities through earnings gained from national or international markets. They may also reduce spending by locals elsewhere, and set the conditions that may attract investment for the future. Perhaps the most important theme of modern geography is the inherent interdependence of modern economies, based on the complementarity of labour roles between different activities in increasingly distant places. Conveying these realities and conflicts is a major challenge for geography as a teaching discipline. They depend on the quality of human resources, the control of investment, the circulation of incomes, the provision of information and the exchange of goods, all guided by the influence and interests of private firms and public institutions. If it accepts the challenge, the discipline should remain close to everyday experience while also improving society's understanding of the extended networks of relationships upon which it increasingly depends. Not only should geography therefore remain part of the teaching curriculum for the next century, but it needs to be increasingly central to it.

REFERENCES

Allen, J. (1992) 'Services and the UK space economy: regionalization and economic dislocation', *Transactions, Institute of British Geographers*, NS 17, pp. 292–305.

Allen, J. and Massey, D. (1988) *The Economy in Question*. London: Sage/Open University (see especially 'Towards a post-industrial economy?', pp. 91–135).

Bromley, R. and Thomas, C.J. (1993) *Retail Change: Contemporary Issues*. London: UCL Press.

Daniels, P. (1983) *Service Industries in the World Economy*. Oxford, Blackwell.

Daniels, P. (1985) *Service Industries: A Geographical Appraisal*. London, Methuen.

Gershuny, J. (1978) *After Industrial Society: The Emerging Self-service Economy*. London: Macmillan.

Marshall, J.N. and Wood, P.A. (1995) *Services and Space: Key Aspects of Urban and Regional Development*. Harlow, Longman.

Williams, C.C. (1997) *Consumer Services and Economic Development*. London, Routledge

Wood, P.A. (1991) 'Conceptualising the role of services in economic change', *Area*, vol. 23, pp. 66–72.

Part Two

The Geography Curriculum: Development and Planning

Key elements of the curriculum process are discussed in the first section of this part; that is planning, strategies, evaluation and assessment. In the second section a number of current issues affecting the modern geography curriculum are considered. In particular multimedia, education for sustainability and citizenship have been at the forefront of public (and political) debate in the last few years. However, the final chapter in this section is the key issue for the middle manager (head of department) – that is how to cope with an increasingly dynamic educational environment and nurture the limited resources, including human, at his/her disposal. Again this is a partial collection of topics but these are certainly of key importance at the time of writing in 2000.

Chapter 9

National Curriculum geography: new opportunities for curriculum development?

Eleanor Rawling

INTRODUCTION

The first version of the National Geography Curriculum for England, published in 1991 (DES, 1991), was greeted with considerable concern by the geography education community, since it largely ignored the developments in curriculum planning which had taken place during the 1970s and 1980s and, consequently, inhibited the role of teachers in school-based curriculum development (Rawling, 1996). The five content-led attainment targets, 183 statements of attainment, overlapping programmes of study and highly prescriptive details of topics and places to be studied comprised so weighty a structure that further professional development seemed unnecessary.

Since 1991, there have been two reviews of the National Curriculum as a whole – the Dearing Review 1993–95 and the review undertaken by the Qualifications and Curriculum Authority 1998–2000. In both these reviews, the Geography Order has undergone simplification and reduction and, as will be shown, despite the rhetoric of minimal change, significant restructuring has occurred. This chapter will seek to highlight the important changes which have taken place in 1995 and 2000, and to assess them from a curriculum development point of view. In the final chapter of his book, *Beyond the National Curriculum*, Lawton (1996) uses the terms 'empowerment' and 'professionalism' against which to assess past, present and future opportunities for curriculum development by schools. I interpret 'empowerment' to mean the existence of an enabling and integrated curriculum framework for the subject with clear opportunities for schools to participate in decision-making about curriculum content, pedagogy and assessment. 'Professionalism' refers to the extent to which the work of teachers, their role in planning and the status of the subject are valued within the education system. These two broad criteria will be used to analyse the situation for geography since 1991. Some suggestions will also be given for ways in which teachers can re-engage with school-based curriculum development. It will be argued that the National Geography Curriculum for 2000 England[1] is a 'very different beast' from its predecessors, providing greater opportunities for the creative interpretation and development which are crucial if geography is to maintain its status and a strong contribution to the school curriculum of the twenty-first century.

EMPOWERMENT

Curriculum development experience in the 1970s taught us that there are a number of factors essential to providing a workable curriculum system capable of being a vehicle for developing high quality teaching and learning in geography. Table 9.1 outlines these factors and also expresses them in question format. In brief, teachers need to know:

- what is considered to be the subject's distinctive purpose in the curriculum;
- what big ideas or aspects of the subject provide an organising framework;
- whether there are minimum national content requirements and how much freedom of choice is left to teachers;
- about the approach to learning and how it is integrated with the development of skills and knowledge; and
- what outcomes are expected in terms of pupil achievement.

Table 9.1 The needs for an effective curriculum system for any school subject

• Aims and rationale for the subject in the school curriculum	What is the subject's distinctive purpose in the curriculum? Why teach it?
• Key questions, aspects or ideas of the subject identified as the basis for selecting and developing content	What are the big ideas or major subdivisions of the subject which can provide an organising framework?
• A clear statement of the minimum content to be taught to each age group	What is the minimum national content requirement for the subject for each age group?
• An approach to learning and skill development which is integrated with the content	How do pupils learn 'how to find out' in the subject and to develop investigative skills as they study the content?
• Outcomes or expectations for pupil achievement clearly specified	What should pupils know, understand and be able to do as a result of teaching and learning the required content?
• Procedures and guidance for teachers on how to use the curriculum system and develop their own school-based courses and schemes of work	How can teachers implement the curriculum system and develop courses/schemes of work appropriate to their own school and pupils?
• Guidance for teachers about formal national testing requirements and suggested procedures/advice about informal assessment for learning	What are the formal assessment requirements and how can teachers also use assessment to further pupil learning?
• Recognition of the subject's contribution to wider dimensions (e.g. special education, equal opportunities) and matters of concern to society (e.g. work-related learning, literacy, citizenship)	How can the subject's potential contribution to wider curriculum dimensions be developed effectively, without distorting the subject?

In order to implement the framework, they will also need:

- advice on curriculum and assessment planning; and
- guidance on using the subject to develop wider curriculum dimensions considered important by the government and society at large.

Table 9.2 compares the performance of the 1991 (DES), 1995 (DfEE and QCA) and 2000 (DfEE and QCA, 1999) National Geography requirements against the first five of these criteria. As a result of the politicised process of its formation and the strong

Table 9.2 Comparison of the 1991, 1995 and 2000 Geography Orders

Criteria	*1991 Geography Order*	*1995 Geography Order*	*2000 Geography Order*
1. Aims/rationale	No rationale for National Curriculum and no aims provided for Geography Order – though Geography Working Group did provide aims in its final report (1990).	No rationale for whole curriculum and still no explicit aims for Geography Order, although para. 1 of Order gives flavour of each Key Stage (KS).	Values, aims and purposes are given for the school curriculum and the National Curriculum, and the Geography Order has an overall rationale ('the importance of geography') and aims/purposes for each KS ('during the KS . . .').
2. Key ideas/aspects	Attainment targets and statements of attainment focus predominantly on content. Key ideas/aspects not drawn out, though hinted at in some statements of attainment.	Places, themes, skills division of programmes of study give greater coherence to the content, and general ideas receive some recognition in level descriptions.	Four key aspects of geography are identified and the general ideas and areas of knowledge, understanding and skills to be developed are outlined in PoS.
3. Minimum content	Content entitlement for each age range overlaps confusingly because programmes of study (PoS) repeat content from statements of attainment.	Each PoS more clearly identifies the content for the KS, although specific topics and general ideas are still mixed up together.	Specific topics/content to be studied (para. 6) are clearly distinguished in each PoS from the general ideas/understandings, skills to be developed (paras 1–5).
4. Integrated approach to learning	Geographical enquiry is mentioned at beginning of each PoS, but not explained or integrated into statements of attainment or PoS	Geographical enquiry process is included as para. 2 of each PoS and as a section in each level description but it is not named.	Geographical enquiry is clearly outlined as one of four key aspects of geography and explicitly described for each PoS. It is linked with skills and integrated with content.
5. Outcomes for pupil achievement	Statements of attainment are intended to be the basis for assessment but they are mainly factual content or specific skills, so broader outcomes (e.g. enquiry approach) or higher intellectual skills (e.g. analysis, evaluation) are marginalised. Testing requirements never fully developed.	Eight-level scale introduced. Geography level descriptions set out broad outcomes for pupil achievement. SCAA guidance clarifies how four key aspects of geography are represented and explains 'best fit' process for summative assessment. Further implementation left to schools and LEAs.	Eight-level scale retained and very minor changes made to level descriptions to emphasise sustainable development education and enquiry. Confusions about the distinction between summative and formative assessment remain.

influence of 'New Right' ideology, the National Geography Curriculum of 1991 failed to meet most of these criteria (Rawling, 1992). It provided no rationale, and the key aspects and ideas of the subject were lost in the mass of detailed content. Because each Programme of Study (PoS) was made up of level-related content direct from the 183 statements of attainment, there were substantial overlaps between the PoS and so no clear content entitlement for each key stage. Geographical enquiry was mentioned by name but was not incorporated in the attainment targets nor explained in the PoS. Assessment had been virtually ignored by the Geography Working Group (GWG) so the content-specific statements of attainment caused difficulties both for teachers and for the various test development consultants attempting to design KS1 Standards Assessment Tasks (SATs) (1991/2) and KS3 tests (1993/4). In both cases, political decisions were eventually taken not to proceed with formal assessment of geography – but not before the nightmare situation left by the GWG had been confronted head-on. The Final Report of the GWG (DES and WO, 1990) had contained a diagram grandly entitled 'The curriculum system for geography 5–16' (p. 9). In fact, as I have explained (Rawling, 1992) the 1991 Geography Order did not make curriculum sense and this diagram was an afterthought included in an attempt to suggest that consultation concerns about curriculum planning had been addressed. Ironically, recognition of the difficulties teachers faced during implementation (e.g. NCC, 1992; OFSTED, 1993, 1996a and b; SCAA, 1997a) have provided one of the main justifications for geography to undergo more extensive structural change.

During the Dearing Review led by Sir Ron Dearing 1993–94, both the Geographical Association and the Council of British Geography campaigned for structural changes to be made to the Order and, indeed, the Dearing Final Report contained a separate paragraph (4.39) which sanctioned such an approach despite the fact that the whole Dearing exercise was publicised only as a 'slimming-down'. The 1995 Order was able to dispense completely with the content-loaded ATs, to merge the content into three broad categories of places, themes and skills, and to clarify the role of the PoS alongside the new level descriptions. The restructured requirements went some way towards highlighting more general ideas in geography and distinguishing these from the specific content. A major achievement was to reintroduce geographical enquiry activities in paragraph 2 of each PoS – though the political sensitivity of this term even in the mid-1990s is reflected in the fact that the term geographical enquiry is never used in the 1995 Statutory Order!

The 2000 Review (promised by Sir Ron Dearing after the five-year moratorium on curriculum change) was undertaken by yet another 'quango' – the Qualifications and Curriculum Authority resulting from SCAA's merger with the National Council for Vocational Qualifications in 1998. This review has taken the structural changes a very significant step forward, despite the statement that this was to make minimal changes only, comprising content reduction rather than more fundamental changes for all non-core subjects (QCA, 1997). Although the consultation version published in May 1999 showed little significant change, during May/June 1999 the Geography Order was completely restructured to a model that focused directly on the four key aspects of geography, making a clear distinction between these and the specific content required to illuminate these key aspects. This model is now genuinely more of a national framework and probably owes more to the curriculum projects in structure than it does to the original 1991 Geography Order. During consultation, primary teaching organisations requested greater consistency with other subjects such as history, and this was one argument used to justify this change in the model. Geographical enquiry, named and explained in considerable detail, now includes values enquiry and occupies a key position at the beginning of each PoS, while sustainable development education and the global dimension also receive explicit recognition in geography because of the Labour government's concern to address these in the curriculum. For Key Stage 3, for example, paragraph 5 of the PoS specifically requires that pupils should be taught to 'explore the idea of sustainable development and recognise implications for people, places and environments and for their own lives'. With the 2000 Geography Order, the situation has then come full circle, providing a national framework for the subject which finally makes curriculum sense, highlights geography's wider curriculum contribution and leaves teachers considerable freedom to vary specific content and the emphasis given to particular aspects of geography and learning.

Despite the continuing grip of a National Curriculum, it can be argued that a more progressive educational agenda, derived directly from project experience, has been able to re-establish itself in the geography curriculum framework and so to re-empower teachers. To explain how and why this has happened, it is necessary to look at the changing character and functioning of the central curriculum agency and its relationship with the subject community.

RE-EMERGENCE OF A MORE PROGRESSIVE CURRICULUM

The appointment of Gillian Shepherd as Secretary of State for Education (1994), and Nick Tate's appointment as Chief Executive of SCAA (1994) signalled the beginning of a period in which the curriculum and assessment body was able to give greater stress to curriculum matters. As Lawton (1996) comments, it was clear that the Dearing Review was shifting the emphasis away from delivery of a fully prescribed entitlement curriculum and back to recognition of teachers' responsibility for developing a balanced curriculum from a minimum national framework. Given this, SCAA was able to interpret its role more creatively after 1994 and to operate more consultatively. Significantly the SCAA Corporate Plan for 1995–98 recognises in Aim 1 the need to identify and undertake 'development work to support the National Curriculum', in addition to its work in monitoring, commissioning tests and regulating the public examination system. In this developmental capacity, the SCAA (and later QCA) Geography Team was able to develop a strategy for subject support and an increasingly fruitful relationship with the subject associations and the geography teaching community. This has been reflected during the 1993–99 period in regular updating meetings, publication of a termly subject 'Update', and involvement of subject experts and consultative groups in all its work. SCAA/QCA officers have also attended subject association committee meetings as observers. Another result has been the production of a whole range of curriculum-focused guidance publications from the SCAA and QCA. Exemplification of Standards for Geography at KS3, Expectations in Geography at KS1/2 and Optional Tests and Tasks for Geography at KS3 have all incorporated a strong element of curriculum planning and a framework of geographical enquiry, despite their rather unpromising assessment-focused titles. Curriculum Planning at Key Stage 2 and Geographical Enquiry at Key Stages 1–3 were more ostentatiously focused on curriculum matters. The aim has been to highlight and improve elements of good curriculum practice, particularly where the Order was lacking. The most obvious examples are geographical enquiry and the four aspects of geography (see Table 9.3) The significance of these publications is that at national level, they have laid the groundwork for necessary structural changes to the Geography Order, while within the geography community they have established a more productive and professional discourse about the geography curriculum. The Geographical Association (GA), and also to a lesser extent the Royal Geographical Society with Institute of British Geographers (RGS-IBG), have been able to redirect their energies into curriculum support (see, for example, the GA's Geography Guidance[2] series and special issues of *Primary Geographer* and *Teaching Geography*), working with the SCAA/QCA Geography Team to enhance a National Geography Curriculum which, from the subject community's point of view, has steadily improved since the 1991 version.

Table 9.3 Re-emergence of more progressive educational features in the 1990s

SCAA/QCA publications	*Characteristics*
Exemplification of Standards KS3 (1996) Expectations in Geography KS1/2 (1997) Optional Tests and Tasks (1996)	Enquiry reinstated and four aspects of geography (i.e. underlying structure/ideas) introduced.
Curriculum Planning at KS2 (1997) Geographical Enquiry KS1–3 (1998)	Explicit reference to curriculum planning and the role of the teacher.
Geography and IT (1995) Geography and Use of Language (1996) Teaching Environmental Matters in the NC (1996)	Geography's wider contributions and dependence on active enquiry teaching/learning.

Of course, there is still the problem that teachers may find it difficult to recognise and capitalise on this new 'empowerment' after ten years of being National Curriculum technicians. In addition, two remaining problems may be identified with the curriculum framework provided by the 2000 Order. One is its continuing failure to integrate assessment meaningfully into the curriculum system. Given the decision to retain the eight-level scale and to make only minor adjustments to the level descriptions, the geography level descriptions provide a reasonable basis for the end-of-key-stage assessment function. Unfortunately, as with other subjects, it is not clear to teachers how assessment may be used more formatively. The recent HMCI *Assessment Report for 1996–97* (HMCI, 1998) revealed that use of assessment information to inform curriculum planning for instance, was unsatisfactory in 49 per cent of schools at KS3. Many teachers feel pressure (often exerted by the school's senior management) to focus only on summative assessment and to 'level' pupils' work termly or even for individual tasks. As Broadfoot (1996) points out, the prevailing emphasis on assessment for 'performativity' has meant that the central agencies have not given any lead in using assessment to improve learning, despite the publicity given to the Assessment Reform Group's reports, *Inside the Black Box* and *Beyond the Black Box* (Assessment Reform Group, 1998 and 1999). Secondly, neither of the two reviews of the National Curriculum undertaken in the 1990s have allowed any consideration of the changing nature of geography and of new ideas and approaches which might be fruitfully incorporated in the Order. The 1991 version represented a very traditional, almost Victorian, view of the subject; academic geography has meanwhile changed beyond all recognition since the mid-1980s, taking on postmodernism, newer cultural approaches (the 'cultural turn'), gender issues, a reinvigorated study of places and many dynamic developments in the environmental area. In this sense, it is not only science and maths (recognised in the QCA's 1999 Consultation Report to the Secretary of State) which require a major reconsideration as school subjects, but also school geography if it is to play its part in educating young people for the twenty-first century.

PROFESSIONALISM

The experience of the curriculum development period confirmed that school-based curriculum development flourishes when the national framework for a subject is clear but sufficiently minimal to allow professional interpretation and development at school and classroom levels. The 1991 Order did not respect this balance, seeming to take over all levels of curriculum planning as a result of its prescriptiveness and to leave no obvious role for the teacher. Lambert (1994) suggested that, in this respect, the geography National Curriculum called into question the whole nature of teacher work as previously understood, giving a new stress on the technician role of delivering a pre-planned curriculum – 'the direct message to these teachers seems to be less autonomy and more conformity'. Teachers received this message both from the content and the structure of the Geography Order. The situation was to some extent ameliorated by the compensatory support role taken on by the Geographical Association and by many LEAs providing guidance publications which imposed a curriculum planning framework on the content-laden geography requirements. OFSTED inspection evidence for the early 1990s showed that the best quality teaching and learning and highest standards of pupil attainment were invariably found in departments which saw their role as more than just 'delivery' of national requirements. Roberts' research (1995) confirmed that teachers who had already been involved in curriculum development (pre-NC) found this easier to take on than those who had not. After the Dearing Review, the Geography Order presented a more obviously minimal framework and the 2000 review has resulted in even greater reductions.

During the 1990s a number of other developments have helped to restore the confidence of geography teachers in their professional role. In particular, the SCAA/QCA guidance materials already mentioned (Exemplification, Expectations, Optional Tests and Tasks, Curriculum Planning, Geographical Enquiry) have followed the GA's compensatory line, bringing back into circulation well-established curriculum planning ideas from the pre-1991 period. The curriculum planning process diagram on the KS2 planning leaflet, for instance, is directly descended from the projects' curriculum planning approaches. Such publications generally receive good reviews from the subject community and *Teaching Geography* has increasingly published more optimistic planning and development articles (e.g. King, 1999). As already explained, the mid-1990s have also witnessed a closer and more rewarding professional relationship developing between SCAA/QCA officers and the subject associations.

Other developments have also reinforced the view that the geography education community was valued, despite the difficulties caused by the Order. For instance, the

SCAA Information Technology guidance and Use of Language publications all offered a relatively high-profile role for geography. The joint DfEE and DoE initiative on environmental education resulted in an SCAA publication *Teaching Environmental Matters in the National Curriculum* which, while not presenting a very radical view of environmental education, at least promoted the importance of geography's role (see Table 9.3). The GA's successful work with the Department for Education's IT in Schools Unit in 1993 also resulted in major funding for a GA led 'Geography and IT Project', significant because, despite the narrowness of the original Geography Order, 'the DfE has recognised that lasting curriculum change will only be made if teachers are given . . . adequate resources and guidance to implement the framework effectively in their own schools' (Rawling, 1996). In a sense, the Geography/IT project was an example of the more targeted curriculum development 1990s style.

In the wider national context however, the 1991–2000 period has given mixed messages about the importance of teacher professionalism. In the immediate 1991–94 period, there seemed to be few opportunities for teachers to meet and plan the new curriculum in a cooperative 'project style' approach. The ethos of ERA ran counter to this, stressing the responsibilities of individual schools and teachers. Other parts of ERA (e.g. local management of schools, opting out) were designed to dismantle all the structures (such as LEA consortia) which had given teachers the necessary support to work on curriculum matters. A National Curriculum Council INSET Task Group report in 1991 said that 'the National Curriculum has initiated a major curriculum development exercise in geography. The publication of the statutory Orders is only the first step, the subsequent follow-up is crucial'. It went on to recommend the establishment of regional and local support structures providing opportunities for teacher interaction and 'shared interpretation of the geography National Curriculum'. Not surprisingly given that Trevor Higginbottom, a former director of one of the Schools Council Projects, chaired the group, this sounded too much like the 1970s style progressive solution, and the report was filed and ignored by the NCC, although the GA did establish its own system of regional support in the 1990s.

After 1995, despite the rhetoric about flexibility and the role of schools and teachers in implementing the curriculum, the focus has remained on individual schools and, with the Labour government after 1997, central control has been reinforced by an increasing range of externally and internally set targets (Bell, 1999). Performance is inspected and checked by OFSTED and publicly disseminated by means of league tables. As many commentators have noted, such a system elevates a narrow view of performance above a broader view of professionalism. In this situation, the old-style INSET opportunities stressing teacher cooperation and teamwork become less relevant, the emphasis changing to a 'hard-nosed' swopping of 'tips for teachers' or learning how to address the latest statutory requirements. These changes are subtle but pervasive. For geography, for example, not only are in-service education opportunities less frequent at LEA and national level, but those that exist tend to focus on the technicalities of delivering or assessing a national requirement, rather than exploring exciting ways of teaching and learning or finding out about new developments in the academic subject. Even the much heralded Schemes of Work for Geography at KS1/2 (DfEE and QCA, 1998, revised 2000) and KS3 (DfEE and QCA, 2000), though undoubtedly serving to raise the profile of geography and to incorporate good practice, run the risk of being accepted uncritically as the 'government approved' interpretation of the curriculum. In fact, the process of their development has revealed a continuous debate about curriculum principles. The subject consultants and QCA subject officers have wished to make them a model of good curriculum planning while the Standards and Effectiveness Unit (SEU) of the DfEE, as coordinators of the project, have viewed them predominantly as manuals for the approved interpretation of the National Curriculum. The first stance genuinely recognises teacher professionalism; the second, reflecting the Labour government's 'nannying' approach to teachers – is no more likely to increase professionalism or raise standards than the Conservative government's more overtly hostile approach. Equally significantly, the circumstances surrounding the Schemes of Work reflect the growing prominence of the SEU and may signal a more restricted approach to policy implementation in the future (see Rawling, 2000a; 2001 forthcoming).

Probably the biggest current issue for geography educators is the declining status of the subject at national level. From the high point of 1987 when geography was accepted as a National Curriculum subject, the 1990s has seen the gradual dismantling of the broad entitlement curriculum and the consequent downgrading of geography. In primary schools, geography's position has progressively been marginalised as emphasis has been focused on the core subjects of English and Maths. The national inspection regime, national tests and the introduction of the National Literacy and National Numeracy Strategies have reinforced the curriculum hierarchy in England, as did the government's announcement in 1998 that the full programmes of study need not be taught in the non-core six (geography, history, design and technology, art, PE and music) to allow greater immediate emphasis on literacy and numeracy. Two reviews of the National Curriculum, although ostensibly slimming the curriculum, have only significantly reduced content for the 'non-core' subjects. Not surprisingly, OFSTED inspections (1999a) and monitoring by the National Curriculum agency (SCAA, 1997) have found that, despite some good practice and excellent support from the subject association, overall geography is not accorded high priority in schools.

For geography in secondary schools, the most severe blow to status came as a result of the Dearing Review in 1994. Geography was dropped from the compulsory KS4 curriculum and, subsequently, had to compete for curriculum time with other National Curriculum subjects (e.g. history), non-National Curriculum subjects (e.g. business studies) and the newly created general vocational qualifications (e.g. leisure and tourism). The latest Review for 2000 has failed to make the situation more flexible and instead has added to the already full statutory requirements by introducing a new Citizenship Subject Order and a framework for Personal, Social and Health Education. The inevitable decline in numbers of pupils opting for GCSE geography is taking place with 8.5 per cent and 3.12 per cent and 2.21 per cent reductions in candidates being registered in 1998, 1999 and 2000 respectively, and fears for the likely negative impact on take-up of 16–19 courses. In 1999, candidates for geography A-level showed a significant 6.02 per cent reduction – the first time since 1994 that geography has registered a reduction rather than an increase at this level (Walford, 1999) – and this was followed by a 12.05 per cent reduction in 2000. This situation leaves geography in England secure only at KS3 (11–14 year olds) but OFSTED inspections note some signs of poor quality teaching and learning at this key stage (OFSTED, 1999b), which may be exacerbated by reduced staffing and resourcing if lower status in schools becomes an accepted fact.

Overall, the irony of the last ten years is that while geography won a place in the National Curriculum in the late 1980s, it proved to be at the expense of the curriculum framework for school geography. More recently in the 1990s, while the geography education profession has focused its attention, successfully, on ameliorating the faulty curriculum system, the subject has been progressively losing status as a direct result of central policies supposedly designed to improve the school curriculum. A joint Teacher Training Agency/RGS-IBG report summarising the proceedings of a conference held to investigate the growing problem of teacher supply in geography noted that 'The quality and status of geography in schools was raised frequently during the conference, as a major issue affecting intending teachers' views of geography teaching', and consequently recommended that 'The geography subject community should consider giving geography a high profile "re-launch" as a National Curriculum subject at Key Stages 1–3 in order to raise the profile of the subject to intending teachers' (Rawling, 2000b).

RE-ENGAGING WITH CURRICULUM DEVELOPMENT

Starting from the traumatic events of the Geography Working Group and the low point of publication of the 1991 Order, the geography education community has been able to influence the making of some very significant changes to the structure of the 1991 Geography Order. Arguably the Geography National Curriculum now owes more in structure to the curriculum development movement of the 1970s than it does to the original Geography Working Group, providing a clear minimum national entitlement with appropriate opportunities for development at school and classroom levels. What is more some of the essential features of good practice developed during the 1970s and 1980s, such as a focus on key aspects and ideas in the subject, the promotion of geographical enquiry approaches and opportunities for the subject to contribute to wider skills and cross-curricular matters, have now been reinstated. What is now required is for geography teachers generally to recognise and implement school-based curriculum development from this framework if the ominous signs of curriculum decline are to be halted and even reversed. The paragraphs which follow identify how the National Geography Curriculum 2000 (NGC 2000) may be used more creatively.

1. The NGC 2000 provides a clear structure for curriculum development activities, as explained on page 12 of the Geography National Curriculum handbook (DfEE and QCA, 1999). In this respect, teachers now have the 'tools' to undertake a curriculum planning job (see Table 9.4). For each programme of study, the Knowledge, Skills and Understanding section presents the important ideas and understandings which should be developed (e.g. KS3 Places (d) – how and why changes happen in places, and the issues that arise from these changes). This section is organised around the four aspects of geography (geographical enquiry and skills, knowledge and understanding of places, knowledge and understanding of patterns and processes, knowledge and understanding of environmental change and sustainable development). The Breadth of Study section lists the minimum specific content which must be taught in order to develop the required knowledge, skills and

Table 9.4 The National Geography Curriculum 2000

Knowledge, Skills and Understanding (paras 1–5 of the PoS)	*Breadth of Study (paras 6 and 7 of the PoS)*	*Level Descriptions (levels 1–8 and exceptional performance*
Four aspects of geography provide the underlying structure and identify the important ideas and understandings to be developed: • geographical enquiry and skills; • knowledge and understanding of places; • knowledge and understanding of patterns and processes; • knowledge and understanding of environmental change and sustainable development.	The specific content to be used as the context for developing the important general ideas and understandings (i.e. list of topics/places). The scales and contexts to address during the work (i.e. local–global range of environments). The need to include fieldwork and topical issues	Nine level descriptions (levels 1–8 and exceptional performance) present the expectations for pupil performance The level descriptions provide the basis for making judgements about pupils' performance at the end of Key Stages 1, 2 and 3.

understandings (e.g. for KS3 Places – two countries in significantly different states of economic development). It also outlines the required scales of study, contexts and environments to be covered and the need for fieldwork (and for KS3 study of topical issues). The level descriptions present the expectations for pupil performance at the end of the key stage.

2. Geographical enquiry is clearly outlined as an active, questioning approach to teaching and learning, which includes values enquiry and is integrated with the development of geographical skills. It is also explained that geographical enquiry and skills are developed and used when studying the required content, and not separately.
3. The importance of locational knowledge is clearly signalled in the programmes of study (within the knowledge and understanding of places) and appropriate examples are given. However, teachers have the opportunity to amend this according to the courses they run and the changing global situation.
4. The NGC is obviously only a minimum entitlement and, in this sense, it is important to highlight the freedoms available to teachers, that is:
   - the freedom to add other topics of the teacher's own choice which are not listed in the Breadth of Study section, as long as they fit the criteria of scale, contexts and environments – for example the study of weather at KS2, to reinstate a topic which many teachers regretted losing, and to extend physical geography and the opportunities for observational work; a local area or local region study at KS3 to maximise opportunities for local issues, multicultural work and development of citizenship;
   - the freedom to vary the balance of emphasis during the study of required topics, as long as the ideas outlined in the four aspects are still addressed, for example, at KS2, greater time and depth may be allocated to the environmental issues compared with water or settlement; at KS3 greater emphasis may be given to population and settlement studies rather than to economic activity;
   - the freedom to draw on new ideas and approaches in geography, e.g. to bring in a feminist perspective during the study of development; to bring in new ideas

from cultural geography when studying settlement and population; to give a local and community perspective to issues of environment and development.

- the freedom to adapt the geography curriculum to address other curriculum priorities, e.g. to use a range of texts and sources of information when studying places in order to assist the development of literacy; to choose specific local issues which have a political dimension and allow community action in order to address citizenship and sustainable development education requirements; to introduce work-related learning opportunities and links with local businesses for students who wish to develop vocational courses alongside geography.

It is not enough merely to understand this situation and to recognise the possibility of taking on these new curricular freedoms. It is, in my view, essential that we do so. Only by creatively expanding and developing the minimal geography requirements will it be possible for us to ensure that:

1. the signs of curriculum decline are reversed so that geography remains popular in schools and is seen as a relevant subject, meaningful to the lives of young people;
2. teachers are provided with the motivation and stimulus to enjoy their teaching and to raise the quality of teaching and learning they offer (this applies as much to primary as to secondary teachers, although it is recognised that primary non-specialists will need help in undertaking curriculum development);
3. the subject is enabled to address wider curriculum concerns, e.g. citizenship, personal, social and health education, literacy, numeracy;
4. geography in schools remains linked to and part of the wider geographical education community, which includes geographers in universities and teacher education, and geographers in business and the professions.

CONCLUSION

This chapter has argued that because of significant changes to the geography National Curriculum framework, teachers are now 'empowered' in Lawton's meaning of the word to undertake creative school-based curriculum development. The situation is more favourable than at any time over the last ten years. While the curriculum framework ('empowerment') has improved, the 'professionalism' of teachers and the status of school geography have not been significantly revalued in society at large. Our continuing inability to throw off the image of geography as a marginal utilitarian subject is one of the unhelpful legacies of the 1991 Order. However, it is suggested that, to a certain extent, the renewal of professionalism is in our own hands. With strong support from the subject community and a greater dialogue with colleagues in higher education, it is not only possible but crucial for the future of the subject that we re-engage with school-based curriculum development.

The author gratefully acknowledges the support of the Leverhulme Trust during 1999–2000, which made possible the research on which this chapter is based.

NOTES

1. Note that as a result of devolution and the existence of a separate curriculum and assessment agency (ACCAC) Wales is no longer subject to the same policy-making processes as England. Despite the initially similar Geography Order in 1991, the geography requirements for England and Wales now show significant differences.
2. The Geography Guidance Series is a source of quick reference and practical help to teachers, edited by R. Bowles (primary) and C. Speak (secondary) from 1997.

REFERENCES:

Assessment Reform Group (1998) *Inside the Black Box: Raising Standards through Classroom Assessment*. University of Cambridge School of Education and the Assessment Reform Group.

Assessment Reform Group (1999) *Assessment for Learning: Beyond the Black Box*. University of Cambridge School of Education and the Assessment Reform Group.

Bell, L. (1999) 'Back to the future: the development of educational policy in England', *Journal of Educational Administration*, vol. 37, no. 3, pp. 200–28.

Broadfoot, P. (1999) 'Empowerment or performativity: English assessment policy in the late twentieth century'. Paper delivered to the BERA Assessment Reform Group Symposium, British Educational Research Association Conference, September 1999, Brighton.

Department for Education (1995) *Geography in the National Curriculum*. London: HMSO.

Department for Education and Employment and Qualifications and Curriculum Authority (1998, revised 2000) *A Scheme of Work for Key Stages 1 & 2: Geography*. London: QCA.

Department for Education and Employment and Qualifications and Curriculum Authority (1999) *Geography: the National Curriculum for England KS1–3*. London: DfEE and QCA.

Department for Education and Employment and Qualifications and Curriculum Authority (2000) *A Scheme of Work for Key Stage 3: Geography*. London: QCA.

Department of Education and Science (1991) *Geography in the National Curriculum (England)*. London: HMSO.

Department of Education and Science and Welsh Office (1990) *Geography for Ages 5–16: Proposals of the Secretary of State for Education and Science and the Secretary of State for Wales*. London and Cardiff: HMSO.

HMCI (1998) *Assessment Report 1996–97*. London: Stationery Office.

King, S. (1999) 'Using questions to promote learning', *Teaching Geography*. vol. 24, no. 4, pp. 169–72.

Lambert, D. (1994) 'The National Curriculum: what shall we do with it?', *Geography*, no. 342, vol. 79(1), pp. 65–76.

Lawton, D. (1996) *Beyond the National Curriculum: Teacher Professionalism and Empowerment*. London: Hodder & Stoughton.

National Curriculum Council (1992) 'Implementing National Curriculum Geography', unpublished report of the responses to NCC questionnaire survey. York: NCC.

OFSTED (1993) *Geography, Key Stages 1, 2 and 3: The Second Year, 1992–93*. London: HMSO.

OFSTED (1996a) *Subjects and Standards. Issues for School Development Arising from OFSTED Inspection Findings 1994–95 Key Stages 1 and 2*. London: HMSO.

OFSTED (1996b) *Subjects and Standards. Issues for School Development Arising from OFSTED Inspection Findings 1994–95 Key Stages 3, 4 and Post 16*. London: HMSO.

OFSTED (1999a) *Primary Education 1994–98: A Review of Primary Schools in England*. London: HMSO.

OFSTED (1999b) *Standards in the Secondary Curriculum 1997–98*. London: HMSO.

Qualifications and Curriculum Authority (1997) *The Next Steps in Developing the School Curriculum May 1998–September 2000*. London: QCA.

Rawling, E. (1992) The making of a National Geography Curriculum', *Geography*, no. 337, vol. 77(4), pp. 292–309.

Rawling, E. (1996) 'The impact of the National Curriculum on school-based curriculum development in secondary geography', in Kent, W.A., Lambert, D.M., Naish, M. and Slater, F.A. (eds), *Geography in Education: Viewpoints on Teaching and Learning*. Cambridge: Cambridge University Press, pp. 100–32.

Rawling, E. (2000a) 'Ideology, politics and curriculum change: reflections on school Geography 2000', *Geography*, vol. 85(3).

Rawling, E. (2000b) 'Understanding geography and teacher supply'. Report of a Conference held in April 1999, Royal Geographical Society and Teacher Training Agency.

Rawling, E. (2001 forthcoming) 'The politics and practicalities of curriculum change 1991–2000: issues arising from a study of school geography in England', *British Journal of Educational Studies*.

Roberts, M. (1995) 'Interpretations of the Geography National Curriculum: a common curriculum for all?', *Journal of Curriculum Studies*, vol. 27, no. 2, pp. 187–205.

School Curriculum and Assessment Authority (SCAA) (1997) *Monitoring the School Curriculum: Reporting to Schools*. London: SCAA.

Walford, R. (1999) 'Geography: a precarious position. Analysis of summer 1999 examination results'. Paper presented to Council of British Geography, November 1999.

Chapter 10

Teaching styles and strategies

David Balderstone

Although there has been increasing standardisation in recent years of the aims and content of geographical education in England and Wales, teaching geography remains a very personal activity. Geography teachers can still exercise autonomy in their selection of teaching strategies and learning activities. Thus, it is easier to determine what geography teachers teach than to influence how they deliver this content (Roberts, 1996, p. 237).

However, as Slater (1987, p. 55) asserts, the selection of teaching strategies is 'as important as selecting content'. Successful teaching involves knowing what to do to bring about the desired learning and being able to do it. One of our main professional concerns as geography teachers should be to learn how to set up learning activities and use different teaching strategies to bring about the aspects of learning in geography that we intend for our pupils. Thus geography teachers are also 'learners', developing their knowledge and understanding of processes of teaching and learning in the subject (Lambert and Balderstone, 2000, p. 233).

We could be forgiven for thinking that teaching is now anything but a personal activity. In the late 1990s, the debate has shifted away from the content of the curriculum towards a focus on methods of teaching. The introduction of programmes for developing literacy and numeracy in the primary years based on the use of specific teaching strategies provides the clearest indication of this policy trend. However important this context, it is not the purpose of this chapter to analyse the influence of educational policy upon classroom practice in geography. This author shares Margaret Roberts' belief that geography teachers still have considerable freedom to decide 'how they are going to teach and how their pupils are going to learn' (1996, p. 232).

We begin by considering some of the contexts shaping current discussions about teaching strategies, before outlining some of the frameworks that have been used to describe teaching strategies. Finally, some thoughts about the ways in which geography teachers might develop their pedagogic knowledge are explored in order to raise important professional development issues.

CONTEXTS AND CONCERNS

What teachers do to ensure that pupils learn, the 'craft' of teaching, is often referred to as pedagogy. In defining pedagogy as 'any conscious activity by one person designed to enhance learning in another', Watkins and Mortimore (1999, p. 3) emphasise the importance of the relationship between teaching and learning. They contend that an emphasis on only the teacher's role and activity would be more appropriately described by the term 'didactics'.

In exploring different conceptions of pedagogy, Watkins and Mortimore (ibid.) suggest that there have been four main phases in the development of our understanding, but recognise that the transition between these has not represented a smooth progression:

1. A focus on different types of teachers which attributed impact to a teacher's personal style, the underlying purpose perhaps being to identify 'good' and 'bad' approaches.
2. A focus on the contexts of teaching which added organisational and managerial aspects of teachers' classroom work to the view of pedagogy. This view of pedagogy established a 'more sophisticated approach to understanding the complex interactions of pupils and teachers' (ibid., p. 4) with the classroom being seen as an 'activity system'.
3. A focus on teaching and learning reflecting a shift away from 'transmission–reception' models towards a view of effective learners being able to develop a better understanding of their own learning. This view is partly the result of our 'increased awareness of the need to think of learners as active constructors of meaning' (ibid., p. 7).
4. Current views of pedagogy which offer more complex and integrated models which specify relations between the different elements: teachers, learners, classrooms and other contexts, content, views of learning and learning about learning (Watkins et al., 1996). Central to such a conception is the creation of learning communities in which 'knowledge is actively constructed, and in which the focus of learning is sometimes learning itself' (Watkins and Mortimore, 1999, p. 8).

We are starting to see a growing interest in pedagogy in education at the level of policy, practice and research. Some would argue that pedagogy has, until recently, been a neglected issue even though it affects the way in which learners are taught (Millet, 1999; Mortimore, 1999). Anthea Millet, the former Chief Executive of the Teacher Training Agency in England and Wales (herself a former geography teacher), argued that this is partly due to teachers' understandable fears of treading on each other's 'professional toes'. 'I am always struck by how difficult they find it to talk about teaching and how unwilling some of them are to talk about teaching at all. They prefer to talk about learning as if there is no relationship between the two' (1999, p. 4).

Hallam and Ireson (1999, p. 69) contend that the controversy about pedagogy is inevitable because there is a lack of understanding about the relationship between the 'learning of the individual' and the 'activities of the teacher'. For practical reasons, the assessment of teaching tends to focus on the skills of the teacher and pupils' learning outcomes. Hallam and Ireson (ibid.) also argue that research has tended to focus on either teaching or learning because of the 'difficulty of capturing the tenuous relationship between the two'. They conclude that to become an 'effective pedagogue', a teacher needs to acquire 'a complex body of knowledge, extensive practical skills and the means of evaluating them' (ibid., p. 88).

Although there is a fairly extensive literature about approaches to the teaching of geography, there seems to me to be an ill-defined body of pedagogic knowledge within geography education. In broad terms, most of the debate within geography education during the 1960s and 1970s focused on the nature of the subject discipline and its educational potential. Although there was interest in approaches to learning geography and the creation of appropriate curriculum materials, little attention was given to the rationale for and principles guiding the effective use of different teaching strategies.

Graves (1971) did provide a discussion of teaching strategies in geography stressing the importance of the relationship between teaching and learning when attempting to achieve geographical objectives. He argued that 'any method which is successful in reaching the objective is a good method. There is no point in being doctrinaire about a particular method, if in fact it is not resulting in pupils learning what they are supposed to be learning' (ibid., p. 6). Graves distinguished between 'teaching methods', which he described as a 'series of procedures', and 'techniques of teaching geography' (see Figure 10.1). 'Techniques' refer to what we understand by teaching strategies whereas 'procedures' describe the general approach to teaching adopted by the teacher.

The Schools' Council projects (Geography for the Young School Leaver 14–16, Geography 14–18 and Geography 16–19) made highly significant contributions to curriculum development in geography in the 1970s and 1980s. One of the main aims of these projects was to encourage approaches to learning geography that would enable pupils to develop a range of abilities and skills in the process of gaining knowledge and understanding. These projects advocated particular styles of teaching which reflected their educational aims and philosophy. Through this process of school-based curriculum development, they sought to influence the teaching styles and strategies used by geography teachers. Roberts (1996, p. 235) illustrates this point by

Methods of Teaching Geography:

A. Verbal Learning and Real Understanding
B. Guidance and Discovery in Learning Geography
C. Thinking in Geography

Techniques of Teaching Geography:

A. Classroom Techniques
   (i) The oral lesson using a textbook and atlas
   (ii) The non-oral working lesson
   (iii) The use of medium- and large-scale maps
   (iv) Using pictures and photographs
   (v) The use of other audio visual aids
   (vi) The case study approach
   (vii) The transformation of data
   (viii) Games and stimulation
   (ix) Programmed learning

B. Fieldwork Techniques
   (i) Types of Fieldwork in the Lower Secondary School
   (ii) Investigations in the Upper Secondary School

Figure 10.1 The methods and techniques of teaching geography (Graves, 1971).

quoting Renwick (1985), who suggests that the Geography for the Young School Leaver project

> encouraged the move away from didactic methods of teaching to experiential learning . . . the project particularly encourages the move towards a discovery/investigative approach in situations well structured by the teacher. The teacher is encouraged to be a guide and stimulus, and to abandon the traditional expository approach in favour of more 'open learning'.

Through the late 1970s and the 1980s concern focused on the role of geography as a medium for education. Frances Slater's (1982) *Learning through Geography* was an influential text providing teachers with guidance on how to structure learning activities. The identification of key questions guided planning and the development of the learning process. Classroom activities and teaching strategies were suggested for working towards generalisations or the resolution of conflicting viewpoints. The important role of language in learning was also discussed.

In a similar way, *The Geography Teacher's Guide to the Classroom* (Fien, Gerber and Wilson, 1984) provided examples of classroom activities as well as practical advice on specific curriculum issues and teaching strategies. Once again the emphasis was on geography as a 'medium for education'. However, this was one of the first texts for geography teachers that explored the application of specific teaching strategies in geography.

While the 'handbooks' produced for geography teachers by the Geographical Association (Boardman, 1987; Bailey and Fox, 1996) have provided guidance about some teaching strategies, the need to fulfil a variety of purposes means that they lack any in-depth discussion of many pedagogic issues. They consider approaches to teaching and learning in geography and strategies for using different resources, but provide only limited guidance about different aspects of learning in geography and little insight into relationships between teaching and learning in the subject. This is perhaps understandable given the need to address a multitude of other curriculum issues.

One of the most significant recent developments in teaching and learning in geography has been the attention being given to the need to develop pupils' ability to think through geography. Leat (1997, p. 143) argues that there has been 'too much emphasis on substantive aspects of geography and not enough on the intellectual development of pupils.' This author shares David Leat's concern about the preponderance of 'busy work' in many geography classrooms and about the failure of many geography textbooks, and much geography teaching, to challenge pupils (ibid., p. 143). This is due to a lack of attention being given to the nature of pupil learning through geography and to pedagogic relationships between teaching and learning in the subject.

One of the consequences of the increasing standardisation of the curriculum is that the content of school geography has changed little in recent years and we have also seen the emergence of the 'textbook as curriculum' in many schools. The danger is that such 'textbook curricula' require 'minimal skilled intervention' by the teacher and can thus diminish 'teacher professionalism' (Leat, 1997, p. 144). The 'Thinking through Geography' project (Leat, 1998) offers teaching strategies and learning activities designed to promote pupils' intellectual development through more stimulating and challenging geography lessons. It also makes a significant contribution to our understanding of pedagogy in geography through its focus on 'fundamental concepts' in geography. Giving some attention to how pupils develop their conceptual understanding should help geography teachers to understand more about the use of teaching strategies that promote cognitive development. Geography teachers need to learn more about how certain strategies can provide appropriate challenge which is an essential prerequisite of intellectual development. They also need to develop debriefing skills that help pupils to explore their own thinking (metacognition).

Educational policy

The educational policy context also exerts a significant influence on how we view teaching. Watkins and Mortimore (1999, p. 13) comment on how politicians and policy-makers have been taking an increasing interest in the 'details of pedagogy'. More recently, the emphasis on the development of 'evidence-based policy' in education has led to a focus on actions which policy-makers claim will achieve particular results. This approach can be seen in the introduction of literacy and numeracy strategies in primary schools in England and Wales. The effectiveness of these strategies in achieving the desired improvements in literacy and numeracy will be monitored, creating some interesting relations between teachers, academic researchers and educational policy-makers.

'Standards' which define aspects of a teacher's work have been introduced. The *Standards for the Award of Qualified Teacher Status* in England and Wales (DfEE, 1998a) outline the 'standards' that need to be achieved by trainee teachers if they are to gain Qualified Teacher Status. Initial teacher training courses are required to assess all trainees to ensure that they meet all of these standards. Within a section on 'Planning, Teaching and Class Management' there is a requirement for trainee teachers to demonstrate that they 'use teaching methods which sustain the momentum of pupils' work and keep all pupils engaged' (ibid., p. 8). A range of objectives, related to different aspects of learning, are stated for these 'methods' but no strategies are specified. Trainee teachers are also required to 'evaluate their own teaching critically and use this to improve their effectiveness' (ibid., p. 9). It remains to be seen whether subject specific exemplifications of these standards will be developed and if so what they might say about teaching strategies in geography.

In addition to this, an even more prescriptive 'initial teacher training National Curriculum' was introduced for the use of information and communications technology in subject teaching (DfEE, 1998b). This curriculum requires that all trainee teachers are 'taught' and 'able to use' 'effective teaching and assessment methods' relevant to the use of ICT in their subject teaching. Their 'knowledge and understanding of, and competence with information technology' must also be developed. It is perhaps interesting that direct reference is made to pedagogy in this latter area. Trainee teachers are required to 'demonstrate that they are competent in those areas of ICT which support pedagogy' in their subject teaching and specific strategies or applications are set out.

National Standards for subject leaders have also been introduced (TTA, 1998) but have yet to be made statutory. These standards are part of a policy which seeks to promote 'improvements in the quality of teaching and leadership which will have the maximum impact on pupils' learning' (ibid., p. 1). Subject leaders are seen as having a key responsibility for 'teaching and learning' in their subject. They are required to 'secure and sustain effective teaching of the subject, evaluate the quality of teaching and standards of pupils' achievements and set targets for improvement' (ibid., p. 10). The Geographical Association's (1999) guidance on these standards advocates that subject leaders in geography should plan opportunities for a variety of teaching and learning styles and strategies. It identifies some questions that subject leaders should consider in relation to the use of these strategies (ibid., p. 9):

- Which of these strategies do you use in your school/department?
- How often do you use these strategies?
- How do you know that they are used in other classes?
- Which are planned for, and which are followed incidentally?
- Are they planned with continuity and progression in mind?
- How can you make these accessible to all (noting, for example, gender, ethnicity, ability)?
- How might you plan to introduce a new approach?
- What constraints might there be to developing new strategies?
- How might you overcome these constraints?

It remains to be seen how the work of subject leaders in geography will be judged against these standards. For example, there are undoubtedly subject leaders who can successfully evaluate teaching in their subject, identifying effective practice and providing guidance on the 'choice of appropriate teaching and learning methods to meet the needs of the subject and of different pupils' (TTA, 1998, p. 11). However, what range of teaching styles and strategies will be deemed to be 'appropriate' and by whom? The standards also appear to require subject leaders to develop their own pedagogic knowledge and skills, but will there be a professional development culture, processes and support in place to enable this to occur?

Another new policy which could have important implications for teaching and learning is the introduction of the notion of 'Advanced Skills' teachers who are rewarded for their classroom expertise. Part of the role of being an 'Advanced Skills' teacher involves sharing this expertise both within and between schools. Although there appear to be fairly rigorous procedures for assessing teachers' capabilities, the criteria for awarding 'Advanced Skills' status in relation to pedagogy are unclear at the moment. What range of teaching strategies must teachers use effectively? To what extent do they understand the nature of the relationships between their teaching and their pupils' learning? Do they understand the principles underpinning effective use of particular strategies and are they able to communicate this understanding to the teachers with whom they are supposed to share such practice? Do they possess the skills and strategies needed to promote effective professional development for other teachers?

Effective teaching

There is already an extensive body of research literature about effective teaching. Some of this research has concentrated on identifying particular features of teaching and learning which contribute to school effectiveness (Mortimore, 1994). Doyle (1987) argues that pupils achieve more when teachers employ a structured approach to their teaching, provide pupils with plenty of opportunities to practise, monitor progress and check understanding with frequent direct questioning, and provide continuous feedback on this progress. Research into 'effective' departments in secondary schools has also emphasised the importance of structuring and feedback in contributing to effective teaching (Harris, Jamieson and Russ, 1995). This research also drew attention to the value of teaching strategies and learning activities that encourage cooperative learning as well as underlining the importance of using a variety of styles and strategies.

Evidence from the inspection of geography lessons raises some important issues about teaching strategies. Reviews of this evidence have highlighted possible relationships between the use of particular teaching strategies and standards of achievement in geography (Smith, 1997; Ofsted, 1998). Low standards of achievement often result from insufficient use being made of practical and investigative work (such as fieldwork), or of strategies and geographical contexts that promote thinking. Furthermore, Smith (1997, p. 126) suggests that in such situations:

> There is sometimes a narrowness in the range of teaching methods characterised by over-long expositions, over-directed styles inhibiting curiosity and initiative and discussions mediated by and through the teacher, all of which reduce opportunities for developing thinking in an uncritical context. Also, some teachers intervene too quickly and then provide an answer in their own words.

Such comments illustrate the importance of pedagogy, of the need for geography teachers to understand more about the principles underpinning effective use of different teaching strategies. They also highlight the need for effective subject leadership as well as the creation of a professional development culture and processes which enhance teacher professionalism and promote further improvements in the quality of geography teaching.

FRAMEWORKS FOR DESCRIBING AND ANALYSING TEACHING STYLES

The term 'teaching style' is used to describe the way in which geography is taught. It has an important influence on the educational experience of pupils in geography because it affects how they learn geography. A teacher's teaching style is determined by their 'behaviour' (their demeanour and the way in which they relate to pupils) and the strategy that they choose to bring about the learning intended.

Some teachers often feel that certain teaching styles and strategies are more appropriate for them because they suit their personality and reflect their philosophy of teaching. However, it is now generally accepted that teachers need to develop a repertoire of different styles and strategies. This is because they need to consider the characteristics and needs of their pupils (their attitudes, abilities and preferred ways of learning) and the intended learning outcomes, as well as their own preferred ways of teaching. They draw upon their own body of pedagogic knowledge about how teachers teach and how pupils learn. Teachers' personal qualities and their approaches to classroom management influence the way that they teach. The nature of the learning environment that they work in (classroom appearance and layout), the size of the class and the availability of appropriate learning resources will also have a significant influence on the decisions that they make about their teaching.

Many of the terms that are used to describe different ways of teaching are not always helpful. Terms such as didactic, teacher-directed, whole-class, practical and experiential provide what are at best only general descriptions.

When used to describe teaching styles, terms such as 'progressive' and 'traditional' are value-laden and stereotypical extremes. For example, one view of progressive teaching might be that it is enquiry-based, child-centred, concerned with problem-solving and therefore represents a forward-looking and effective approach to teaching. However, another view might be that it is 'trendy' and lacking intellectual substance. Traditional teaching may be seen as being old-fashioned, autocratic, didactic and lacking creative opportunities, or as being reliable and effective at maintaining academic standards. Opinions about the relative strengths and weaknesses of different styles of teaching vary and such descriptions only give a partial view of how a teacher may be teaching.

As mentioned earlier, research in the past has often focused on the relationship between different styles of teaching and the effectiveness of pupil learning. This often leads to more value being placed on one style than another because it is believed to be more effective or, as Roberts (1996, p. 235) also suggests, because it relates more to the researchers' 'particular educational aims and philosophy'.

The Schools Council projects described earlier set out to influence the styles of teaching used by geography teachers through the process of school-based curriculum development. The 14–18 Bristol Project, which sought to influence geography for high achieving pupils during the 1970s, identified three styles of classroom interaction (see Figure 10.2) but indicated a strong preference for an interactionist style of teaching geography. The weaknesses of the transmission and structured learning approaches were highlighted while greater emphasis was placed on the significance of values in

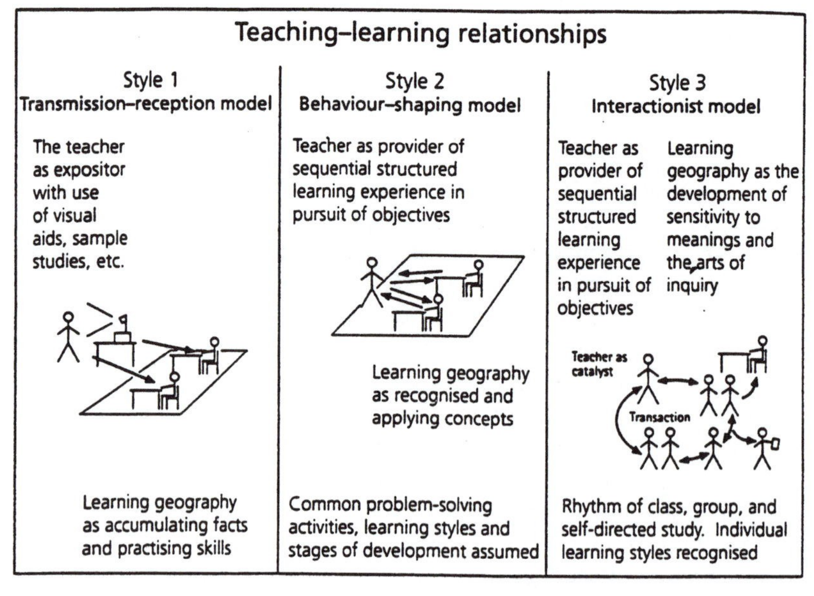

Figure 10.2 Alternative styles of teaching and learning in geography (Tolley and Reynolds, 1977, p. 27).

decision-making and on the deeper learning processes inherent in the interactionist model.

Another influential curriculum development, the Schools Council 16–19 Geography Project, advocated an 'enquiry-based' approach to teaching and learning and envisaged a continuum of approaches (see Figure 10.3). Although this provided 'scope for an effective balance of both teacher-directed and more independent enquiry' (Naish et al., 1987, p. 46), the project's view of enquiry-based learning focused predominantly on structured problem-solving and open-ended discovery.

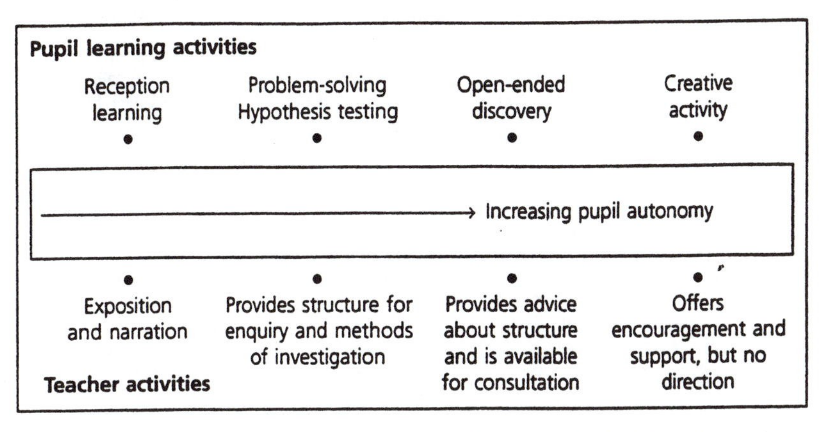

Figure 10.3 The teaching and learning continuum (Naish et al., 1987, p. 45).

It is clear that there is often a gap between the rhetoric and ideals espoused about teaching styles and what actually happens in the classroom. Pragmatism and an understanding of particular school contexts and cultures lead teachers to adapt the teaching styles and strategies that they use. However, this could lead to a belief that you cannot use particular styles or strategies with pupils in certain school contexts. This would of course deprive pupils of opportunities to learn in different ways.

Roberts (1996) introduced a different framework for looking at teaching styles and strategies in geography. She shows how the 'participation dimension' (see Figure 10.4) can be used as an analytical tool to enable teachers to 'engage critically' with their own practice. She has adapted this framework so that it can be used to interpret and analyse different styles of teaching and learning in geography (see Figure 10.5). Using this framework it is possible to imagine what geography lessons consistent with particular styles of teaching and learning might be like. She argues that teachers can adapt their strategies so that they operate across different styles depending on the context in which they are working (ibid., p. 238).

In the closed style the learners are passive as the teacher controls the selection of content and the way it is presented to them. This content is presented as 'authoritative knowledge' to be learnt by the pupils. The teacher decides how this content or 'data' is to be investigated by prescribing the procedures to be followed. The pupils follow instructions presented in textbooks and worksheets or through whole-class teaching. The learning outcomes or key ideas and generalisations are predetermined by the teacher and accepted by the pupils as valid conclusions.

Framed styles of teaching and learning are guided by more explicit geographical

	← Closed	Framed	Negotiated →
Content	Tightly controlled by teacher. Not negotiable	Teacher controls topic, frames of reference and tasks; criteria made explicit	Discussed at each point; joint decisions
Focus	Authoritative knowledge and skills; simplified, monolithic	Stress on empirical testing; processes chosen by teacher; some legitimation of student ideas	Search for justifications and principles; strong legitimation of student ideas
Students' role	Acceptance; routine performance; little access to principles	Join in teacher's thinking; make hypotheses, set up tests; operate teacher's frame	Discuss goals and methods critically; share responsibility for frame and criteria
Key concepts	'Authority': the proper procedures and the right answers	'Access': to skills, processes, criteria	'Relevance': critical discussion of students' priorities
Methods	Exposition; worksheets (closed); note-giving; individual exercises; routine practical work. Teacher evaluates	Exposition, with discussion eliciting suggestions; individual/group problem-solving; lists of tasks given; discussion of outcomes, but teacher adjudicates	Group and class discussion and decision-making about goals and criteria. Students plan and carry out work, make presentations, evaluate success

Figure 10.4 The participation dimension (Barnes et al., 1987).

questions. The focus of the geographical study or enquiry is still determined by the teacher, but pupils are encouraged to generate their own questions. Presenting pupils with questions, problems to be solved or decisions to be made creates a 'need to know' with pupils (Roberts, 1996, p. 243). The resources and content are still selected by the teacher but they tend to be presented as 'evidence' to be interpreted.

In this framed style, teachers help pupils to develop their understanding of the processes and techniques involved in geographical enquiry. Evaluation is also important as pupils need to understand the strengths and limitations of different sources of information and techniques for presenting or analysing this data. Conflicting information or viewpoints should be explored so that pupils can come to different conclusions when analysing this information.

When using negotiated styles of teaching and learning, teachers identify the general theme to be studied but the pupils generate the questions that will guide their enquiry either individually or in groups. As well as negotiating these questions the teacher will provide guidance about the methods and sequence of enquiry, and about the suitability of proposed sources of information. The pupils collect this information independently and select appropriate methods to present, analyse and interpret this data. It is helpful to review the sources and methods selected because the processes of learning are often as important as the learning outcomes themselves.

Stage of teaching and learning	Closed	Framed	Negotiated
Questions	Questions not explicit or questions remain the teacher's questions	Questions explicit, activities planned to make pupils ask questions	Pupils decide what they want to investigate under guidance from teacher
Data	Data selected by teacher, presented as authoritative, not to be challenged	Variety of data selected by teacher, presented as evidence to be interpreted	Pupils are helped to find their own data from sources in and out of school
Interpretation	Teacher decides what is to be done with data, pupils follow instructions	Methods of interpretation are open to discussion and choice	Pupils choose methods of analysis and interpretation in consultation with teacher
Conclusions	Key ideas presented, generalisations are predicted, not open to debate	Pupils reach conclusions from data, different interpretations are expected	Pupils reach own conclusions and evaluate them
Summary	The teacher controls the knowledge by making all decisions about data, activities, conclusions. Pupils are not expected to challenge what is presented	The teacher inducts pupils into ways in which geographical knowledge is constructed, so that they are enabled to use these ways to construct knowledge themselves. Pupils are made aware of choices and are encouraged to be critical	Pupils are enabled by the teacher to investigate questions of concern and interest to themselves

Figure 10.5 A framework for looking at different styles of teaching and learning in geography (Roberts, 1996, p. 240).

Roberts' (1996) discussion of how this framework can be used to analyse different approaches to teaching and learning in geography is illustrated with examples from a variety of geography lessons and fieldwork activities. Further examples illustrating how the framework might be applied when interpreting geographical fieldwork can also be found in Lambert and Balderstone (2000).

The choice of fieldwork approach and strategies to be used will depend on the purpose that the teacher has in mind for this fieldwork. The purpose may be to develop knowledge and understanding 'about' the environment or to develop practical skills and provide activity-based learning experiences 'through' the environment. Alternatively, the aim might be to promote education 'for' the environment with its agenda for social change leading to more sustainable lifestyles. Job, Day and Smyth

(1999, p. 14) provide a summary of the purposes and strategies of local fieldwork (see Figure 10.6). They contend that the 'best fieldwork teachers have an awareness of the full range of strategies and a clear view of the purposes of the fieldwork and can vary their approach according to the needs of students and the available environments' (ibid., p. 13). These approaches are certainly not mutually exclusive and it is clear that several draw upon elements from a variety of available strategies.

Field teaching and field research can bring about a range of desirable educational

Strategy	Purposes	Characteristic activities
The traditional field excursion	• Developing skills in geographical recording and interpretation • Showing relationships between physical and human landscape features • Developing concept of landscape evolving over time • Developing an appreciation of landscape and nurturing a sense of place	Students guided through a landscape by teacher with local knowledge, often following a route on a large-scale map. Sites grid-referenced and described with aid of landscape sketches and sketch maps to explore the underlying geology, topographical features, the mantle of soil and vegetation and the landscape history in terms of human activity. Students listen, record and answer questions concerning possible interpretations of the landscape.
Field research based on hypothesis testing	• Applying geographical theory or generalised models to real-world situations • Generating and applying hypotheses based on theory to be tested through collections of appropriate field data • Developing skills in analysing data using statistical methods in order to test field situations against geographical theory	The conventional deductive approach involves initial consideration of geographical theory, leading to the formulation of hypotheses which are then tested against field situations through the collection of quantitative data and testing against expected patterns and relationships. More flexible variants of this approach encourage students to develop their own hypotheses based on initial field observations, thereby incorporating an inductive element.
Geographical enquiry	• Encouraging students to identify, construct and ask geographical questions • Enabling students to identify and gather relevant information to answer geographical questions and offer explanations and interpretations of their findings • Enabling students to apply their findings to the wider world and personal decisions	A geographical question, issue or problem is identified, ideally from student's own experiences in the field. Students are then supported in the gathering of appropriate data (quantitative or qualitative) to answer their key question. Findings are evaluated and the implications applied to the wider world and personal decisions where appropriate.
Discovery fieldwork	• Allowing students to discover their own interests in a landscape (rather than through a teacher) • Allowing students to develop their own focus of study and methods of investigation • Encouraging self-confidence and self-motivation by putting students in control of their learning	Teacher assumes the role of animateur, allowing the group to follow its own route through the landscape. When students ask questions these are countered with further questions to encourage deeper thinking. A discussion and recording session then identifies themes for further investigation in small groups. This further work has arisen from students' perceptions and preferences rather than those of teachers.
Sensory fieldwork	• Encouraging new sensitivities to environments through using all the senses • Nurturing caring attitudes to nature and empathy with other people through emotional engagement • Acknowledging that sensory experience is as valid as intellectual activity in understanding our surroundings	Structured activities designed to stimulate the senses in order to promote awareness of environments. Sensory walks, use of blindfolds, sound maps, poetry and artwork are characteristic activities. Can be used as an introductory activity prior to more conventional investigative work or to develop a sense of place, aesthetic appreciation or critical appraisal of environmental change.

Figure 10.6 Fieldwork strategies and purposes (Job, Day and Smyth, 1999, p. 14).

outcomes. The practical nature of tasks such as observing, collecting and recording data helps pupils to acquire new skills and develop 'technical competency' in a range of fieldwork and data-handling skills. The use of focused investigations and carefully structured approaches to geographical enquiry can help pupils to transfer these skills and frameworks to their own independent investigations. There may also be some gains in conceptual understanding and the development of technical and specialised vocabulary will usually be strengthened.

However, much of the potential of fieldwork for generating pupil-centred learning can be lost if the focus of study, data collection techniques and sites have been predetermined by the teacher rather than arising from pupils' own field experiences and perceptions. Job (1999) argues that when hypothesis-testing approaches are used the development of conceptual understanding depends more on processed data rather than on direct field experiences. He draws attention to Harvey's (1991) research into pupils' experiences of fieldwork at A-level which suggests that the quest for generalisations dominating the more heavily quantitative approaches to fieldwork can result in a neglect of 'sense of place'.

Job (1999) provides examples of a variety of less structured fieldwork activities that can be used to encourage deeper thinking about landscapes and environmental issues. These activities can provide starting points for fieldwork investigations raising pupils' awareness of an environment based on their own personal experiences and perceptions. The objective of this 'engagement with places at an emotional or sensory level' is to develop pupils' 'sense of care and concern about places and landscapes' (Job, 1999, p. 156) which is a vital element of any deeper environmental perspective. Art, poetry and literature can all help to provide such sensory experiences and develop pupils' 'sense of place'.

Figure 10.7 is a graphical summary of the different approaches to geographical fieldwork outlined by David Job. Each approach is distinguished by its focus, and the extent to which it relies upon measurement and data collection or more qualitative forms of experience. A more comprehensive review of these different fieldwork styles and strategies can be found in Job (1999) and Job, Day and Smyth (1999).

UNDERSTANDING DIFFERENT TEACHING STRATEGIES

One of the important features of successful teaching is variety. It is widely accepted that to be effective teachers need to develop a repertoire of teaching styles and strategies that they can use successfully in different situations. Teachers use different strategies to achieve different learning outcomes, to promote different learning styles or processes, and to respond to the variety of ways in which pupils learn. Pupils will not thrive and achieve their potential on a monotonous diet no matter how it is presented. An important part of being a geography teacher involves finding out how these different teaching strategies foster different types of mental activity and the degree to which particular mental activities bring about learning in the subject.

Wragg (1997, p. 86) describes 'teaching' as 'whatever teachers do to ensure children learn'. Teaching strategies are the specific methods, techniques or procedures employed by teachers to bring about this learning. Over the years there have been many different approaches used to define, describe and classify these teaching strategies. Each approach has its limitations and drawbacks not least because of the complex variations

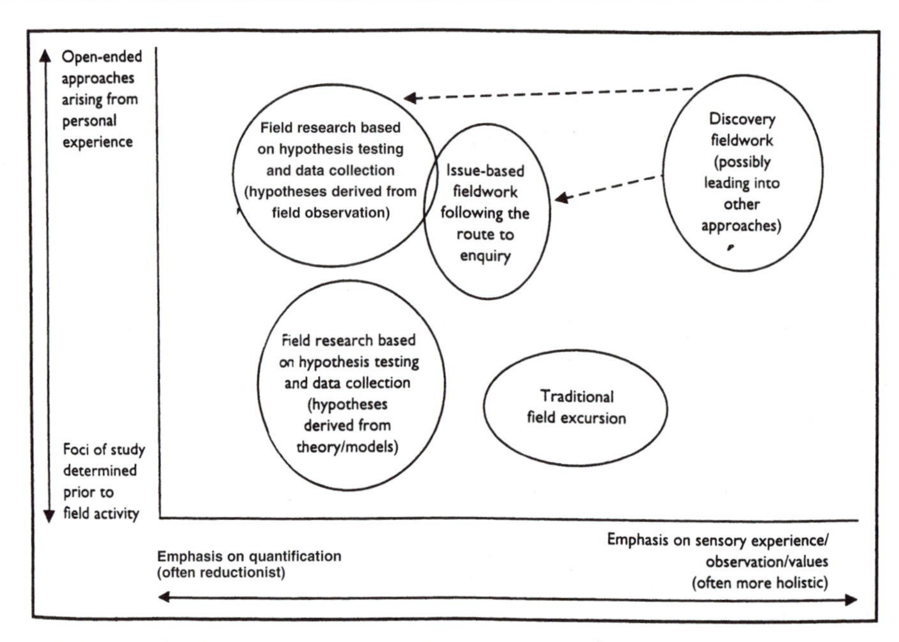

Figure 10.7 Graphical representation of fieldwork approaches (Job, 1999, p. 23).

between different school and subject contexts. Wragg (1997) identifies five general categories of teaching strategies:

- telling and explaining;
- discovery and invention;
- teachers' questions;
- feedback;
- group or team work.

Elsewhere, an attempt is made to explore in some detail the main groups of strategies used in the teaching of geography (Lambert and Balderstone, 2000). These groupings are certainly generic but they are felt to have particular relevance to geography teaching:

- exposition;
- questioning;
- collaborative strategies;
- games, simulations and role plays;
- values education strategies;
- problem-solving and decision-making;
- developing thinking skills.

This represents an attempt to identify some of the important principles guiding the effective use of different teaching strategies in geography education. It draws upon work already undertaken within geography education and elsewhere to provide advice for trainee teachers of geography. However, it recognises the need for more focused and illuminative research to be carried out to inform our understanding of the different strategies used to teach geography. To exercise the professional judgement that Roberts (1996) and others value so strongly, geography teachers need to understand how and when they can use different teaching strategies effectively.

DEVELOPING PEDAGOGIC KNOWLEDGE IN GEOGRAPHY EDUCATION

Geography in education has made considerable advances in the last thirty years or more. This discussion has tried to show how curriculum concerns, particularly in relation to the nature of the subject discipline and the planning of the geography curriculum in schools, have dominated development efforts during that period. The 1980s saw a welcome shift in focus towards a concern for the learning that takes place through a geographical education and especially for developing the crucial role of geographical enquiry in this learning. Increasing standardisation of the geography curriculum at all levels in schools has been centre stage over the last decade leading to calls from many for renewed curriculum development endeavours and innovation. Other important issues such as the contribution of a geographical education to global citizenship and the development of pupils' critical thinking skills are also deserving of our attention.

But geography teachers should not neglect their own professional practice and should continue the process of developing their pedagogic knowledge that they began during their initial training. Graves (1997) argues that teachers adapt an essentially pragmatic attitude towards teaching methods selecting strategies that are in harmony with their objectives. But pragmatism should not be our only concern and, as Graves himself rightly warns, 'consolidation does not mean stagnation' (ibid., p. 30).

There is a growing body of research on teachers' professional learning (Brown and MacIntyre, 1993; Calderhead, 1988) which needs to be extended and more fully utilised. Geography teachers need to develop their knowledge and understanding of processes of teaching and learning in geography. There are no short cuts to acquiring this pedagogic knowledge. Initially, trainees begin to develop this knowledge through observation of experienced practitioners at work in the classroom supported by advice from mentors and other teachers. However, there are dangers of oversimplification in this model of professional learning if these mentors and practitioners themselves have a limited understanding of pedagogic relationships. Teacher education could be enriched through further development of techniques of classroom observation and coaching which would enhance the pedagogic knowledge of both trainees and experienced teachers.

There is a growing awareness of the complexity of classroom processes and of the different ways of interpreting and influencing these processes. This usually begins during initial training as trainee teachers become less concerned with their own performance and start to recognise what Tony Fisher describes as a 'complex interplay of three specific types of knowledge': knowledge about learners, knowledge about geography and pedagogic knowledge (1998, p. 32). Fisher summarises these interrelationships between teaching and learning in geography in a useful dynamic model in which teaching is 'seen as both a causal and an enabling activity' (see Figure 10.8).

Central to the development of a geography teacher's pedagogic knowledge is the need to build up a broad repertoire of teaching styles and strategies. Receptiveness to

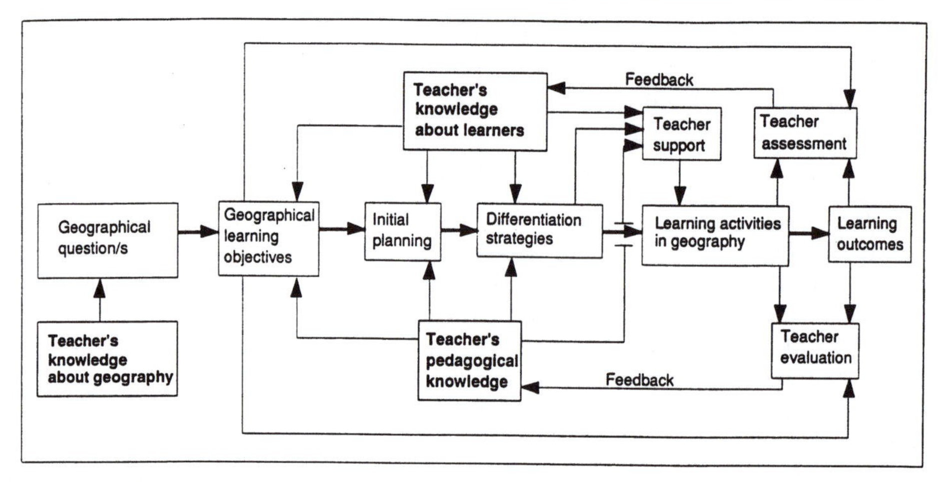

Figure 10.8 The 'teaching and learning complex' – a model of teaching for learning in geography (Fisher, 1998, p. 3).

ideas about different approaches and a willingness to be flexible, imaginative and take risks can help to enrich one's pedagogic knowledge. David Leat describes geography as 'an enormously eclectic borrower' with geography teachers being 'inclined to play fast and loose in applying ideas and techniques' (Leat and McAleavy, 1998, p. 113). It also puts geography teachers in a better position to promote the intellectual development of their pupils and respond to the concerns reported earlier in this chapter about the lack of challenge in many geography lessons (Smith, 1997). Leat and McAleavy (ibid.) assert that 'teaching thinking strategies and pedagogy can add substantially to the repertoire of teachers and schools to make changes in the classroom without which raising attainment becomes an end without a means'.

Teacher education implies something more than just 'training' and I have always felt that professional growth requires 'attitude' as much as 'knowledge, understanding and skills'. In this context, 'attitude' is appropriately summed up by Romey and Elberty Jr (1984, p. 315):

> Past successes pose a danger to person-centred education in geography. Once something 'works' we tend to want to use the techniques over again in order to repeat the success ... [I]f an approach works, rejoice, but then approach the next question freshly, on its own terms and seek a new perspective. Abandon 'techniques' that get to feel like formulas, and search for freshness as if you have had no past experience. Mistakes? Yes, mistakes must continue to be made if progress is to continue. Failure to make mistakes generally means failure to grow. Teachers must join their students in exploring all possible paths, including what may appear to be dead ends, if better paths are to be found. It is amazing how often a 'safe' path becomes a blind alley and an unlikely, overgrown trail leads to a previously unknown highway.

There is also something about successful teaching that is difficult to put your finger on. The interplay between effective teaching and successful learning has sometimes been described as 'artistry'. The idea of artistry recognises that teaching is a highly creative and personal activity:

> There is a striking quality to fine classrooms. Pupils are caught up in learning; excitement abounds; and playfulness and seriousness blend easily because the purposes are clear, the goals sensible and an unmistakable feeling of well being prevails.
>
> Artist teachers achieve these qualities by knowing both their subject matter and their students; by guiding the learning with deft control that itself is born out of perception, intuition and creative impulse.
>
> (Rubin, 1985, p. v)

I hope that this brief discussion has outlined the nature of the challenge facing geography education in relation to pedagogy. There is a need to extend research into this important area and find ways of making such research accessible to classroom practitioners in a form that they can understand and value. Developments in teacher education – and by this I go beyond that of just initial teacher education – need to be underpinned by enquiry. Effective strategies must be found to disseminate the outcomes of such enquiry and ensure that they inform pedagogy in geography education in schools. Until they are it is unlikely that some of the concerns expressed about the value of educational research will be addressed.

REFERENCES

Bailey, P. and Fox, P. (eds) (1996) *Geography Teachers' Handbook*. Sheffield: Geographical Association.

Barnes, D., Johnson, G., Jordan, S., Layton, P., Medway, P. and Yeoman, D. (1987) *The TVEI Curriculum 14–16: An Interim Report Based on Case Studies in Twelve Schools*. University of Leeds.

Boardman, D. (ed.) (1987) *Handbook for Geography Teachers*. Sheffield: Geographical Association.

Brown, S. and MacIntyre, D. (1993) *Making Sense of Teaching*. Buckingham: Oxford University Press.

Calderhead, J. (1988) *Teachers' Professional Learning*. London: Falmer Press.

DfEE (1998a) *Standards for the Award of Qualified Teacher Status in England and Wales*. London: HMSO.

DfEE (1998b) *Initial Teacher Training National Curriculum for the Use of Information and Communications Technology in Subject Teaching*. London: HMSO.

Doyle, W. (1987) 'Research on teaching effects as a resource for improving instruction', in Wideen, M. and Andrews, I. (eds), *Staff Development for School Improvement*. Lewes: Falmer Press.

Fien, J., Gerber, R. and Wilson, P. (1984) *The Geography Teacher's Guide to the Classroom*. Melbourne: Macmillan.

Fisher, T. (1998) *Developing as a Geography Teacher*. Cambridge: Chris Kington Publishing.

Geographical Association (1999) *Leading Geography: National Standards for Geography Leaders in Secondary Schools*. Sheffield: Geographical Association.

Graves, N. (1971) *Geography in Secondary Education*. Sheffield: Geographical Association.

Graves, N. (1997) 'Geographical education in the 1990s', in Tilbury, D. and Williams, M. (eds), *Teaching and Learning Geography*. London: Routledge.

Hallam, S. and Ireson, J. (1999) 'Pedagogy in the Secondary School', in Mortimore, P. (ed.), *Understanding Pedagogy and Its Impact on Learning*. London: Paul Chapman.

Harris, A., Jamieson, I. and Russ, J. (1995) 'A study of "effective" departments in secondary schools', *School Organisation* 15(3), pp. 283–99.

Harvey, P. (1991) 'The role and value of A-level geography fieldwork: a case study'. Unpublished PhD thesis, Department of Geography, Durham University.

Job, D. (1999) *New Directions in Geographical Fieldwork*. Cambridge: Cambridge University Press.

Job, D., Day, C. and Smyth, T. (1999) *Beyond the Bicycle Sheds*. Sheffield: Geographical Association.

Lambert, D. and Balderstone, D. (2000) *Learning to Teach Geography in the Secondary School: A Companion to School Experience*. London: Routledge.
Leat, D. (1997) 'Cognitive acceleration in geographical education', in Tilbury, D. and Williams, M. (eds), *Teaching and Learning Geography*. London: Routledge.
Leat, D. (1998) *Thinking through Geography*. Cambridge, Chris Kington Publishing.
Leat, D. and McAleavy, T. (1998) 'Critical thinking in the humanities', *Teaching Geography*, 23(3), pp. 112–14.
Millet, A. (1999) 'Why we need to raise our game', *The Independent*, 11 February.
Mortimore, P. (1994) 'School effectiveness and the management of effective learning and teaching', *School Effectiveness and School Improvement*, 4(4), pp. 290–310.
Mortimore, P. (ed.) (1999) *Understanding Pedagogy and Its Impact on Learning*. London: Paul Chapman.
Naish, M., Rawling, E. and Hart, C. (1987) *Geography 16–19: The Contribution of a Curriculum Project to 16–19 Education*. Harlow: Longman.
Ofsted (1998) *Standards in the Secondary Curriculum 1997/98: Geography*. London: HMSO.
Renwick, M. (1985) *The Essentials of GYSL*. Sheffield City Polytechnic, GYSL National Centre.
Roberts, M. (1996) 'Teaching styles and strategies', in Kent, A., Lambert, D., Naish, M. and Slater, F. (eds), *Geography in Education: Viewpoints on Teaching and Learning*. Cambridge: Cambridge University Press.
Romey, W. and Elberty, W. Jr (1984) 'On being a geography teacher in the 1980s and beyond', in Fien, J., Gerber, R. and Wilson, P. (eds), *The Geography Teachers' Guide to the Classroom*. Melbourne: Macmillan.
Rubin, L. (1985) *Artistry and Teaching*. New York: Random House.
Slater, F. (1982) *Learning through Geography*. London: Heinemann.
Slater, F. (1987) 'Steps in planning', in Boardman, D. (ed.), *Handbook for Geography Teachers*. Sheffield: Geographical Association.
Smith, P. (1997) 'Standards achieved: review of geography in secondary schools in England, 1995–96', *Teaching Geography*, 22(3), pp. 123–4.
Tolley, H. and Reynolds, J. (1977) *Geography 14–18: A Handbook for School-based Curriculum Development*. London: Macmillan Education.
TTA (1998) *National Standards for Subject Leaders*. Teacher Training Agency.
Watkins, C. and Mortimore, P. (1999) 'Pedagogy: what do we know?', in Mortimore, P. (ed.), *Understanding Pedagogy and Its Impact on Learning*. London: Paul Chapman.
Watkins, C., Carnell, E., Lodge, C. and Whalley, C. (1996) *'Effective Learning' School Improvement Network: Research Matters'*. Institute of Education, University of London.
Wragg, E (1997) *The Cubic Curriculum*. London: Routledge.

Chapter 11

Using assessment to support learning

David Lambert

INTRODUCTION: ASSESSMENT IN EDUCATION

This chapter sets out to examine the potential of 'formative assessment' to promote learning in geography classrooms (Torrance and Pryor, 1998). Written by a geographer and for geography educationists, the chapter nevertheless necessarily engages in discussion at a general and often system-wide level. Geography teachers operating in different systems around the world, who may have different assumptions about the value of assessment practices of various kinds, are invited to consider the implications of the points raised in this chapter. There is a need to experiment with sustained effort in order to translate the general principles discussed here into effective day-to-day classroom practice. The chapter is written in the profound belief that such effort will be richly rewarded, but (to re-emphasise the point) pupils as well as teachers will be at different 'starting points' depending on the range of theoretical debate and developments in practice characterising particular system contexts.

There is not sufficient space in this chapter to consider in any detail the pros and cons of formative assessment in relation to its distant relative, 'summative assessment'. Though writing from an English perspective, a system that has experienced a substantial rise in the use of external summative testing and examinations in recent years, formative assessment tends to be subservient to summative assessment the world over. The latter tends to dominate our thinking about assessment in education (Black, 1998; Stobart and Gipps, 1997), and it will simply be taken as read that:

- summative assessment has its place in education, mainly in the form of end-of-course tests and external examinations; but that
- it should be kept in its place, because it can exert influence that is not always educational.

In concentrating on formative assessment the chapter does not, therefore, adopt an 'anti-testing' stance, though there are certainly debates to be had over the efficacy of particular forms of external, summative assessment and the purposes to which data thus obtained are put (see Black, 1998; Gipps, 1994; Davis, 1998, 1999). The position that *is* taken up here centres on the question of what balance needs to be struck between different kinds of assessment practice (Lambert and Lines, 2000), and the implications for geography teachers who, in accepting the above assertions, also accept the need to raise the specifically educational functions of formative classroom assessment. Allowing assessment in education to be dominated by tests serves to overemphasise the administrative and bureaucratic functions of assembling assessment data at the expense of developing assessment processes serving educational ends.

The closing years of the last century were a turbulent time for those with an interest in the relationship between learning and assessment, that is its educational function. Around the world there have been responses of various kinds to the perceived international pressures of globalisation, often manifest in moves to centralise education infrastructures such as curriculum and assessment (see Naish, 1990) and to use assessment as the measure – and sometimes the means – to raise standards. In England and Wales, the introduction of a national curriculum following the Education Reform Act of 1988 provided the platform for a quite extraordinary rise in regular testing of children from the age of 5 in the so-called 'core subjects' of English, mathematics and science. Teachers of other subjects, including geography, were (and are) also expected to provide criterion-referenced summative assessments on the children they have taught, by a process known as 'teacher assessment' based on centrally laid down Level Descriptions of attainment (see Butt et al., 1995; Hopkins et al., 2000; Lambert, 1996; 1997a).

Furthermore, all subjects in England and Wales, including geography, are examined at 16 years old and beyond by the vast 'examinations industry' (Lambert and Lines, 2000) including GCSE and A-level public examinations. These examinations seemed to have acquired ever higher stakes: examination results are now published in the form of league tables, policy-makers are increasingly demanding that schools, and the teachers who work in them, be judged by 'value added' statistics (using predominantly test results) and the present government has introduced 'performance related pay' as an element of its radical policy suite designed to raise expectations and standards among teachers, parents and pupils. Thus, all teachers are increasingly aware of the power exerted through the 'results' they (or more accurately, their pupils) achieve, which is possibly why assessment matters are often discussed generically rather than in a subject-specific way – and why questions concerning summative testing tend to dominate teachers' thinking. Of course, it is not sensible to examine assessment in geography education without recourse to general principles. This chapter will, therefore, attempt to remain clearly focused on geography classrooms while at the same time refer to evidence derived from wider sources. But we are not going to discuss, and therefore contribute to, the mounting material on testing and examinations in geography or beyond, but concentrate on explicating the potential of teachers using *classroom assessment* to support learning, now widely referred to as 'formative assessment'.

IDENTIFYING FORMATIVE ASSESSMENT

Possibly in reaction to the dangers of the narrowing, teaching-to-the-test mentality that can begin to mount when high-stakes[1] summative testing begins to dominate the minds of pupils, parents and teachers, there has been a surge of interest in formative assessment. A recent issue of the professional journal *Teaching Geography* (*TG*) contained three articles discussing in various ways the role of assessment in enhancing learning.

While one of these (Hopkins, 2000) remained rooted in the traditional context of making sense of, or interpreting for its readership, statutory duties and responsibilities, and another focused on a particular strategy for using assessment information (Hamson and Sutton, 2000), a third (Leat and McGrane, 2000), took the cue from, but radically reworked, several central government pronouncements concerning the relationship between teaching, learning and the curriculum (see Figure 11.1). One can conclude from such re-visioning that the statutory documents (reviewed anew for the launch of 'Curriculum 2000', the most recent formulation of the National Curriculum for England and Wales) should be seen more as a facilitating framework than a set of tightly designed curriculum rules to follow. Leat and McGrane showed how the idea of 'level descriptions' could be adapted and form the basis for assessing, but also supporting the development of, thinking in geography lessons.

However, notwithstanding the encouraging signs for professionals such as Leat and McGrane from the snippets quoted from the Secretary of State for Education in Figure 11.1, and indeed the apparent concern over the present unsatisfactory use of

> We want to develop creativity and high level thinking skills, deepening knowledge and stretching achievement. In short, developing new forms of excellence with diversity . . .
> . . . I have been very impressed by the growing evidence in this country and abroad of the impact on standards of systematic and disciplined approaches to the teaching of higher order thinking skills . . .
> . . . It is not about some loosely defined or woolly approach to study skills. It is about the ability to analyse and make connections, to use knowledge effectively, to solve problems individually and to think creatively. It is about developing mental strategies to take on both academic and wider challenges. Above all, the evidence shows that the systematic teaching of thinking skills raises standards.

Figure 11.1 'Moving onto something better' from the Secretary of State for Education and Employment (Blunkett, 2000).

> *A. The limits of assessment competence in geography classrooms according to the Office for Standards in Education (Ofsted):*
>
> '. . . day-to-day assessment . . . is weak and the use of assessment to help planning of future work is unsatisfactory in one in five schools. What is particularly lacking is marking which clearly informs pupils about the standards they have achieved in a piece of work, and what they need to do to improve; whilst marking needs to be supportive of efforts made, it also needs to be constructively critical, and diagnostic of both strengths and weaknesses.'
>
> (DFEE, 1998)
>
> *B. Extract from the Task Group on Assessment and Testing – the vision of a national assessment system:*
>
> 'Promoting children's learning is a principal aim of schools. Assessment lies at the heart of this process. It can provide a framework in which educational objectives may be set, and pupils' progress charted and expressed. It can yield a basis for planning the next educational steps in response to children's needs . . . it should be an integral part of the educational process, continually providing both 'feedback' and 'feedforward'. It therefore needs to be incorporated systematically into teaching strategies and practices at all levels.'
>
> (DES/WO, 1988, para. 3/4)

Figure 11.2 Visions of formative classroom assessment.

classroom assessment by teachers reported by Ofsted (see Figure 11.2), it seems that interest in formative assessment among the *policy-makers* may only be skin deep. In David Blunkett's full article, reference to assessment was limited to external test outcomes, the introduction of yet more tests in the core subjects (for every year in Key Stage 3) and GCSE performance. There was at best only tacit acknowledgement of any value attached to low-stakes, day-to-day classroom assessment undertaken by teachers – nor how to understand such processes better and to improve them if they are to be found wanting (and often, they are).

If we take a close look at the Ofsted quotation (Figure 11.2A) we can see that what the inspectorate has in mind in relation to formative assessment is demanding. According to this quotation, Ofsted inspectors look for assessment that:

- helps teachers plan future work;
- informs pupils of the standards they have reached;
- shows pupils what they need to do to improve;
- is diagnostic of strengths and weaknesses;
- is constructively critical.

Interestingly, it is possible to trace the contents of this list, at least in principle, back to the assessment framework devised to underpin the introduction of the 1988 National Curriculum. The hastily convened Task Group on Assessment and Testing (TGAT) produced a ground-breaking report (DES/WO, 1988) which encouraged the kinds of ambitious formative assessment practices that subsequently Ofsted inspectors reported they were looking for. Again, close examination of the TGAT quotation in Figure 11.2B is useful. It recommended assessment practice which:

- informs planning;
- articulates standards ('feedback');
- shows pupils what to do next in order to improve ('feedforward');
- becomes an organic part of teaching and learning.

The two lists and the quotations in Figure 11.2 are remarkably similar. Arguably, the TGAT quote goes a little further in that it equates assessment with teaching, in effect saying that the two cannot be separated, although it may be that teaching is what Ofsted had in mind with the phrase 'constructively critical'. This is, however, a very significant point to contemplate and helps counter the claim that busy teachers have 'no time' to engage seriously with formative assessment practices: this, the argument runs, would be tantamount to saying they have no time to teach effectively! The shift in thinking represented by the quotations in Figure 11.2 takes us away from an assumption that assessment is something done after the teaching is finished and towards the notion that it is integral to teaching; you cannot claim to be teaching without undertaking forms of assessment, and by implication, this assessment activity helps ensure the quality of what is taught and learned (and how). It is this point that Leat and McGrane (2000) have explored so imaginatively.

ASSESSMENT FOR LEARNING

From the above discussion we can begin to identify formative assessment in a way that distinguishes it from assessments that (merely) measure performance; remember the popular adage that 'weighing the baby does not make it grow'. What I mean by this in the classroom context is that the 'assessment of learning', though useful in several respects, does not *itself* help teachers teach better or learners learn better. When we consider definitions of formative assessment, therefore, we need to explore the idea of 'assessment for learning' (Sutton, 1995).

For example, what are the practical implications of the following theoretical positions? First:

> Formative assessment is concerned with how judgements about the quality of student responses . . . can be used to shape and improve the student's competence by short-circuiting the randomness and inefficiency of trial and error learning.
>
> (Sadler, 1989, p. 121)

And secondly:

> . . . for students to be able to improve, they must develop the capacity to monitor the quality of their own work during actual production. This in turn requires that students possess an appreciation of what high quality work is [and] that they have the evaluative skill necessary for them to compare with some objectivity the quality of what they are producing in relation to the standard.
>
> (ibid., p. 119)

Among the many discussion points that can be derived from such statements, three very important realisations stand out, confirming what we noted from our deliberations of the TGAT and the Ofsted reports (in Figure 11.2). Each carries significant implications for classroom practice:

- Formative assessment has to take place during a course of study so that the learner has a chance to make a difference; some commentators would urge us to go beyond the preposition 'during' and describe formative assessment as an organic *part of* effective teaching.
- Effective formative assessment is in essence a form of *communication*, a conversation between pupils and teachers consisting of analysis, hints and suggestions in the form of feedback and feedforward. As with most conversations, the bottom line is that the participants are getting to know each other better – their motivations and preferences, and the expectations teachers and students have of each other.
- Genuine formative assessment involves the learners so that they grow to understand that assessment is not just something done to them, but something that is part of their learning action. This means students being involved in *self-assessment*. For this to stand any chance of working successfully students need to be familiar with the success criteria relating to the work and how to apply them.

Despite the persuasiveness of such 'theoretical' positions it remains the case that assessment for learning (that is, formative, classroom assessment) is a very poorly developed relation to the assessment of learning. The Assessment Reform Group (ARG) maintains that the former is utterly dominated by the latter, possibly to a damaging degree:

> A clear distinction should be made between assessment of learning for the purposes of grading and reporting, which has its own well-established procedures, and assessment for learning which calls for different priorities, new procedures and a new commitment. In the

> recent past, policy priorities have arguably resulted in too much attention being given to finding reliable ways of comparing children, teachers and schools.
>
> (Assessment Reform Group, 1999, p. 2)

The importance of the ARG's position is perhaps plain to see, but is one which seems to require enormous courage or ambition on the part of teachers and pupils to act upon, despite the tacit support from Ofsted and others who take predominantly a professional/educational interest in assessment rather than an administrative/bureaucratic one.

On the other hand, if assessment for learning can be undertaken successfully, as the ARG urges, then surely we do not need to be too worried about the high-stakes summative tests which assess the product of learning. Pupils who have been taught to be deeper, more confident thinkers can surely achieve better test scores than otherwise they would have done. The ARG certainly think so, continuing,

> The important message now confronting the educational community is that assessment which is explicitly designed to promote learning is the single most powerful tool we have for both raising standards and empowering lifelong learners.
>
> (ibid., p. 2)

The basis for making this statement is the research evidence to which we now should turn, for it helps underpin what we have been arguing here. Evidence helps teachers to nurture that 'act of faith', and enables them to invest the necessary time and energy in developing formative classroom assessment strategies.

RESEARCH EVIDENCE

Partly in response to the overriding attention paid to testing, especially at the policy level, Black and Wiliam (1998a, 1998b) undertook an extensive review of research conducted internationally on formative assessment. The principal motive was to find whether internationally accumulated research provided convincing evidence that formative assessment 'worked'. The absence of such evidence, in a form that was available and accessible to wider professional and public audiences, was thought to be a major stumbling block to the promotion of formative assessment, allowing politicians especially to rely on exhorting the 'rigour' of external tests as the means of 'raising standards'. The ARG refers to Black and Wiliam's review, stating that assessment research has 'proved without a shadow of doubt that, when carried out effectively, informal classroom assessment with constructive feedback to the student will raise levels of achievement'. (1999, p. 1). This claim is placed in stark contrast to another statement that '[t]here is no evidence that increasing the amount of testing will enhance learning' (ibid., p. 2)

It is unusual in the field of education that research can communicate such a clear, unambiguous message. We need to be careful, however, to ensure that we 'hear' this message accurately. Among the findings synthesised and summarised from several hundred research articles and reports, Black and Wiliam showed broadly that effective formative assessment produces significant 'learning gain'. Translated into more familiar terms, understandable to secondary teachers in England and Wales, the authors calculated that formative assessment, incorporating effective feedback strategies, could increase pupils GCSE performance by one or two grades. Furthermore, research seemed to suggest that resulting raised levels of performance were greater among lower attaining pupils, a particularly resonant finding in the context of the English education system which traditionally has a persistent, long tail of underachievement in comparison with other comparable systems. Developing effective formative assessment practices can help rectify this system failure.

Among the main research findings are the following headlines, all of which deserve some consideration in the context of geography classrooms:

- Although formative assessment has become a familiar term in schools, its implications are not well understood. Marking pupils' work regularly and conscientiously may not always have formative impact. Rather than being formative, marking can appear to be little more than 'serial summative' assessment.
- Neither teachers nor students readily adopt formative assessment processes when they perceive this to mean adding to their existing practice. The breakthrough occurs when it is understood to be part of teaching and learning. As we have seen, this seems to require a leap of faith by both teachers and pupils.
- Pupils need to be trained in self-assessment so that they can understand learning goals. This may take some time to achieve. The aim would be to:
  - break the pattern of passive learning;
  - make learning goals ('the overarching picture') explicit;
  - establish the: 'desired goal – present position – way to close the gap' mentality in pupils.
- Feedback should be about the particular qualities of pupils' work, with advice for improvement. This may be one of the most difficult professional skills for teachers to acquire. As Black and Wiliam note, much pupil feedback tends to be 'social and managerial' in purpose and not *subject-specific* in nature. Learning how to engage pupils, sometimes individually, with subject-specific feedback requires deep thinking on the part of the teacher. The content has to be worthwhile, relevant and non-trivial (that is, worth learning!). Furthermore, feedback should avoid comparisons with other pupils so that the work is the object of focus, not the class 'pecking order'. It should also encourage:
  - creating a culture of success;
  - pupils to take risks, make mistakes and use such occasions as learning opportunities;
  - reconstruction of the teacher–pupil 'contract of contentment' (where neither is challenged by the other.
- Opportunities for pupils to express their understanding have to be built into the teaching – to initiate interaction and allow the teacher to build up knowledge of the learners. Thus:
  - teaching and assessment are indivisible;
  - choice of tasks (chosen teaching strategy) has to be justified in terms of the learning aims they serve.
  - teachers can change what they do in the light of what they learn about the students through listening to them.

It is arguably this final innocuous point that goes to the heart of what is meant by effective formative classroom assessment. Thus assessment is concerned with 'getting to know' pupils (see Lambert, 1997b; Rowntree, 1987), and then being prepared to change what we do with them in geography lessons as a result of what we learn. To be able to respond constructively in this way is one of the 'standards' for the initial training of teachers laid down by the government (DfEE, 1998). It is one of the most demanding requirements of initial teacher trainees.

CONCLUSION: PRIORITIES FOR GEOGRAPHY EDUCATION?

To conclude this discussion, I wish to speculate on how a departmental team of geographers may interpret their developmental priorities in relation to enhancing their day-to-day assessment practice. As was emphasised at the start of this chapter, how this is done needs to take into account other pressing assessment requirements, such as preparing pupils for external examinations or teachers assessing the National Curriculum levels for pupils at the end of Key Stage 3. What we also noted was that although it is relatively easy to find advice on both these issues, whether from commercially published sources (such as Balderstone and King, 1998), the awarding bodies themselves or from government agencies (such as SCAA, 1996), assistance for developing practical classroom assessment is usually harder to obtain. Circumstances are further complicated by the self-evident truth that subject teams tend to be at different starting points, and in entirely different educational contexts, making it difficult to generalise about priorities. There could be many small-scale action research projects, or even Masters degree dissertations, hidden away in what Black and Wiliam referred to as the classroom (or departmental) 'black box'.

Nevertheless, it is possible to make one speculation about a particular set of actions likely to repay big dividends on the investment of time and energy. This centres on the establishment and maintenance of National Curriculum 'standards portfolios' of geography attainment. A full discussion of how to do this, and the approach to assessment underpinned by them, can be found elsewhere (Lambert and Balderstone, 2000; Lambert and Lines, 2000) as there is not the space here to do so in sufficient detail. Fundamentally, standards portfolios are ring binders in which is assembled a selection of pupils' work which, *in toto*, illustrates what the departmental team considers to be the standard at any particular 'level'. In practice, the department requires a portfolio for National Curriculum levels 3, 5 and 7 – by definition, if colleagues can agree these levels then they also are probably close to agreeing levels 2, 4, 6 and 8 as well.

The strength of standards portfolios lies in the selection of pupils' work. The Level Descriptions are abstract and general and therefore difficult to gain purchase on, but the pupils' work 'speaks' plainly about pupils' real capacities. Selection is clearly subjective, but 'moderated' by the level descriptions and other teachers' interpretations of what they mean. Colleagues can expect to argue over what value they are prepared to give to pieces of work (note, the 'work', not the pupils), and it is unlikely that a portfolio for any particular level will ever finally be settled: judgements will always be contingent. Of course, such contingency is a source of strength not weakness: it forces the teaching team to consider and reconsider the nature of achievement in geography, and from such work teachers can derive increased clarity of subject-specific feedback in their work with pupils.

All manner of important practical concerns need to be sorted out, including those governing how meaningful feedback can be woven into lessons and how to prepare the pupils, before classroom assessment can begin to achieve its potential. However, the much harder task is to identify what 'meaningful feedback' consists of. Standards portfolios can provide the basis for determining this in relation to the National Curriculum. But being flexible assessment instruments, standards portfolios could also provide alternative versions of 'progress', for example tracing conceptual development or, as in the case of Leat and McGrane (2000) referred to earlier, thinking capacity. There is perhaps some interesting research and development work to be done in this field of geography education.

NOTE

1. The concept of high-stakes testing probably originates from analysis in the USA. The term is a useful one for all education systems, denoting how some tests *really matter* in a public sense, because job prospects or future educational opportunities depend directly on the test outcome. Research has shown that when testing operates in high-stakes conditions the impact on teaching can be so great as to distort healthy teaching and learning relationships.

REFERENCES

Assessment Reform Group (1999) *Assessment for Learning: Beyond the Black Box*. Cambridge: University of Cambridge School of Education.

Balderstone, D. and King, S. (1998) *GCSE Bitesize Revision: Geography*. London: BBC.

Black, P. (1998) *Testing: Friend or Foe? Theory and Practice in Assessment and Testing*. London: Falmer Press.

Black, P. and Wiliam, D. (1998a) 'Assessment and classroom learning', *Assessment in Education*, vol. 5, no. 1, pp. 7–74.

Black, P. and Wiliam, D. (1998b) *Inside the Black Box*. University of London, Department of Education, Kings College.

Blunkett, D. (2000) 'Moving on to something better', *Teaching Today: NASUWT Termly Review*, no. 25, Spring, pp. 6–7.

Butt, G., Lambert, D. and Telfer, S. (eds) (1995) *Assessment Works*. Sheffield: Geographical Association.

Daugherty, R. (1995) *National Curriculum Assessment: A Review of Policy 1987–1994*. London: Falmer Press.

Davis, A. (1998) *The Limits of Educational Assessment*. Oxford: Blackwell.

Davis, A. (1999) 'Educational assessment: a critique of current policy', *Impact No. 1*. Philosphy of Education Society of Great Britain.

DES/WO (1988) *Task Group on Assessment and Testing: A Report*.

DfEE (1998) *Teaching: High Status, High Standards. Requirements for Courses of Initial Teacher Training*. Department for Education and Employment: Circular 4/98.

Gipps, C. (1994) *Beyond Testing: Towards a Theory of Educational Assessment*. Brighton: Falmer Press.

Hamson, R. and Sutton, A. (2000) 'Target setting at Key Stage 3', *Teaching Geography*, vol. 25, no. 1, pp. 8–11.

Hopkins, J. (2000) 'Assessment for learning in geography', *Teaching Geography*, vol. 25, no. 1, pp. 42–3.

Hopkins, J., Telfer, S. and Butt, G. (eds) (2000) *Assessment in Practice*. Sheffield: Geographical Association.

Lambert, D. (1996a) 'Assessing pupils' attainments and supporting learning', in Kent, A. et al.

(eds), *Geography in Education*. Cambridge: Cambridge University Press, pp. 260–87.

Lambert, D. (1997a) 'Teacher assessment in the National Curriculum', in Tilbury, D. and Williams, M. (eds), *Teaching and Learning Geography*. London: Routledge, pp. 255–66.

Lambert, D. (1997b) 'Assessing, recording and reporting pupils' progress and achievement', in Capel, S., Leask, M. and Turner, T. (eds), *Starting to Teach in the Secondary School*. London; Routledge, pp. 172–92.

Lambert, D. and Balderstone, D. (2000) *Learning to Teach Geography*. London: Routledge.

Lambert, D. and Lines, D. (2000) *Assessment in Education: Perceptions, Purpose, Practice*. London: Falmer Press.

Leat, D. and McGrane, J. (2000) 'Diagnostic and formative assessment of students' thinking', *Teaching Geography*, vol. 25, no. 1, pp. 4–7.

Naish, M. (ed.) (1990) *Experiences of Centralisation*. British Sub-Committee of Commission for Geographical Education, IGU, University of London Institute of Education.

Rowntree, D. (1987) *Assessing Students: How Shall We Know Them?* London: Kogan Page.

Sadler, D. (1989) 'Formative assessment and the design of instructional systems', in *Instructional Science*, vol. 18, pp. 119–44.

SCAA (1996) *Consistency in Teacher Assessment: Exemplification of Standards (Geography)*. London: School Curriculum and Assessment Authority (now the Qualifications and Curriculum Agency).

Stobart, G. and Gipps, C. (1997) *Assessment: A Teacher's Guide to the Issues*. London: Hodder & Stoughton.

Sutton, R. (1995) *Assessment for Learning*. Salford: R.S. Publications.

Torrance, H. and Pryor, J. (1998) *Investigating Formative Assessment*. Milton Keynes: Open University Press.

Chapter 12

Evaluating geography departments and their staff

Sheila King

THE DEVELOPMENT OF EVALUATION IN EDUCATION

Evaluation relates the consequences of actions to the original aims of the action and assesses the value of actions and behaviour. In education, the purpose of evaluation is to improve the quality of student learning, a purpose which recent UK governments have put at the heart of their education policies. This chapter is concerned with the evaluation of geography departments and their staff as a whole rather than specific aspects such as the curriculum, textbooks and other resources. Readers who wish to delve into these areas should begin by examining the work of Kent (1996, pp. 167–90), Martin and Bailey (1996, pp. 235–47) and Cambers (1996, pp. 279–95). Also, this chapter is written predominantly from the UK perspective, a country which has seen its evaluation systems develop rapidly in recent years. However, I have made references to some other countries' evaluation systems, mainly those of other English-speaking countries.

Evaluation is very much part of the working day of UK schools. The drive to improve pupils' standards as shown through external examinations such as GCSE, vocational and A-level results and by the end of key stage assessment tests and tasks has led to a plethora of initiatives to monitor and evaluate what pupils and their teachers do within the classroom. It would not be uncommon to find heads of geography who in the course of last year have:

- systematically monitored and evaluated geography teachers' marking;
- observed colleagues working within the classroom;
- had their own lessons observed by other members of the department and a trainee teacher;
- prepared for and led their staff through OFSTED inspections;
- produced and begun to implement development plans based on the OFSTED findings;
- appraised one of their geography staff; and
- worked with colleagues at meetings to improve schemes of work.

The development of evaluation within education is well documented in the literature but beyond the scope of this short chapter. Kent (1996, pp. 133–6) summarises this literature and describes Nisbet's three recent phases of development (see Skilbeck, 1984):

Phase 1 (1960s)	Evaluation was integral to curriculum development but often tagged onto curriculum projects. The contrasts between summative and formative, 'hard' and 'soft' evaluations began to be debated.
Phase 2 (1970s)	Evaluation had become a profession with massive spending on innovation and evaluation, particularly in North America. Evaluation was seen as a control mechanism.
Phase 3 (1980s)	Greater participation of schools in the evaluation process with self-evaluation introduced in an attempt to close the gap between policy and practice.

The 1990s continued to see evaluation becoming 'big business' in education with many new centres, e.g. International School Effectiveness and Improvement Centre (Institute of Education 1994–), and journals, e.g. *Quality Assurance in Education* (1994–), dedicated to evaluation.

Some types of evaluation work use hypothetico-deductive methodology which judges whether an innovation has reached the required standard by measurement and prediction (quantitative data). Others use social anthropological approaches which are concerned with description and interpretation (qualitative data). Both have their place in educational research. The former is used when large amounts of data exists or can feasibly be collected, such as with national examination grades. The latter is often used in a case study approach perhaps using classroom observation techniques to reveal information about teacher and pupil activities.

Government policies that make schools more accountable are indicative of the priority given to evaluation in recent years. In the UK, the Office for Standards in Education (OFSTED), set up in 1992, symbolises these policies and has had a massive impact on education at all levels within England and Wales. No sector of education from pre-school to teacher training is free from inspection and publication of the findings.

SCHOOL OFSTED INSPECTIONS

OFSTED inspections are likely to continue to monitor and evaluate the work of schools and departments in England and Wales for the foreseeable future, and therefore it is appropriate to consider how these inspections have changed since their introduction. Section 10 of the School Inspections Act 1966, still in place today, states that the key focus points on which all school inspections must report are:

- the educational standards achieved by the school;
- the quality of the education provided by the school;
- whether the financial resources made available to the school are managed efficiently;
- the spiritual, moral, social and cultural development of pupils at the school.

(OFSTED, 1999a, p. 4)

The first inspections began in 1992 with all maintained schools inspected by July 1998. Initially there was widescale protest from a range of professionals in the education system who complained of a bureaucratic, cumbersome process which did not help schools to make rapid and productive use of the report findings. Many school staff found the stress of preparing for and undergoing the inspection unacceptable. It was therefore not surprising that changes were made once the new inspection system had 'bedded down'.

In 1995 a revised framework (OFSTED, 1995) gave greater openness during both the data collection and judgemental stages. Inspectors were encouraged to communicate their findings with teachers as the inspection evolved, a dialogue presumably intended to put staff at their ease. They were allowed to help teachers to improve their work through identifying what they felt did and did not work, something which had been discouraged during the first cycle of inspections. The inspectors' findings could be explained to individual teachers, to senior managers and to the governing body. At the same time report writing was made clearer, more direct and more useful to parents. Inspectors were told to elaborate judgements and make their reports come more alive.

Generally these changes were seen as improvements by the teaching profession and as schools began the second cycle of inspection, many teachers felt less threatened and the most forward-looking departments saw that the findings could be useful to improve their work. Research into teachers' views of the inspection process has been limited and the results variable. Ouston, Earley and Fidler (1996, p. 167), in their conclusions to a variety of case studies and contributions by several researchers, were surprised at how positive most schools were about inspection. In contrast the National Union of Teachers (1998) found overwhelming dissatisfaction among questionnaire returns from 1250 headteachers and deputy headteachers. Inspectors were not seen to be supportive or motivational, there were concerns about fairness and accuracy of judgements and the 'ends did not justify the means' (p. 3).

In January 2000 a third framework for inspecting schools was introduced. The most significant changes are:

- the introduction of short, 'light touch', three-day inspections for the most effective schools as judged by previous inspections and examination results;
- shorter advanced notice of an inspection, i.e. eight weeks;
- the way in which lesson observations are recorded and evidence and judgements presented: Figure 12.1 illustrates an observation form with prompt questions, inserted by one inspection team, Brookbridge Education, to help their inspectors. Inspectors are now encouraged to 'tell the story' as they write their lesson observations rather than to use a defined set of headings into which evidence had to be sorted.

Undoubtedly in the early 1990s teachers found the new system of inspection incredibly stressful. By March 2000 the process and its associated pressures have become more familiar and the process no longer attracts the bad press it received in its early days. Several things are likely to have helped reduce these pressures. Initially many schools invested huge amounts of time before an inspection in writing schemes of work and departmental policies. These have largely been done and now need regularly 'tweaking' rather than wholesale rewrites. Understandably teachers in their first cycle of inspection feared the unknown and often 'played safe' in their lessons planned for the inspection week. Teachers now know what to expect and with the help of school and external training courses have learnt how best to present their departments. Finally, changes to the inspection process itself as outlined above have done much to make the process more 'human' and accountable.

The UK is not alone in placing the evaluation of teachers' work high on their agenda. Australia, Canada and the USA have state rather than national education systems.

GUIDANCE ON COMPLETION OF OBSERVATION FORMS
(For all subjects. Subject-specific criteria to be added by individual inspectors)

Reg OFSTED number		DfEE school no.		Observation type
Year group(s)		Grouping		Present/NOR
Subject codes		Accreditation		Observation time
Teacher's status		Lesson type		Support teacher/staff

Context of the observation
- Brief summary of lesson content activities and organisation; role of support staff
- Details of work sample inspected

Teaching
- Teacher's subject knowledge and knowledge of SAT, GCSE, A-Level, GNVQ requirements
- Expectations (for full range of ability in class)
- Effective planning
- Methods and organisation to achieve lessons aims for all pupils
- Pace
- Class management and discipline (including group work if used)
- Use of time and resources
- Assessment (marking): use of assessment to modify teaching
- Checking for understanding
- Homework to reinforce/extend

Response
- Are pupils interested, engaged enthusiastic?
- Concentration (including when working individually and in groups); attentive to the teacher
- Behaviour (on entry, during lesson and on departure)
- Relationships with teacher and with other pupils (including those with different abilities, gender or ethnicity)
- Respect for feelings and belief of others
- . Initiative and taking responsibility

Attainment
- Overall in relation to end-of-key-stage expectations (i.e. is level of work now right for a year group that will hit the target?) Consider in national and school context.
- NC ATs covered and level achieved (where appropriate)
- Skills/knowledge/understanding shown (what pupils can do?)
- Any skills/knowledge/understanding weak?
- Literacy and development (if any) during lesson
- Number skills and use/development (if any)
- Note especially any variations in attainment by pupils with different levels of ability, gender or ethnicity

Progress
- Progress made during the lesson:
  - gains in knowledge, skills, understanding,
  - specific mastery of new material.
- Progress made over time (evidence of books and other pupils' work) indicating how many seen

Other significant evidence
- Use of IT and its level/quality
- Support for pupils with SEN (indicate whether statemented) by class teacher or support teacher
- Significant impact of accommodation, resources, timetable, etc.
- Equal opportunities

Figure 12.1 OFSTED pro-forma pre-2000 with guidelines for completion (adapted from a guidance sheet issued by Brookbridge Education).

States within the USA and Canada, for example, offer guidance which district education boards then use to form their own policies. Evaluation is usually a quality assurance process which forms an accreditation system in relation to standards and also assures quality for pupil admission to higher education. Evaluators review and pass judgement on the academic qualifications of teachers, class sizes and the curriculum.

PREPARING A GEOGRAPHY DEPARTMENT FOR AN INSPECTION

Familiarity with the inspection process and how best to prepare a department is paramount in reducing the stress and pressure on staff. It is a good idea to read the inspection framework (see OFSTED, 1999a), though some of it can be daunting! An example of the criteria which inspectors use for judgements about teaching is given in Figure 12.2. A growing amount of work specifically related to geography has now been published offering departments help in preparing for an inspection (see Campion et al., 1997, and Harris, 1996). Figure 12.3 offers one useful checklist adapted from Harris (1996). Davidson (1996) uses the observation of one geography lesson to show how OFSTED criteria could be used to develop good classroom practice.

SELF-EVALUATION AND DEPARTMENTAL REVIEW

Of course OFSTED inspections, long or short, are only one part of the evaluation with which schools engage. The departmental review has become regular and established

How well are pupils or students taught?

In determining their judgements, inspectors should consider the extent to which teachers:

- show good subject knowledge and understanding in the way they present and discuss their subject;
- are technically competent in teaching phonics and other basic skills;
- plan effectively, setting clear objectives that pupils understand;
- challenge and inspire pupils, expecting the most of them, so as to deepen their knowledge and understanding;
- use methods which enable all pupils to learn effectively;
- manage pupils well and insist on high standards of behaviour;
- use time, support staff and other resources, especially information and communications technology, effectively;
- assess pupils' work thoroughly and use assessments to help and encourage pupils to overcome difficulties;
- use homework effectively to reinforce and/or extend what is learnt in school;

and the extent to which pupils:

- acquire new knowledge or skills, develop ideas and increase their understanding;
- apply intellectual, physical or creative effort in their work;
- are productive and work at a good pace;
- show interest in their work, are able to sustain concentration and think and learn for themselves;
- understand what they are doing, how well they have done and how they can improve.

Figure 12.2 The criteria which inspectors use for judging about teaching (based on OFSTED, 1999a).

Before the inspection ensure that:

- There is an updated departmental handbook containing:
  - statement of aims;
  - policies on Assessment, Recording and Reporting (ARR), Special Educational Needs (SEN), fieldwork arrangements, discipline procedures, reward strategies and any others;
  - schemes of work;
  - staff details with job descriptions;
  - arrangements for appraisal;
  - details of INSET records;
  - departmental timetables;
  - departmental development plan; and
  - details of capitation and spending.
- Check the departmental minute book is up to date and easily available.
- All staff are familiar with the handbook and know and use the policies.
- All marking is up to date and follows the ARR policy.
- Check that issues raised during the previous inspection have been addressed and prepare evidence to show the inspector how.
- Prepare samples of pupils' previous work that you would like the inspector to see, for example field and course work, models or ICT work which may not be kept in exercise books.
- Check displays are complete and well presented. Plenty of pupils' work should be displayed and classrooms should be overtly geographical.
- You may also wish to try some interdepartmental observations so staff feel more used to being observed and gain knowledge of the observation procedure and criteria.

During the inspection (assuming a long inspection, not one of the short inspections)

- Try to meet the inspector as early on as possible. Arrange an interview during which you can answer questions and describe the department's strengths (and weaknesses?).
- Some lessons will be observed, normally for at least 30 minutes, and if possible a short oral feedback will be given. It is inevitable that a teacher's best lessons during the inspection are not observed!
- Provide the inspector with some information on each class. This should include number on roll and present, grouping and ability range, context indicating previous and next lesson, and at least an outline plan of the lesson.
- At the end of the inspection the head of department (sometimes head of faculty) receives feedback from the subject inspector. A senior member of staff is present to take notes. You are invited to dispute incorrect facts and figures and you can also comment on judgements but inspectors will not necessarily alter those judgements.

After the inspection

- Organise a departmental or school celebration of the hard work.
- Discuss the departmental feedback with other geography staff.
- Analyse the written paragraphs when they are published and prepare a departmental action plan to address any weaknesses. Feed these into the departmental development plan.

Figure 12.3 Checklist for a departmental approach to an OFSTED inspection (based on an earlier version by Harris, 1996).

practice within many schools. A small team comprising senior management and departmental staff is set up and all members of the department have some opportunity to feed into the work. As self-evaluation has, since January 2000, become a key part of the new OFSTED inspection procedure, the OFSTED format is likely to become a key part of any future departmental review. Figure 12.4 summarises the key questions which could drive such a departmental self-evaluation which would then feed into the full departmental review. Campion et al. (1997) state that self-review is intended to help departments to create a balance between consolidation and innovation. They also claim that inspection evidence indicates that departmental self-review, along with target and budget setting, are often the weakest parts of a school's planning cycle (ibid., p. 171). By involving schools and their subject departments in evaluating their own work it is intended that the process will be more meaningful and the outcomes will have a greater impact in securing educational improvement. Departmental reviews identify priorities for improvement, monitor provision and evaluate outcomes. A mixture of evaluation methodologies need to be used including statistical analysis, interviews, work scrutiny and classroom observation.

Examination results provide an appropriate starting point to a review of standards. GCSE and A-level results together with any trends in data from KS3 teacher assessments, vocational examinations and annual tests are measurable outcomes and can often be compared to data from other similar schools and the national picture. The use of computerised systems has had an impact on how quickly and effectively such data can be analysed. Ethnic and gender differences can be examined from the same data if it is input in an appropriate way.

Where schools use performance targets and predicted grades, these can be analysed. The school Performance and Assessment Report (PANDA) provides helpful data too. One useful criteria used by inspectors but more rarely by departments compares how pupils achieve in their GCSE geography compared to the average of all their other grades at GCSE. A departmental head may congratulate his or her team if there is a significant positive difference or look for reasons why the situation has occurred if there is a significant negative difference.

The data utilised above is quantitative, but qualitative data collection is also valuable. For example, in spite of schools' attempts to mix classes within year groups teachers may regularly claim that 8X is 'particularly dull', 8Y 'a really lovely class' or 8Z 'much less able than the other year 8s'. Questions frequently asked at school or departmental level are:

- Why is Mr T's class consistently gaining lower results that expected?
- Why are 8B's end of term tests scores higher than those for other Y8 geography classes?

A head of department may use an interview with the class teachers or classroom observation to seek answers.

Departmental reviews may be driven by a whole-school focus or an issue which is causing concern within the department itself. Typically such reviews focus on:

- raising the achievement of one group of pupils – the most able, boys or an ethnic group;
- identifying features of good teaching;
- one aspect of teaching, for example the extent to which pupils are encouraged to think and be challenged during lessons;
- an aspect such as assessment, resourcing, leadership and management.

The characteristics of the school
What are the main characteristics of your geography department, and what features have changed since the last inspection? What levels of attainment do pupils have when they join your department?

Monitoring and evaluation processes
What steps do you take to monitor the performance of your department and evaluate the quality of teaching?

The overall effectiveness of the department
What do assessment and other performance data tell you about the strengths and weaknesses of your department? Considering this analysis – are there any other aspects of pupils' achievements you consider important, and making comparisons with departments similar to yours, what can you say about the overall effectiveness of your department?

Improvement since the last inspection
Taking into account the key issues and other headline judgements from your department's last inspection, and the internal and external evaluations you have undertaken since, what are the main improvements that have taken place and what has contributed to them? What remains to be done?

Priorities for development
What are your department's most significant educational priorities and targets? How are they decided and acted upon, and how are their outcomes evaluated?

Pupils' personal development
How do your department teachers keep track of pupils' personal development? How well do you think pupils' attitudes, values and personal development reflect the aims of the department?

Teaching and learning
How do you go about improving the quality of teaching and learning in your department? How do you judge the impact of what the department does? Which areas of teaching and learning give you the most pride? In which areas does work still need to be done?

What the department offers its pupils
How does your department make sure that its curricular and other provision, in the broadest sense, match the interests, aptitudes and special needs of pupils? What specific provision do you make for particular groups of pupils?

Equality of opportunity
How do you set about ensuring that your department provides equal opportunities for all?

Guidance and support
What contributions do your procedures for caring for and supporting pupils make to their development of new knowledge, understanding and skills, and to their personal development? How do you judge the effectiveness of these procedures?

Partnership with parents
How do you evaluate the effectiveness of the relationships your department has with the parents of your pupils? How do you make use of the resulting information?

Leadership and management
What formal and informal methods do you have to help you understand how effective you and the other senior managers are in raising standards? How have these improved the way your department is led and managed?

The governing body
How well informed is the governing body about the work of the department, including the outcomes of monitoring and evaluation? How well does the governing body use this information to shape and support the department's direction and provision?

Financial planning
How do you ensure that planning for improvement and financial planning are fully integrated? How does your department build in the principles of best value?

Figure 12.4 Questions to guide a department self-evaluation (adapted from Form S4, The Headteacher's Statement, supplied by OFSTED, 1999b).

Such foci often benefit from carefully constructed lesson observation methods of data collection (see King, 2000).

One outcome of a departmental self-review is a clear departmental development plan with details of targets, how those targets will be met, by whom and by when and with success criteria. Costs should also be included to aid prioritisation.

A departmental review can also make good use of the OFSTED summative reports that are published and which describe the strengths, weaknesses and issues found nationally in school geography (see OFSTED, 1999c, and Smith, 1997). Departments should find it useful to examine the latest findings, highlight the key points and then discuss the extent to which their own department's OFSTED feedback and work agrees. Alternatively a department meeting could focus on the characteristics of good geography teaching. Teachers could arrive at the meeting with a copy of the OFSTED (1999c) document highlighted to identify good and poor characteristics and the discussion could focus on the extent to which the department shows the good characteristics and how further improvements can be made.

RESPONDING TO GOVERNMENT INITIATIVES

Each year a new government initiative seems to be introduced to add yet another item to the department's list of 'things to do'. A changing National Curriculum, citizenship, the literacy and numeracy strategies and training in information and communications technology (ICT) are recent examples. An effective strategy is to use a department meeting or training session to identify where the department is, where it wants to be and what action can be taken to move it forward.

STAFF REVIEWS AND APPRAISAL

Evaluating the work of individual staff has long been a contentious issue among teachers and teaching unions within the UK. After numerous pilot studies during the 1980s a national appraisal scheme was eventually published (DES, 1991). However five years later a report from TTA/OFSTED (1996) which used a range of evidence from inspections, internal evaluation including lesson observation, value-added work and external test results reached the conclusion that the lesson observation aspect of the appraisal process was not wholly effective. Arrangements for appraisal in schools were considered to be slack and to lack rigour. This was perhaps unsurprising when highly experienced and trained inspectors compare their approach to appraisal observation by teachers who are rarely given more than a few hours' training. Horne and Pierce (1996) in their study of 200 schools in four LEAs, also concluded that teacher appraisal lacked rigour and failed to contribute to the improvement of teacher effectiveness in the classroom.

Good appraisal may be useful to all concerned but there is no doubt that appraisal poorly planned and followed up is not only ineffective but creates bad feeling within an already overworked staff. Clear outcomes linked to action plans, which are well supported financially and in terms of time, are necessary to make appraisal a respected procedure.

Wragg (1999) suggests that before any appraisal takes place several questions should be addressed:

1. What is the principal purpose of the exercise?
2. Who will observe whom and with what focus?
3. What kind of preparation will be necessary (training of observers, briefing of teachers)?
4. Under what conditions should observations take place (how often, on what days, with what classes or groups)?
5. What formats will be used (freehand note-taking, checklist, semi-structured schedule)?
6. By whom and according to what principles will the format be devised?
7. What form of debriefing and discussion will take place after observations?
8. What record of appraisal will be kept and who will have access to it?
9. What targets will be set for the future?
10. What will be done to support teachers seeking to improve what they do as a result of appraisal, and how will the achieving of targets be monitored?

Observers engaged in appraisal should delay making any judgements until joint discussions have taken place. In essence the process is that the observer should 'record what is happening, *agree* what has happened, *reflect* (with the teacher) on what has been recorded and finally *encourage* him/her to interpret the information' (Moore, 1998). Very recent government initiatives such as accelerated pay thresholds and Advanced Skills teachers seem likely to make the process of making judgements about many teachers' work more common, though no less controversial, than ever before.

Despite its precarious introduction, appraisal seems set to stay. One of the most recent references to school appraisal (see DfEE, 1999, pp. 15 and 16) states that 'all teachers will be appraised and many will have senior management responsibilities for appraisal'. Recent government initiatives such as the two-layer pay structure and the more selective Advanced Skills teachers use teacher effectiveness as part of the selection process. However, it is a reflection of the changing stance of teacher unions that many teachers who would formerly have opposed them are accepting these initiatives. The government aims to provide teachers with guidance and training on techniques such as lesson observation skills. Unless it does so appraisal in the UK is likely to continue to be viewed negatively by teachers.

In contrast to the UK, the USA teacher appraisal – or 'teacher assessment' as it is called – is being led by the profession (unions and associations). The Interstate New Teacher Assessment Consortium (INTASC) and National Board for Professional Teaching Standards (NBPTS) have produced recommendations for performance assessments over the course of one year which are linked to salary increases. Teachers who achieve this standard are seen as experts and are more easily able to work in other states across the US.

In other countries, appraisal is more strongly linked to salary. One of the largest school boards in Canada, the York Region District School Board, has recently issued draft plans for a teacher effectiveness process 'to support continuous improvement in teacher practice' as part of an 'ongoing cycle of professional growth and development' (York Region District School Board, 2000). The emphasis is on the teachers' performance rather than the department or school as in the OFSTED procedures described above. It is proposed that senior members of staff observe lessons and make criteria referenced judgements under a number of specified categories. There is scrutiny of a teacher's own personal development plans and their outcomes as demonstrated within a portfolio. The proposed portfolio is a 'purposeful collection of work which exhibits efforts, progress and achievements in one or more areas over an extended period of time' and guidance is given as to how it can be compiled.

IMPROVING AN INDIVIDUAL TEACHER'S OWN WORK

Self-evaluation can also apply to the work of individual teachers and according to Kent (1996, p. 136) 'has been and remains one of the most effective long-term ways of securing educational improvement'. Many effective teachers regularly check the variety and regularity with which they use different teaching strategies and resources. Usually teachers who attend training courses outside of school are asked to complete a sheet to evaluate the quality of teaching, resources and accommodation. Rarely do these same teachers ask their pupils to do the same. Some good practitioners build evaluations such as that illustrated in Figure 12.5 into their lessons and work units. The results are a useful aid to developing better practice. Another route to developing good practice is through classroom observation. It is my belief that observers learn a great deal about their own practice as they analyse and reflect upon the classroom activities and relate what they see in synthesis with their own work. Fortunately many schools are now building observation into the work of all teachers, not just senior and departmental managers, although for most it is a constant problem to create time for this within hectic school schedules.

CONCLUSIONS

Teachers, and the departments and schools in which they work are likely to remain the subject of much evaluation work, both through OFSTED inspections and other government, school and departmental initiatives. Teachers can improve their ability to self-evaluate and to develop mechanisms for monitoring and improving the work they and their departments and schools do. This chapter has outlined the development of evaluation and considered ways in which geography departments can evaluate themselves in order to meet the requirements of new inspection procedures and in order to monitor and improve their effectiveness.

Hargreaves (1994, pp.423–36) argues that as an indirect result of recent educational reforms, a new professional and institutional development has emerged in some schools. This can be expressed in two propositions:

- there is little significant school development without teacher development; and
- there is little significant teacher development without school development.

To improve schools, Hargreaves argues, one must be prepared to invest in professional development; to improve teachers, their professional development must be set within the context of institutional development.

In the UK, within the last ten years, government initiatives, particularly inspection by OFSTED, have bullied teachers into having their work evaluated by outside agencies rather than persuading them to engage in it voluntarily. The introduction of national evaluation systems has not been smooth, but schools and teachers now accept that external inspection through OFSTED is likely to stay and that evaluation – and in

An Evaluation of the Unit 'Cities in LEDC'

Please help us to understand how you feel about the work we have done and to make changes to improve this unit for next year. (You may look at your books!)

Choose from these three, VERY, OK or NOT VERY. If you missed a lesson write ABSENT.

Lesson	**How interesting?**	**How much learnt?**
Fastest growing cities in the world		
Differences between cities in LEDC and MEDC		
Inequality in LEDC cities		
Shanty towns – an integral part of the city		
High rise in Caracas and Singapore		
Shanty town game		

Now tell us about the activities we ask you to do. Do you learn a lot from them? Do you like doing them? Do you find them easy? . . . or hard? Again use, VERY, OK, NOT MUCH or EASY/HARD

Activity	**Learn from**	**Like doing**	**Easy/Hard**
Talking in pairs or groups			
Using photos			
Watching video clips			
Drawing maps and diagrams			
Reading and using textbooks			
Using graphs and statistics			
Using cartoons			

Now tell me about my teaching. Ring any option that applies; you can ring more than one

Books are marked:	**Often**	**Not often enough**		
Marks and comments are:	Helpful	Not very helpful	Too short	
The amount of homework set is:	About right	Too much	Too little	We should have longer to do it
The teacher talks:	Too much	Too little	Just right	Uses too many words I don't understand
The teacher explains what we have to do:	Always clearly	Usually clearly	Sometimes confusing	I often need you to explain again
The pace of the lessons is:	Too rushed	Too slow	Just right	Mixed
I understand the work:	Always	Mostly	Sometimes	Not very often
The number of handouts is:	Too many	Too few. They are helpful	About right	

Now ring any words or phrases that best describe your teacher (i.e. me!)

Fair Unfair | Strict Not very strict | Punctual | Not punctual

Likes her work | Does not like her work

Concerned about me | Not very concerned about me

Figure 12.5 An example of an end-of-unit evaluation.

particular self-evaluation – is a key part of improving standards. Forward-looking schools, geography departments and individual teachers should build it into their regular work.

REFERENCES

Cambers, G. (1996) 'Department self-assessment', in Bailey, P. and Fox, P (eds), *Geography Teachers' Handbook*. Sheffield: Geographical Association, pp. 279–95.

Campion, K., Carter, R. and Krause, J. (1997) 'OFSTED revisited: how to make the best use of prior experience', *Teaching Geography*, vol. 22, no. 4, pp. 170–2.

Davidson, G. (1996) 'Using OFSTED criteria to develop classroom practice', *Teaching Geography*, vol. 21, no. 1, pp. 111–14.

Department for Education and Employment, (DfEE) (1999) Green Paper: *Teachers Meeting the Challenge of Change – A Technical Consultation*. London: DfEE.

Department of Education and Science (DES) (1991) *School Teacher Appraisal: A National Framework*. London: DES.

Hargreaves, D.H. (1994) 'The new professionalism: the synthesis of professional and institutional development', *Teaching and Teacher Education*, vol. 10, no. 4, pp. 423–38.

Harris, C. (1996) 'Managing and benefiting from an OFSTED inspection', in Bailey, P. and Fox, P. (eds), *Geography Teachers' Handbook*. Sheffield: Geographical Association, pp. 291–6.

Horne, H. and Pierce, A. (1996) *A Practical Guide to Staff Development and Appraisal*. London: Kogan Page.

Kent, A. (1996) 'Evaluating the geography curriculum', in Kent, A. et al., *Geography in Education*. Cambridge: Cambridge University Press.

King, S. (2000) *Into the Black Box: Observing Classrooms*. Sheffield: Geographical Association.

Martin, F. and Bailey, P. (1996) 'Evaluating and using resources', in Bailey, P. and Fox, P. (eds), *Geography Teachers' Handbook*. Sheffield: Geographical Association, pp. 235–47.

Moore, J. (1998) 'The role of observation in teacher appraisal', in Tilstone, C. (ed.), *Observing Teaching and Learning*. London: Fulton.

NUT (1998) OFSTED: *The Views of Headteacher and Deputy Headteacher Members of the National Union of Teachers*. London: NUT.

OFSTED (1995) *Guidance on the Inspection of Secondary Schools*. London: HMSO.

OFSTED (1999a) *Inspecting Schools: The Framework*. London: HMSO.

OFSTED (1999b) *Handbook for Inspecting Secondary Schools with Guidance on Self-evaluation*. London: HMSO.

OFSTED (1999c) *Standards in the Secondary Curriculum 1997/8 – Geography*. London: HMSO.

Ouston, J., Earley, P. and Fidler, B. (eds) (1996) *OFSTED Inspections: The Early Experience*. London: Fulton.

Skilbeck, M. (1984) *School-based Curriculum Development*. London: Harper & Row.

Smith, P. (1997) 'Standards achieved: a review of geography in secondary schools in England, 1995–96', *Teaching Geography*, vol. 22, no. 3, pp. 125–6.

TTA/OFSTED (1996) *Review of Headteacher and Teacher Appraisal (Summary of Evidence)*. London: TTA/OFSTED.

Wragg, E. C. (1999) *An Introduction to Classroom Observation*, 2nd edn. London: Routledge.

York District School Board (2000) 'The teacher effectiveness process'. Unpublished draft, pilot document.

Chapter 13

Information and communications technology

Stephanie Jackson

INTRODUCTION

This chapter aims to briefly review historical and political stages of the incorporation of technology into education, as well as debates about the future. It concludes with the description of an innovative research and development project that illustrates one way in which technology could be incorporated into future geography classrooms. The chapter will focus on Britain and technology in general, and whenever possible the arguments and discussions will be placed in the context of geography education and related to Europe.

DEFINITIONS

There is more than one aspect in which technology can be incorporated into education, therefore, general discussions about technology and education can be ambiguous if the context in which the word 'technology' is used is not clearly defined. According to Lewis (1999, pp. 148–9), the word 'technology' can refer to any of the following when used in an educational context:

- technology as a curriculum area in itself (IT skills for students, word processing, using e-mail, etc.);
- technology as the presentation of learning material for students, with occasional additional functions such as assessment;
- technology as the administrative and managerial infrastructure (finance, personnel, etc.);
- technology as a learning system through which teaching and learning are managed, transacted and recorded regardless of the location of the student.

Although each of these definitions relate to technology in an educational context, this chapter will focus primarily on the second and fourth definitions, namely as a way in which information is presented to students and the use of technology as a dynamic learning system.

To clarify the use of the terms information technology (IT) and information and communications technology (ICT) in this chapter, the definitions by Pickford and Hassell that King (2000) refers to have been adopted. According to their work IT and

ICT are defined as follows:

> 'IT' refers to the students' knowledge and understanding of the technology and their ability to apply it, as stated in the IT National Curriculum.
>
> 'Information and communications technology' refers to the computing and communications that support teaching and learning, where the focus is on the curriculum subject being taught, not on the technology skills. ICT is not just about computers: it also covers the use of fax machines, tape recorders and cameras. (King, 2000, p. 3)

This chapter will focus primarily on ICT rather than IT.

BRIEF OVERVIEW OF HISTORICAL DEVELOPMENTS

ICT in education is not a new topic – even in the 1960s 'there was some use of large mainframe computers in teaching, but only on a very small scale' (Twells, 1996, p. 14).

In 1970, the *British Journal of Educational Technology* (*BJET*) was established in order 'to bring about in education the "white-hot technological revolution"' (Hawkridge, 1999, p. 293). Two viewpoints that were expressed in the first edition were that 'the economic justification for CAI [computer-aided instruction] (or any educational innovation) was difficult' (Hawkridge, 1999, p. 294), and a 'very limited use of the computer was foreseen at present in education up to the age of 16' (Duke, 1970, quoted in Hawkridge, 1999, p. 294). Although *BJET* is a British journal, it was intended from the beginning that it would have an international representation. In the first year it had articles 'about activities in Africa, America and Australia, as well as Britain' which illustrates an international interest in educational technology (Hawkridge, 1999, p. 293).

By the late 1970s the 'advent of micro-electronics' meant that the 'costs and potential of computers made their use in schools a viable proposition' (Twells, 1996, p. 14). However, in geography classrooms the 1970s are looked back upon as a decade in which 'only a minority of geography teachers were touched by computing' (Kent, 1992, p. 164).

In the 1980s the emphasis on the use of computers in UK classrooms grew. According to Kent (1992, p. 164), 'throughout these eras, geography has been a front runner in grasping the pedagogic potential of the new technology'. Evidence of this is that as early as 1983, *Teaching Geography* established a Computer Page 'with articles and reviews of software', and there 'has been a steady flow of books aimed at supporting and encouraging the use of computers in geography' since the early 1980s (Kent, 1992, p. 164). This is also a time period in which 'case studies of how microcomputers could be used in geography lessons at secondary level' as well as 'subject specific, pre-written programmes of software, supplying a limited amount of knowledge and often involving mechanistic forms of learning' were characteristic, and the 'emphasis in geography began to move away from using the computer as a calculative tool towards simulation' (Twells, 1996, p. 15).

The 1990s has been a time period in which the Internet has had an impact on society and schools. One way of measuring the impact is by the increase in the number of schools that are connected to the Internet. In 1996 it was estimated that between 2000 and 3000 schools and colleges were connected to the Internet in the United Kingdom (Durbin and Sanders, 1996, p. 15), but by 1999 it was estimated that up to 12 000 of the 32 000 schools were connected (Cole, 1999). This increase is not only taking place in schools in the United Kingdom, it is an international phenomenon as suggested in the following quote:

> The Internet's pace of adoption eclipses all technologies before it. Radio existed for 38 years before it gained 50 million listeners and television took 13 years to reach that point. But the Internet crossed that line in four years: in 1994 three million people were connected and by March 1998 the figure was 119 million. Traffic on the Internet doubles every 100 days.
>
> (Lynch, 1998, quoted in Joo, 1999, p. 245)

This exponential increase in the number of Internet connections is from home users as well as schools and businesses. The Internet provides access to a variety of resources such as websites with international data, e-mail and chatroom facilities, and live web cameras showing everything from volcanic eruptions to game park watering holes in Africa. These resources enable teachers and students to obtain a diverse amount of information that can be incorporated into teaching and learning. This can be valuable for subjects like geography.

Past predictions

Throughout these decades, there have been several debates about and predictions of the use of ICT in education in the future. One example is that 25 years ago a lecturer from the University of London, Institute of Education took part in a debate at a mathematics conference where academics argued over whether students would be able to afford calculators for use in school mathematics lessons. He reflected on the irony of that debate in comparison to the discussions that had just taken place during a seminar of the Digital Technologies Research Group at the University of London, Institute of Education in December 1999. Debates like the one about the calculators in the past have grown into present-day discussions about multimedia computers with Internet connections.

The same questions have arisen throughout the history of technology and education: What is happening in the field of technology? Which ICT should be incorporated into schools? What are the costs? Can equal access to the resources be provided for the students and teachers? How can the ICT contribute to teaching and learning? It is useful to review past predictions at a time in which we are striving to predict what education will be like in the future.

In reference to geography education in particular, the following statements are a selection of predictions, made by a panel of experts in 1988, who were asked to predict the likely status of technology in the geography classroom by 2000:

- Computers will be regarded as a routine resource similar to paper, pencil or book and used in all areas of the curriculum.
- Teachers will be keen to use the new technology, will be adequately trained and will play a more facilitating role in classrooms where more pupil-centred and enquiry learning will be used.
- The technology will play an emancipatory role, removing boring mechanical tasks and encouraging sophisticated graphicacy skills via the use of graphics packages, plotters, three dimensional projections, digital mapping and the like.
- The most significant change predicted by the experts is the greatly increased use of word processors by pupils.

- Electronic mailing, either for teachers to share ideas and teaching resources or by pupils to communicate with other children, is unlikely to be used much more than at present.

(Allen, 1988, quoted in Kent, 1992, pp. 173–4)

Other predictions were made by the experts about the changes in types of software and how a 'closer affinity between educational and industrial software will emerge' (Allen, 1988 quoted in Kent, 1992, p. 173), as well as teachers gaining access to huge on-line databanks, 'more accurate and realistic' computer simulations, and cheaper and easier access to interactive videos' (Kent, 1992).

The extent to which these predictions have become true can be debated. This author would argue that there has been an increase in the use of word processors by pupils in general; however, there is still a great need for training teachers and for better provision of equipment in schools before it is regarded as a 'routine' resource for all students and teachers. An interesting point to note, however, is that although e-mail is mentioned in the predictions, there is not an overt mention of the Internet.

Political change

Government initiatives have been a driving force in the incorporation of ICT into education in England and Wales. Milestones in the history of the incorporation of ICT into education can be determined by different government programmes that provided software, hardware or training for the teachers. Although it is recognised that the European Commission has also had an impact on the incorporation of both hardware and software technologies into classrooms across Europe, it is not within the bounds of this chapter to review them.

Table 13.1 is based upon and lists the main ICT government initiatives as compiled by Watson (1997). It is evident from the extensive list of initiatives, spanning over two decades, that a large amount of effort and funding have been put into ICT and education. Although the table of initiatives ends in 1995, the government initiatives did not. Since 1998, an overall sum of more than £1 billion has been invested in order to meet the following British government targets for ICT by 2002:

- serving teachers should generally feel confident, and be competent to teach, using ICT within the curriculum;
- all schools, colleges, universities and libraries and as many community centres as possible should be connected to the NGfL [see below];
- most school leavers should have a good understanding of ICT;
- the UK should be a centre for excellence in the development of networks;
- general administrative communications to schools should be electronic, not paper based.

(Hassell, 1999, p. 92)

The consultation process for the National Grid for Learning (NGfL) was started in 1997. It is a large-scale initiative that aims to serve 'as an architecture of content' by providing 'links to information, advice and learning resources' (NGfL, 2000, website page ending/learner). The NGfL is for learners of all ages, rather than just students in schools. It collates information and resources from a wide range of locations such as

Table 13.1 The main ICT government initiatives as compiled by Watson (1997)

Year	*Programme*	*Description*
1973–1977	National Development Programme in Computer Assisted Learning (NDPCAL)	• First national project in the UK funded to explore the role of computers, particularly in HE • 35 projects developing and evaluating CAL materials • one school geography project • Council for Educational Technology established by the government at the end to continue to act for it in further matters related to educational computing
1973–1990	Computers in the Curriculum Project (CIC)	• Funded by the Schools Council • Aim was to explore the role of computers for secondary schools • Geography was included • Development of educational software with related curriculum materials • Engaged active classroom teachers in formative evaluation
1980–1986	Microelectronics in Education Programme (MEP)	• National project: covered curriculum development, teacher training, and resource organisation • New curriculum based subjects being developed • Traditional subjects being supported • Strong emphasis on regional projects
1986–1988	Micros in Education Support Unit (MESU)	• To bring together accomplishments of the MEP for each of the three divisions • Worked directly with LEAs and higher education institutions rather than schools
1987–1992	Information Technology in Schools	• Education support grants to LEAs for the provision of advisory teachers and hardware • A grant to NCET (National Council for Educational Technology) for training the new advisory teachers, to provide professional support for LEAs and teacher training institutions on the use of IT across the curriculum • LEA training grants for in-service training, required to produce a policy statement for developing IT in schools over five years starting April 1988
1988	Formation of the NCET (National Council for Educational Technology)	• The MESU was terminated two years earlier than planned and was subsumed by the newly expanded CET to form the NCET • Developed courses and training materials for advisory teachers associated with the IT in Schools government initiative
1989–1995	IT in the National Curriculum	• Incorporation of IT into the National Curriculum • IT was the only 'cross-curricular' subject to be incorporated into the enacted orders of the National Curriculum • Following the Dearing revision in 1994 it was eventually identified as a separate subject

libraries, museums, health and leisure ... services at local, metropolitan or regional level(s) (NGfL, 2000, website page ending/edulife).

In reference to schools, 'the grid is more than just the Internet of course, and there are high hopes that schools will use it to share resources, ideas and experiences' (Cole, 1999). Nevertheless, some educators are questioning the long-term commitment of the government. One headteacher from London stated that 'the NGfL funding is a short-term boost but there are long-term issues on sustaining the investment for ICT when the money runs out. It is going to put a lot of pressure on school budgets' (Cole, 1999). This is something that could be an issue of concern in the future.

Although the NGfL is a very broad initiative, there is ample opportunity for geography teachers to use the grid in order to access a variety of resources such as a database of educational software, CD-ROM reviews, advice on safely using the Internet in the classroom and on-line discussion areas.

The incorporation of ICT into education is being taken seriously by the government. There is a large amount of funding in ICT for education, as well as statutory obligations for students in primary and secondary schools to use computers and other forms of ICT in the classroom.

National governments and the European Commission are spending extensive amounts of money on integrating the use of ICT into classrooms. The arguments for doing this are that it will allow students to access a greater amount of information, motivate their learning, provide them with the skills that they need to work in a society of the future and provide them with a wider range of resources to inform their decision-making and knowledge base. The British government's commitment is considerable because it believes that 'investment in Britain as a learning society which makes the maximum creative use of new technologies to raise educational standards, improve the quality of life and significantly enhance international competitiveness' is very important (NGfL, 2000, website page ending/govern).

Sponsoring research and development projects that create innovative ways of incorporating technology into education on a larger scale are one of the ways in which the European Commission is spending millions of euros. In reference to geography education in particular, projects like 'Eurogame', which is described in detail later in the chapter, and HERODOT, which trains and supports geography teachers in using the Internet to teach geography, are just two of the many European projects that are being sponsored.

THE DEBATE

Introduction

From this brief historical and political overview of the incorporation of ICT into education, it is evident that this has become an increasingly important issue. However, the perception of how ICT should be incorporated into education is changing. The focus is no longer solely on incorporating ICT into our existing education system, it is looking at teaching and learning first and devising valuable ways of using ICT to enhance this process. On some levels, teachers are still thinking about how to integrate ICT into their classrooms in order to fulfil legal requirements, by just using a computer as a resource to support a student's learning in a 'traditional' style. However, the very nature of teaching and learning is being questioned with the rapid rate in which ICT is being developed and used more universally, along with the evolving needs of students, parents, governments and teachers.

The past

In general the literature over the past 15 years, from both teachers and researchers alike, has focused primarily on how to integrate specific software packages or hardware products into the classroom, such as Davies' (1996) suggestions for using the Internet in a structured/planned way for classroom teaching, and O'Grady's (1996) suggestions for handling data with computers. The use of ICT in education has been justified by some of the arguments that are represented in Table 13.2 that was created by quoting from the work of Twells (1996).

Table 13.2 Justifications for the use of ICT in education

Rationale	*Description of argument*
Social	If children need to become literate and numerate they also need to know something about computers.
Vocational	IT should be related to future jobs.
Pedagogical	Children enhance their learning through the use of computers.
'Catalytic'	The use of computers will actually change schools for the better, in terms of both teaching and learning.
Cost-effectiveness	IT can replace teachers and be more cost-effective, ignoring the socialising and humanistic roles of schools.

Source: Twells (1996), pp. 22–3.

In reference to geography education, the literature has covered the types of issues that teachers have been faced with at the chalk face when using ICT. These range from the provision of hardware and software to the most effective ways to use ICT resources in a geography classroom. Articles such as those by Garner (1997) on 'Integrating ICT into schemes of work' and Warner (1994) on 'CD-ROM technology in geography: potential and issues' were written to support teachers in using ICT to teach geography. Writers like Freeman (1997, p. 202) not only provided ideas for ways in which to incorporate ICT into the geography classroom, but argued that ICT could also enhance geography teaching and learning, rather than just to fulfil legal requirements. The basic principles of the ways in which ICT could be used to enhance the geography curriculum (see Table 13.3) later became 'well accepted as fundamental tenets and have been built into the Key Stage 3 Geography guidance produced by SCAA (now QCA) and NCET (now BECTa)' (Hassell, 1996, p. 10). The statements in Table 13.3 'outlined the benefits that ICT could provide' as well as presented ways in which 'students studying geography are entitled to use ICT' (Hassell, 1996).

In addition, there has been research on CAL (computer-assisted learning) in geography. Between the late 1970s and the early 1980s Kent (1984) cited 'fifteen pieces of research' that were primarily 'classroom studies' or programme evaluations with a few focusing on 'curriculum development'. Half of the works cited by Kent were MEd and MA dissertations. Other examples of MA Geography in Education research from

Table 13.3 Ways that ICT can support teaching and learning

- Enhance geographical enquiry skills
- Provide access to a wide range of geographical knowledge and information sources
- Deepen the understanding of environmental and spatial relationships
- Provide experience of alternative images of people, place and environment
- Enable the consideration of the wider impact of IT on people, place and environment

Adapted from Hassell (1996), p. 77.

the University of London, Institute of Education are the work carried out by Leonard (1984) who 'concentrated on a case study' of using the software package RICE FARMING 'with a mixed ability group of third year pupils', Lawler (1986) who 'directed his attention to the ways in which computers can support fieldwork', and Thomas (1985) who 'concentrated on software evaluation' (for full details see Graves et al., 1989, pp. 91–4). More recently studies undertaken on multimedia in secondary school geography (Ingram, 1998) and investigating the use of the Internet in teaching A-level geography (Morris, 1998) have also focused on CAL in geography education.

One thing all of these articles and pieces of research have in common is that the technology has been brought into classrooms within the parameters of the existing educational system. There has been pressure to use ICT in education, and the emphasis has been on how to incorporate ICT into education to enhance teaching and learning within the existing education system and methods of teaching and learning.

However, according to Chambers 'it is clear that such technologies are becoming an intrinsic part of our educational armoury'. 'And yet, as far as their specific educational applications are concerned, such technologies would appear to have only superficial claims as to their capacities for supporting learning and teaching' (Chambers, 1999, p. 151).

Lewis takes this argument further to state that 'the thinking behind the introduction of technology has to date been limited. Its purposes have been narrowly defined as either cost-efficiency or learning effectiveness, or some balance between' (Lewis, 1999, p. 149).

In reference to geography education, Watson (2000) supports these arguments from the evidence found in the case studies that she conducted as part of the ImpacT project, which was 'an evaluation of the impact of information technology (IT) on children's achievements in primary and secondary schools' (Johnson, 1993, p. 1). Watson found that large-scale innovative users of ICT in the geography classroom are people that are personally interested in technology, whereas the majority of teachers 'use IT in their classrooms only when it has a particular resonance with their pedagogic and subject philosophy' (Watson, 2000). Therefore she found that the teachers who were not large-scale users of ICT in teaching geography were willing to use ICT as a resource if the educational benefits outweighed the costs.

Therefore, at present, it has generally been accepted that ICT should be used in the classroom as a resource when it has the potential to enhance teaching and learning. It is this discussion of enhancing teaching and learning that has spurred on an even broader debate that is larger than the issues faced by individual teachers in individual classrooms trying to use ICT. It is a greater debate that addresses the evolving meanings of teaching and learning, as society as a whole is being transformed into a new information age which empowers individuals with access to a wider variety of resources. This debate is not subject-specific – it touches upon all disciplines and levels of education.

The future

While studies of the integration of particular technologies into traditional classrooms within the existing educational structure continue, there are also calls for exploring new meanings of teaching and learning based on an integration of ICT within education. ICT provides a means by which interactive synchronous distance education is possible. Distance education does not only mean university courses that are created for students that work from distant places, it can also be a model in which distant primary secondary students are networked together to work on a single collaborative project for a particular class, or when individual students can go to a chatroom or send e-mails to discuss issues with others in distant places without guidance from a teacher. In considering the possibilities that the technology provides, there is an inherent shift in the meaning of teaching and learning when these technologies are used since the very basis of distance education implies that there is a distance between teachers and students. This distance enables students to have access to a greater variety of materials and influences on their thinking rather than solely depending on the materials and arguments presented by their teachers. These changes in the technological developments are causing a shift that can be referred to as a move from traditional teaching to constructive learning, as defined in Table 13.4.

Table 13.4 Traditional teaching vs. constructive learning (Lewis, 1999, p. 142)

Traditional teaching	Seeks to transmit fixed, well-structured knowledge with a firm external control of content, sequence and pace of learning; for many this continues to be of value because it is seen to confer rigour and respectability on the learning process.
Constructive learning	Stresses active, outcome-oriented and self-regulated learning, where meaning is negotiated, multiple perspectives are encouraged and learners map their way through an ever-changing information and knowledge landscape.

Lewis argues that constructive learning has become the core of recent educational philosophy, and the teaching styles need to match the learning. Teachers can no longer view ICT as a separate entity that can be incorporated into the classroom to teach content to students, they need to look at ICT in conjunction with teaching and learning to develop a fulfilling and useful curriculum. By using ICT in a constructive way, the teacher not only increases the amount of content, he or she is also equipping students with a wide range of sophisticated skills that are enhanced by the ICT. The discussion has opened up to 'how technology can facilitate learning, particularly through learner-centred and collaborative approaches and the development of skills' (McConnell, 1999, p. 177). For example, this is supported by Chambers, from his research into how 11-year-old students navigate through an encyclopaedic CD-ROM in order to answer specific questions that they were given, who illustrated that new technologies not only assist learners in finding specific information but they also 'enhance a range of skills associated with deep level processing and meaningful learning such as metacognition, problem solving and critical thinking' (Chambers, 1999, p. 151).

This change from traditional/conventional teaching to constructive/networked learning is being referred to as a paradigm shift in teaching and learning in education. The debate 'argues that technology needs to be thought of much more radically as the means by which our schools, colleges and universities will respond to the challenges they currently face. This requires visionary thinking and the construction of scenarios which generate the energy and will to act' (Lewis, 1999, p. 149).

McConnell has even proceeded to define 'networked learning' which is 'the convergence of information technology with communication technology for the purposes of education and training' which 'creates opportunities for people to learn and communicate with each other in new and flexible ways' (McConnell, 1999, p. 177). This is based on his argument that we are moving from conventional (traditional) teaching and learning, through second-generation (distance) teaching and learning, and into a virtual or networked distance learning (McConnell, 1999, p. 178).

'Are the world wide web and multimedia technologies only to feed a reproducing model of learning? Or have they the potential to facilitate a transforming model of learning?' These are the questions raised by Dahlgren (1984, quoted in Chambers, 1999, p. 151). This idea of learning refers not just to the relationship between teaching and learning in the classroom, but to distance learning, life-long learning and virtual learning as well.

The causes

One reason for this shift to an expanding definition of teaching and learning is the fundamental changes on both public and private levels, with efficiency being a driving force. A major aspect of this relates to educating future members of the workforce. The following statements that support this viewpoint were highlighted by Lewis from a report that was written by Lewis and Merton (1996):

- Private and public sector organisations are adopting flatter, more devolved structures that require employees to be more flexible, autonomous and responsive to change, capable of learning fast and making decisions independently yet within a corporate framework.
- They have to operate more remotely, yet at the same time communicate often and purposefully with others in their networks.

(Lewis and Merton, 1996, quoted in Lewis, 1999, p. 141)

It is argued that these changes in expectations of the workforce in both public and private sectors have contributed to 'the importance of independent learning' (Lewis, 1999, p. 141)

Another external factor is students' access to information on the Internet and other forms of ICT outside of the classroom where 'information is no longer structured only in a simple, linear, logical fashion: it is becoming fragmented, multi-channelled and simultaneous' (Lewis, 1999, p. 142). This access to external information and the way students are receiving it affects how they learn and their responses to different teaching styles. Students are attending lessons with a wide range of experiences, and with the growth of the Internet they can have access to information from all over the world without leaving their home.

Some of these fundamental arguments in the debate are not completely new, as Papert was discussing 'how learning to communicate with a computer may change the way other learning takes place' back in 1980 (p. 6). However, technology has progressed so rapidly that the potential opportunities for innovative ways of teaching and learning, coupled with the evolution in the ways in which people are obtaining and processing information, have increased the pressures on moving away from traditional methods of teaching to more constructive learning.

Cybergeography

The impact of ICT is not only taking place at the teaching and learning level, it has also spurred on the creation of a new field of geography – cybergeography. According to Donert, 'studies of the evolving information environments have led to the development of a new discipline . . . which investigates the impact of virtual places on people's lives in the real world' (2000, p. 37). As an increasing number of people of all ages and backgrounds are interacting in virtual worlds, this is causing effects on the real world, like people who know more about their neighbour in a cybervillage or friend in a chatroom than they do about their physical neighbour next door. It is a new area of study in the field of geography that is in its infancy.

A PROJECT OF TODAY FOR CLASSROOMS OF TOMORROW

The following project is a recent example of an innovative way in which ICT is being incorporated into the geography classroom. The prototypes allow geography students to work with other geography students from around Europe in a geography decision-making exercise. Besides the prescribed learning aims and objectives, the potential affective learning that takes place between the collaborating European teachers and students is also enormous. For example, by working with students from other European countries, the geography students are provided with the opportunity to 'get to know' their peers and to gain an understanding of what is important to them within and beyond the prescribed content of the game. This type of game has the potential to be a valuable tool for teaching geography, as it creates links with students and teachers from different cultures and backgrounds. The technology itself also causes students to work together in an on-line cooperative manner which is an increasingly important skill for the workforce of tomorrow.

'Eurogame'

'Eurogame' was a two and a half year European Commission funded project, which started in January 1998. The main aim of 'Eurogame' was to design and create on-line, multimedia, multi-lingual educational game prototypes that teach the regional geography of Europe through cooperative learning. Geography academics, pedagogy academics, software developers and publishers from five different European countries worked along with 14 pilot teachers from four of the countries to design, create and evaluate three game prototypes during the project period.

This project was commissioned to develop leading-edge technology to incorporate

ICT into the geography classroom by enabling students from different European countries to work together cooperatively by means of Internet connections in order to make decisions on issues related to the regional geography of Europe. Also, by playing together they could gain a better understanding of one another's viewpoints, opinions and perceptions, as well as possibly build distant relationships, which are all important factors in creating a more integrated Europe.

Both strategy and adventure game prototypes were developed, the former as two different role-plays for 16–19 year olds, and the latter as a game for 12–14 year olds. At the time of writing, the first prototype, an off-line version created to develop the architecture of the game, had been developed and evaluated by the pilot teachers and the second prototype was in the process of being evaluated. The third prototype was still under development.

In the second prototype, the first on-line version, there are four roles in each game. Each role can be played by a small number of students working on one networked computer. The computers are networked together so that each of the roles could be played from different classrooms in different countries. In order to play the game, students have to learn how to share their information with their team-mates via a newsgroup in a language that they can all understand.

The first impressions of the second prototype are that the students are motivated to play the game and to work with team-mates in other countries in order to make decisions. The technology enables students to access an extensive range of data such as photographs, tables, GIS maps and relevant websites, as well as providing them with electronic tools that assist them in analysing the data in order to make informed decisions.

Projects like 'Eurogame' help to create integrated teaching and learning strategies for future geography classrooms.

CONCLUSIONS

The incorporation of ICT into education has been an issue for several decades. The discussions have ranged from debates about whether ICT should be used in classrooms, to how it could be incorporated into the classroom, and to why it is or isn't being used in the classroom. All of these past debates and discussions have been constrained by trying to incorporate ICT into *existing* educational structures.

Today academics are thinking of the whole issue on a broader level without the constraints of the current education system. ICT not only contains a number of powerful tools, but it is these tools that are causing the relationships between teachers and students to evolve. The traditional teaching approach is being threatened by the pressures for a change to constructive learning and potentially to networked learning. This change is causing a shift in the thinking about teaching and learning for the future. Although this debate is about education as a whole, projects such as 'Eurogame' illustrate the potential of this type of teaching and learning for geography classrooms of the future.

REFERENCES

Chambers, P. (1999) 'Information handling skills, cognition and new technologies', *British Journal of Educational Technology*, vol. 30, no. 2, pp. 151–62.

Cole, G. (1999) 'Technology to fire the imagination', *Times Educational Supplement*, 8 January.

Davies, G. (1996) 'Guides for the perplexed', *Times Educational Supplement*, 22 March.

Donert, K. (2000) 'Virtually geography: aspects of the changing geography of information and communications', *Geography*, vol. 85, part 1, pp. 37–45.

Durbin, C. and Sanders, R. (1996) 'Geographers on the Internet', *Teaching Geography*, vol. 21, no. 1, pp. 15–19.

Freeman, D. (1997) 'Using information technology and new technologies in geography', in M. Tilbury and D. Williams, (eds), *Teaching and Learning Geography*. London: Routledge.

Garner, D. (1997) 'Integrating IT into schemes of work', *Teaching Geography*, vol. 22, no. 2, pp. 90–1.

Graves, N. et al. (1989) *Research in Geography Education: MA Dissertations 1968–1988*. Institute of Education, University of London.

Hassell, D. (1996) 'Using ICT in coursework', *Teaching Geography*, vol. 21, no. 2, pp. 77–80.

Hassell, D. (1999) 'Will you get some training?', *Teaching Geography*, vol. 24, no. 2, pp. 92–3.

Hawkridge, D. (1999) 'Thirty years on, BJET! And educational technology comes of age', *British Journal of Educational Technology*, vol. 30, no. 4, pp. 293–304.

Ingram, P. (1998) 'Multimedia in secondary school geography: a critical understanding of the present state of use', unpublished MA dissertation, University of London Institute of Education.

Johnson, D. (1993) 'Executive summary', in Watson, D. (ed.), *The ImpacT Report: An Evaluation of the Impact of Information Technology on Children's Achievements in Primary and Secondary Schools*. London: University of London, King's College.

Joo, J. (1999) 'Cultural issues of the Internet in classrooms', *British Journal of Educational Technology*, vol. 30, no. 3, pp. 245–50.

Kent, W.A. (1984) 'Research in computer assisted learning', in Graves, N. (ed.), *Research and Research Methods in Geographical Education*. London: University of London Institute of Education.

Kent, W.A. (1992) 'The new technology and geographical education', in Naish, M. (ed.), *Geography and Education: National and International Perspectives*. London: University of London Institute of Education.

King, S. (ed.) (2000) *High-tech Geography – ICT in Secondary Schools*. Sheffield: Geographical Association.

Lewis, R. (1999) 'The role of technology in learning: managing to achieve a vision', *British Journal of Educational Technology*, vol. 30, no. 2, pp. 141–50.

McConnell, D. (1999) 'Guest editorial: networked learning', *Journal of Computer Assisted Learning*, vol. 15, no. 3, pp. 177–8.

Morris, S. (1998) 'An investigation into the use and potential of the Internet (WorldWideWeb) in the teaching of A-level geography', unpublished MA dissertation. London: University of London Institute of Education.

National Grid for Learning (NGfL) website pages:
http://www.dfee.gov.uk/grid/challenge/edulife.htm
http://www.dfee.gov.uk/grid/challenge/govern.htm
http://www.dfee.gov.uk/grid/challenge/learner.htm

O'Grady, C. (1996) 'Making the most of fine weather', *Times Educational Supplement*, 18 October.

Papert, S. (1980) *Mind-Storms: Children Computers and Powerful Ideas*. New York: Basic Books.

Twells, P. (1996) 'Information highways: the present and possible future implications for the teaching and learning of geography in schools', unpublished MA dissertation. London:

University of London Institute of Education.
Warner, H. (1994) 'CD-ROM technology in geography: potential and issues', *Teaching Geography*, vol. 19, no. 4, pp. 184–5.
Watson, D. (1997) 'Information technology in geography classes: the appearance and the reality of change', unpublished PhD thesis. London: King's College London School of Education, University of London.
Watson, D. (2000) 'Issues raised by research into ICT and geography education', in Kent, A. (ed.), *Research Forum 2: Information and Communications Technology*. London: University of London Institute of Education.

Chapter 14

Geography teaching for a sustainable society

John Morgan

> For large numbers in Britain today, the new century is not a source of hope. The predominant mood, if anything, is of fear. People are anxious about the future, about the world they are leaving for their children. They see, with a profound understanding quite missing from national political life, the growing crisis of humankind's impact on the natural environment, as the simultaneous growth of material consumption and population generates inexorably greater pollution and resource degradation. They witness poverty, famine and conflict in distant places and know that we cannot disclaim responsibility. They see the fabric of British society tearing under the strain of inequality and the glorification of me-first materialism. They forsee a world in which people live increasingly barricaded lives, fearful of others, besieged by crime; in which material wealth offers no substitute for the lost quality of community life.
>
> (Jacobs, 1996, p. 1)

Michael Jacobs' words were written for 'The Real World Coalition', and were part of what was described as 'a major statement of public concern from over 30 of the UK's leading voluntary and campaigning organisations'. The statement is important for a number of reasons. The first is the way that it links a wide range of issues together in a broader vision of sustainability than simply concern for the environment. Instead, the statement seeks to link issues of sustainability, social justice and democratic renewal. The second is the extent to which such arguments are generally accepted. Jacobs cites a number of examples as evidence that many people care about the morality of their society, and wish to act upon it. These include the continued growth of 'green' consumerism and ethical investment, political protests based on animal welfare and the loss of the countryside, the growing debate about corporate ethics, and the high levels of participation in Britain's voluntary sector:

> For most people, ethical motivations of these kinds reflect a desire to live in a moral society: one which cares for its less fortunate members, for its natural environment and for the idea of community. They reflect the feeling which many people who have not themselves been hurt – who many even have done personally very well – have had in recent years, that there is something deeply uncomfortable about living in a society which tolerates homelessness and rising poverty, racial discrimination and environmental destruction. We have been told in these years that what matters is personal consumption and rising material living standards. It seems to us that many people recognise that there is more to life than this: more to their own personal development, and more to building a good society.
>
> (Jacobs, 1996, p. 123)

What the Real World Coalition is suggesting is that there exists a groundswell of feeling towards a better world, and more inclusive and socially just ways of living. I think it can be argued that, in the British context, school geography taps into, and reflects, this widespread 'structure of feeling'. To offer just two examples where the language of geography educators matches that of the Real World Coalition, the position statement of the Geographical Association 'Geography in the Curriculum' (1999) states that among the aims of a geographical education are: 'to develop in young people a knowledge and understanding of the place they live in, of other people and places, and of how people and places inter-relate and interconnect'; and 'to develop an informed concern for the world around us and an ability and willingness to take positive action, both locally and globally'.

Similarly, the Geovisions group, which was set up to raise the debate about the future of geography and how it related to global dimensions, development perspectives and human rights, suggested that geography should provide:

> An entitlement for all school pupils to a school geography that enables them to make sense of the world and themselves as players in the world.

and:

> To develop the knowledge, skills and values young people require to exercise and extend their rights and responsibilities as global citizens and thereby help them develop a sense of identity.

These are laudable and ambitious aims. However, my concern in this paper is the extent to which such aims are realised in school geography. My argument is that the desire to teach geography for a 'sustainable society' – a more inclusive and socially just society - is stifled by established approaches to teaching in geography. In *The Impotent Image*, Rob Gilbert (1984) suggests that the social subjects (economics, sociology, geography and history) as taught in schools serve to promote ideological views of the world. He argues that:

> Images in the present subjects are remnants of the past, related to social structures of the time. In geography the commercial and environmental emphases derive from an imperial and Darwinist milieu. The abstract models of location analysis, the market and functionalism are associated with positivism and the 'end of ideology' faith in technocratic planning. Market analogies and functionalism gloss over the role of power in social relations, as does the pluralist ideology from which they arose. Whiggish ideas of progress and harmony are upheld by neglecting the persistence of injustice.
>
> (Gilbert, 1984, p. 229)

Gilbert's argument is that the images of economy, society and polity in the social subjects fail to provide students with a critical understanding of the world. This is explained by the notion of ideology. He suggests that subjects such as geography promote a conservative view of the world that accepts existing social relations and serves to deny any discussion of alternative ways of organising society. Geography thus plays an important part in promoting 'false consciousness' and legitimising capitalism. While a focus on ideology offers one explanation of how conservative ideas come to dominate in geography teaching, it tends to gloss over the question of how such ideologies are produced and reproduced. In what follows, I want to suggest that we can begin to comprehend the difficulties we face in realising such goals as teaching for a sustainable society through a consideration of the wider social and political context in which we work.

THE POLITICAL GEOGRAPHY OF CONSENSUS

Mohan (1999), echoing political economists, argues that during the period from 1945 to the mid-1970s the economic and social geography of Britain was shaped by a broad consensus comprising, among other things, a commitment to full employment, Keynesian techniques of economic management, the welfare state and a strong regional policy. Gamble (1989) describes the political geography of the consensus. He notes that it was underpinned by a particular territorial code and by a set of political institutions. Both Labour and Conservatives were national parties seeking power at the centre of a unitary state and using national ideologies and national appeals to win support throughout the country. While both parties appealed to different sections of the population, and had clear bases of regional support, they shared agreement on many aspects of policy.

In this context of broad consensus or 'one-nation' politics, supported by a background of economic growth and Britain's pre-eminence in world affairs, it is unsurprising that geography took on many of the assumptions and outlooks that characterised the wider polity, society and culture. A look at several texts widely used in courses on the UK's human geography at the start of the 1970s provides an interesting view of the way the subject dealt with its concerns. For example, Stamp and Beaver's (1971) influential textbook amounted to a detailed description of Britain's physical resources and their exploitation, and detailed accounts of the physical characteristics of places. The book gives around 350 pages to the description of heavy industries, and the geographical patterns of these are explained in terms of their location factors. It would be hard to imagine a similar text today, not least because little of the industry described by Stamp and Beaver remains. House's *The UK Space* took a different approach. House (1973) placed a considerable degree of faith in the capacity for planning. He spoke of the possibility of 'more comprehensive regional planning', and concluded that 'the necessary further management of the UK space . . . will not be feasible without . . . greater and more decisive public intervention to channel market forces in the national interest'. The faith in rational planning is also found in Chisholm and Manners's (1971) book on the *Spatial Problems of the British Economy*. They discuss how 'geographical space' is becoming a new dimension of public concern and policy:

> The undoubted achievement of the welfare state in demolishing the principal bastions of inequality have exposed more vividly than ever before the causes for equalitarian public concern, amongst which are several characterised by their spatial as much as by their social nature.
>
> (Chisholm and Manners, 1971, p. 16)

The answer to solving these spatial problems is planning, to provide a 'more relevant framework for the administration of public decisions' (p. 19).

Like all texts, these books were a product of their time. Viewed from the standpoint of the beginning of the twenty-first century we are struck by some of the important lacunae. For instance, in the texts I have mentioned here, political geography hardly warrants a mention, and the role of the state is not explicitly considered except as a tool for making things happen. Social polarisation, poverty and other planes of division are absent, despite the 'rediscovery of poverty' in other disciplines from the mid-1960s onwards. The UK's geography is discussed with little reference to its place in the wider world. Again, despite the growth of an environmental lobby, there is little sense that these concerns impinged on the geographical imagination. Environmental issues receive little attention other than resource inventories and consideration of how to maximise their supply and use.

These textbooks reflect a discipline that was only just beginning to engage with social issues and break out of its regionalist and determinist legacies (Mohan, 1999). These core texts had an influence on the school textbooks of the time. But there is also a wider context in which these books were written. They reflect what now appears as an era of steady growth, social harmony and rising prosperity, and political consensus. Their timing is important, since they appeared before the world economic recession of 1973/74. The sense of a 'world we have lost' comes through clearly in the preface to the third edition of *The UK Space* in 1982. House notes that the book, which had begun, in the 1970s, as a 'national stock-taking', became a 'commentary and interpretation of dramatic and rapidly shifting trends':

> The great debate has shifted in focus, from growth to stabilization or the counteracting of decline, from environmental enhancement to its protection, from regional equilibrium to regional economic survival, from devolution to resisting the centralizing power of the State, and from full employment to the consequences of mass unemployment.

The tone of House's conclusion to the 1982 edition is less upbeat. He expresses the hope that the abrupt end to regional planning in 1979 will be no more than a passing phase so that the country can return to prosperity and strengthen social harmony by the end of the century.

These texts can be read as the products of an earlier style of geography, but, more importantly, as products of a particular political era. The gap between 1973 and 1982 was only a decade, but it was a decade in which many of the old certainties about economic, social, political and cultural life in Britain were eroded. In 1982, it may have been possible to imagine that normal service would soon be resumed.

In these conditions, school geography served to offer a particular perspective on the world. The approach that developed in the postwar period has been described as one of 'enlightened traditionalism' (Beddis, 1983). School geography provided students with knowledge of the physical and human environments. In relation to human geography, this was largely a description of patterns of population, settlement and economic activity, realised through the study of places and regions. Where explanations for these patterns were offered, these tended to be framed in terms of ideas about environmental determinism. Social issues were largely ignored, which reflected a number of factors, including ideas about the strict academic division of labour, the professional responsibility of teachers to be neutral and avoid controversy, and the general climate of consensus, planning and the belief in progress. From the 1960s, however, geography was subject to important changes. This was linked to a series of factors that there were influencing the school curriculum including: government pressure for more and better scientists, the anticipated raising of the school leaving age to 16, the amalgamation of grammar and secondary modern schools into comprehensives, and the demand for student participation. One response to these changes was the introduction of more scientific and quantitative approaches that were increasingly found in university courses. These ideas were seized upon by heads of department in some schools in order to argue for greater resources and gain the prestige associated with a more 'scientific' approach. In line with ideas about technocratic management of resources and environment by the state, school geography took on perspectives from the wider discipline that stressed the importance of management and planning (Huckle, 1985).

In summary, dominant forms of geography education in the postwar period served to project and reproduce images of a settled society, largely based on consensus and the idea of the possibility of progress and harmonious relationships between people and environment. In many ways this reflected the human geography of the United Kingdom. With the onset of economic recession in the 1970s and the renewed 'crisis of capital', these images of the UK's geography were shattered, with important implications for geography teaching.

THE POLITICAL GEOGRAPHY OF CRISIS

Eighteen years later, House's conclusion in *The UK Space* appears overoptimistic. Instead of the hoped-for return to the older certainties about regional planning, prosperity and social harmony, the decade that followed saw the publication of a whole series of geographical texts that charted the 'break-up' of Britain. The titles of these are indicative of the mood of many geographers in this period: Hudson and Williams' (1995) *Divided Britain*, Lewis and Townsend's (1989), *The North–South Divide*, Cloke's (1992) *Policy and Change in Thatcher's Britain*, and Johnston et al.'s (1988) *A Nation Dividing?* These books (often made up of collections of edited chapters) can be read as part of the geographical Left's attempt to make sense of the changes that took place under Mrs Thatcher's governments. There were some important changes taking place here. The old Marxist political-economic approaches were rapidly merged with developments in other disciplines that were attempting to account for the decline of Labour politics and the new landscape of Britain. Much of this work was involved in mapping the changes but some geographers were concerned to offer accounts of the changes, a task which meant engaging with social and political theory. These accounts pointed to the fact that the Conservative government inherited in 1979 a country divided in various ways – by class, gender, race and location. They argue that it was to become even more divided in the 1980s. However, these accounts tend to point to the political intent involved in the widening of these divisions. Hudson and Williams, writing at the end of a decade of Thatcher's policies, argued that 'the North–South divide has deliberately been redefined and enhanced as part of the political strategy of Thatcherism. It was and is intimately connected to its electoral prospects' (p. 165).

There is insufficient space here to fully document the policies that were adopted under the Conservative governments. However, it is worth noting the ways in which the national space economy was altered. Martin and Sunley (1997) argue that under the postwar consensus the national economy was the key geographical unit of economic organisation, accumulation and regulation. There was also a degree of spatial centralisation of the economy and integration via welfare policies designed to foster consistent national standards across the regions of the UK. The economic policies of the period were aimed at the redistribution of wealth with the effect of reducing inter-regional income differentials through public expenditure and public employment. The reversal of these policies in the 1980s had important consequences. The exposure of the national economy to external influences in the form of globalisation means that regions within Britain have been exposed to the intense competition and uncertainties linked with the global economy. Individual regions and localities are more prone to external shocks. The privatisation of public industries and the shake out in public employment have exacerbated the problems and the shift in welfare ideologies have had serious implications for particular social groups in these areas.

It is not possible here to provide a full summary of the work done by geographers in documenting the effects of the break-up of consensus. However, Table 14.1 does attempt to convey some of the issues that were covered. The contents of the books

Table 14.1 Contents of texts that mapped the impact of Thatcherism

Lewis and Townsend (1989) *The North–South Divide:*
- Owner-occupied housing: a north–south divide
- The growth of financial centres and the location of non-financial HQs
- The geography of ill-health and health care
- The privatisation of education
- The division in voting patterns

Mohan (1989) *The Political Geography of Contemporary Britain:*
- Nationalism in a disunited kingdom
- Changing electoral geography
- The crisis of local government
- Deindustrialisation and state intervention
- Changing geography of trade unions
- The politics of race and segregation
- Women in Thatcher's Britain
- Transport policy
- The political geography of housing
- The geography of health care
- Policing the recession
- Environmental politics and policy in the 1980s

Cloke (1992) *Policy and Change in Thatcher's Britain*:
- Changing political relations
- The changing local state
- Changing planning relations
- The economy
- Housing
- Transport
- Health
- The city
- The countryside
- The environment
- Spatially uneven development
- Social divisions, income inequality and gender relations

listed reflect a concern with four major areas. First, there is a sense of economic change. Britain's economy is subject to deindustrialisation and manufacturing decline, which is only partly offset by the development of new types of work. These changes are seen as important because of their uneven impact on regions and localities in Britain. Second, there is a focus on the changing political relations of the British state. There is a recognition of the pressures for devolution in the context of heightened economic division, attempts to reassert central political control at various levels of the state, and the moves to reduce public expenditure and open up areas previously dominated by state provision to market forces. Third, there is a focus on the social effects of these developments, with a concentration on divisions along axes of race and gender. Finally, the environment is recognised as an important area of political tension and debate. These add up to a renewed agenda for geographical study.

The re-emergence of the crisis of capital from the late 1960s was marked in education by debates about the purposes of schooling. A particular concern for geography educators was how schools could incorporate the concerns of a large number of working-class children previously excluded from schools. The incorporation of newer groups of previously excluded groups of students due to comprehensivisation and the gradual spread of a public sector ideology among teachers led to alternative visions of the potential for school geography. As Huckle (1985) argued: 'While the majority of school geographers were preoccupied with the "new" geography, others were employing humanistic and structuralist philosophies to design lessons on such topics as environmental issues, global inequalities and urban redevelopment' (p. 301).

The type of geography education being advocated was a form of political education that was less concerned with the defence of geography per se than with the development of a broader social education. The flavour of these alternatives can be seen in the issues of the journal *Contemporary Issues in Geography and Education* published by the Association for Curriculum Development between 1984 and 1987. The concerns mirrored those of the geographical Left: racism, sexism, wealth and poverty, environmental degradation, war and conflict. Geography teachers were engaging in wider debates about the nature of the school. These new developments were the subject of critique by the New Right in the 1980s, and this critique was accompanied by calls for the return of traditional subject-based teaching. In terms of geography, this 'discourse of derision' (Ball, 1994) took the form of an attack on progressive teaching methods that meant that children no longer knew where places were. The place of geography in the school curriculum became the subject of public debate in the 1980s when the Secretary of State for Education, Sir Keith Joseph, addressed the Geographical Association and challenged geographers to justify the place of the subject in the school curriculum. In relation to geography the argument was about the extent to which the teaching of content – by which was meant 'facts' – was being undermined by a focus on values and attitudes.

It is now perhaps possible to understand the context in which Gilbert's assessment of the school geography curriculum was made. In the 1980s – in the midst of profound economic, social and political change – geography continued to provide images of the world that relied on older models of explanation. Machon (1987) provides an interesting account for the reluctance of geography teachers to take on board newer perspectives in human geography. He suggests that while the introduction of the quantitative revolution was readily incorporated into syllabuses and textbooks, the results were uneven. In physical geography the new approaches made real advances in understanding possible. In human geography, though, the models and quantitative approaches did not generate explanation. However, continued change was inhibited by the memory of previous upheavals and the constraints of precise syllabuses. The result was a 'period of consolidation' and the retention of a crudely positivist human geography. In addition changes in the context of education inhibited reform in school geography. Machon suggests that the incorporation of child-centred approaches to education (which were actively embraced by the new geography) brought with them an increased awareness of the sensibilities of pupils, especially with issues of race, religion, class and gender. There was thus a fear of offending parental sensibilities and the common sense was to keep politics out of the classroom. The effect of this was to be tempted to handle only socially validated 'controversial' issues (for example, the impact of motorways, London's third airport).

Machon concludes that teachers are essentially conformist, for their work is frequently defined in terms of service to others at the same time as involving a socialising and accrediting role. The stress on the importance of subject matter, the establishment of uniform and distancing patterns of authority and an acceptance that some issues are 'not suitable for the children' means that many controversial issues, explanatory models and radical perspectives are off limits in the geography classroom. This 'slows the pace of change in political, economic and social processes and underwrites the status quo'.

Similarly, Goodson (1994) reminds us that at the very moment that the 'nation' is seen to fragment or become increasingly divided, the state seeks to promote the idea of a national curriculum. This begs the question of whose 'nation' is being promoted? Goodson argues that the re-establishment of 'traditional' forms of geography reflects the interests of middle-class parents. Thus, despite the official rhetoric of the national curriculum and the much vaunted claim that geography teachers have a great deal of freedom to interpret the curriculum in diverse ways, school geography harks back to traditional approaches and there are few alternative voices to be heard. The result is that many of the recent developments in geography that might enable teachers to teach about the issues raised by Jacobs in a serious way are marginalised in school geography.

TOWARDS SUSTAINABILITY

The geography of the UK is undergoing significant changes (Gardiner and Matthews, 2000). The imagined solution to the 'crisis' of the 1970s inaugurated by Thatcherism has been largely accepted by the new Labour government. The political geography of (the old) consensus is in the process of being replaced, and though there are clear signs of the direction we are headed, the outcomes of these changes are not yet known. However, in almost all areas of economic and social policy, important questions are being discussed. This is an exciting time to be teaching geography. However, there are real problems in the teaching of these issues, since they require a deeper understanding of politics and sociology than is common among geography teachers. Where these topics are engaged, they tend to be treated in a descriptive manner, something that has been aided by the greater availability of detailed statistics and information systems. For example, Daniel

Dorling's (1995) excellent *A New Social Atlas of Britain* provides a wealth of information about a whole range of issues. However, there is a danger of geography teachers falling into the trap of 'cartographic fetishism' whereby the focus is on ever more detailed mapping of social patterns at the expense of any real analysis of the social and political processes which produce these patterns. In order to overcome this problem, there needs to be a focus on analysing academic and political debates about these patterns. Allen et al. (1998) argue that space should be understood as the 'product of social relations ... the product of the networks, interactions, juxtapositions and articulations of the myriad of connections through which social phenomena are lived out'. This is admittedly a difficult idea to grasp, but what it means is that we need to pay attention to the processes (economic, political, social and cultural) that lead to the formation of human geographies, and the ways in which geographies shape social processes. For example, rather than simply map the patterns of social inequality in cities, we need to understand how categories of 'rich' and 'poor' are socially constructed, how they came to be coded in these ways, how they are contested and so on. The following paragraphs outline three areas in which geography can contribute to teaching for a 'sustainable society'.

Work

A major concern in sustainable societies is work. This relates to the availability of paid employment, the role of unpaid employment and issues to do with the quality of the work available to people. Geography teaching could provide students with an understanding of the changing nature of work in the contemporary world. This should focus on a range of scales from the local to the global. The focus would be on the various explanations for these changes, and developing students' knowledge of various theories about the economy. In addition students would learn about the ways in which governments seek to provide work. There needs to be a more wide-ranging discussion of the nature of work in contemporary societies, drawing on debates about the desirability of different types of work and the social relations that are involved in them (McDowell, 1999). In all this study, less emphasis should be placed on description and more on examining the various theories and debates about the world of work.

Social divisions

Students need to examine the extent to which social divisions are compatible with the achievement of a sustainable society. They need to be introduced to the way in which social divisions occur along lines of race, gender, age and class (Philo, 1995). In geography an important dimension of division is location. While there is a need to understand the empirical bases of these divisions, of equal importance is an understanding of the social processes that work to cause these divisions. These areas might include a study of inequalities in the provision of health and education, as well as the construction of groups such as the 'underclass'. The focus in this work would be on what might be done to reduce these social divisions (see Hill, 2000).

Environment

School geography has laid claim to the study of the environment in the school curriculum. In this, it has tended to focus on providing students with an understanding of a range of environmental issues and introduced them to the ways in which such problems can be managed. There is a large body of literature that teachers can draw upon in these areas. However, teaching for a sustainable environment raises important questions about the way these issues are handled in geography. The environment tends to be seen in physical terms rather than as a social construction. There is generally an avoidance of political issues in the study of these issues, and explanations fail to take into account the complex social causes of the problems (Huckle and Sterling, 1996).

CONCLUSION

This chapter is intended as an addition to the debate about the contribution geography can make to teaching for a sustainable society. I have argued that Rob Gilbert's statement about the failure of school subjects such as geography to provide students with plausible accounts of the social world must be understood in the context of the politics of the school curriculum. Geography as taught in schools largely reflects the conditions of an earlier era of consensus. While human geographers have developed more critical perspectives to explain the changing nature of society in the 1980s and 1990s, leading to a more politicised and theoretically inclined geography, school geography retains older representations of society and space, excluding topics and theories that might have provided relevant explanations. Following Goodson (1983), this is perhaps less the result of ideological imposition from above than the efforts of teachers in schools to retain the academic status of their discipline. However, it does reflect the social interests of geography teachers who tend to favour traditional approaches to their subject, as well as the policies of gatekeepers. Goodson suggests that one way of understanding our work as teachers is to gain a historical perspective on the type of subject positions available to us as teachers – in other words, to reflect upon the ways in which we habitually think and act as geography teachers are constructed for us. In doing so, we may come to understand our own social location as geography educators and reflect upon alternatives.

REFERENCES

Allen, J., Massey, D. and Cochrane, A. (1998) *Rethinking the Region*. London: Routledge.
Ball, S. (1994) *Education Reform: A Critical and Post-structural Approach*. London: Routledge.
Beddis, R. (1983) 'Geographical education since 1960: a personal view', in Huckle, J. (ed.), *Geographical Reflection: Reflection and Action*. London: Oxford University Press, pp. 10–19.
Chisholm, M. and Manners, G. (ed.) (1971) *Spatial Policy Problems of the United Kingdom*. Cambridge: Cambridge University Press.
Cloke, P. (ed.) (1992) *Policy and Change in Thatcher's Britain*. Oxford: Pergamon.
Dorling, D. (1995) *A New Social Atlas of Britain*. Chichester: Wiley.
Gamble, A. (1989) 'Thatcherism and the New Politics', in Mohan, J. (ed.), *The Political Geography of Contemporary Britain*. London: Macmillan, pp. 1–17.
Gardiner, V. and Matthews, H. (2000) *The Changing Geography of the United Kingdom*. London: Routledge.
Gilbert, R. (1984) *The Impotent Image: Reflections of Ideology in the Secondary School Curriculum*. London: The Falmer Press.
Goodson, I. (1983) *School Subjects and Curriculum Change*. Beckenham: Croom Helm.
Goodson, I. (1994) *Studying Curriculum*. Buckingham: Open University Press.
Hill, D. (2000) *Urban Policy and Politics in Britain*. London: Macmillan.

House, J.W. (ed.) (1973) *The UK Space: Resources, Environment and the Future*. London: Wiedenfield & Nicholson.
Huckle, J. (1985) 'Geography and schooling', in Johnston, R. (ed.), *The Future of Geography*. London: Methuen.
Huckle, J. and Sterling, S. (eds) (1996) *Education for Sustainability*. London: Earthscan.
Hudson, R. and Williams, A. (1995) *Divided Britain*. Chichester: Wiley.
Jacobs, M. (1996) *The Politics of the Real World*. London: Earthscan.
Johnston, R., Pattie, C. and Allsopp, J. (1988) *A Nation Dividing? The Electoral Map of Britain 1979–87*. Harlow: Longman.
Lewis, J. and Townsend, A. (eds) (1989) *The North–South Divide*. London: Paul Chapman.
McDowell, L. (1999) *Gender, Identity and Place: Understanding Feminist Geographies*. Cambridge: Polity Press.
Machon, P. (1987) 'Teaching controversial issues: some observations and suggestions', in Bailey, P. and Binns, T. (eds), *A Case for Geography*. Sheffield: Geographical Association.
Martin, R. and Sunley, P. (1997) 'The post-Keynesian state and the space economy', in Lee, R. and Wills, J. (eds), *Geographies of Economies*. London: Arnold, pp. 278–89.
Mohan, J. (1999) *A United Kingdom? Economic, Social and Political Geographies*. London: Arnold.
Philo, C. (ed.) (1995) *Off the Map: The Social Geography of Poverty in the UK*. London: CPAG.
Stamp, L.D. and Beaver, S. (1971) *The British Isles: A Geographic and Economic Survey*. London: Longman.

Chapter 15

Citizenship: the role of geography?

Paul Machon and Helen Walkington

CITIZENSHIP AND THE NATIONAL CURRICULUM

Teachers of civics worldwide will be surprised that only now does citizenship appear in England's schools, so central is it to most national curricula (http://www.inca/org.uk/). Almost as surprising has been the speed at which the introduction, consultation and development of this new addition to England's National Curriculum (NC) has taken place. It was only in November 1997 that a government White Paper, *Excellence in Schools* (DES, 1997), set out the initial terms of reference, the Advisory Group's first and final reports appearing within one year (QCA, March and September 1998). The QCA/DfEE Proposals were published in May–June 1999 (DfEE, 1999) and the Bill passed through the Commons in February 2000. This speed should not imply that this was an uncontested process or one incapable of producing surprises. Indeed it is with one of these that our tale starts, for the 1999 Proposals looked for 'the opportunities for developing a citizenship order in relation to the teaching of history, *geography* and English' (p. 14 – our emphasis).

GEOGRAPHY!

In Britain's schools, but interestingly not its universities, geography teaching is largely apolitical, working instead within long-established traditions that have underpinned the status quo. Contentious issues, if they are dealt with at all, are located in narrowly defined areas that inhibit the active involvement of pupils in the events themselves. There are exceptions to this, particularly in development education, environmental geography and the continuing debate about 'values' in geography. But such work is always limited by the choices teachers make within their own schools and the structural limits to choice such as examination syllabi and specifications. But these exceptions remind us that geography does have the potential to convey the contentious and political. Its content, after all, describes distributions, locating and accounting for differences (in short is relational) with profound political implications – Dicken and Lloyd's 'access to goods and proximity to bads' (1980, p. 281–361). Finally there is also geography's distinctive claim that here is a discipline that locks the use of natural worlds into the beliefs and actions of our social worlds.

The lack of experience that many geography teachers have in dealing with the political and contentious is a concern for citizenship education. One cause of this lack of experience is the way that disciplines are constituted – what is legitimate subject matter and what is not – and in school geography politics is so often excluded. Subjects build boundaries around themselves within which an orthodox body of work develops and significant transformations occur to new concepts that cross those borders to become absorbed in another discipline. This, we argue here, now has to happen to the political concept of citizenship in geography.

THIS CHAPTER

This chapter's concern is to reflect upon citizenship, a concept with the capacity (and now the opportunity) to 'cross those borders' and then to consider how citizenship may be taught through geography. This chapter comes from collaboration between a geographer and a political scientist and seeks to examine how these two disciplines can inform teachers of geography who wish to engage in citizenship education and to reflect upon that engagement. The opening section provides a theoretical account of citizenship, locating the NC proposals in a particular liberal and democratic tradition, before turning to a brief critique of such assumptions. It is our belief that an understanding of the formal political concept of citizenship is crucial to the development of critically reflective practitioners and we hope that some geographers will explore one of the many excellent introductions to political theory such as McClelland's *A History of Western Political Thought* (1998). However, at this point we think that it is important to note that political theory is properly a branch of moral philosophy, that is here we are primarily concerned with values. Consequently the final section develops the idea that how citizenship is taught through geography is at least as important as what is dealt with in the classroom. In both sections our aim is to begin a process of reflection amongst geography teachers in ways that we hope will allow the subject of geography to acquire this new material while maintaining its descriptive and explanatory power.

CITIZENSHIP

Citizenship is not a static concept but has evolved as social settings change. However, at its core, is the concept's concern with the iterative relationship between an individual's duties to the state within which they live and the rights they can expect to receive in return. Here the classical literature usually starts by describing the politics of the early Greek city-states – but our focus is the modern state.

One account of the development of the modern state is the story of the democratisation of social power (Mann, 1993) and the construction of systems to institutionalise and regulate that power. Some argue that modern states are defined by the possession of a single source of authority, deriving legitimacy from the people and operating through an efficient bureaucracy. What results must meet two demands: protecting the population from danger (both from within and without) and ensuring its own long-term future by doing this effectively. Here education plays a fundamental and geography a particular role in establishing parts of such hegemony. In the nineteenth century, for example, British geography was concerned with empire, informing and preparing the population to participate in an economy that enjoyed inexpensive supplies of raw materials, protected markets and frequently service overseas in the army and navy. None of this means that modern states become alike – quite the opposite, for as different state forms develop their varied history, the choice of political strategies and the ideologies employed in the search to find legitimacy ensure difference as well as similarity.

In much of Europe, North America and wherever a similar state form evolved, what developed can be described as liberal and representatively democratic. In these states the dominant economic system is capitalist (hence liberal), with the political system electing party-based representatives, often working in oppositional ways reflecting capitalism's tensions. These representatives are subject to periodic change by mass voting. Marshall (1950) offered a taxonomy of citizenship in such states as possessing three components, civil, political and social. The first permits individual freedom, most clearly expressed in terms of ownership and property. The second ensures the right to participate in mass voting and the right to hold political office. The last ensures the citizen's right to be part of society, usually expressed in terms of its standard of living. As a consequence of this last component the provision of welfare and education becomes a state's concern, for such provision ensures a continuing legitimacy with a citizenry who come to expect that their welfare and education will be protected. This is not to say that the state has to do the providing, but it is to say that it must assure that provision is made, even if that is through market processes. Presented in this way Marshall's description of citizenship is plain and desirable enough. However, in practice progress to this point has been slow, especially where citizenship was defined in exclusive terms, that is by defining a citizenry by excluding 'outsiders'. This approach was and is, at least initially, an easier political balance to maintain (Birnbaum and Katnelson, 1995), especially in states that developed strongly nationalist politics. In such states populist politics, mass culture and shared sentiment (see Figure 15.1) can combine to produce a polity that is united across other social distinctions like social class. It is also significant that no established power ever willingly relinquished its advantages to others on such a journey. It would be straightforward to present a history of the last centuries as the confrontational expansion of citizenship and there are echoes of this in much school geography.

At one level the symbolism of Jean-Jacques Waltz's cartoon in Figure 15.1 is clear enough even without its accompanying text. The sense of loss and sacrifice is accompanied by the sentimental image of the young girl dressed in the folk costume of a better time that has already passed. But the picture's resonance is far greater for those in the Alsace who have taken Waltz's work as somehow defining who they are, so much so that he has become *l'oncle Hansi*.

Proceeding from such accounts 'active citizenship' (Bendix, 1998) urges vigilance against the loss of rights or the expansion of duties without a concomitant increase in rights. Equally dangerous would be the development of an apathetic citizenry (or 'passive', Bendix again) because this threatens to relinquish power to the state by neglect. Rights can be eroded by the state itself – importantly liberal formulations of citizenship do not conceive of the state as intrinsically good but much more as a necessary evil upon which the cautious citizen keeps a suspicious eye.

The desire to include citizenship in the NC is driven by a concern about political apathy or disengagement and the threat that this poses to social inclusivity. This is

Figure 15.1 Cartoon by Jean-Jaques Waltz.

detailed in the Final Report in terms of falling voting figures among the young, although it is acknowledged that the figures themselves are disputed. It is therefore no surprise that the Report is firmly located within the liberal and democratic tradition that has been described. As the Final Report notes:

> The benefits of citizenship education will be: for pupils – an entitlement in schools that will empower them to participate effectively as active informed, critical and responsible citizens; . . . for society – an active and politically-literate citizenry convinced that they can influence government and community affairs at all levels.
>
> (QCA, 1998, p. 9)

LIBERAL FOR WHOM?

The liberal democratic account of citizenship has critics, however unproblematic the account may seem to have been so far. Some of the criticisms, we suggest here, are of particular importance to those now charged with teaching citizenship within the NC and are also relevant where civics is already taught.

Citizenship – at least the classical liberal formulation of it – is an abstract political concept. It tends to be presented as a series of opposites: state and individual, market and consumer, rights and duties. It has also been noted that classical liberalism is suspicious of the state and this locates three critical themes that we now touch upon: the location of social power, the state's desire to protect itself and the risk that liberalism poses to an individual's rights.

Because the concept is an abstract one liberal citizenship is rather poor at describing the material and unequal distribution of social power. An individual's power is always likely to be limited by the greater power of others. This can be seen in structured ways in social differentiation based on socio-economic class, ethnicity, gender and age. Many of the 'limits' are market-based and so appear to operate through inviolable and natural laws. Market forces, it is frequently argued, remove jobs from parts of the world where labour is expensive and relocate them where it is cheaper, so underpinning 'globalisation'. Other inequalities, for example in the quality of publicly provided education, are tacitly authorised by the state (Goodin and LeGrand, 1987).

The impact of all these inequalities is seen in differences in the provision of goods, access to finance and the standard of services provided. These combine to produce distinctive spatial patterns of production and consumption. Among the key services is education, where differentiated provision threatens any formation of a meritocracy. The spatial inequalities that result could be an important focus of school geography – but raise a thorny issue. Presenting the evidence of such spatial inequalities is relatively straightforward, but teachers would be hard-pressed to provide students who recognised themselves as victims of these inequalities with the ability and the optimism of spirit to respond to the challenges positively – which we may term *empowerment*. Indeed, providing an authentic and credible account of an individual's weak position without empowerment would be doubly alienating and so even more likely to disenfranchise.

Earlier in the chapter much was made of the 'state's management of its own authority'. This is effected in part by ensuring an appropriate standard of living for people, meeting Marshall's 'social' element of citizenship. This is not easy in capitalist states where losers outnumber winners and the taxation of the latter may be a disincentive to their enterprise. The state's task is approached by endeavouring to establish inequality as both legitimate and 'natural' so that its presence remains unremarkable and unchallenged – even by the losers. It is a conventional criticism of education that schools play a part in constructing this ideology and operate as both agents and microcosms of the state. Certainly they can be concerned with their own authority and at times even against the interests of pupils as classic studies like Willis (1977) showed. This locates a key difficulty, for teaching citizenship is the search for reflection, participation and action – but within structures that are often profoundly authoritarian.

Again the material difficulty remains that rights to citizenship are linked to one's social power and social power is directly related to the inequalities that people experience. Classical liberalism portrays the state as some sort of neutral referee, managing the inevitable tensions and arbitrating between those in dispute on the worth of the case. This neutrality is challenged if the state's relationship with business and the effect of insider pressure groups, the media and others with power are examined. This also happens at a global scale, where the role of multinationals is an important part of any account of why development has been so hard to effect in much of the world. This reminder of the relative power of some states and some companies may cause the neutral-liberal model of the state to be replaced with one that sees the state behaving with both bias and independence. As a result, at times, the state will ally itself with the powerful, and then on other occasions will act against them in pursuit of its own legitimacy – precisely the sort of arbitrary behaviour that so alarms classical liberals about the state.

Finally, classical liberalism, being suspicious of politics, sees 'being a citizen' as only one aspect of life and not central to it, for, it follows, privileging 'the private' must reduce citizenship's importance. Placing the individual first also makes it harder to encourage them to take courses of action that are for others, or universal, and far easier to create individuated, or particular, decision-makers even when it can be demonstrated that those decisions are against the common good. In practice people live between these two states – perhaps this is a description of a modern citizen – without either category being fully distinct. As important, no one is able to be entirely private because the aggregated results of all those individual and self-serving decisions will eventually damage the common good so extensively that its impact will re-enter and put at risk the private realm. This would threaten the sustainability of any social system, and any state.

'DEEP' CITIZENSHIP

The challenge posed by this critique is whether it is possible to form another view of citizenship, one that establishes links between public and private actions so that personal or particular decision-making takes into account universal concerns – indeed they become one. If it is possible to form such a view the real challenge is to prepare students for this, rather than the more passive, shallow or narrowly liberal citizenship.

To be a citizen in the neutral-liberal sense is to describe a very limited form of citizenship, one that elevates self-interest, reduces political activity to infrequent voting and so reduces universalistic decision-making. An alternative, sometimes called 'deep citizenship', argues that the particular and the universal must not be separated, that political reflection is central to doing this and that politics is more central to life that classical liberalism maintains (Clarke, 1996). Such an approach would require students to reflect upon the consequences of all their actions, and here knowledge of the natural and social worlds would be crucial. It would also be important because such an approach could reduce the penetration into students' thinking of the 'Eichmann prinzip' (pp. 91–2), the abdication of moral decision-making to others: 'I'm not responsible, I'm only a technician; I'm only following orders.'

CITIZENSHIP THROUGH GEOGRAPHY

The previous section has considered how a liberal notion of citizenship can be extended to take into account 'deep' notions of the concept. It has raised theoretical issues of relevance to a teacher of geography engaging in education for citizenship. However, Shermis and Barth (1982) noted that despite good theoretical knowledge of citizenship it remains difficult to influence practice. The following section considers how citizenship can inform the teaching of geography at secondary level. This section includes some practical strategies. The section also emphasises the importance of reflection with regard to the practice of teaching citizenship through geography.

Geography and citizenship share many common concepts and skills (see Table 15.1), but perhaps the area of most significant overlap is within the realm of teaching about values and attitudes. All forms of education take place in a particular social context and are inherently value-laden. Geography, as with any other subject, can therefore be viewed as a vehicle for values education (Slater, 1994) or moral teaching (Smith, 1995). However, within geography there are many different approaches available to the teacher and the methodology adopted in the classroom in particular conveys clear as well as subtle values messages. Citizenship education, through geography, can be viewed as a structured values education entitlement for students within which the simple transmission of values from teacher to learner is avoided and where students are encouraged to think and then behave independently and critically. This aim is made explicit in the Final Report (QCA, 1998, p. 13): 'Citizenship education is education for citizenship, behaving and acting as a citizen, therefore it is not just knowledge of citizenship and civic society; it also implies developing values, skills and understanding.'

Table 15.1 Some of the values, concepts and skills shared by citizenship and geography education

Values and attitudes	*Concepts*	*Skills*
• Social justice	• Interdependence	• Critical thinking
• A sense of place	• Sustainability	• Decision-making
• A sense of community	• Change	• Reflection
• Empathy	• Place	
• Respects and values diversity	• Cultural diversity	

We have noted that central to the notion of being a reflective citizen is the idea that young people must have an understanding of how the world works. In particular we would argue that this understanding of geographical processes, simultaneously economic, social, environmental, physical and political, is fundamental, informing reflection, decision-making and participation in society. The discipline also has the potential to begin to develop in young people a sense of their role as global citizens responsible for the outcomes of their actions because of the subject's sophisticated sense of scale (Machon, 1998). This returns us to the theme of all personal or private actions having social or public consequences. Geography's distinctive spatial perspective is able to develop a realisation that local (or private) actions result in global (universal) or geographically dispersed consequences. This notion is central to the themes of globalisation and interdependence, linking citizenship and geography at secondary level (QCA, 1999). The work of Massey and Jess (1995) reveals the importance of conveying a global sense of place. Thus to understand our own locality we must understand how it is linked to other places. This reinforces the importance of actions at the local level to our global future. The lesson idea outlined in Box 1 reflects these concepts.

Box 1 – Lesson: 'Local Actions - Global Consequences' (Year 12/13)

All actions have consequences.

- Ask students to brainstorm everyday actions that they feel may have environmental consequences, for instance using a mobile phone, recycling or throwing away a drinks can, buying sweets.

Local actions can have far reaching consequences.

- In pairs plot with annotated arrows a single action and all the consequences or connections to other spatial scales on a diagram made of concentric circles indicating differing scales from local (inner circle) to global (outer circle).

Sometimes actions today only have consequences later – the activity can be repeated with short-term, medium-term and long-term impact circles if desired.

- Consider how the scale at which some consequences are felt allows people to 'forget' that their actions have impacts elsewhere.
- Now ask the students to think of the way that their own behaviour connects them to the wider world (for example, the spatial impact of their consumer decisions, especially in relation to multinational companies).

Introduce the concept of 'ecological footprint' – an individual's environmental impact on the world. (NB: Environmental impacts can be positive as well as negative.)

- Consider with the students how the scale of their impacts are great (large footprints), whereas the impact of people in rural areas in the developing world, for instance, remain at a local or regional level (small footprint).

The lesson described in the box opens up a critical perspective on taken-for-granted geographical descriptions of phenomena such as globalisation and relationships between the core and periphery and can begin to account for these patterns in political terms. Geography is well placed to demonstrate that spatial inequalities and unsustainable environmental diseconomies are related to the aggregated behaviour of individuals. From this viewpoint students can then begin to consider whether 'globalisation' is, as the term suggests, really an indomitable, worldwide force following an implacable logic. They can also begin to critically examine how individual behaviour contributes to these social outcomes and so consider their own behaviour.

Introducing the concept of core–periphery relationships warrants a further comment. In Friedman's theory (1966) it was argued that growth and prosperity in the core eventually 'trickled down' into the periphery. So, for example, countries in the developing world involved in the production of food for UK supermarkets would eventually benefit from a process of 'development'. A second trickle-down mechanism suggests that in the core, success would raise direct costs like land and labour and indirect costs like congestion and pollution and so begin the transfer of investment to the periphery. In short the logic of market structures would do their work. Again this account is a narrowly liberal one that plays down the part that people (or agents) can play among larger structures. But there is another – and a critical – interpretation of the same phenomenon. In this second account the power of the core is exerted over the periphery in terms of powerful individuals and agencies which allocate growth to their own advantage. So, for example, desirable rural landscapes have been preserved for leisure and recreation, while flows of labour and capital develop that preserve the periphery's subservient status. In this account trickle-down now conspicuously fails to work and the outcome is a spatially differentiated one, for example as 'North' and 'South' in the UK or indeed at a global scale, creating resistant regional disparities. For geography teachers the significance of this example is that when teaching geographical theories or concepts it is important to develop the contestability of the theoretical accounts that are used. In this way the critical skills of students will be enhanced.

PARTICIPATION

The QCA (1999) document that outlined the legal requirements for citizenship education at Key Stages 3 and 4 described citizenship education as giving 'pupils the knowledge, skills and understanding to play an effective role in society at local, national and international levels' (p. 12). The obvious implication that this has for encouraging students to participate in activities reveals a clear agenda for active learning and therefore any planning of citizenship education through geography must pay great attention to the teaching methods adopted. The content of the citizenship curriculum (QCA, 1999) corresponds closely to specific geographical themes. At Key Stage 3, for example, the topic of population and migration can be used to give pupils a greater understanding of the diversity of national, regional, religious and ethnic identities in the UK. Similarly, while learning about sustainable development pupils can gain a greater understanding of the environmental implications of the world as a global community. However, it would be possible to teach about migration and sustainability in such a way as to bypass these opportunities for citizenship education, the difference primarily being made in decisions about the approach in the classroom. Roberts (1996) evaluated different teaching styles and strategies on a continuum of increasing learner participation. Lynch (1992) noted the importance of real participation in learning and Hart (1992) extended this work by defining citizenship education as being where the facilitative role of the teacher ensures pupil–centred learning rather than manipulation or tokenism in relation to the teacher's own agenda.

For example, a teacher could encourage his or her pupils to collect data about their families as far back in their family trees as they can. This would be a genuine geographical enquiry whatever the scale of the movement and migration that was uncovered, and provide information about changing patterns of marriage, of family size and life expectancy. Significantly the children are participating in their own learning, are researchers, are taking responsibility for the collection, analysis and presentation of their data and will be working collaboratively. In contrast the same teacher could adopt a more didactic style with students following this work with a data response activity leading to geographical but not necessarily contextual, holistic or personally meaningful learning. The difference in method is the difference between an encounter with some attributes of being a citizen through geography and teaching geography in isolation.

Box 2 below provides lesson ideas which are pupil centred to ensure citizenship as well as geographical learning takes place. Such activities encourage learners to create their own geographical knowledge, making it personally meaningful.

Box 2 – Activity: 'Relying on Other People and Places' (Years 7–9)

Homework

- Ask the students to choose one place in their house, for example a cupboard in the kitchen, a wardrobe. Then they should find out where all the items in this place are made.

Classwork

- Provide an outline map of the world on which the students should plot the places as accurately as possible.

Follow-up work

- As a challenge, students could be asked to design a local product which can be made, sold, marketed and packaged in the local community. This may inspire them to consider what life would be like if we weren't interdependent with other people and places.

This activity can draw out key issues of fair trade, trade embargoes/sanctions and their effects on people's lives. It would also be a good opportunity to introduce a simulation exercise to promote cooperative skills.

The research results in Table 15.2 show the relationship between educational aims and classroom approaches for two groups of practitioners. It shows that those who aimed only to teach geography (Group A) did so in a descriptive way, whereas those whose aims extended also to conveying elements of citizenship consistent with geography teaching (Group B) relied upon participatory classroom methods (e.g. role-play, collaborative group work, simulation and discussion). This research is reported more fully elsewhere (Walkington, 1999a, 1999b).

Table 15.2 Teachers' aims and practice

	Group A only	*Shared by teachers in Groups A and B*	*Group B only*
Aims	Knowledge and comparative skills	Increase cultural awareness and have positive images, values and attitudes.	Critical thinking. A global perspective. Develop an understanding of citizenship
Practice	Objective description through information gathering	Images and values through discussion. Promote a positive image, giving a cultural focus.	Issues-based learning to develop critical thinking through experiential activities with a citizenship aim. Pupils are actively involved in their own learning

Participatory practice is also emphasised in Oxfam's curriculum for Global Citizenship (1997) and such active methods are shared with education for sustainability, development education and environmental education.

REFLECTING ON PRACTICE – RESEARCH FINDINGS

The importance of reflecting on one's practice has been highlighted by many authors (see, for example, Pollard and Tann, 1993). The model shown in Figure 15.2 was used as a tool to stimulate reflection on the methods used to convey geographical themes. These methods were described as two extremes: 'How' type methods which focused on teacher-led description and 'Why' type methods, which revolved around enquiry-based learning with a high level of learner control. Each type of teaching method had accompanying descriptors tailored to the specific geographical topic being studied. The model was used by individual teachers placing a vertical line in the place that they felt best represented their practice, so for example line A represents a predominantly 'How' type teacher, the dotted line is an even balance between How and Why type approaches and line B a predominantly 'Why' type teacher. The line then became the starting point for a conversation about their aims, practice, desired practice and constraints upon achieving this.

The use of the How–Why model with 25 teachers had the following outcomes:

- Teachers clarified their actual and desired practice and how these differed. This initiated thinking about how practice could be developed.
- The constraints on desired practice were identified.
- Teachers considered a range of alternatives to their existing practice (by reading the descriptors of alternative types of practice).
- Teachers were able to clarify, through conversation, the philosophical commitments behind their educational aims.
- All teachers reported the desire to increase the proportion of their practice that was described as 'Why' type, a view consistent with an approach to teaching geography which could incorporate citizenship.

Teachers clearly benefited from structured thinking and discussion about methodological aspects of their practice, which could be replicated by members of staff within geography departments as a form of professional development.

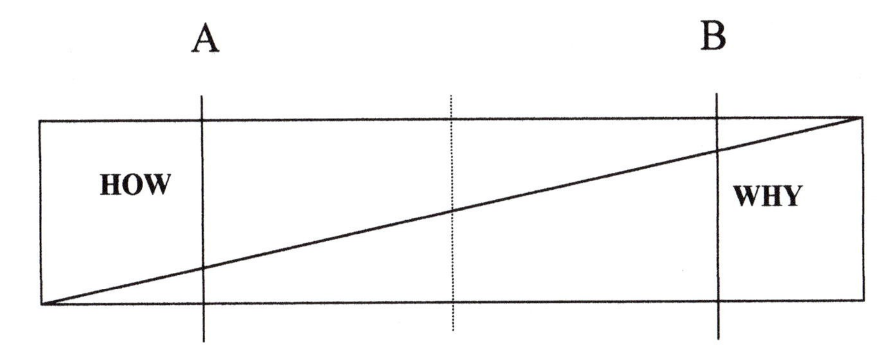

Figure 15.2 The How-Why model for teacher reflection.

CONCLUSION

This chapter began by arguing that, as citizenship becomes part of what geography teachers cover in their classrooms, there will need to be an encounter with political theory and the incorporation of some of its insights into geography. A liberal formulation of citizenship was then set out and with it the contemporary perception of disengagement among the young and the risk of a too passive citizenry within a too strong state. Such a formulation, the argument continued, permitted a ready acceptance of inequalities as they seemed to be 'naturally' structured into society. This led to a critique that suggested that the opening definition of citizenship had been too narrow and that, to avoid the inherent dangers in such a definition, private decision-making must more thoroughly consider the impact of those decisions in the public sphere – termed 'deep citizenship'. These considerations could begin to be explored by geography teaching that allowed learners to reflect upon their actions. Such work drew upon the experience of values education as well as geography's ability to deal with the distribution of inequalities and relational connections and its tradition of considering both the physical and social world. The chapter concluded with some detailed references to classroom settings where such considerations were central and it was further noted that the process of teaching is as important as the content taught.

REFERENCES

Bendix, R. (1996) *Nation-Building and Citizenship*, 3rd edn. New Brunswick, NJ: Transaction Publishers.

Birnbaum, P. and Katnelson, I. (1995) *Paths of Emancipation: Jews, States and Citizenship*. Princeton, NJ: University of Princeton Press.

Clarke, P.B. (1996) *Deep Citizenship*. London: Pluto Press.

DES (1997) *Excellence in Schools*. London: HMSO.

DfEE/Qualifications and Curriculum Authority (1998) *The Review of the National Curriculum in England. The Secretary of State's Proposals*. London: DfEE/QCA.

Dicken, P. and Lloyd, P.E. (1980) *Modern Western Society: A Geographical Perspective on Work, Home and Well-Being*. London: Harper Row.

Friedmann, J. (1966) *Regional Development Policy: A Case Study of Venezuela*. Cambridge, MA: MIT Press.

Goodin, R.E. and LeGrand, J. (1987) *Not Only the Poor*. London: Allen & Unwin.

Hart, R. (1992) *Children's Participation: from Tokenism to Citizenship*. Florence, Italy: UNICEF, International Child Development Centre.

Lynch, J. (1992) *Education for Citizenship in a Multicultural Society*. London: Cassell.

McClelland, J.S. (1998) *A History of Western Political Thought*. London: Routledge/Taylor & Francis.

Machon, P. (1998) 'Citizenship and geographical education', *Teaching Geography*, vol. 23, no. 3, pp. 115–17.

Mann M. (1993) *The Sources of Social Power, Volume II. The Rise of Classes and Nation-States, 1760–1914*. Cambridge: Cambridge University Press.

Marshall, T.H. (1950) 'Citizenship and social class', in *Sociology at the Cross-Roads* (1963), London: Heinemann.

Massey, D. and Jess, P. (eds.) (1995) *A Place in the World? Places Cultures and Globalisation*. Oxford: Oxford University Press in association with the Open University.

National Curriculum Council (1990) *Education for Citizenship. Curriculum Guidance 8*. York:

National Curriculum Council.
Oxfam (1997) *A Curriculum for Global Citizenship*. London: Oxfam.
Pollard, A. and Tann, S. (1993) *Reflective Teaching in the Primary School: A Handbook for the Classroom*. London: Cassell.
Qualifications and Curriculum Authority (1998) *Education of Citizenship and the Teaching of Democracy in Schools*. London: QCA.
Qualifications and Curriculum Authority (1999) *Citizenship: The National Curriculum for England Key Stages 3–4*. London: DfEE/QCA.
Roberts, M. (1996) 'Teaching styles and strategies', in Kent, A. et al. (eds), *Geography in Education: Viewpoints on Teaching and Learning*. Cambridge: Cambridge University Press.
Shermis, S.S. and Barth, J.L. (1982) 'Teaching for passive citizenship: a critique of philosophical assumptions', *Theory and Research in Social Education*, vol. 10, no. 4, pp. 17–37.
Slater, F. (1994) 'Education through geography: knowledge, understanding, values and culture', *Geography*, vol. 79, pp. 147–63.
Smith, D.M. (1995) 'Moral teaching in geography', *Journal of Geography in Higher Education*, vol. 19, no. 3, pp. 271–83.
Walkington, H. (1999a) 'Reflections of places, reflecting on practice: on the teaching of a developing locality in primary school geography', unpublished PhD thesis. University of Reading.
Walkington, H. (1999b) *Theory into Practice: Global Citizenship Education*. Sheffield: Geographical Association.
Willis, P. (1977) *Learning to Labour: How Working Class Kids get Working Class Jobs*. Farnborough: Saxon House.

Chapter 16

Managing a geography department

Charlie Carpenter and Ian Langrish

INTRODUCTION

The saying 'Jack of all trades, master of none' is not too far removed from the requirements needed to manage geography in the secondary school curriculum today. The role of subject manager involves a considerable amount of organisational skill in juggling a wide range of responsibilities for both people and resources. The Office for Standards in Education highlighted the crucial role of heads of department in their report on 'Subject Management in Secondary Schools – Aspects of Good Practice: 'The management role of the head of department in secondary schools is crucial if the quality of teaching is to be high and pupils of all abilities are to make good progress' (OFSTED, 1997). Underpinning the work of the head of department is the need to raise the quality and standards of teaching and the learning experiences of pupils to enhance pupil attainment. This is against a background since the 1988 Education Reform Act and the introduction of the National Curriculum of increasing political intervention in the school curriculum and continual changes to public examination syllabuses and requirements. Running a secondary school geography department therefore constantly provides a challenge. This is reflected in the example of a job description shown in Figure 16.1 for the role of the head of department (see also Wiegand, 1989). Further guidance on managing geography in schools is also to be found in the Teacher Training Agency's National Standards for Subject Leaders (1998) and Leading Geography – National Standards for Geography Leaders in Secondary Schools (Geographical Association, 1999).

Geography teaching at Key Stage 4/GCSE (General Certificate of Secondary Education) and Post-16 level is an increasingly competitive situation within the curriculum with numbers taking geography courses steadily declining in recent years. Market forces, pupil perceptions about fashionable subjects and media influences mean that geography needs to be rigorously and positively promoted, and sold to both parents and pupils in an informed and challenging manner. The advent of the Geographical Association's 'Geography Action Week' provides opportunities to offer activities that develop a broader interest level in the subject beyond the classroom norm and the GA has produced a range of publications to assist geography departments in promoting the subject (see Kent, 1999). Use of poster displays focusing on 'Why study Geography?' and geography careers information (see Palot, 1999) together with

JOB DESCRIPTION – Head of Department

MAIN PURPOSE OF THE JOB:

- To ensure the development of pupils by teaching the curriculum, with due regard for the aims and objectives of the school and the needs of individual pupils
- To manage your department within the limitation of the resources allocated

1. RELATIONSHIPS

1.1 Responsible to:

- The head

1.2 Responsible for

- The pupils in your charge;
- The staff in your department.

1.3 Important relationships

- Pupils
- Parents
- Other members of staff
- Governors
- Staff in other schools
- Your link person on the Management Committee

MAIN RESPONSIBILITIES OF THE JOB

2.1 Curriculum

- Preparing, reviewing and keeping up to date a departmental handbook to include schemes of work for all classes and all years; bearing in mind the school's objectives
- Monitoring marking, homework setting and progress for each teaching group
- Keeping up-to-date with latest curriculum developments, especially the National Curriculum and changes
- Being involved in the school's curriculum development process
- Taking note of equal opportunities
- Taking responsibility for any student teachers within the department
- Ensuring that for external examinations, the entries, moderating procedures, coursework submission, attainment targets and records of achievement are completed and at the correct times and that records are kept
- Ensuring that for internal examinations the papers are set, reproduced, marked and moderated correctly
- Advising the timetable team on staffing and room requirements
- Producing a departmental development plan for inclusion in the School Development Plan
- Reporting to governors
- Promoting the use of ICT in the department
- Setting annual examination result targets

2.2 Pupils

- Ensuring that pupils are set subject-specific targets
- Fostering interest in the subject with the aim that it continues beyond the school day
- Taking responsibility for discipline in the department
- Tutoring your form as specified in the Staff Handbook
- Teaching Personal and Social Education to your form

2.3 Staff
- Holding exchange-of-ideas sessions and minuted departmental meetings (at least six per year in addition to INSET time) (circulating minutes to head, deputy head and link person)
- Being involved in the appointment of members of the department and advising on their professional development
- Delegating clearly to members of the department such matters as may be appropriate to their experience and scale allowances and helping to prepare job descriptions
- Helping new members of the department, especially NQTs
- Being involved in the creation of school deadlines and ensuring they are met
- Observing lessons and providing written and verbal feedback
- Working with your link person to ensure that quality of delivery is maintained at all times

2.4 Resources
- Creating a visually attractive departmental area
- Ordering all the resources needed for the department and keeping a stock book up to date
- Keeping accounts and preparing budgets for the departmental expenditure
- Ensuring that the fabric of the departmental area and adjacent corridors is maintained to the highest possible level
- Ensuring that published safety procedures appropriate to the department are adhered to

2.5 Other responsibilities
- Implementing the school's policies and promoting the school's aims and objectives

2.6 Miscellaneous
- Undertaking other duties as may reasonably be expected
- In addition, to carry out the responsibilities and duties of a Main Scale Teacher, when undertaking the teaching of pupils

NB: This Job Description allocates duties and responsibilities but does not direct the particular amount of time to be spent on carrying them out and no part of it may be so construed.

Source: Tiffin School.

Figure 16.1 Job description – head of department.

promotional leaflets for pupils and parents offering comprehensive advice are a must if the subject is to maintain its mainstream status.

MANAGING PEOPLE

The individual subject teachers that comprise the departmental team are the most important elements in the delivery of high quality teaching and learning. A key role of the head of department today is to engender a cooperative spirit and sense of corporate responsibility among all the department's staff (Cambers, 1996). Developing a common ethos regarding the aims, approaches and delivery of geography within the classroom together with adopting a leadership style that encourages teamwork is a critical starting point. Colleagues within a department need to have a sense of involvement and ownership, 'belonging to the team', including part-time or non-specialist staff and student teachers. Shared decision-making and equitable delegation of departmental tasks, bearing in mind the varying workloads and experiences that different members of the department may have, together with effective communication and discussion opportunities through regular, well planned and documented department meetings, help develop a sense of involvement and collective responsibility for geography matters within a secondary school. Department meetings provide a useful vehicle for the discussion and review of new textbooks plus other teaching resources together with a forum for reflecting on good classroom practice. This will often follow on from the sharing of ideas and experiences of the delivery of a particular lesson or sequence of new lesson plans using modified or innovative approaches. Part of the remit of middle managers in secondary schools today involves the purposeful monitoring of overall standards of teaching and learning and that within a department they are being maintained and where necessary improved. Good practice includes the sharing of classroom resources and experiences together with regular monitoring of classroom performance, using an agreed set of criteria and guidelines. This needs to be a two-way process between the head of department and other members of the geography team and will help inform in-service training and professional development requirements, notably with newly qualified teachers (NQTs).

Regular shared moderating of marking will also ensure standards of assessment are being applied equally across all teaching groups.

Subject managers within secondary schools are also responsible for the appraisal of staff within their departments. While involving objective and judgemental observations this process can provide a valuable opportunity to discuss professional development and provide insight into a colleagues in-service training needs. Appraisal discussion meetings enable staff to step back from their day-to-day activities and reflect on their classroom practices and subsequently identify areas for development, with identified timescales and realistic and achievable targets. Given the increased emphasis on 'lifelong learning' to enhance subject knowledge as well as teaching and learning skills, and the need for NQTs to develop Career Entry Profiles that will act as a record of their professional development, the role of appraisal takes on an increasing importance.

Working with student teachers within a department can bring fresh approaches and inject new ideas to geography teaching and involves frequent discussion and feedback sessions on their observed lessons. In addition, with geography teachers now in short supply direct contact with a teacher training institution can help staff recruitment in schools.

Particularly important in the smooth running of a department is the need for all its members to be aware of the various school policies that apply to their teaching and how they are implemented within geography. This includes strategies for dealing with the special educational needs of individual pupils, literacy and numeracy policies, and the homework and assessment/marking policy. These together with schemes of work and exam syllabi/specifications are best assembled within the departmental handbook along with departmental records on exam results and resource listings, etc. The departmental handbook is a key information source not only for the members of the geography department but also the school's senior management team and external agencies such as OFSTED. It needs to be user friendly in layout and organisation to make it easily accessible and understandable to those unfamiliar with the work of a department. These may include newly qualified or student teachers joining a department.

A further important area of documentation is the development of a standards portfolio of examples of pupil work. This is particularly valuable for moderation of a range of varying standards of pupil work and assessments at KS3 for teacher assessment of National Curriculum Levels of Attainment, required at the end of Year 9. It is also useful to retain, from previous years, samples of students' GCSE and A-level coursework to compare and maintain marking standards from one year to the next during internal moderation meetings.

A major focus for change within schools is the departmental development plan. In producing and reviewing the development plan process all members of the department need to be involved in the establishment of areas for further development and their related, measurable and achievable targets. This document is a key vehicle for managing curriculum change.

MANAGING THE CURRICULUM AT KEY STAGE 3

Prior to the 1988 Education Reform Act geography teachers enjoyed an enormous degree of freedom in determining their local school curriculum. Following the introduction of the National Curriculum schools have been required by statute to provide a programme of study that conforms to a national template. For many geography departments this undoubtedly caused a great deal of concern and stress. There were genuine fears that the introduction of a National Curriculum would lead to a highly content-driven syllabus which presented little opportunity for teacher-based creativity. The subsequent amendment of the National Curriculum, most recently with the introduction of 'Curriculum 2000', has further added to the workload of teachers.

While many geography departments work collaboratively in the detailed planning which is now required in order to construct a working programme of study, a great deal of pressure continues to fall on the head of department. Increasingly subject leaders are placed under a conflicting set of pressures to provide a challenging and dynamic curriculum which captures the interest and imagination of children while at the same time satisfying national requirements. As Cambers (1996) noted, heads of department 'must accept that their management is open to intrusive public scrutiny'. Schools are now subject to regular inspection by OFSTED with subsequent reports readily available within the public domain. OFSTED inspectors now expect to see evidence for the teaching of good geography. While, as Luker (1996) observed, what 'constitutes good geography is open to debate', the requirements of the National Curriculum are relatively straightforward.

It is essential that heads of department conduct a regular audit of their geography programme of study to ensure that there is clear evidence to show that the curriculum laid down by the department is actually taught and that it conforms to national requirements. QCA (1999) in the Curriculum 2000 geography document emphasised the inclusive nature of the National Curriculum, which carries with it 'an entitlement for learning, which must be an entitlement for all pupils'. While it is relatively easy to construct a curriculum which satisfies the National Curriculum in terms of overall content, it is far more difficult to implement a curriculum which is accessible to children of all levels of ability. This requires a very practical approach to the need for differentiation.

The management of the curriculum places a particular pressure on subject leaders in the small school where the geography team may well include just one or two full-time teachers. In reality the curriculum planning will differ little in its demands from that of a large school employing three or four full-time geographers. The difference lies in the scope for collaborative work.

The problem of the primary/secondary interface provides an additional challenge for the school geographer. The introduction of national literacy and numeracy initiatives has tended to squeeze certain subjects within the primary curriculum. There is now strong evidence to show that the time given to geography at Key Stages 1 and 2 has been reduced. This has to some extent been confirmed by the revised National Curriculum, which has significantly reduced the subject content at this level. Despite this a great deal of excellent geography is being taught at primary level. Geography cannot be seen in isolation – children are now entering Key Stage 3 with greatly enhanced word and number skills and with well developed investigative skills. There is considerable evidence to show that many children fall back in terms of achievement following their transfer to secondary school. While there are undoubtedly many reasons for this there is good reason to believe that the secondary curriculum and in particular teacher expectations are in part responsible. There is a particular need to ensure progression following transfer and to ensure that the stimulating environment of the primary classroom is maintained into the secondary phase.

The attitude that entry into the secondary school marks the point where the real study of geography begins has been all too prevalent in the past. The proper introduction of the National Curriculum both in the primary and secondary phase should militate against this but in practice far more is required. There is a need for dialogue between primary and secondary teachers. The need is for regular meetings between subject leaders with a shared approach to curriculum planning. An excellent approach is to develop a unit of work that spans the period of transition. Not only does this enable children in Year 6 to demonstrate their capabilities but it also presents an opportunity for continuity.

While it is relatively straightforward for secondary schools which draw their children from a small number of primary schools, it is far more difficult for those who take their children from a large number of schools scattered over a wide area. Such schools are not exclusively rural; many urban schools have an increasingly large catchment area. Under such circumstances it may well be necessary to focus on one or two key feeder schools.

RESOURCE MANAGEMENT ISSUES

Teaching resources, ranging from textbooks to Ordnance Survey map extracts and video tapes of educational programmes, are the bread-and-butter tools of the trade for geography teaching. However, organising their efficient storage, use and distribution poses a variety of problems, not least dependent on the classroom layouts and availability of departmental resource areas or storage facilities. Further issues involve consideration of how to finance the purchase, updating and replacment of teaching resources over time.

Resources (books and equipment)

Textbooks, whether issued to individual pupils or used as class sets, represent expensive investments for any geography department and therefore maximising effective usage and ensuring their prolonged lifespan is an important task. Many departments regard a 4–5 year life for regularly used texts to be the norm and this can be enhanced through the use of protective plastic covers, readily available from many publishers and other suppliers, and storage in plastic boxes for moving books between rooms. Book storage is space consuming and therefore optimisation of shelf space and use in both classrooms and departmental storage areas is important. Certain categories of departmental book stock, such as dictionaries, atlases and reference texts, may be stored within classrooms for immediate pupil access, although security of such items may be a consideration worth bearing in mind. It is also extremely valuable for staff, and (possibly) sixth formers, to have access to a range of textbooks and journals for their own use and research in a departmental library. The efficient organisation, storage and ease of accessibility of such materials is improved through well-labelled and indexed (A4 or foolscap, cardboard or plastic) magazine storage boxes. The use of computer-based spreadsheets or databases can also aid departmental records in both this and all other areas of resource storage.

It is not only in the departmental area that a subject manager is responsible for geography texts but also in liaising with the school library or learning resources centre to ensure that up-to-date and relevant books to the geography curriculum are available to pupils.

While the book stock in most geography departments will collectively comprise their biggest financial investment audio-visual and computer equipment will individually constitute high-value items that need to be stored securely and ideally security marked. High-cost lockable television and video recorder storage boxes are available as well as mobile trolley systems that enable equipment to be utilised in more than one room. As well as ensuring the secure storage of such valuable pieces of equipment, a department needs to have a booking system, based around timetabled lessons for the use of such items. Secure storage is also advisable for fieldwork equipment, such as tape measures, flow meters, ranging poles, etc. that is only used on occasions through the year. Again a system of cataloguing and recording their use and return is essential to avoid items going astray, particularly where sixth-form students may be involved in borrowing items for their own personal studies. Many schools also have outdoor weather stations containing valuable recording instruments which may need security to be taken into account. One solution many have adopted is the use of roof-top sites, particularly suitable for automatic electronic recording equipment.

Specialist storage facilities are likely to be needed for full size map sheets and posters/wall display materials. These may include either conventional flat map chest storage drawers or upright hanging storage systems. Smaller multiple exam map extracts and folded maps require less spacious or specialist facilities but need to be catalogued and stored efficiently. Frequently used map extracts, as well as other paper-based teaching resources, may benefit from lamination in protective plastic at relatively low cost.

Day-to-day consumable stationery and paper resources need to be readily available within the classroom and this is likely to include photocopiable teaching materials. A well-managed filing cabinet system is useful here plus lockable cupboards for paper and exercise books plus scissors and paste etc. Where consumable photocopy resources such as outline maps are used who is responsible for monitoring stock levels and arranging replacements is a further management issue that will need resolving.

An often overlooked teaching resource is the classroom itself, which can enhance and provide a highly stimulating environment to motivate and interest pupils in the topics or issues they are studying. Regularly changed and careful choice of posters, wall maps or other visual display material aids pupil understanding, engenders an interest in the subject and helps develop a greater sense of place. When planning and developing displays use of professionally prepared materials, including typed/computer-generated labels and graphics, provide a lead to the pupils in their own presentation of work. Pupil work is also an invaluable source of material to brighten and enliven any classroom environment and engenders a sense of pride and care in the work. Although it is not always feasible in all schools, if departments have a suite or group of classrooms allocated for their teaching the designation of separate rooms for Key Stage 3, Key Stage 4 and sixth-form teaching enables wall displays to be directly linked to the current themes being delivered and can be directly referred to in classroom teaching.

Finance issues

Basic accountancy skills are seldom mentioned in job descriptions for subject managers but dealing with money matters is a routine part of the head of department's role. This involves a range of responsibilities from the relatively mundane ordering of items for purchase from departmental budget capitation allowances to possibly generating additional income from alternative sources, e.g. charitable sources, car boot sales, parent-teacher associations or national supermarket chain promotions. Policies need to be agreed upon for deciding how available finances are to be spent, with decision-making being a consultative process across the staff within a department. Budgeting for replacement of lost/damaged book stock and or equipment needs to be built into this process and increasingly schools are linking an element of departmental allowances to departmental development plans which they have to bid for and compete with other areas of the curriculum. Other resource issues with a financial dimension that affect departments include considerations about the maintenance and decoration of classrooms and equipment, the fact that computers and videos do break down on occasion, plus furniture requirements. While these issues tend to be dependent on whole school budgets and resources, nevertheless a subject manager needs to be aware of policies and procedures in dealing with any problems in these areas. Keeping track of how money is spent is an important consideration and use of computer-generated spreadsheets makes this relatively straightforward.

MANAGING ICT WITHIN THE GEOGRAPHY DEPARTMENT

There is a clear expectation within the revised National Curriculum (1999) that the use of ICT will be incorporated into the geography programme of study at Key Stage 3. The new orders (page 9) require the selective use of CD-ROM and the Internet 'to find information about places and environments', plus the use of e-mail to communicate and exchange information and the use of spreadsheets and databases to 'handle and present geographical data'. There is also an expectation that children will be given access to geographic information systems (GIS), remote sensing and datalogging.

This is both a sophisticated and challenging requirement for any geography department, and one which raises many issues for the subject leader. The key issues centre around the availability and management of resources, staff competence and training and the integration of ICT into the geography programme of study.

Resource provision is frequently the most serious problem for the geography department. There are still many schools where the computer provision is concentrated in one or two areas, the use of which is heavily dominated by computer studies and IT, with other subjects bidding in competition for the very limited remaining time. If ICT is to be effectively integrated into the geography curriculum there must be proper, regular access to computer facilities, ideally under the management of the geography department. A lone computer at the back of the geography room cannot provide adequate access. Equally, in the present financial environment, it is extremely difficult for geography departments to establish their own facility. There is an acute need for long-term planning which must be shared with senior management.

The departmental development plan must allow for the progressive extension of facilities. A GIS can be based on one computer, which can also act as the download point for an automatic weather station which can provide an ideal opportunity for children to use datalogging. Even one access point to the Internet within the geography department is better than none at all. Clearly there will be a need to start small and think big.

It is essential that the use of ICT is fully integrated into the programme of study and that throughout Key Stages 3 and 4 there is clear progression in the children's work. An example showing one school's approach to the problem of integrating a progressive programme of ICT into the geography scheme of work at Key Stage 3 is shown in Figure 16.2. This is not intended to present an ideal model but is rather a practical attempt to encapsulate good practice.

The underlying planning cannot be carried out in isolation; it is essential to work alongside other colleagues to ensure continuity across the curriculum. In the case of the example shown, the head of department is a member of the school's IT across the curriculum working party which works alongside the IT coordinator in the planning of ICT on a whole-school basis.

However creative and imaginative the use of ICT in the geography programme of study, much will depend on the individual teacher's ICT capability and in particular their level of competence. Although beginning teachers are now required to reach a demanding level of ICT competency the position with serving teachers is very different. The New Opportunity Fund (NoF) training programme has ambitiously set out to ensure that all teachers in England and Wales reach a demanding set of standards but has failed to meet the needs of many. The prime focus of the NoF programme has been on the application of ICT rather than the acquisition of basic generic skills, which is particularly needed by many serving teachers.

The head of department not only has to ensure that his or her own skills are adequate but also that those of the remaining members of the department meet the desired level. It is essential that levels of staff competence are assessed accurately and that the INSET needs of colleagues are identified. Again the head of department cannot do this in

Year	Autumn Term	Spring Term	Summer Term
Year 7	*Croydon Tourist Brochure* Internet (pre-set hyperlink) *Local land use* – Digital camera + Microsoft Publisher to produce report	*Weather* – Datalogging/automatic weather station. Local weather investigation – preparation of a report – Word	
Year 8	*Plate Tectonics* – CD-ROM – research topic using Violent Earth report using Word	*Migration* – Preparation of report using Excel and Word (Table and Chart pasted from Excel into Word)	*Fieldwork Project – Rye* Collection of data – the use of a database to store data and assist in analysis (FLEXIDATA2)
Year 9	*Global Climates* – Virtual classroom link – local environmental study – exchange with Australian children via. the school website	*Population* – Population Trends – using Excell to model change.	*Preparation of a fieldwork report – Spitalfields* – Integrated report using digital images, Excel, Word and Publisher. Internet – to obtain secondary data.

Projected developments – School Year 2000/2001:
Year 7 – Virtual classroom project – local studies project – exchange with Australian children via e-mail
Year 9 – The use of a GIS system based on the Local Studies package

Figure 16.2 Edenham High School – current use of ICT within the Key Stage 3 geography programme of study.

isolation – there is a genuine need for senior management support in this.

At the very least there will be a need for an effective departmental policy for the use of ICT. The implementation of a successful policy takes considerable time and must form a key element within the departmental development plan.

FIELDWORK MANAGEMENT

Out-of-classroom activities now form an integral part of geography learning, ranging from litter surveys or microclimate studies around the school grounds to residential field weeks in foreign localities. Fieldwork should be fun and 'a refreshing change from the predictable routines of the school and the "virtual" or "simulated" reality of the book, slide and video' (Bland et al., 1996). The application of geographical skills and enquiry is an integral requirement of the National Curriculum at KS3 (11–14) in England and Wales: 'in developing geographical skills, pupils should be taught: to select and use appropriate fieldwork techniques, for example land use survey, and instruments' (DfEE, 1999). The collection of first-hand data in the field is a compulsory component of all GCSE and A-level exam syllabi/specifications:

> AS and A level specifications in geography should require students to undertake investigative work, based on evidence from primary sources, including fieldwork, and secondary sources; . . . should require students to develop the ability to: identify, select and collect – using a range of techniques – quantitative and qualitative evidence from primary sources, including fieldwork.
>
> (QCA, 1999)

All of these opportunities greatly enhance children's learning experiences at first hand but present a potential minefield of problems for those responsible for their supervision and organisation. This is particularly the case as a result of changes in legislation following tragic accidents on school trips at Lyme Bay and Land's End in the last ten years.

Advance planning goes a significant way to ensuring successful fieldwork for both day trips and residential visits. A reconnaissance trip to sites to be used to check potential risks and hazards is a significant part of preparation. It is now a legal requirement under the Management of Health and Safety at Work Regulations 1992 for local authorities and school governing bodies to carry out a risk assessment of sites to be used in any off-site visit. This involves assessing sites to be used in the following terms:

- What are the hazards or potential hazards? (A *hazard* is any situation that may cause harm to someone and a *risk* is the chance that someone may be harmed by the hazard.)
- What safety measures can be taken to reduce risks to an acceptable level?
- What are the steps to be taken in an emergency? (For example, where is the nearest public phone and hospital emergency and accident department?)

(See Holmes and Thomas (2000).)

The Cambridge Local Examinations Board together with the Field Studies Council have produced a highly informative video tape on *Managing Fieldwork Safely* (OCR, 1999). Anyone planning residential or any other fieldwork ought also to consult *Health and Safety of Pupils on Educational Visits* (DfEE, 1998) along with *Fieldwork in Action 1–3* (May, Richardson and Banks, 1993; May and Cook, 1993; Thomas and May, 1994). Forward planning for any school trip benefits from setting out clearly in advance a timetable of pre-visit administrative tasks to be completed and the timescale involved for this may vary from a few weeks to over twelve months depending on the complexities and exact details involved. Figures 16.3 and 16.4 are examples of how such planning timetables might be laid out, with Figure 16.3 being based on a residential field week taking place at Easter.

For residential visits accommodation often needs to be booked at least six months in advance, if not longer, and the same applies for some of the more popular London museums. Costs, location and accessibility, availability of and size of meeting/work rooms, quality of catering (geographers march on their stomachs as well as any army!) and the nature of bedroom arrangements (individual bedrooms versus dormitory layouts) are some of the key considerations in choosing appropriate accommodation for residential fieldwork. The precise details of accommodation and travel arrangements together with related costs, plus the programme of activities and insurance cover details etc., must be agreed with school senior management teams and

Time-scale		Action needed	Task done
1st half Summer Term	❑	Provisionally book accommodation (by phone and in writing)	❑
	❑	Complete and return provisional booking forms	❑
1st half Autumn Term	❑	Book coach transfer to destination (NB: confirm cost in writing!)	❑
	❑	Book hired minibuses	❑
	❑	Map out provisional activities programme with Dept	❑
	❑	Calculate costings	❑
	❑	Check LEA/school insurance cover arrangements	❑
	❑	Governors trip application form/risk assessment form	❑
	❑	Update/generate parents' letters	❑
	❑	Develop fieldwork Aims and Objectives summary sheet	❑
2nd half Autumn Term	❑	Issue/collect in parents' letters/consent forms	❑
	❑	Develop teaching/logistical details for any new elements within trip (including Aims & Objectives sheet + overview Key Questions handouts for students + overhead transparencies)	❑
	❑	Check field equipment needs (if necessary order replacements)	❑
	❑	Check OS map needs (if necessary order replacements/updates)	❑
1st half Spring Term January	❑	Write to local planning departments etc. for up-to-date information.	❑
	❑	Book into field sites etc. (e.g. nature reserves, quarries or visitor centres)	❑
	❑	Check stationery needs (if necessary order replacements)	❑
February	❑	Prepare Emergency Phone Nos Contact sheet + procedures	❑
	❑	Discuss worksheet/handout needs and arrange photocopying	❑
	❑	Sort out Student Group lists	❑
	❑	Issue final information details to students/parents	❑
Two weeks before departure	❑	Notice in weekly staff newsletter/noticeboard re students to be away	❑
	❑	Preliminary packing of paper/map rolls etc. (in lessons)	❑
	❑	Notify Finance Office of cash float requirements	❑
Week before departure	❑	Senior Assembly notice re pre-fieldcourse briefing meeting	❑
	❑	Packing of stationery/equipment	❑
	❑	Photocopy parent consent forms (main office)	❑
	❑	Set cover lesson work	❑
	❑	Check First Aid Kit supplies + staff 'comfort' supplies (kettle etc.)	❑
	❑	Pre-fieldcourse Briefing Meeting with students (house rules etc.)	❑
Day before departure	❑	Circulate Emergency Contact Nos lists to Office/Staff Contacts	❑
	❑	Cover lesson work organised	❑
	❑	Check school minibus and refuel etc.	❑
	❑	Collect cash float from finance office	❑
D-day	❑	Collect mobile phones/chargers from office	❑
	❑	Pack vehicles	❑
	❑	Check all students present	❑
	❑	Go!	❑
After trip	❑	Complete and submit for audit by finance office trip accounts	❑
	❑	Review arrangements/programme	❑
	❑	Start planning next trip!	

Source: Tiffin School Geography Department.

Figure 16.3 Residential fieldcourse planning.

Time-scale		Action needed	Task done
Term or 3–6 months ahead	❑	Arrange bookings with field centres/museums etc.	❑
	❑	Complete and return provisional booking forms	❑
	❑	Book transport (coaches/hired minibuses etc.)	❑
	❑	Map out provisional work/activity programme with Dept	❑
	❑	Calculate costings	❑
	❑	Complete school/governors trip application form + risk assessment forms for senior management team	❑
	❑	Create/update parents' letters	❑
One month ahead	❑	Issue/collect in parents' letters/consent forms	❑
	❑	Develop teaching/logistical details for any new elements within trip	❑
	❑	Check field equipment needs (if necessary order replacements)	❑
	❑	Prepare Emergency Nos Contact sheet	❑
	❑	Discuss worksheets/handout needs and arrange photocopying	❑
	❑	Sort out Student Group lists	❑
Two weeks before departure	❑	Notice in staffroom/weekly newsletter re students away etc.	❑
	❑	Notify Finance Office of any cash float requirements	❑
Week before departure	❑	Set cover lesson work	❑
	❑	Check First Aid Kit supplies	❑
	❑	Pre-trip briefing of pupils in lesson	❑
Day before departure	❑	Circulate Emergency Contact Nos lists to School Office/Staff Contacts	❑
	❑	Cover lesson work organised	❑
	❑	Check school minibus and refuel etc.	❑
	❑	Collect cash float from finance office	❑
D-day	❑	Collect mobile phones/chargers from office	❑
	❑	Check all students present and depart	❑
After trip	❑	Review arrangements/programme	❑
	❑	Start planning next trip!	

Source: Tiffin School Geography Department.

Figure 16.4 Day trip planning.

governing bodies where residential visits are involved prior to circulating details to pupils and parents. It is essential at an early stage that as much detail as possible about the trip is forwarded to parents; this includes information about timetabled activities and costs, transport and meal arrangements etc., plus any hidden extra costs that may be involved, such as the hire or purchase of suitable wet weather gear and boots etc. Many schools also now require detailed parental consent forms and parent-student behaviour contract agreements. It is also strongly advisable for foreign-based visits to arrange an information meeting with all parents and pupils involved, in order to provide an opportunity for any queries to be resolved well ahead of the trip. Last but not least the actual programme of geography activities needs to have been planned.

Job (1999) provides a good deal of sound advice on most of the key issues briefly outlined here and in particular on the range of teaching strategies that are available. Depending on the aims and objectives most geography trips are likely to involve elements of pupil data collection and processing activity, visits to sites of geographical interest and field teaching. From day trips to residential field weeks, given the limited amount of time available, precise planning of what the students are actually going to be doing is vital to ensure it is utilised to the full from a geographical point of view. The following key questions need to be tackled prior to organising precise field-based activities:

- What do you want the students to learn from their fieldwork experience?
- How is this best achieved in the circumstances and environmental surroundings?
- How does the fieldwork link/relate to public exam requirements?

Plenty of books are available for practical ideas on actual field activities (see Frew, 1993, and Lenon and Cleves, 1994) as well as regular articles in *Teaching Geography*, published by the Geographical Association (GA). For background geographical information on potential sites/areas to be visited the GA publish a wide range of landform guides to many of the most popular physical fieldwork locations around England and Wales. In human geography the Regions of the British Isles series, originally published by Nelson in the 1960s, provide detailed historical background material along with the Association for the Advancement of Science regional studies, both of which, although out of print, can probably be obtained through library loan services. More recent and up-to-date information is found in Ordnance Survey, Michelin and AA guidebooks. County and local authority planning departments may well have publications dealing with contemporary issues and problems within a particular area.

Once the types of activities are determined resources such as questionnaires or field data recording sheets need to be prepared and any related fieldwork equipment organised. The latter may not all be readily available within a geography department but may possibly be borrowed from other sources within a school. Biologists have equipment like tape measures and quadrants in common, or local authority Teachers' Centres may be able to help. If your trip is based at a permanent outdoor or field studies centre they will very often have a range of equipment available for loan, including wet weather gear for students to hire, but check availability in advance.

In your programme planning don't forget to have poor weather contingency plans, most notably if you are planning fieldwork in exposed or hostile upland or coastal environments. If you do go ahead in wet conditions ensure your students are appropriately clad, including footwear, and check, if on residential visits, what drying facilities are available at your accommodation base.

Also on residential trips, evening programmes need to be organised together with any 'free time' activities. In addition, clear ground rules for students must be set out regarding arrangements for going off-site/reporting back to staff, retirement/quiet times at night, etc. These should be outlined in written communications with parents and agreed in parental consent documentation.

CONCLUSION

The intention of this chapter has been to provide a practical overview of the wide-ranging nature and complexity of tasks undertaken within the secondary school sector by geography subject leaders. The role is a multi-faceted and challenging one that encompasses a broad range of skills incorporating the management of people, staff and students, resources both physical and financial, curriculum change and out-of-classroom activities. Delivery of high quality, stimulating and interesting lessons resulting in successful teaching and learning is dependent on the lead given in all these areas. If the subject is to thrive and continue to be a popular option choice at 14 and 16+ the head of department has to be highly organised and capable of juggling many balls at once. In among all of this one wonders how we find the time to carry out the core role as a classroom teacher.

REFERENCES

Bland, K., Chambers, B., Donert, K. and Thomas, T. (1996) 'Fieldwork', in Bailey, P. and Fox, P. (eds), *Geography Teachers' Handbook*. Sheffield: Geographical Association.

Cambers, G. (1996) 'Managing the departmental team', in Bailey, P. and Fox, P. (eds), *Geography Teachers' Handbook*. Sheffield: Geographical Association.

Department for Education and Employment (1998) *Health and Safety of Pupils on Educational Visits*. London: DfEE.

Department for Education and Employment (1999) *Geography at Key Stage 3 in the National Curriculum*. London: DfEE.

Department for Education and Employment and Qualifications and Curriculum Authority (1999) *Geography: The National Curriculum for England KS1–3*. London: DfEE and QCA.

Frew, J. (1993) *Advanced Geography Fieldwork*. London: Nelson.

Geographical Association (1999) *Leading Geography – National Standards for Geography Leaders in Secondary Schools*. Sheffield: Geographical Association.

Holmes, D. and Thomas, A. (2000) 'Fieldwork and risk management', *Teaching Geography*, vol. 25, no. 2, pp. 71–4.

Job, D. (1999) *New Directions in Geographical Fieldwork*. Cambridge: Cambridge University Press.

Kent, A. (1999) *Promoting Geography in Schools*. Sheffield: Geographical Association.

Lenon, B.J. and Cleves, P.G. (1994) *Fieldwork Techniques and Projects in Geography*. London: Collins Educational.

Luker, K. (1996) 'Managing resources', in Bailey, P. and Fox, P. (eds), *Geography Teachers' Handbook*. Sheffield: Geographical Association.

May, S. and Cook, J. (1993) *Fieldwork in Action 2: An Enquiry Approach*. Sheffield: Geographical Association.

May, S., Richardson, P. and Banks, V. (1993) *Fieldwork in Action 1: Planning Fieldwork*. Sheffield: Geographical Association.

OCR (1999) *Management Fieldwork Safety*. Videotape. Office for Standards in Education (OFSTED) (1997) *Subject Management in Secondary Schools: Aspects of Good Practice*. London: OFSTED.

Palot, I. (1999) *Going Places: A Geography Careers Resource Pack*. Sheffield: Geographical Association.

Qualifications and Curriculum Authority (1999) *GCE Advanced Subsidiary (AS) and Advanced Level (A) Specifications Subject Criteria for Geography*. London: QCA.

Teacher Training Agency (1998) *National Standards for Subject Leaders*. London: TTA.

Thomas, A. and May, S. (1994) *Fieldwork in Action 3: Managing Out-of-Classroom Activities*. Sheffield: Geographical Association.

Wiegand, P. (ed.) (1989) *Managing the Geography Department*. Sheffield: Geographical Association.

Part Three

Research and Geography Teaching: Case Studies of Why and How Research Matters

Underpinning 'reflective' practice is a careful consideration of literature, viewpoints and research findings and so no further justification is needed for this section in a book entitled *Reflective Practice in Geography Teaching*. Again there is a mixture here of overview in Chapters 17 and 24 with other chapters that share recent research findings. In particular Chapters 19–22 bring together experienced academics in geography education with students actively and recently engaged in MA research. Too rarely valuable research work of this type does not reach a wider audience, so it is to be hoped these findings might influence at least discussion about practice, if not practice itself.

Chapter 17

Overview and international perspectives

Rod Gerber and Michael Williams

INTRODUCTION

Across the globe, over the last three decades there has been a dramatic increase in the numbers of researchers in geographical education and their output is evidenced in bibliographies, books and theses, research conferences and symposia, and articles in research journals. A brief glance at the British bibliography (Foskett and Marsden, 1998) and the more recent Internet bibliography produced by the National Council for Geographic Education (2000) in the United States indicates clearly the range of topics that have attracted the interest of researchers and demonstrates a variety of research methods. It is important that research reported in languages other than English should not be ignored and examples of such writing include the work of John Chi-Kin Lee (1998) in Chinese, Hannele Rikkinen (1997, 1998a and 1998b) in Finnish and Juan-Luis Klein and Suzanne Laurin (1999) in French. Many others could be quoted.

In this chapter we sketch out selected features of the context of research in geographical education with particular reference to their culture and community. We highlight the roles of both the Commission on Geographical Education of the International Geographical Union and national organisations. We then seek to identify broad trends in research in geographical education before outlining an agenda for future research studies.

CONTEXT

Elsewhere, we have listed a number of features of the research culture of geographical education (Williams, 1998) and suggested three stages in its development: an incipient stage, an intermediate stage and a mature stage (see Table 17.1). Using this model it is possible for researchers to locate themselves in terms of the stages and indicate lines for progress in a cultural context. Published evidence suggests that most research in geographical education is being conducted at the incipient stage. Obviously, this is not a reflection on either the quality or quantity of the work being undertaken. Further, it does not indicate the influence that any researcher or group of researchers may have upon other researchers, curriculum policy-makers and classroom practitioners. What the model offers is a checklist against which individuals and groups can gauge their progress in establishing and strengthening the research culture of geographical

Table 17.1 Stages of growth in the culture of research in geographical education

Incipient stage	*Intermediate stage*	*Mature stage*
Individuals researching in isolation	Intra-institutional groups	International groups
Idiosyncratic and changing substantive focuses	Stable substantive focuses though subject to personnel changes	Enduring substantive focuses that are unaffected by personnel changes
Unfunded	Funded by local and national organisations	Funded by international organisations
Unsupported by a professional body	Supported on the margins of a national professional body	Central to the work of an international body
Dominated by immediate practical issues	Linking practical and theoretical issues	Dominated by universal theoretical issues
Focused largely on a single sector of a national education system	Focused on more than one sector of a national education system	Focused on lifelong learning in an international context
Undeveloped specialist geographical education research language	Emergence of a specialist geographical education research language	Use of a sophisticated geographical education research language
Absence of textbooks on geographical education research	Introductory textbooks on geographical education research	An array of established textbooks on geographical education research
Lacking close ties with conventional educational disciplines	Developing ties with a number of educational research disciplines	Closely integrated into the educational research community
Lacking any subdiscipline strengths within geographical education	Emergent subdiscipline strengths within geographical education	Established subdiscipline communities within research in geographical education
No infrastructure of research-focused symposia, conferences, web pages, journals and other publications	Developing nationally based infrastructure of research-focused symposia, conferences, web pages, journals and other publications	Well developed international infrastructure comprising symposia, conferences, web pages, journals and other publications
Few opportunities for training in research in geographical education	Limited national opportunities for training in research in geographical education	Many international opportunities for training in research in geographical education

education. 'The fundamental shift is from the relatively isolated individual functioning in one institution to an international group of researchers collaborating on a single project' (Williams, 1998, p. 2).

What the model also highlights is the need for a strong research infrastructure that includes frequent research-focused symposia and conferences with publications appearing in refereed specialist and general journals and on websites. Globally, there is a need for funding agencies, governmental and non-governmental, to include research in geographical education higher in their funding priorities. This is particularly important for those agencies that fund international research projects. Lacking this funding, it is not surprising to find that curriculum revision of geographical education is usually undertaken without recourse to prior research findings. Indeed, some commentators have pointed to the deliberate neglect of the geographical education community in the launching of major reforms, as in Australia (Lidstone, 1998) and the Republic of South Africa (Smit, 1998).

Without doubt, the organisation that has been most influential in progressing research in geographical education beyond the incipient stage for many researchers is the Commission on Education of the International Geographical Union (IGU). In recent years the numbers participating in the symposia on geographical education, held usually before the meeting of the World Congress every four years, has been increasing. More and more participants are attending from more and more countries. In addition, more continental and national symposia are being arranged under the auspices of the Commission. Thus, in 1999, symposia were held in Argentina, England and the United States. Details of the presentations can be read in the publications stemming from these meetings, e.g. *Teaching Geography in a World on Change* (Ostuni et al., 1999), the Proceedings of the conference held in Mendoza, Argentina.

Every four years, the Commission prepares a list of projects proposed by participants, usually in international, collaborative groups. While the Commission lacks the funding to finance these projects, it lends its weight behind submissions for funding made to various bodies. Books, reports and journal articles are the products of these projects and a list of recent publications can be accessed on the Commission's website and listserve page. In 1991, the Commission launched the refereed journal *International Research in Geographical and Environmental Education*, edited by Rod Gerber and John Lidstone. Initially published three times a year, in 1999 a decision was made to extend the issues to four a year, reflecting the increasing number of quality papers being produced. The year 1999 also witnessed the establishment of a new American journal *Research in Geographic Education*, edited by Richard Boehm and David Stea and sponsored by the Gilbert Grosvenor Center for Geographic Education at the South West Texas State University, San Marcos.

At the national level, in various parts of the world researchers in geographical education find organisations that enable them to communicate their interests with their peers and disseminate the findings from their studies. Such national groups include the UDE (University Departments of Education) Geography Tutors Group in England and Wales, the Geographie und Ihre Didaktik Group in Germany, the Australian Geography Teachers Association and the National Council for Geographic Education in the United States. In Europe many national organisations have been brought together under the former European Standing Conference of Geography Teachers' Associations, now referred to as Eurogeo. These organisations arrange national conferences and some publish journals and reports that include research in geographical education.

CURRENT TRENDS

In considering current trends in research in geographical education, the dichotomies listed in Table 17.2 are a useful starting point.

These dichotomies point to differences in motivation and purpose. In particular, they stimulate questions about who are and who should be the beneficiaries of research. Generally, there would appear to be little interest among geographical educators in undertaking research that is narrowly defined in terms of theory construction or the refinement of research methodologies. There appears to a strong interest in practitioner-based research. Much research in geographical education originates in the contemporary school classroom, is not linked closely to a social science discipline and is intended to contribute to improved professional practice. A good example of this pattern can be found in the *Theory into Practice* series of booklets (Dove, 1999; Leat and Nichols, 1999; and Walkington, 1999), edited by Mary Biddulph and Graham Butt and published in 1999. As the blurb for the series states.

> The aim of *Theory into Practice* is to take aspects of current research into geographical education and deliver them directly to the classroom practitioner. Geography teachers from across the professional spectrum will be able to access research findings on particular issues which they can relate to their own particular context . . .

There are perils for researchers who follow too closely a research agenda that is determined by policy-makers and practitioners. As stated elsewhere.

> Research in geographical education ought not, in my opinion, to become a political football used in a game where the goal posts are ever changing. Far better would it be if the research agenda was defined according to concerns for both improved research methodologies and substantive issues of an enduring and universal kind.
>
> (Williams, 1998, p. 6)

The dissemination of research in geographical education has been diverse, but a survey of major databases and key journals reveals that major areas of interest over the past two decades have been as follows.

The development of policy in geographical education

What, how and why general education policies have been used to develop policies in different curricular areas in formal education has been of particular interest in countries

Table 17.2 Dichotomies in research in geographical education

Originating in practice	*Originating in theory*
Designed for a practitioner audience	Designed for a researcher audience
Intended to contribute to improved professional practice	Intended to contribute to improved research
Not linked to a social science discipline	Closely linked to a social science discipline
Single method	Eclectic
Atheoretical	Theoretical
Not rooted in a substantial scholarly literature	Rooted in a substantial scholarly literature

around the world. Without wanting to single out any country in this regard, geographical educators have reported how their policy-makers have proscribed a diversity of policies on such issues as the principles of education for particular levels of education, e.g. for primary or elementary schooling, the implementation of fieldwork in school programmes or what should constitute a school curriculum. Detailed investigations are reported on the nature of these policies, their relationship to prevailing social priorities and the impact of different policies on the type of geographical education that is promoted in such policies. Sometimes, the studies report on the debate and challenges that have resulted from proposals for developing new policies, e.g. how the status of geography is affected by particular policy pronouncements. Limited attempts have been made to produce comparative studies of the variations in these policies and cross-cultural impacts in different regions, e.g. South East Asian countries.

Learning and teaching in geographical education

Research on learning and teaching in geographical education has been quite comprehensive. It reflects a passion by researchers to focus on learning and teaching of school children and, to a lesser extent, students in higher education. It does not reflect a strong interest in learning and teaching in vocational/technical education or lifelong learning. The main sub-areas in learning and teaching that interest geographical educators include: different approaches to learning and teaching; teaching styles; children's development of geographical and pedagogical skills; the development by teachers and students of the basic forms of communication including literacy, numeracy, graphicacy and oracy; children's development of basic geographical concepts; and the development of values through geographical education, especially social and environmental values.

Many of these studies focus on either learning or teaching. Few of them attempt to relate learning to teaching. With the advent of the widespread use of new communications technologies in geography classrooms, the reconsideration of how teachers use these technologies to maximise learning in geography, and how students use these technologies to learn, has drawn the two sides of the teaching–learning experience together. A similar observation can be made about learning and teaching in cross-cultural contexts within countries or regions. Here, case studies of learning and/or teaching geography were reported, but little attempt was made to reflect on any generalisations that may be evident across a range of similar studies in different cultural contexts.

The growing interest in learning and teaching geography in higher education over the past decade is reflected in the increased popularity of the *Journal of Geography in Higher Education* and the number of studies that focus on learning and teaching in university or college geography classes. The increase in the number of interest groups in professional associations for learning and teaching geography in higher education reflects the strong interest in improving learning and teaching across all areas of formal education. Maybe the next wave of interest will be to extend research in geographical education to learning and teaching in vocational education and lifelong learning?

Geography curriculum development

Changes in geography curricula in different countries provoke researchers to study the variations of the changes to previous policies and practices, the implementation of these changes and the impacts of these changes on policy development and practice in learning and teaching in geography. Since most of these changes to curricula occur on a state or national basis it is usual to find many reports of individual curriculum developments. On a similar basis, these reports may be of special curriculum projects that have been developed as a government priority. Often investigations of these changes involve the collection of a considerable amount of empirical data from people who have experienced the change. This has involved the popularising of a range of research methodologies, e.g. case study methodology, naturalistic inquiry, action research, ethnography and phenomenology, to draw out the personal experiences of people implementing a different geography curriculum.

The impact of the diffusion of a curriculum innovation has been the focus of a string of studies in geographical education. This is often the closest that researchers come to thinking about geography curricular changes across different educational environments. An example is the impact of the High School Geography Project from the USA as it related to the investigation of the diffusion of inquiry methodology in the teaching of geography in different parts of the Western world in the 1970s and 1980s.

The implementation of an action research approach to studying curricular changes and developments in geographical education has been very productive. It enabled research studies to become research and development studies as educators conducted investigations into the implementation of a curricular change in geography, reflected on their findings and then improved their curricula on the basis of the results of their earlier study. This practice is in the mainstream of geographical education research in many countries.

Assessment and evaluation in geography

Research into student assessment and wider aspects of evaluation in geography is popular because of the influence of external examination systems in many countries. Studies of the variations in student success in examinations use differing methodologies depending on the goal of the particular study. For example, detailed investigations of student performance on different types of questions in an examination have been conducted using the most comprehensive experimental research designs to search for significant differences in student performance. However, in studies focused on the students' experience of, say, a field-based examination, a more qualitative methodology has been found to be more appropriate.

Investigations searching for the effectiveness and relevance of geography curricula are reported regularly at geographical education conferences. They reflect the continuing thirst to determine the effectiveness of curricular innovations as expressed in different geography programmes. Using accepted techniques for programme evaluation, studies describe and interpret individual programmes based on surveys of participants or interviews with them. Sometimes these evaluations are conducted on a contract basis for an employing educational authority. At other times, professional associations undertake the evaluations on a voluntary basis. Strengths and weaknesses of the programmes are often included in the results of such evaluations. However, few of these evaluations are conducted on a scale broader than the single programme.

Teaching resources

The effectiveness of different types of teaching resources in geographical education has become a very popular research theme. In geography, reported studies have focused on learning and teaching resources, including textbooks, video and audio-visual resources, maps and atlases, games and simulations, and computer software. They include the suitability of the resources for the learner, the clarity of the resources, how they structure the learning, aspects of attractiveness, relevance to the curriculum, and cost.

In studies in higher education, there has been strong interest over the past decade in how learning using remote sensing and Geographic Information Systems (GIS) has occurred and can be improved. At school levels, the emphasis has been more on how textbooks, atlases and individual maps are used and can be effective. In the 1980s, there was strong interest in using games and simulations to promote geographical education. More recently, this emphasis has changed to maximising the effectiveness of computer software and multimedia programmes in geographical education. New types of resources enter the educational market every day ensuring a continuing research focus on their educational qualities

Technology in geographical education

For some educational researchers consideration of technology in geographical education is a part of the section on teaching resources. Specifically this may be true, but it is also true that technology may be considered in the section on learning and teaching. Because of the dramatic growth in the use of advanced communication technologies in geographical education it is worthwhile to consider research into them as a discrete part of the research arena.

In the last decade, a number of geographical education research studies have focused on computers, specialised software for learning, remotely sensed spatial data obtained from earth satellites and the digitising of spatial data through Geographic Information Systems (GIS). However, there is currently a strong research interest in GIS, together with geographical education through the World Wide Web and the Internet, with a focus on multimedia learning.

These studies have placed a new emphasis on the teaching–learning process where teachers have become much more facilitative and learners much more active and independent. Not only have the styles of learning and teaching changed as the result of research into technology in geographical education, but the concept of literacy in geographical education has taken on a broader meaning to include information technology literacy, in conjunction with verbal, oral, graphic and numeric literacies.

Geographical education in differing social contexts

The study of geography in different social contexts has attracted considerable research interest as the role and place of geography in the formal education curriculum have been challenged over several decades. Several studies have been conducted into the role that geography can and has played in the areas of citizenship and political education, development education, intercultural understanding, peace education, industrial and/or business education and vocational education. Some of these studies have sought to demonstrate the differences between geography and other subjects while others have set out to explain how geographical education can contribute to, say, citizenship education. The first set of studies has often taken a defensive stance, whereas the second has been more positive, searching for links between the two types of education that may strengthen them both.

Not totally forgotten, though fewer in number, are studies bridging different cultures on different scales and across regions and countries. These seek to demonstrate variations in geographical education as it has been implemented by different government policies at different administrative levels. When it comes to understanding the variations in the ways that geographical education is planned, implemented and recognised in different cultural settings, then the work of global organisations such as the International Geographical Union becomes very important as a facilitator of cross- and inter-cultural understanding through geographical education (see Naish, 1990).

Geographical and environmental education

While geographical education is researched in differing social contexts, the largest set of comparisons is reserved for studies about geographical and environmental education. Most researchers agree that geography is a discipline that integrates the physical and social sciences. However, many educators believe that the role of geography in environmental education can be explained without having geography operate as a separate subject or discipline. They argue that geography can act as the link or integrator in a holistic approach to learning and teaching the social and physical sciences from a spatial perspective. Consequently, both camps of researchers and theorists have established separate journals to promote their viewpoints, e.g. *Geography* and the *Journal of Geography* promote a specific geographical approach whereas the *Journal of Environmental Education* and *Environmental Education and Information* promote an integrative approach.

RESEARCH FUTURES

There is little doubt that the study of people's interaction with their Earth and with other planets will continue to be an important aspect of human endeavour. Also, there is little doubt that technologies will continue to improve and be applied to formal and everyday learning situations. Geographical education in some form will continue to be important for effective human existence. What then may be some pegs upon which to hang the organisers of future research in geographical education?

The seminal report, *Learning: The Treasure Within* (Delors, 1998), by the International Commission on Education for the Twenty-first Century offers one starting point. In this report, four pillars of education are identified:

1. Learning to know, e.g. acquiring the instruments of understanding, learning to learn and understanding the benefits of lifelong learning.
2. Learning to do, e.g. being able to act creatively in one's environment, having the competence to deal with many situations and working in teams.
3. Learning to live together, e.g. being able to participate and cooperate with other

people in all human activities, managing conflicts and appreciating independence.
4. Learning to be, e.g. being better able to develop one's personality and act with greater autonomy, judgement and personal responsibility.

From these pillars, it may be deduced that international geographical education should seek to achieve the following things:

1. Improving teacher education through searching for new perspectives in geographical education by: developing new ways to bring the world into the classroom; developing new competencies in geographical education; learning what and how to teach; and promoting the professional development of geography teachers.
2. Using the resources of the information society to broaden geographical learning and teaching.
3. Emphasising geographical education that is aimed at improving the art of people living together.
4. Refocusing curriculum development at all levels of formal geographical education to promote pedagogies to promote greater autonomy, judgement and personal responsibility. This would include developing learning strategies that are used in both post-industrial and developing countries such as guided participation.
5. 'Rediscovering geography' as a basis for effective lifelong learning in both formal and non-formal education.

These five clusters of emphasis offer researchers in geographical education a future agenda. Whichever themes they choose, researchers should take very seriously the view that we are groups of people who function within selected environments at differing scales. Therefore, while it is useful to know what one group of people comprehend in their geographical education, it is most important to develop an understanding of how regional groups and the whole world understands and practises geographical education. New communications technologies make international and global considerations much more realistic for researchers in geographical education, permitting cross-cultural studies to be achieved with greater ease. This will require much greater networking among geographical educators around the world thus promoting a global geographical education community of scholars.

REFERENCES

Delors, J. (ed.) (1998) *Learning: The Treasure Within.* Report to UNESCO of the International Committee on Education for the Twenty-first Century. Canberra: UNESCO Publications/Australian National Committee for UNESCO.

Dove, J. (1999) *Immaculate Misconceptions.* Sheffield: Geographical Association.

Foskett, N. and Marsden, B. (eds) (1998) *A Bibliography of Geographical Education.* Sheffield: Geographical Association.

Klein, J.-L. and Laurin, S. (eds) (1999) *L'Education Géographique: Formation du citoyen et conscience territoriale,* 2nd edn. Sainte-Foy, Québec: Presses de l'Université du Québec.

Leat, D. and Nichols, A. (1999) *Mysteries Make You Think.* Sheffield: Geographical Association.

Lee, J. C.-K. (1998) *Theory and Practice in Environmental Education in Primary and Secondary School: Towards Sustainable Development,* published in Chinese. Beijing: Beijing Normal University Press.

Lidstone, J. (1998) 'Cultural studies and geographical education: are we losing the way?', in Ferreira, M., Neto, A. and Conceição, S. (eds), *Culture, Geography and Geographical Education: Proceedings of the Oporto Symposium of the Commission on Geographical Education of the International Geographical Union*. Lisbon: Universidade Aberta.

Naish, M. (ed.) (1990) *Experiences of Centralisation: An International Study of the Impacts of Centralised Education Systems upon Geography Curricula*. British Sub-Committee of the Commission for Geographical Education, London: University of London Institute of Education.

National Council for Geographic Education (2000) *A Bibliography of Geographical Education*. Indiana: National Council for Geographic Education.

Ostuni, J., Lotfi, V., de Grosso, M. and de Becette, R. (1999) *Teaching Geography in a World on Change*. Proceedings of the International Geographic Union Commission on Geographical Education conference, Mendoza, Argentina, 19–24 April.

Rikkinen, H. (1997) *Geography in the Primary School*, published in Finnish. Helsinki: Helsingin Yliopistin Opettajankoulutuslaitos (Department of Teacher Training, University of Helsinki).

Rikkinen, H. (ed.) (1998a) *Geography in the Secondary School*, published in Finnish. Helsinki: Helsingin Yliopistin Opettajankoulutuslaitos (Department of Teacher Training, University of Helsinki).

Rikkinen, H. (ed.) (1998b) *Geography in the Upper Secondary School*, published in Finnish. Helsinki: Helsingin Yliopistin Opettajankoulutuslaitos (Department of Teacher Training, University of Helsinki).

Smit, M. (1998) 'A paradigm shift in geography teaching in South Africa: the outcomes-based approach', in Ferreira, M., Neto, A. and Conceição, S. (eds), *Culture, Geography and Geographical Education: Proceedings of the Oporto Symposium of the Commission on Geographical Education of the International Geographical Union*. Lisbon: Universidade Aberta.

Walkington, H. (1999) *Global Citizenship Education*. Sheffield: Geographical Association.

Williams, M. (1998) 'A review of research in geographical education', in Kent, A. (ed.), *Issues for Research in Geographical Education, Research Forum I*. London: University of London Institute of Education, pp. 1–10.

Chapter 18

Information and communication technologies: researching the reality of use

Deryn M. Watson

INTRODUCTION

It has long been accepted that the introduction and then establishment of change within education depends critically on the role of the teacher (Fullan, 1991). For twenty years there has been a series of national initiatives designed to stimulate, encourage and exhort teachers to use computers in subject classrooms; from the development of computer-assisted learning curriculum materials and a series of in-service courses to the integration of IT into the National Curriculum, the emphasis has been on the benefits to pedagogy. Geographers have taken an active part in this national scene. The Geographical Association has been a keen advocate, with an active working group since 1978, regular software reviews appear in *Teaching Geography* and a range of publications have emerged (Shepherd et al., 1980; Watson, 1984; Fox and Tapsfield, 1986; Kent, 1992).

Nevertheless evidence indicates that the anticipated IT use in schools has not occurred (DES/DfEE, 1989, 1991, 1993, 1995 and 1997; Stevenson, 1997). Change has been patchy and inconsistent (OFSTED, 1995). Indeed, the impact of IT on education is 'a resolutely disappointing one' (Cuban, 1989). Why? What do we know about the few IT users? What do we know about their styles of teaching, in-service involvement or sheer tenacity that makes them adopt the change that others appear to resist? Conversely, what do we know about the rest, who are often characterised as technophobic, conservative and reluctant to accept innovation?

My analysis will draw on data collected initially during the case study work of the ImpacT Project (Watson, 1993; Johnson, Cox and Watson, 1994), during which I spent two years observing the geography lessons of five teachers with seven different classes in five co-educational comprehensives in southern England. I spent time observing their lessons, some of which involved IT, interviewing and talking to pupils, the five teachers and their colleagues. All the teachers were in geography departments where the curriculum delivery was considered 'sound'; geography in these schools was a popular and successful subject. All of the geography department staff tended to work as strong teams, a 'peer group of geographers', with a strong subject subculture (Goodson, 1991). All had rooms that formed a defined geography area, often with a small room which acted as a focal point for the staff during coffee and lunch breaks.

This chapter will explore what research can tell us about the way geography teachers are responding to the use of IT (or ICT) in their geography classrooms. Based on case study research and an analysis of documents over the last 15 years, it will explore the different reflexive practices of these teachers. In particular it will attempt to establish a sense of legitimacy of the professional opinions of both those who do and those who do not use IT in their geography classrooms. I will argue that models of change, whether the cascading of innovation through role models or a focus on the 'deficiencies' of teachers who fail to adopt change, are misconceived.

GEOGRAPHY TEACHERS WHO USE IT

Intuitive and enthusiastic users

The case study teachers, Rita, Zena, Bob, Peter and Steve, were not working in noticeably favourable resource environments. The five schools had a range of hardware that was typical of the national scene at the time – computer rooms of stand-alone or networked micros. The computer rooms were timetabled for use mainly by a declining quantity of computer studies and a growing quantity of IT classes. Indeed the two computer rooms at one school had only one free period a week available for any other class to book. As the head of IT said: 'If the geography class wants to use it, they [the staff] have to arrange a swap with a junior school IT skills class.' Such provision does not make it easy to integrate using IT into subject lessons. Computers have arrived in schools in response to a number of national or local initiatives, often without any coherent internal planning. In such an environment it is possible for a keen user to emerge and determine what is going on. It became clear that these teachers were all such keen users. One notable factor was that these geographers were often responsible for the school acquiring the resources they had. Zena stated: 'Honestly, I think the lead for using computers here has come from me and to the extent that I got a BBC in my room, then I got the satellite stuff in and tried to make sense of it.'

They were confident users of the hardware, but were not enamoured of it. They negotiated the micropolitics of access within their school setting and made the provision work to their advantage. Timetabling caused problems but they overcame them. For instance, Bob booked rooms when he wanted them, and was prepared to negotiate swaps as necessary. However, both the rooms were in different blocks from his own geography suite and he was actively pursuing a policy of getting more machines into his room to ease access.

Peter would pop in and out of the computer room, conveniently next door to his own room, to see if anyone was using it and then decide on the spur of the moment to take his class in for an extra period. Problems with resources were for them an irritant, but not a barrier. Their confidence which drove them to seek access to the computer was not necessarily born out of technical skills, but rather out of the ability to get things to work, either themselves or through others. These teachers overcame any technical problems quite pragmatically – they were annoyed rather than flustered by them. Thus they made the most of the situation in which they found themselves, but this achievement was particularly the teacher's own rather than a collective one.

IT supporting their geography curriculum, both content and process

All five were committed to using IT because they felt it supported their geography curriculum, both content and process. For all of these teachers, the way IT reinforced their normal way of doing things was important. Zena said: 'I don't think I would encourage anything which was going to change the syllabus that we wanted to teach and the way we would do it. I firmly believe that whatever we do supports the geography, not the other way around.'

Each teacher expressed a clear rationale for the use of computers, and this rationale was related to a notion of 'added value' for the pupils. They had no problems pinpointing their purposes, which related both to their perceptions of geography, the particular curriculum they taught, and the style of learning that could be encouraged. Teachers expressed getting the pupils to make decisions and answer questions as one of the main aims for using software.

Rita liked simulations, and in particular ones that included an element of role playing. Zena was quite clear about why she used IT. She used one program explicitly because of the processes it would stimulate. 'It promotes discussion about different viewpoints. So it fits in with issues and debates that we are trying to get going in the third years. If we didn't have SAND HARVEST it would all have been very dry, as all books. . . SAND HARVEST makes them role play and so make decisions.'

Bob actually used software the most out of all the teachers. He had a comprehensive collection of software acquired over the years. He was committed to their value in geography, often as an enquiry exercise directed at the process of learning and not just to acquire certain content. Bob saw lessons using IT as 'all about them generating the question and me responding – not me doing the prompting'. Steve believed that pupils have 'an added motivation when engaged in computer-based activities'.

These teachers were prepared to spend time on IT even when it did not specifically contribute to the assessment of the pupils, and when its use ate into the overall time allocation for the syllabus. These teachers confirm that IT within a subject curriculum framework can deliver the promises that have been extolled. For the successful and confident IT teacher there is clearly a powerful belief in the value of an outcome that is process based. And this belief supports their particular pedagogic philosophy which underpins their work.

There was no doubt that a clear relationship existed in all these teachers' minds between the use of IT and their perception of geography to be learnt, usually at the level of skills, processes and concepts rather than factual knowledge. They selected software which suited them and their purposes best. This was a very individual perspective and suited their individual 'style' as teachers. Yet all the teachers had one overriding reason in common for continuing to use the computer in their geography teaching: they had decided it was valuable in the classroom.

A particularly personal interest and initiative

In probing further the attitude and enthusiasm of the innovators, it became apparent that this was a particularly personal interest and initiative. Those teachers who did use IT were prepared to spend time on it even when for some classes it did not specifically contribute directly to the assessment of the pupils and when its use ate into the overall time allocation into which the whole syllabus had to be fitted. For the successful and confident IT teacher there is clearly a powerful belief in the value of the outcome that is process based. In particular they felt intuitively that they were offering a valuable experience to pupils. Their tone of voice while talking to me – and in contrast to that of their colleagues – was uniformly positive. Often when I arrived the first thing they did was tell me about some of the class work on the computer done when I was not there. How much was this belief also connected with an intuitive enjoyment by the teachers in the process for themselves, perhaps related to the challenge of using the equipment successfully and confidently?

These five teachers came from a variety of backgrounds, career and life histories. Gender was obviously not relevant as two of my IT users were female. Nor was age significant; my teachers ranged from Rita at 27 to Zena in her mid-fifties. There was no common in-service history; most of the teachers had come to their level of expertise through particular efforts made on their own initiative rather than from a directed source. Three had come to using software through their involvement in innovative geography curriculum projects and so had considered using IT from the first with a clear curriculum perspective. The only factors in common were that all five held positions of responsibility, four had taken a further professional development course, e.g. an MA, and all had started from their own efforts, not through an in-service course.

The only real commonality was their own personal interest and enthusiasm and an intuition that through using software in their classes they were both supporting geography teaching and providing a valuable experience for their pupils. Thus it supported their personal professional sense of self (Huberman, 1995).

GEOGRAPHY TEACHERS WHO DID NOT USE IT

Micropolitics of access

This confidence and use of IT was not shared by their geography peer group colleagues. Even with the same hardware in the same physical arrangement, the same software and an expressed willingness to get involved, in reality these colleagues were reluctant to use IT, and articulated a combination of reasons which intervened.

At one school booking the room proved a major bone of contention. Anne said: 'We all want to do it [using the computer] in context. When using BROOK FARM, what happens is while in context of children doing that we find we can't book the room so that weeks go by and they haven't caught up with the piece of work post-dates by the time they do it.'

All the staff (nine in the department) spoke about the problem during a departmental meeting. What had started as a complaint about access – 'problems with booking the room weeks after doing the exercise' – then turned into a complaint at 'having' to use IT. Andy said: '. . . look, I'm not sure this is really geography we are doing, only IT, and I'm not even sure about that. This is so prescriptive – I don't like being told what to do in my lessons.'

Where there were three micros in the geography suite, Hilary said:

> 'I wouldn't mind if I had access to a room, plenty of computers and I knew what I was doing. I wouldn't make a fuss at all. Time and resources are the problems . . . When you have thirty kids what worries me is the organisational aspect in the classroom. What do you get the others to do because you can't go around and help them? You have to keep an eye on the computers so you can make sure they are not making total cock-ups. You have to be in about five places at once and it's quite difficult.

Professional unease

Few of these colleagues were explicit about why for them access to hardware was a problem. Conversations focused on the timetabling issue or organisational arrangements when using a small number of machines. But it became clear that this was deeply intertwined with a sense of professional unease about using computers, part of which was also related to their unhappy experiences in using them.

Both Zena and Bob had tried to support their colleagues by developing worksheets specifically for use with the software and showing how they could fit into the curriculum. All the geography staff were meant to use SAND HARVEST with their Year 9 classes, using worksheets devised by Zena. But she later reported that 'Rosie is terrified of computers. She ended up taking my lesson while I went down and sorted out the computer'.

Dave, another teacher in the same department as Bob, talked about a number of related concerns:

> The use of IT in my experience has been fraught with every classroom management difficulty that teachers have not yet grasped. The reasons for doing – we always felt perhaps that using the computer would excite children and that in some cases with simulations it might actually make things easier, particularly when dealing with calculations of profits and so on, so that the children don't make mistakes with that sort of thing. I found the children puzzled by the software and I found it very strange that there are very few programs so far that naturally hook children. Children can be very casual about computers, much less serious about them than they are about classroom work – they won't explore the possibilities in depth, they skate superficially over the problem and say they're finished or they find they can't do it. On only one or two occasions can I remember children getting really excited about what they were doing, but I don't know whether that's a failure on my part.'

Steve was aware that his colleagues did not use data handling as much as he did. 'I can't force people . . . stand over them. They have made, I think, quite a lot of progress but you will always come up against what I'm sure you knew all the time – this notion of the time factor and how much time is involved to make yourself reasonably confident.' He also related their reluctance to face a range of issues: 'Some staff will take it on and are motivated – some are in too much haste so we get a negative feedback. And there isn't the right equipment at the right time . . . '

Peter's colleague John also suggested that the computers themselves were not the problem:

> I and my colleagues make good use of computers themselves personally, word processing and so on. And I think it's a very difficult department where all of us have got other responsibilities. And so we need therefore to be very careful of the way we use time . . . The thing is, it's not really a question of not wanting to use them, but it's a question of priorities. And I do feel that I need a lot of time to really become completely familiar with the software, and what I would like to have is the opportunity to work on individual lessons rather than on a system generally.

Anne displayed a similar reluctance:

> Oh, a lot has been directed by Bob to give you the incentive to do it, but since then I use things that I feel I tried and they have worked. I'm not happy to just experiment with a class without having done it myself so I find it quite onerous in that things that I have used, used the weather depression one, but before I could use that I spent a long time getting to grips

> with how to work the program, but also preparing resources, so I'm not very favourable. I feel I need to know exactly what I'm doing. Because of that I haven't used as many because time dictates, don't have enough time to prepare.

Clearly a variety of factors make using IT in the curriculum problematic: in essence it did not work for them, so they were rejecting the innovation on personal professional grounds.

MODELS OF CHANGE

Myth of the role model

Competing demands made it difficult for the innovative teachers to pass on their knowledge and experience to colleagues – the cascade model of training. Extraneous pressures squeezed out teacher collaboration and curricular development. As John said, 'much of our curriculum planning takes place in snatched conversations as we pass on the stairs'. Huberman (1995) has noted, 'school scheduling provides little slack time for exchanges that are not purely functional – most exchanges are to do with what Yinger (1987) call the "language of practical action", as opposed to a forum for presenting practice in larger more visible patterns.' Is the amount of time required for the adoption of IT the critical factor?

At Bob's school, the large geography department met formally once a fortnight. They felt that sometimes the software Bob showed them 'was not up to much'. Anne went further:

> He's done one for IT on volcanoes but I've not used it. That's not a criticism of Bob. I find that because he's ahead of us in IT, when he prepares things he thinks he's done it so that anyone can use it, but in reality, often the rest of the department don't feel happy with it. I'm very much at child level, so if I can work it certain children won't find it difficult.

Anne was anxious that I should understand the point underlying her reservations: 'I haven't been intentionally negative, but when people have actually looked at something and tried it, and felt it not worthwhile, they have said that they don't feel they want to use it again. But because Bob's able to make it work for him, he can't see the problem.'

Basically Anne was saying there was a credibility gap. The department accepted Bob's enthusiasm and related it to the way he worked, but were cautious about whether it was for them. All were articulating strong personal perceptions as to why IT was not for them. Indeed it became increasingly apparent that rather than aid a cascade of knowledge throughout the peer group, the innovator had contributed to their colleagues' reluctance.

It would seem that this is the reality behind Fullan's (1991) statement that 'In many ways the more committed an individual is to the specific form of change, the less effective he or she is'. This credibility gap between the innovator and their colleagues makes a nonsense of the notion of a role model. Much of the in-service strategy for the adoption of IT has been structured on the basis that one user will cascade their knowledge skills and enthusiasm to other members of their department.

But in these departments, the notion of the teacher as a rational and familiar exemplar of change simply did not work. Indeed, the characterisation of an innovator as someone different, someone who takes risks and explores the new, makes them an unlikely person to provide a safe and comfortable role model from which the innovation will cascade.

Barrier of the deficit model

And so the professional perspectives of the teachers in these five departments provide us with a conundrum. Teachers use IT in their classrooms only when it has a particular resonance with their pedagogic and subject philosophy. And yet the same pedagogic and subject philosophy supports and underpins their colleagues' professional judgement not to use the innovation. These teachers all expressed reasons that have become associated with the failure of IT innovation (van den Akker, Keursten and Plomp, 1992; Pelgrum and Plomp, 1991): a lack of good software or time to explore the software, negative experiences in the classroom that had 'put them off', and it not being worth the amount of extra effort required. I would maintain that these are sensible and legitimate professional concerns.

The dominant research relates the apparent reluctance of teachers to use IT in their classrooms to a 'deficit model' of teachers, who are characterised as technophobic, too traditional in their teaching style and reluctant to adopt change. Willis (1992) asks: 'Why do some teachers, when faced with an opportunity to begin using technology in their classroom, treat it more like a disease to be avoided than a promising aid to effective instruction?' His language indicates the inadequacies of teachers rather than of the innovation. The PLAIT report, an evaluation of the use of laptops (Gardner et al., 1992), was concerned to find that curriculum requirements alone do not sustain daily use. Although laptops were distributed to all pupils, their relatively sparse use was put down to

> . . . the inability of the wider teaching community to stimulate and extend the frequency of computer usage in the classroom. Indeed usage in some cases may not be frequent at all. Teachers are not felt to be sufficiently IT-literate to easily and effectively integrate IT into their teaching . . . It is therefore unlikely that the frequency of usage will be greatly extended by innovations in teaching methods until teachers themselves are as literate in IT techniques as the pupils are expected to become.

At no stage do they address the possibility that the perceived barriers by the teachers may be sensible ones.

For the 'resisters' the questions of training, access and control were overshadowed by the problem of time – time to learn and explore, time to gain confidence and time to reflect on the potential for their pedagogy. Teachers need time to reflect and consider the implications of the new. Olson (1995), when identifying a range of teachers' concerns on the difficulty of achieving interaction between computer use and existing practice, raised the problem that teachers are not provided with enough time to reflect on practice and change. He believed teachers appear to be expected to take substantial risks in accommodating IT in their teaching that threatens their classroom ethos. He and Duchateau (1995) noted the value of computers in that they may help teachers to confront their experience; change involves not just the adoption and integration of the technology, but personal reflection and adaptation as well. Ridgeway and Passey (1995) considered that the advocates of computers, through overambitious claims and an underestimation of practical constraints, sow the seeds of their own failure, challenging teachers' fundamental values and practices.

In the last ten years there have been 44 articles in *Teaching Geography* (vols 15–24) specifically associated with using IT in geography classrooms; 75 per cent were written by members of the GA IT working group. Many focus on how IT can support the curriculum, whether it be with satellite imagery or through using the Internet. An increasing number relate to the integration of IT into schemes of work. Rudd (1994) reported on a large survey of the then current situation with regard to IT and geography – insufficient hardware, problems of access and poor quality software all featured in the respondents' concerns. Most used IT only once or twice a term; only 11 per cent had received any INSET on more than two days. The DfEE national survey of software for curriculum use (Freeman, 1997) noted that there were a number of areas key to geographers where appropriate software was sadly lacking. My case study research was in the early 1990s, but the last DfEE statistical review of IT use in classes reported again that less than 10 per cent of geography teachers used software regularly in their classes. The reality has not changed.

We have had similar problems with innovation in geography in the past. It was a common mistake of many of the Schools Council Projects to assume that the materials produced, would inherently work and be used only in the style which the project teams intended and espoused. However, Roberts (1996) reported that research had shown a gap between the ideals of the curriculum projects of the 1970s and actual practice.

Thus we have here a substantial gap between the rhetoric of IT use, advocated by both the government and the GA, and the reality of classroom use. In this chapter I have argued that research evidence suggests there should be less emphasis on the use of the computer as a curriculum artefact, and more on the time professionals need to address their legitimate concerns. Cuban (1986), writing about the use of machines by teachers, refers to the 'exhilaration, scientific credibility, disappointment, blame cycle'. I would argue that the cycle does not necessarily operate in a linear fashion, and that the conundrum of the legitimate professional concerns of the teachers in my research schools reflects the conflicts of different parts of the cycle. Attention should rightly focus on the barriers to change, but the current rhetoric surrounding the barriers does not appear to address the professional concerns of the majority of geography teachers.

REFERENCES

Cuban, L. (1986) *Teachers and Machines – the Classroom Use of Technology since 1920*. New York: Teachers College Press.

Cuban, L. (1989) 'Neoprogressive visions and organizational realities', *Harvard Educational Review*, vol. 59, no. 2, pp. 217–22.

DES/DfEE (1989, 1991, 1993, 1995, 1997) *Survey of Information Technology in Schools*. London: DES/DfEE.

Duchateau, C. (1995) 'The computer: ally or alien?', in Watson, D. and Tinsley, D. (eds), *Integrating Information Technology into Education*. London: Chapman & Hall.

Freeman, D. (1997) 'A review of software for geographers', *Teaching Geography*, vol. 22, no. 4, pp. 196–7.

Fox, P. and Tapsfield, A. (eds) (1986) *The Role and Value of New Technology in Geography*. Sheffield: Geographical Association.

Fullan, M. (1991) *The New Meaning of Educational Change*, 2nd edn. London: Cassell.

Gardner, J., Morrison, H., Jarman, R., Reilly, C. and McNally, H. (1992) *Pupils' Learning and Access to Information Technology*. Belfast: Queen's University of Belfast.

Goodson, I. (1991) 'Teachers' lives and educational research', in Goodson, I.F. and Walker, R. (eds), *Biography, Identity and Schooling*. London: Falmer Press.

Huberman, M. (1995) 'Professional careers and professional development: some intersections', in Guskey, T.R. and Huberman, M. (eds), *Professional Development in Education: New Paradigms and Practices*. London: Teachers College Press.

Johnson, D.C., Cox, M.J., and Watson, D.M. (1994) 'Evaluating the impact on pupils' achievements', *Journal of Computer Assisted Learning*, vol. 10, no. 3, pp. 138–56.

Kent, W.A. (1992) 'The new technologies and geographical education, in Naish, M. (ed.), *Geography and Education*. London: London University Institute of Education.

OFSTED (1995) *Information Technology: A Review of Inspection Findings, 1993/94*. London: HMSO.

Olson, J. (1995) 'Classroom ethos and the concerns of the teacher', in Watson, D.M. and Tinsley, D. (eds), *Integrating Information Technology into Education*. London: Chapman & Hall.

Pelgrum, W.J. and Plomp, T. (1991) *The Use of Computers in Education Worldwide*. Oxford: Pergamon Press.

Ridgeway, J. and Passey, D. (1995) 'Using evidence about teacher development to plan systemic revolution', in Watson, D.M. and Tinsley, D. (eds), *Integrating Information Technology into Education*. London: Chapman & Hall.

Roberts, M. (1996) 'Teaching styles and strategies', in Kent, A., Lambert, D., Naish, M. and Slater, F. (eds), *Geography in Education: Viewpoints on Teaching and Learning*. Cambridge: Cambridge University Press.

Rudd, M. (1994) 'IT in geography: present and future', *Teaching Geography*, vol. 19, no. 3, pp. 138–9.

Shepherd, I.D.H., Cooper, Z. and Walker, D.R.F. (1980) *Computer Assisted Learning in Geography: Current Trends and Future Prospects*. London: Council for Educational Technology, with the Geographical Association.

Stevenson, D. (ed.) (1997) *The Future of Information Technology in UK Schools*. London: McKinsey and Company.

van den Akker, J., Keursten P. and Plomp, T. (1992) 'The integration of computer use in education', *International Journal of Educational Research*, vol. 17, no. 1, pp. 65–76.

Watson, D.M. (ed.) (1984) *Exploring Geography with Microcomputers*. London: Council for Educational Technology.

Watson, D.M. (ed.) (1993) *The ImpacT Report: An Evaluation of the Impact of Information Technology on Children's Achievements in Primary and Secondary Schools*. London: King's College London.

Willis, J. (1992) 'Technology diffusion in the "soft disciplines": using social technology to support Information Technology', *Computers in the Schools*, vol. 9, no. 1, pp. 81–118.

Yinger, R. (1987) 'Learning the language of practice', Curriculum Enquiry, vol. 17, no. 3, pp. 293–318.

Chapter 19

Research into geography textbooks

Norman Graves and Brendan Murphy

INTRODUCTION

Why should research on textbooks be worthwhile? Perhaps a prime reason is that textbooks are a reflection of the society that produced them. The ethos of a society, its culture, the issues which arise at any particular time, the technological stage of the society, all these tend to be manifest in textbooks whether they are concerned with mathematics, science, history or geography. For example: nationalistic fervour is often present in both history and geography textbooks; economic problems concerning the distribution of industry are to be found in geography textbooks; the use of examples of financial dealings are found in mathematics textbooks; environmental issues feature in science textbooks; the very techniques used in printing and publishing are revealed in all textbooks – indeed the progress made by electronic media is thought by some to threaten the very existence of textbooks. Of course, not all authors conform to the norms of any given society, and some stand out as being divergent.

More specifically in relation to geography, textbooks tend to reveal the authors' conception of the discipline and its educational purpose. Looking at the evolution of textbooks over time, it is possible to see how and why what is taught has evolved and what relation school geography bears to geography at a higher level. Further, the pedagogical techniques employed in textbooks alert one to the way the subject was used to fulfil (or not to fulfil) the aims and objectives of education. Inevitably the content of textbooks mirrors to a large extent the nature of the education system into which they are embedded; for example in England and Wales at present, no book is likely to be successful unless it reflects the content of the National Curriculum. This has been true for a long time, of course, in many countries where the curriculum has always been laid down centrally by the government. In fact textbooks have not infrequently been used to reinforce the ideology favoured by the government of the day. This was particularly true of Nazi Germany prior to the Second World War and of the Union of the Soviet Socialist Republics until its demise in 1991. But whether consciously undertaken by the 'guidance' given to authors by government ministries of education or, less consciously, by individual writers who have simply internalised the current ethos of their society, all geography textbooks tend to reflect the cultures of the societies which they serve. An interesting case is that of nineteenth- and early twentieth-century French geography textbooks where patriotism is a recurring theme.

THE DEVELOPMENT OF RESEARCH ON TEXTBOOKS

Most research concerned specifically with geography textbooks is of relatively recent origins, though in the United States of America, research began in the second decade of the twentieth century. In Europe research on textbooks in general is something of an academic novelty, though some work was begun in the interwar years on the revision of history textbooks, as these were seen to be a source of international friction. UNESCO continued this work in the post-Second World War period starting with international conferences in 1950–51. Dr Georg Eckert in Germany with the cooperation of German teachers set up the International Institute for School Textbooks in Brunswick, which collected large numbers of textbooks in history, geography and modern languages. These were commented on by teachers and other educationists, with a view to correcting inaccuracies and misconceptions. This movement towards the revision of textbooks with a view to improving international understanding began in the 1950s, was also aided by the Council of Europe and continues to this day (Eckert, 1964). The study of textbooks as an academic pursuit began in the USA where at present there is an extensive literature on the subject. An international review of textbook research may be found in Glammer's (1986) *Textbook Research: An International Perspective*, though this is mainly concerned with the work of bodies like the League of Nations and UNESCO. To our knowledge the first general book in Europe devoted to the study of textbooks was not published until 1992 and that was in France (Choppin, 1992), to be followed in 1993 by Johnsen's *Textbooks in Kaleidoscope* published in Norway. Chris Stray, one of the foremost British researchers into textbooks, developed his ideas on the historical sociology of textbook writing and production, through an analysis of classics 'primers' (Stray, 1993). The British Textbook Colloquium which consists of a group of academics interested in the study of textbooks published its first Newsletter in 1989, which subsequently became, in December 1993, the journal *Paradigm* containing refereed articles.

RESEARCH ON GEOGRAPHY TEXTBOOKS

The first bibliography of British sources on geographical education, which deals with the period 1870 to 1970, was published in 1972 (Lukehurst and Graves, 1972). Admittedly a selective bibliography, it contains only 36 entries on textbooks out of a total of 1402 entries. Of these, 17 date from the post-Second World War period, nine from the interwar period, nine from the early part of the twentieth century and only one was written in the last years of the nineteenth century. Most of the articles referred to in the bibliography were written to help teachers to choose books for use in their teaching. Some were reviews of books, and some consisted of what the authors thought were the characteristics of a good geography book or atlas. A comment made by André Hanaire (1965), author of a chapter on 'Teaching Materials' in the *UNESCO Source Book for Geography Teaching* sums up the attitude of teachers to textbooks:

> There is no such thing as a perfect textbook. The teacher plays a primordial part. Whatever book he has, it is for him to make his own selection from the material offered. He must use it according to his conception of the lesson and he must supplement it as he thinks necessary.

On the other hand, the perceived need for making sure that geography textbooks did not contain inaccuracies or biased material when they described 'foreign' countries led a number of scholars to make studies of textbooks and to make recommendations for their revision. Some of these early works are listed in Marchant's (1967) *Geography Teaching and the Revision of Geography Textbooks and Atlases*, which also reports on four conferences held on geography textbook revision under the aegis of the Council for Cultural Cooperation of the Council of Europe. The main aim of these conferences was to eliminate what were seen as factual inaccuracies in textbooks.

The second bibliography on geographical education (Foskett and Marsden, 1998) contains somewhat more entries on textbooks than the first: 66 entries out of a total of 3708, though admittedly not all came from British sources, but most do date from the 1980s and 1990s. Thus there is little doubt that writing about geography textbooks is essentially a twentieth-century phenomenon, and research on such textbooks is a development that belongs to the post-Second World War period.

Of the later research, can one discern any general trend or common thread? Certainly some of the outstanding concerns, as we saw earlier, were those of researchers who were anxious to document and ultimately to eliminate bias in geography textbooks. Apart from the work of the Council of Europe and the George Eckert Institut (the new name of the former International Institute for School Textbooks), a number of individual workers have devoted much effort in this direction, as for example David Hicks (1980) who documented ethnocentric bias, Bill Marsden (1990) who pointed to the many imperialistic attitudes extant in many prewar textbooks, and Rex Walford (1989) and David Wright (1986a) who pointed to the tendency of textbooks to portray Third World people as 'backward' as a result of their illustrations concentrating on exotic and primitive techniques in agriculture and industry. More recently Teresa Ploszajska (1998) attempted to show that imperialistic attitudes existed alongside the desire to develop citizenship education, in other words that while imperial attitudes still dominated there was a concern also to develop attitudes of responsibility towards other people. Rob Gilbert (1984) described the extent to which textbooks omitted to consider important issues of race, class and gender, and so by omission reinforced establishment ideologies. Textbooks, he argued, seldom asked critical questions about society and its practices. Another line of research lies in attempts to find out how teachers actually use textbooks. In this domain John Lidstone (1990) has been the main protagonist. His observations based on a sample of ten teachers showed that most teachers used textbooks as a primary source of data, but did not extensively use the questions and activities proposed in the books; neither did they expect their pupils to read the books independently. Teachers valued the diagrams in textbooks as an aid to exposition, but rarely used these in questioning pupils; photographs in textbooks were not extensively used by teachers although pupils valued them. Allied to this is the search for a means of evaluating textbooks to which David Lambert (1996) and David Wright (1986b) have signally contributed. There has also been the beginnings of research using content analysis of geography textbooks (Acheson, 1994) and research into how textbooks on particular aspects of geography are actually conceived (Lester, 1996). This latter arises partly out of more general research on discourse analysis. Teresa Ploszajska (2000) has undertaken a critical analysis 'of relations between popular geographical and imperial discourses' through the study of nineteenth- and early twentieth-century textbooks. Brendan Murphy (1999) has examined recent textbooks with a view to finding out how far the activities for pupils they contain reflect a concern for values education (see below). A review of research which concentrates on geography textbooks has been published by the British Sub-Committee of the International Geographical Union's Commission on Geographical Education (Kent, 1998). It contains useful chapters on writing about textbooks by Bill Marsden, on rediscovering textbook pedagogy by David Lambert and on the way primary school textbooks have changed since 1945.

SOME CURRENT ISSUES IN GEOGRAPHY TEXTBOOK RESEARCH

Despite the recent growth of access to multimedia and the Internet, the textbook remains the principal teaching resource used in the geography classroom. It is the textbook that establishes much of the material conditions for teaching and learning and it is the textbook that often defines what is legitimate knowledge to pass on. The amount of space in professional journals and books on geography teaching which has been devoted to the textbook, however, remains dramatically less than that given to other teaching and learning resources such as computers.

What little attention has been given to textbooks has often focused on criticisms of the textbook rather than on its effective use in the classroom. John Lidstone (1992) suggests that much of this criticism is ill-founded, being often a matter of the worker criticising his tools rather than acknowledging that there may be some failing in the way in which they are used. Textbooks, it has been suggested, are composed of expository text that must be learned by pupils and so are equated with the worst mode of the 'reception' model of learning. Textbooks have also been criticised as consisting entirely of the results of geographical enquiry presented as findings to be learned by pupils. Authors are thus presenting students with their interpretations of evidence, rather than presenting evidence and encouraging students to make their own interpretations. Lidstone contends that most textbooks published during the 1980s contained a wide range of data sources in the form of text, maps, diagrams, tables, graphs and photographs taken from newspapers, government reports, journals and the publications of special interest groups and included activities that were designed to encourage pupils to create their own interpretations based on the source material provided. He quotes the Prefaces and Introductions of the then current generation of textbooks as revealing statements such as: 'Data is provided to be thought about and analysed and worked on' (Beddis, *A Sense of Place*, Oxford, 1982, quoted in Lidstone, 1992, p. 180).

A detailed survey of the activities contained in the textbooks of the 1980s would be necessary in order to establish whether such claims were borne out, and is beyond the scope of this chapter. It is sufficient to note that it was the stated intention of those authors to encourage discussion, thought and analysis among pupils. The equivalent statements by textbook authors and their publishers in the 1990s, however, perhaps reveal a different set of priorities. On the back cover of David Waugh's 1994 *The Wider World*, the publishers claim that the textbook 'delivers National Curriculum and GCSE geography in a stimulating, clear and readable manner', while pupils 'are encouraged to test their understanding and knowledge in a range of assessment material' (Waugh, 1994). In Keith Grimwade's *Discover Human Geography*, published the same year, a note

'To the Teacher' states that, 'Enquiries help pupils to record important information and to develop their understanding of the themes covered' (Grimwade, 1994). Kemp et al.'s, *Access to Geography*, meanwhile, features 'themes, topics, and case studies drawn from the National Curriculum programmes of study' (Kemp et al., 1995).

Perhaps the trend evident in the textbooks of the 1980s, away from a reception model of learning and towards one in which pupils are seen as actively engaged in their own learning, has to some extent been reversed in the 1990s by the impact of the National Curriculum. Textbooks currently available for use at Key Stage 3 overwhelmingly refer to the National Curriculum in their introductions or sleeve notes and many of them claim to 'deliver' the curriculum!

The work of the well-respected geographers who wrote the books of the past may be regarded as reflecting the dominant ideology of their times. Textbooks may implicitly present knowledge about the world as fixed in structure and may lead pupils to regard a particular world-view as uncontroversial or even incontrovertible. Pupils may be given selective access to ideas and information that may predispose them to think and act in certain ways and not consider possibilities, questions or actions not promoted by the textbook. Geographical knowledge is chosen, organised and presented on the basis of subjective decisions by people who hold particular value positions. It is not indisputable and subject to universal laws in the positivist sense. The aim of geographical education, therefore, should not be to impart a predetermined and particular world-view, but to develop pupils as autonomous, informed and critical agents, who think for themselves.

RESEARCH ON GEOGRAPHY SCHOOL TEXTBOOKS: AN EXAMPLE (MURPHY, 1999)

In order to think about the values underpinning currently used geography textbooks at GCSE, a broad analytical framework was developed from Margaret Roberts' (1996) framework for thinking about teaching style and strategy. Roberts' framework was based on a categorisation suggested by Barnes et al. (1987), in an interim report evaluating the TVEI curriculum. The report suggested three 'styles' of teaching and learning: closed, framed and negotiated, the main factor used to determine style being the amount of control teachers maintained over subject content and activities. It also suggested that action at different ends of the spectrum is underpinned by different educational values. This 'participation dimension' was adapted by Roberts and applied to geographical education. This framework was refined in order to provide a means of categorising the activities contained within the textbook along a broad continuum ranging from purely closed activities, through activities that could be categorised as being framed in style to the most open type of activity (see Table 19.1).

Since the activities contained within a textbook relate to the text, thinking about them and the values that underpin them allows us to think about the values and assumptions about knowledge that underlie the text. Activities at the closed end of the framework are those in which pupils are the passive recipients of and dependent upon the author's knowledge. Such activities may merely require pupils to repeat information contained in the text or may require them to process information into a different form, as when pupils are asked to read data from a graph or to draw a graph from data given. Activities at the closed end of the framework present data as authoritative and not to

Table 19.1 A framework for analysing the activities contained in geography textbooks

	Textbook activities require pupils to . . .	Pupils are . . .
Closed	repeat information contained in the text;	passive dependent
	process information from different sources or process information into a different form;	
	think about information and begin to ask questions, although these will remain the author's questions.	
Framed		
	Activities are designed to make pupils ask their own questions.	
Open	Activities are designed to make pupils evaluate the data and ask their own questions about its validity.	active enquiring independent

be challenged; they lead pupils to conclusions that have been predetermined and which are not open to debate. Activities that can be categorised as framed are those which encourage pupils to think about the information and begin to ask questions, although these may remain the author's questions. Such activities may engage the pupils with a variety of data, which may be presented as evidence to be interpreted. Pupils may be presented with conflicting evidence or viewpoints and led to reach their own interpretation. At the open end of the framework, activities are designed to allow pupils to ask their own questions, evaluate the data and ask questions about its validity. Pupils could be encouraged to find their own data from sources beyond the textbook. Pupils will be encouraged to reach their own conclusions and evaluate them. Here, pupils are actively engaged in their own learning, and are learning to be independent of textbook author and teacher.

In this research, four textbooks were scrutinised with reference to the activities suggested on 'Aid' and 'Flooding'. Here, only references to 'aid' in two of those textbooks will be examined. In David Waugh's *The Wider World* (1994), 'aid' is dealt with within a chapter on 'World Development'. Pupil activities come in the form of one page of questions at the end of the chapter. There are six pupil activities specifically on 'aid', grouped together as one 'stepped' question, with marks allocated to each task in the manner of a GCSE question (p. 167). The first task is a straight closed question that merely requires the pupils to repeat the information given in the text on the differences between bilateral, multilateral and voluntary aid. The next two tasks appear at first to be more 'open' and to require pupils to give their own opinion. On closer examination, however, the tasks also fall at the extreme 'closed' end of the framework, merely requiring pupils to find and repeat information supplied in the text. Having described the differences between the three types of aid (6 marks), the pupils are then asked, 'Which type of aid do you think is best for the recipient country?' (1 mark), and asked to give reasons for their answer (2 marks). A note at the head of the question refers pupils to pages 160 and 161. Here, the different types of aid are described, but whereas the descriptions for bilateral and multilateral aid are purely negative, giving no advantages, that for voluntary aid is purely positive. So, for example, in the case of bilateral aid, we are told that 'the donor country benefits by increasing its trade', while 'the recipient country falls further into debt'. In the case of bilateral aid, we are told that 'theoretically, there should be no political ties', but that 'recently, these organisations have taken it upon themselves to withhold aid if they disagree with the economic and political system within a country'. Voluntary aid, by contrast has 'no political ties', and voluntary organisations are 'usually the first to provide food, clothing and shelter following a major disaster'. It is obvious which answer the author requires the pupils to give. Far from inviting pupils to come to a conclusion about the pros and cons of each type of aid, the question is in fact requiring pupils to find and repeat the opinion expressed by the author on page 160.

In Kemp et al.'s *Access to Geography 5* (1995), aid is dealt with in two double-page spreads, one a general section on 'International aid', the other a 'case study' of Bangladesh. The section 'Choices for Bangladesh' includes a role-play activity in which pupils take the parts of the Bangladeshi prime minister, finance minister and ministers for education, health, and trade and industry. Each group has to discuss six proposed aid programmes and choose three of them, giving the reasons for their choice. The six aid programmes include large- and small-scale industrial projects, a scheme to develop agriculture, cyclone protection and rural health education. They are funded through bilateral, multilateral, voluntary and Bangladeshi government aid. This task falls in the middle of the framework, requiring pupils to think about the information and to begin to ask questions. Although these remain the authors' questions, the pupils are engaged in making decisions and evaluating choices. The pupils are dependent upon the information that is provided by the authors, but this is not framed in such a way as to present pupils with easy and obvious choices between 'good' and 'bad' aid programmes. Indeed, the activity is structured in such a way as to encourage pupils to appreciate the different points of view and different interests that can come into play when decisions about spending aid money are made.

Overall, the four textbooks considered are dominated by activities of the closed type (see Tables 19.2 and 19.3). David Waugh's *Wider World* is the most closed in character, while Kemp et al.'s *Access to Geography* has most activities of an open character and the widest range of activities when categorised in this way. All of the textbooks have at least some range of activities, however, and it should be borne in mind that, although the textbook activities were broken down into individual tasks for the purposes of the summary tables, these would not all be of equal weight in terms of pupil time. It is interesting to note that, overall, there is a rather narrower range of activities on flooding than on aid and that, although three of the textbooks ask pupils to choose between different flood prevention options, there is no real attempt in any textbook to introduce a values and attitudes dimension to this topic.

Flooding, apparently, is a less controversial issue than aid, at least in the eyes of this sample of textbook authors. It is interesting to ask why this is so, as this may hold the key as to why all of the textbook activities are dominated by closed tasks. The lack of a values dimension to flooding, and the way in which values regarding aid are dealt with, suggests that the textbook authors themselves have only a limited notion of what

Table 19.2 Pupil activities on 'aid' summarised

	Waugh	Bowen & Pallister	*Grimwade*	*Kemp et al.*
Textbook activities require pupils to . . .				
1 repeat information contained in the text	*****	*******	***	*
2 process information from different sources or process information into a different form	****	***	**	
3 think about information and begin to ask questions, although these will remain the author's questions	*	*	**	**
4 activities are designed to make pupils ask their own questions			*	
5 activities are designed to make pupils evaluate the data and ask their own questions about its validity				

Note: Each asterisk represents one pupil activity or task.

values education is. The authors, we would suggest, see values and attitudes as consisting of 'points of view' of which the pupils need to be aware in order to answer certain questions in the examination. Thus, whereas 'aid' is a controversial topic about which pupils should have a 'view' (chosen from one of two polar positions), 'flooding' is a non-controversial topic where the need for pupils to be aware of, and express, attitudes does not arise.

CONCLUSION

As the previous section indicates research on geography textbooks is actively being undertaken though it is still in its infancy. However, a start has been made. Currently more attention is being paid to the textbooks as a reflection of the society which produced them, to the extent to which they reflect the true state of the discipline at the research level, to the values implicit in their content and to the way textbooks are being used.

REFERENCES

Acheson, D.A. (1994) 'An analysis of how changing viewpoints in geography at university level have influenced school textbooks', in Slater, F. (ed.), *Reporting Research in Geography Education,*

Table 19.3 Pupil activities on 'flooding' summarised

	Waugh	Bowen & Pallister	*Grimwade*	*Kemp et al.*
Textbook activities require pupils to:				
1 repeat information contained in the text	*******	**	******	*
2 process information from different sources or process information into a different form	*	*******	***	
3 think about information and begin to ask questions, although these will remain the author's questions	*	**	**	
4 activities are designed to make pupils ask their own questions				
5 activities are designed to make pupils evaluate the data and ask their own questions about its validity				

Note: Each asterisk represents one pupil activity or task.

Monograph No. 1. London: University of London Institute of Education.

Barnes, D., Johnson, G., Jordan, S., Layton, D., Medway, P. and Yeomans, D. (1987) *The TVEI Curriculum 14–16: An Interim Report Based on Case Studies in Twelve Schools*. University of Leeds.

Bowen, A. and Pallister, J. (1999) *Understanding GCSE Geography*. Oxford: Heinemann.

Choppin, A. (1992) *Les Manuels Scolaires: Histoire et Actualité*. Paris: Hachette.

Eckert, G. (1964) 'International textbook revision', in Bereday, G.Z.F. and Lauwerys, J.A. (eds), *Year Book of Education 1964*. London: Evans Brothers.

Foskett, N. and Marsden, B. (eds) (1998) *A Bibliography of Geographical Education: 1970–1997*. Sheffield: Geographical Association.

Gilbert, R. (1984) *The Impotent Image: Reflections of Ideology in the Secondary School Curriculum*. Lewes: Falmer Press.

Glammer, P.E. (1986) *Textbook Research: An International Perspective*. University of East Anglia, School of Education.

Grimwade, K. (1994) *Discover Human Geography*. London: Hodder & Stoughton.

Hanaire, A. (1965) 'Teaching materials' in *Unesco Source Book for Geography Teaching*. London: Longmans/UNESCO.

Hicks, D. (1979) *Bias in Geography Textbooks: Images of the Third World and Multi-ethnic Britain*, Working Paper No. 1. London: University of London Institute of Education.

Hicks, D. (1980) 'Bias in books', *World Studies Journal*, vol. 1, p. 3.

Johnsen, E. B. (c.1993) *Textbooks in Kaleidoscope: A Critical Survey of Literature and Research on Educational Texts*. Oslo: Scandinavian University Press.

Kemp, R., Mason, R., Carvin, P. and Carvin, Z. (1995) *Access to Geography 5: GCSE*. Oxford: OUP.

Kent, W.A. (ed.) (1998) *Issues for Research in Geographical Education, Research Forum 1: Textbooks*. London: IGU Commission on Geographical Education/University of London Institute of Education.

Lambert, D. (1996) 'The choice of textbooks for use in secondary school geography departments: some answers and further questions', *Paradigm*, vol. 21.

Lester, A.J. (1995) 'Conceptualising social formation: producing a textbook on South Africa', PhD thesis. University of London Institute of Education.

Lester, A. (1996) 'Textual discourse and reader interaction: writing a text on the historical geography of South Africa', in Slater, F. (ed.), *Reporting Research in Geographical Education*, Monograph No. 3. London: University of London Institute of Education.

Lidstone, J. (1990) *Researching the Use of Textbooks in Geography Classrooms*. Internationale Schulbuchforschung 12.

Lidstone, J. (1992) 'In defence of textbooks', in Naish, M.C. (ed.), *Geography in Education: National and International Perspectives*. London: University of London Institute of Education.

Lukehurst, C.T and Graves, N.J. (1972) *Geography in Education: A Bibliography of British Sources*. Sheffield: Geographical Association.

Marchant, E.C. (ed.), (1967) *Geography Teaching and the Revision of Geography Textbooks and Atlases*. Strasbourg: Council for Cultural Cooperation of the Council of Europe.

Marsden, W.E. (1990) 'Rooting racism into the educational experience of childhood and youth in the nineteenth- and twentieth-centuries', *History of Education*, vol. 19, no. 4, pp. 333–53.

Murphy, B.P. (1999) 'To what extent is the way in which geography is presented in GCSE textbooks informed by a concern for values education?' Unpublished MA dissertation, University of London Institute of Education.

Ploszajska, T. (1998) 'Representations of imperial landscapes and peoples in popular geography texts, 1870–1944', in Naish, M. (ed.), *Values in Education*. London: IGU Commission on Geographical Education/University of London Institute of Education.

Ploszajska, T. (2000) 'Historiographies of geography and empire', in Graham, B and Nash, C. (eds), *Modern Historical Geographies*. Harlow: Longman, Pearson Educational.

Roberts, M. (1996) 'Teaching styles and strategies', in Kent, W.A., Lambert, D., Naish, M. and Slater, F. (eds), *Geography in Education: Viewpoints on Teaching and Learning*. Cambridge: Cambridge University Press.

Stray, C. (1993) 'Quia nominor leo: vers une sociologie historique du manuel', *Histoire de l'éducation*, no. 58, May.

Walford, R. (1989) 'On the frontier with the New Model Army: geography publishing from the 1960s to the 1990s', *Geography*, vol. 74, part 4, pp. 308–20.

Waugh, D. (1994) *The Wider World*. Walton-on-Thames: Nelson.

Wright, D.R. (1986a) 'Racism in school textbooks', in Punter D. (ed.), *Introduction to Contemporary Cultural Studies*. London: Longman.

Wright, D.R. (1986b) 'Evaluating textbooks', in Boardman, D. (ed.) *Handbook for Geography Teachers*, Sheffield: Geographical Association.

Chapter 20

The renaissance of geography education in the USA

Joanne Clark and Joseph P. Stoltman

AN INTRODUCTION TO GEOGRAPHY EDUCATION IN THE UNITED STATES

The United States has approximately 45 million students enrolled in kindergarten through secondary school. In such a huge educational system, change occurs slowly, often in orchestrated steps. However, some changes arrive practically unnoticed, and this was the case with the changes in the teaching of geography within the United States in the two decades following World War II.

Geography as a separate subject had all but disappeared from the American schools by the beginning of the 1980s. The aspects of the subject that were being taught were often delivered by teachers who themselves had little or no academic background in the discipline. Geography was subsumed mainly in the social studies curriculum where it was ill defined without clear content or methodology, and had received scant attention for many decades.

Numerous studies at the time revealed the extent of geographic ignorance among Americans and it became apparent that much work was to be done if geographical education was to enjoy a revival in the school curriculum.

The geography community, led by the prestigious and wealthy National Geographic Society was spurred into action and a turnaround for geography was called for. What followed was a richly funded and well-supported national campaign to improve the quality and quantity of geography taught in schools.

This chapter starts by tracing the history of geography education in the United States, focusing on the circumstances leading to geography's decline and then to the period of revival. The ongoing campaign to bring about a revival of geographical education in the United States is then examined in detail. The range and nature of the initiatives, policies and projects implemented on geography's behalf, both on a national level and in the case-study area of Michigan, are outlined

The chapter concludes that although much progress has been made, there is still a long way to go. On a national level geography has moved from a very weak, ignored and neglected condition, to a position of increasing status and power. On an individual school level, however, geography remains the underdog of subjects despite the large-scale projects and the rigorous policy-making of the national campaign.

GEOGRAPHY – FROM STRENGTH TO DECLINE

Pre-twentieth-century geography – a period of strength

Geography was not always a subject of low status in America. In fact during the eighteenth and nineteenth centuries geography was regarded to be an integral part of the school curriculum. Writing in 1784, Jedidiah Morse described geography as 'A science no longer esteemed as a polite agreeable accomplishment only, but as a necessary and important part of education'.

In the 1830s a number of American states passed laws requiring the teaching of geography, particularly physical geography, in their schools (Stoltman, 1986) and by 1840 almost 50 geography school textbooks had been published. *Harper's School Geography* of 1875 stated 'The study of geography is now, much more than at any former period, an essential element in education. It is second in importance only to reading, writing and rudimentary arithmetic'.

Geography education in the early twentieth century – the decline begins

At the start of the twentieth century, geography held a strong position in the school curriculum, but things began to change quite drastically following a National Education Association (NEA) curriculum review in 1911. The NEA report and recommendations led to general science and earth science consuming the physical aspects of school geography courses and the emerging discipline 'social studies' the social and human aspects of the subject.

The social studies movement strengthened during the 1920s, but the position of geography within it began to weaken. This was especially so following a social studies curriculum initiative, led by a group of history teachers. The project had the aim of developing social studies course materials and the organizing committee approached subject specialists from all areas of social studies for input. All replied favourably, except for the prominent geographers who decided not to take part in the discussions, believing that geography should not just be a part of social studies but a subject in its own right. As a result 'geographers did not gain a prominent role in the early stages of the social studies movement. In fact quite the contrary occurred' (Libbee and Stoltman, 1994).

From the 1930s and 1940s, geographical education in schools can be described as suffering a spiral of decline, a decline that was to profoundly affect the quality and provision of geographical education in the future. At this time social studies courses were continuing to thrive while separate geography courses continued to disappear and 'special interest groups in geography comparable to those that had been concerned with the subject as a separate offering in 1892 and 1904 had little to say' (Libbee and Stoltman, 1994).

The status of geography in the social studies curriculum began to diminish after World War II for many reasons. First, at this time only a few teachers were majoring in geography at undergraduate level (Natoli, 1994) and as a result less curriculum time was being devoted to the study of geography than the other social studies subjects like history (Stoltman, 1989). Also, university geography departments were giving less time to the training of teachers in favor of specialist research and the problem of the lack of trained geography teachers was further exacerbated. The quality of the geography teaching suffered and with it pupil learning and interest in the subject.

This lack of geography expertise in the teaching of social studies, coupled with crowded social studies, science and mathematics curricula marked the start of a downward trend which resulted in the continuing marginalization of geographical education and a tradition of geography in the school curriculum becoming increasingly forgotten.

Concern over geography's waning status within social studies was voiced as early as in the 1950s. In 1953 the Association of American Geographers (AAG) expressed the concern that, 'Our nation does not provide the majority of its young men and women with the necessary knowledge of the geography of the United States and that of other countries in the world as a whole' (Barrs, 1988).

In 1965 Mayo summarized geography's situation at that time. Some of his conclusions are reported in Figure 20.1.

By the middle of the 1970s, the status of geography had hit rock bottom. A survey in 1973 showed that less than half of the nation's schools had geography courses, of which most were junior high schools (Lanegran, 1989). Enrolments in geography courses in the mid-1970s had dropped to just 9 per cent of all secondary pupils, compared with 14 per cent in 1961 (Stoltman, 1989) and by the 1980s not one state required geography to be taught as a separate subject for high school graduation.

Many geographers of the time, notably Gilbert Grosvenor, Chairman of the National Geographic Society, agreed something had to be done to improve the quality and standing of geography in the school curriculum.

A RENAISSANCE FOR GEOGRAPHY

The catalyst

In contrast to the gradual decay and neglect school geographical education suffered for much of the twentieth century, the attempted revival of the subject has been much more of a dynamic process.

- Physical geography has been neglected almost completely.
- Even in the relatively sparse offerings of human geography, factual material is left out in favor of the interest-centered appeal.
- As a fused content subject, geography is not given equal time with history or other social sciences.
- Geography does not exist into the senior high school, except rarely, and it is even left out in the junior high school to a large extent.
- There is indifferent teaching in social studies concerning geography due to the lack of preparation of the teacher whose background is usually primarily in history courses.
- The chronological approach inherent to history wins out over the spatial or geographical approach.
- There is a lack of understanding on the part of the school administrators and teachers as to what geography is and what it should encompass.
- There is a lack of adequate class time in the curriculum for both history and geography on equal time levels.

Figure 20.1 Problems for geography in the social studies school curriculum (Mayo, 1965).

For many years the American geography community was aware of the poor quality and low status of geographical education. However, it was not until the 1980s that any significant action was taken on geography's behalf.

At this time numerous surveys were revealing the extent of geographical ignorance in the country. Concerned and embarrassed by these findings, the President of the National Geographic Society (NGS), Gilbert Grosvenor, brought geography to the attention of the media by condemning the absence or failure of geography teaching in America. Grosvenor called for a 'turnabout' in attitudes toward geography and then helped to stimulate this turnaround by throwing the considerable weight and resources of the NGS into a Geography Education Program.

An initial NGS grant of $20 million was used to provide a 'permanent and expanding source of financial support for exemplary education programs' (Grosvenor, 1995). Also, to encourage others to join the cause for geography, the NGS offered an additional $20 million as a 'challenge grant' where every individual and corporate contribution to the Geography Education Program would be matched by an equal amount from the challenge grant. More than $15 million has been raised as a result of this.

Although less cash rich, academic geography organizations, most notably the Association of American Geographers (AAG) and the National Council for Geographic Education (NCGE) were equally determined to help improve the quality and quantity of geography education in schools. Working both independently and with the NGS these organizations have implemented a wide range of initiatives.

STRATEGIES TO IMPROVE THE QUALITY AND QUANTITY OF GEOGRAPHY EDUCATION

The *Guidelines for Geographic Education*

The first successful attempt to provide educators and teachers with a conceptual base for organizing the structure of the core of geography in schools was given in the *Guidelines for Geographic Education* (NCGE, 1984).

The Guidelines, developed by a joint committee of the AAG and the NCGE, proposed that geographical education should include five key themes (Location, Place, Relationships within Places, Movement and Regions) and that these themes should be recurrent throughout the curriculum and represented at all levels in schools.

The Guidelines provided social studies teachers, who quite likely had no academic background in the subject, with a structure for geography curriculum planning. Natoli (1994) suggests that the Guidelines', 'subsequent adoption as the content vehicle for teacher networks and their use by textbook publishers, map producers, and curriculum developers in geography and social studies are evidence of their legitimacy'.

GENIP

GENIP, the Geographic Education National Implementation Project, was formed in 1985 when the National Council for Geographic Education (NCGE) and the Association of American Geographers (AAG) agreed to combine efforts with the National Geographic Society (NGS) and the American Geographic Society (AGS) to implement the recommendations of the Guidelines nationwide. It was the first time in the twentieth century that these four groups had joined together with the purpose of achieving a common goal – the reintroduction of geography into the curriculum (Boehm, 1997).

GENIP was initially set up to implement the Guidelines by distributing them to schools, teachers, State Education Department officials and the media across the United States. Today, GENIP continues to provide outreach on behalf of geography to educators and policy-makers across the United States and is active in providing expertise and leadership in the development of policies relating to geography education (GENIP, 1999).

The National Geographic Society Education Program

The Geography Education Program is at the 'heart' of the National Geographic Society's effort to put geography back in the nation's classrooms. The program, working with the National Geographic Society Education Foundation, utilizes resources from across the Society to improve geography instruction.

The NGS Geography Education Program focuses its resources in five strategic areas (see Figure 20.2). The State Alliance Network is described as the 'cornerstone' of the National Geographic Society's Education Program (Grosvenor, 1995). The network was initiated in 1985 and is a partnership between teachers, professional geographers, other education professionals, state officials and the public, working to improve geography's place in the schools of the United States.

Since 1985, the Alliance network has expanded across the country. Today, the Alliance involves more than 150 000 teachers and hundreds of academic geographers, and spans all states of America as well as Puerto Rico, The District of Columbia and Canada. Reviewing the progress of the Alliance movement in 1995, Gilbert Grosvenor stated 'we have gone from just a handful of geography professors and a small cadre of devoted teachers to an entire army of dedicated professionals intent on restoring geography to the curriculum and equipping their students with a solid understanding of the world'.

Typically, the State Alliances are based in the geography departments of state universities and are coordinated by university geography professors. The NGS Education Program provides each State Alliance with financial support, educational materials and teacher training. In return they are required to raise matching funds, usually from private sector investment, and to develop geography education programs in schools, colleges and universities across the state.

1. A grassroots network of State Alliances of teachers, professors and educational administrators.
2. Teacher training workshops and institutes.
3. Development of innovative educational materials.
4. Outreach to decision-makers.
5. Increasing public awareness through vehicles such as Geography Awareness Week and the National Geography Bee competition.

Figure 20.2 The five key strategies of the Geography Education Division of the National Geographic Society (Grosvenor, 1995).

The State Alliances also have responsibility for providing social studies teachers with instruction in geography. This geography training takes place through summer institutes, two-week all expenses paid training courses designed to provide social studies teachers with geography subject knowledge and teaching skills.

Graduates of the summer institutes are given the title 'Teacher Consultant'. Trained teacher consultants are expected to become active in their local State Alliance and are also encouraged to share what they have learned by leading in-service training sessions in schools in their home area (see Figure 20.3).

Geography for Life: National Geography Standards

The 1989 'America 2000' summit and the 1994 'Goals 2000: the Educate America Act' both included geography as one of the essential disciplines in which students should achieve 'world-class competency' by the year 2000.

The voluntary National Geography Standards were developed to help teachers to achieve these 'world-class' standards by suggesting what students should know and be able to do at the end of three benchmark grades: grade 4, grade 8 and grade 12 (equivalent to years 5, 9 and 13).

The *Geography for Life* document (NGSP, 1994) represents the first federal government attempt to provide State Education Departments, school officials and teachers with guidance as to what should be included in the geography curriculum. Stoltman (1999) suggests 'The reinvigoration of geographic education in the US has been greatly enhanced by the national content standards and assessment at both the state and national level'. (An outline of the content of the *Geography for Life: National Geography Standards* is provided in Figure 20.4.)

Unlike the English National Curriculum, the Geography for Life standards are

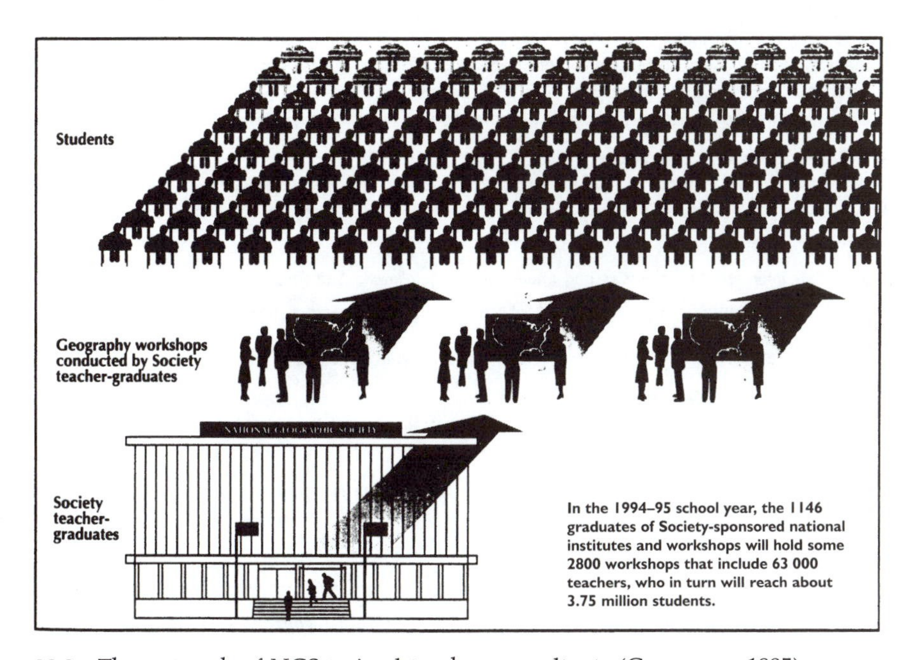

Figure 20.3 The outreach of NGS trained teacher consultants (Grosvenor, 1995).

The Six Essential Elements and their related Geography Standard

Element 1. The World in Spatial Terms.
Geography studies the relationship between people, places, and environment by mapping information about them into a spatial context.

The geographically informed person knows and understands the following Standards:
1. How to use maps and other geographical representations, tools, and technologies to acquire, process, and report information from a spatial perspective.
2. How to use mental maps to organize information about people, places, and environments in spatial context.
3. How to analyze the spatial organization of people, places, and environments on the Earth's surface.

Element 2. Places and Region
The identities and lives of individuals and peoples are rooted in particular places and in those human constructs called regions.

The geographically informed person knows and understands the following Standards:
4. The physical and human characteristics of places.
5. That people create regions to interpret Earth's complexity.
6. How culture and experience influence people's perceptions of places and regions.

Element 3. Physical Systems
Physical processes shape the Earth's surface and interact with plant and animal life to create, sustain, and modify ecosystems.

The geographically informed person knows and understands the following Standards:
7. The physical processes that shape the patterns on the Earth's surface.
8. The characteristics and spatial distribution of ecosystems on the Earth's surface.

Element 4. Human Systems
People are central to geography in that human activities help shape Earth's surface, human settlements and structures are part of Earth's surface, and humans compete for control of Earth's surface.

The geographically informed person knows and understands the following Standards:
9. The characteristics, distribution, and migration of human populations on the Earth's surface.
10. The characteristics, distribution, and complexity of the Earth's cultural mosaics.
11. The patterns and networks of economic interdependence on the Earth's surface.
12. The processes, patterns, and functions of human settlement.
13. How the forces of co-operation and conflict among people influence the division of control of Earth's surface.

Element 5. Environment and Society
The physical enviromnent is modified by human activities, largely as a consequence of the ways in which human societies value and use the Earth's natural resources, and human activities are also influenced by Earth's physical features and processes.

The geographically informed person knows and understands the following Standards:
14. How human actions modify the physical environment.
15. How physical systems affect human systems.
16. The changes that occur in the meaning, use, distribution, and importance of resources.

Element 6. The Uses of Geography
Knowledge of geography enables people to develop an understanding of the relationships between people, places, and environments over time – that is, of Earth as it was, is, and might be.

The geographically informed person knows and understands the following Standards:
17. How to apply geography to interpret the past.
18. How to apply geography to interpret the present and plan for the future.

Figure 20.4 The content of the *Geography for Life: National Geography Standards* (NGSP, 1994).

voluntary, not mandatory, and the extent to which the recommendations are implemented varies state by state and indeed from school to school.

In the United States education is the responsibility of Education Department Officials in each state. The State Education Departments (SEDs) are fiercely autonomous and there is a general reluctance to accept or adopt any federal initiatives. As a result it has been a challenging task for national and state level geography organizations to change the content of geography taught in each state in line with the national standards document.

The state geography Alliances have been active and have worked with SEDs on advisory committees to help instigate change. Also, GENIP, NCGE and NGS have worked with State Education Departments in an advisory capacity. There have been successes: some states have almost entirely adopted the content of the geography standards, and other states have adapted the standards to fit in with the existing curriculum. However, in too many states few changes have been made.

Even where states have adopted the concepts and content of *Geography for Life*, the problem remains that the majority of social studies teachers in the USA have little or no academic background in geography and teachers without prior geographic academic work found the content standards challenging (Stoltman, 1999).

Resource development

The development of quality resources has been a priority in the campaign to bring about a renaissance of geography education.

In 1999 a new division of the National Geographic Society, devoted to the development of educational products for the school arena, was created. The division is responsible for producing maps, videos, workbooks, overhead transparencies, activity books, CD-ROMs, mixed media kits and a website designed for teachers. It is intended that the Education Products Division will work with the Alliance network to establish the further needs and requirements of teachers.

The Association for American Geographers has also been active with the development of the ARGUS (Activities and Readings in the Geography of the United States) and ARGWorld (Activities and Resources in the Geography of the World) teaching materials.

Mission Geography is another large-scale curriculum development project. The National Aeronautic and Space Administration (NASA) is collaborating with the Geography Education National Implementation Project (GENIP) and its constituent organizations on this project. The goal is to produce three publications containing curriculum support materials that link NASA's missions and results with the National Geography Standards.

Advanced Placement Courses

In the USA high school students can take what are known as Advancement Placement Courses. These courses are available to highly academic students in grades 11 and 12 (years 12 and 13) and if passed provide the students with credit for their future undergraduate degree course.

The development of the first Advanced Placement Course in human geography, to be introduced in the academic year 2000–01, is further evidence of the increasing status of geography. The exclusion of a geography option from the Advanced Placement system was symptomatic of the perceived low value of the subject in the past and the development of the human geography course 'is drawing new attention to the importance of high school geography' (S. Bednarz, in Clark, 1999).

Private sector involvement

Another most impressive and unique element of the national campaign to revive geography in the United States is the support given by the private sector and other organizations. Organizations such as NASA, the National Science Foundation, BANK ONE, Delta Airlines, Apple Computers, IBM, Chrysler, Nissan and the Environmental Systems Research Institute have all been involved and have contributed significant financial resources, time and expertise to geography education projects.

Organizations such as these have become generous benefactors and powerful allies who could be crucial to the future success of the campaign. The decision of NASA to list geography alongside mathematics and technology as the three educational foci of NASA education programs, for example, is an illustration of how outside organizations can be important advocates for geography.

MICHIGAN CASE STUDY

Geography in Michigan schools

During the period from 1993 to 1999 the State of Michigan was engaged in a major reform of its state supported, K–12 educational system.[1] Geography was affected because of its role within the social studies curriculum. The Michigan Geographic Alliance was providing considerable leadership and service to Michigan education within the K–12 social studies. The many initiatives of the Alliance were designed to improve the teaching and learning of geography in the schools by providing professional preparation for teachers, materials for use in the classroom, and a public service program that heightened the awareness of the importance of geography education within the schools and the state. The overarching focus of improved geographic education was to prepare a more informed citizenry, both present and future, that would participate in the public issues being addressed. The principal focus on citizenship as the outcome of social studies education is widely accepted within Michigan. Geography is not taught to make young people miniature geographers, but to provide them with information, conceptual foundations and perspectives that will enable them to make informed decisions when a geographic perspective is helpful.

As in many other states, the Michigan Geographic Alliance became active during the early and enlightened period of reform, rethinking and reorganization of education when new ideas were accommodated and classroom reforms could be observed in upgrades of content, new materials and fresh approaches to enhancing the potential of geographic education. The Alliance had an important service to deliver, that of developing a significant geographic perspective among the students within the state through high quality instruction within K–12 classrooms. The Alliance, with the assistance of the National Geographic Society, the Michigan Department of Education and the Kellogg Foundation, had developed a cadre of Alliance trained teachers and embarked upon the challenge with considerable enthusiasm. The initial five years of

Alliance activities included annual summer workshops for teachers, in-service teacher development workshops during the school year, presentations at state, regional and national meetings, and membership on the policy-making groups that were formulating the future of social studies education. Alliance Teacher Consultants were well positioned on the key policy groups, including the Michigan Task Force for Social Studies Education, the Michigan Educational Assessment Program and the Michigan Task Force for the Development of Content Standards in Social Studies. The demands were great to meet the needs expressed by teachers and which school curriculum designers faced with educational reform, and the rewards were great. Geography education, through the Michigan Geographic Alliance, was boosted to a high-profile educational service provider.

In 1996, the reform movement had begun to implement the priorities and public policies that were formulating the future for Michigan education. Within social studies, geography was identified as one of the core academic subjects that all Michigan K–12 students should study. In addition to its placement among the core disciplines, it was designated as one of four core social science disciplines to be included on a statewide assessment of all students at 5th, 8th, and 11th grades in social studies. The importance of geography within Michigan K–12 education was clearly established and the future prospects to make important contributions to the educational mission of the state were in order.

Despite the operation of a successful Geographic Alliance since 1991, the actual status of geography within the curriculum in Michigan was not well known at this important juncture in the educational reform movement. What changes were necessary? What types of improvements were needed and expected? How would the Michigan Geographic Alliance know if it had been successful in five or ten years with the improvement of geography in the schools? Each of these questions came back to the realization that baseline data regarding how geography was functioning within the social studies curriculum was required if progress along the reform course was to be documented.

In 1996–97 the Alliance began to systematically collect baseline data from each of the 556 local educational authorities (school districts) within Michigan to ascertain change. What have we learned that has been helpful?

1. Geography is in the social studies curriculum. This clearly informs the Alliance of the ground rules for geography in the school. It is part of an integrated curriculum and must be viewed that way if geography teaching is to be enhanced.
2. In half the school districts there is no individual responsible for overseeing the development, scope and sequence of the social studies curriculum. It is the responsibility of a committee in most of those school districts, or left to develop by chance. The void is easily filled with enthusiastic, informed teachers. Geographic Alliance teachers have assumed considerable responsibility in designing and developing a geographically strong social studies curriculum in many school districts where other personnel have not been readily available.
3. When there is an individual, such as a curriculum coordinator or supervisor with responsibility for social studies, somewhat less than 25 per cent, on average, of that person's assigned time is actually devoted to social studies. The role of teacher consultants with in-service professional development and curriculum design and

writing experience is a major asset within the school district. It builds good personnel and working relationships when Alliance teacher consultants provide expertise in geography.

4. As the need for additional in-service professional development of teachers in response to the educational reform has increased, the Michigan Geographic Alliance (MGA) in-service professional activities have increased significantly. The MGA had an in-service network in operation beginning in 1992, and it continued to receive calls for workshops and institutes at a statistically significant level between the 1996–97 and 1998–99 school years. The provision of in-service professional development for the MGA has increased to the point where in any given year, in-service activities are being provided to approximately 25 per cent of the 556 school districts within the state. Since school districts not provided with the Alliance professional development program in prior years are continuing to call for assistance, the Alliance has probably had an impact on nearly every school district in a period of five to six years. This is a short timeframe in terms of systemic reform of the educational programs within the State of Michigan.

What lessons have been learned within Michigan that are helpful to others? There are many, but three are of most importance. First, the decision-making and policy-making arenas of education, whether at the local or state level, must be impacted by geography education. To fail to do this is to fail! Second, a strong cadre of teachers willing to work towards a common goal is crucial. This also necessitates clearly identifying the common goal. Third, there must be either real or perceived benefits in the classroom. While real benefits are better since they can be documented, the perceived benefits will hold the organization steady and on course for a time, but eventually the benefits of geography education from the reform must be apparent to parents, teachers and the community at large.

GEOGRAPHY EDUCATION IN AMERICA TODAY

Strengths, weaknesses, opportunities and threats

It is clear that the aspiration of achieving a 'renaissance' for geographical education in America's schools is a vision shared by all of the major national geography organizations of the United States.

The commitment of the organizations involved is unquestionable. The continuing financial support given to the development of geographical education and the magnitude and wide range of the projects introduced is astounding. As Boehm (1997) stated 'never before in recent history has the profession been so unified in its requirement for quality geographical education'.

The financial resources and influence of the National Geographic Society have allowed for the unprecedented development of large-scale and widespread geography education projects, such as the Alliance network, the Geography Bee and the Geography Awareness Week activities.

Other geography organizations, most notably the Association of American Geographers, the National Council for Geographic Education and the Geography Education National Implementation Project, have also made a significant undertaking to improve the quality and quantity of geographical education provided in American schools. The AAG has developed an impressive teacher resource on the geography of the United States in the ARGUS CD-ROM and the ARGWorld project, once completed, will provide a world geography resource CD. The NCGE continues to develop curriculum projects and resources for teachers. GENIP also continues to be active in providing expertise and leadership in the development of policies relating to geography education.

Clearly, the campaign to bring about a renaissance of geographical education is well established. However, the financial undertaking is evidently greater than was first appreciated. Gillbert Grosvenor (Chairman of the National Geographic Society) in his article 'In sight of the tunnel: the renaissance of geography education' (1995) states: 'In fact, after nearly 10 years of effort and 80 million dollars spent at the Society alone, it will be some time before we see the light at the end of the tunnel; in fact, we have only just come in sight of the tunnel itself.'

So, how much success has this multi-million dollar campaign achieved and to what extent can it be said that a renaissance for geographical education is taking place?

At a national level the campaign to bring about a renaissance of geographical education appears to be thriving. However, at state level the extent to which progress has been made is much less obvious and success varies dramatically across the country.

The extent to which progress is made on a state level is influenced by many different factors. First and foremost, the revival of geographical education is most dependent on the strength and power of the individuals involved in the campaign. The effectiveness of the State Alliance coordinators, the positions of influence they hold within State Education Departments and the extent to which SEDs are compliant and willing to change the geography curriculum are all factors fundamental to success in each state. A large army of active teacher consultants within each state is also crucial, but perhaps more important still is that among them, a dedicated and committed core of individuals exists to take on leadership and managerial roles.

Historical and geographical factors in each state can also affect the ease to which geographical education can be reintroduced into the curriculum. For example, the historical position and status geography holds within each state curriculum and the power and sway of other competing curriculum interest groups can affect the extent to which progress can be made. Also, the physical size and diversity of a state can affect the reintroduction of geography into the curriculum.

All of these factors together can ensure an improved position for geography within each state and if any one link in the chain is weak the progress made can be limited.

At individual school level it becomes even more problematic to judge the extent to which the campaign to bring about a revival of geographical education has been successful. In the absence of a complete national assessment, the yardstick against which progress can be measured is based largely on small-scale studies and anecdotal evidence. From these sources it is widely accepted that although there are schools which have made great advancements in geography education there are many more schools in which little progress has been made. The biggest problem remains that geography continues to be taught as part of social studies courses. Social studies teachers generally have very little or no academic background in geography, so the subject remains marginal for many teachers and their students.

When considering the overall picture, it is clear that geographical education has

STRENGTHS

- All of the major geography organisations are committed to bringing about a renaissance of geography.
- Geography has many wealthy and/or influential advocates, e.g. National Geographic Society and NASA.
- The National Geographic Society has vowed to continue work for geography education until 'substantial progress' has been made.
- The public perception of the National Geographic Society in general is very positive this has good ramifications for the geography campaign.
- Public awareness campaigns continue to maintain the campaign for geography in the media spotlight.
- The Alliance Network is very strong and is spreading the geography message across the country.
- Many thousands of social studies teachers have received geography subject and teacher training as a result of NGS initiatives.
- The federal government has recognized the importance of geography education and the development of a government supported national standards document. *Geography for Life* provides a framework for geography curriculum development.
- The perception of geography as a neutral or apolitical subject means few oppose 'renaissance' initiatives.
- The development of the first Advanced Placement Course in geography is evidence of the subjet's increasing status.
- University enrolments in geography are already increasing.

WEAKNESSES

- The lack of geography subject knowledge of existing social studies teachers is a major problem for the renaissance of geography. NGS two-week training courses are a start but only affect a small proportion of teachers and can not provide extensive coverage.
- The lack of geography content in many initial teacher training courses is a great cause for concern. There have been some pockets of progress, e.g. in Michigan it has been agreed that social studies teacher training courses will include a minimum of two geography units (for some, this represents a 200 per cent increase).
- The extent to which *Geography for Life*, the national geography standards have been adopted varies from state to state. The extent to which they are introduced in each state is very dependent on the power and influence of individuals.
- There is some criticism that the National Standards are content heavy and difficult to interpret, especially considering that so many social studies teachers have no academic background in geography. At state and individual school level much of the burden of campaign work continues to rest on the shoulders of individuals.
- There has been no overall evaluation to measure the success of initiatives to date.

OPPORTUNITIES

- The National Geographic Society promises to continue to apply its resources toward eradicating geographic illiteracy until 'we can actually see that light at the end of the tunnel' (Grosvenor, 1995).
- The political, media and private sector influence of the National Geographic Society can be further exploited.
- A successful Alliance network is already in place. Strong links are forming between Alliance members and State Education

THREATS/PROBLEMS

- Even after 15 years of activity and in excess of $100 million spent, the status, quality and quantity of geography taught in schools remains a concern.
- In the majority of American classrooms, geography still continues to be taught as a strand in social studies courses rather than a stand-alone subject.
- The size and diversity of the USA makes change difficult to achieve.
- The self-governing nature of each state also

Department officials and other state decision-makers. This can help to further the geography cause.

- *Geography for Life*, the national ,geography standards, provides a guide as to what should be taught throughout the school system. Further opportunity comes through encouraging state adoption of these standards.

means it is notoriously difficult to being about changes of any kind on a national scale.

- Due to the autonomous nature of each state, the widespread adoption of *Geography for Life*, the national geography standards cannot be guaranteed.
- The current educational focus on developing basic skills of literacy and numeracy is a potential threat to geography education.

Figure 20.5 Strengths, weaknesses, opportunities and threats/problems surrounding the campaign to bring about a renaissance of geography education in the USA (adapted from Clark, 1999).

come a long way over the past twenty years. On a national level geography has moved from a very weak, ignored and neglected condition to a position of increasing status and power. On an individual school level, however, geography remains the underdog of subjects in spite of the large-scale projects and the rigorous policy-making of the national campaign. Progress has been made, but much work is to be done if the campaign is to begin to affect geographical education where it really makes a difference, at grassroots level in the classrooms of the schools of America.

The campaign for the renaissance of geography education has great strengths, but also many problems to overcome as summarized in Figure 20.5. The strengths, weaknesses, opportunities and problems/threats surrounding the campaign to bring about a renaissance of geographical education in the United States of America must eventually be accommodated by the larger educational structure of the individual schools and teachers. When this occurs, then a true rebirth of the discipline in kindergarten through secondary education will be underway.

NOTE

1. K–12 = Kindergarten to grade 12 (i.e. reception class to year 13).

REFERENCES

Association of American Geographers, (1993) *Activities and Readings in the Geography of the United States (ARGUS)*. Washington, DC: Association of American Geographers.

Barrs, D. (1988) 'School geography in the USA', *Teaching Geography*, vol. 13, pp. 4–6.

Bednarz, S. Downs, R. and Vendor, J. (1999) Geography education in America. Draft paper.

Boehm, R.G. (1997) 'The first assessment: a contextual statement', in Boehm R.G. and Petersen, J.F. (eds), *The First Assessment*. San Marcos, TX: Grosvenor Center for Geographic Education.

Boehm, R.G. and Petersen, J.F. (1997) *The First Assessment*. San Marcos, TX: Grosvenor Center for Geographic Education.

Clark, J.K. (1999) 'A study to review progress in the renaissance of geographical education in the USA', unpublished MA dissertation. London: University of London Institute of Education.

Committee on Geographic Education, National Council for Geographic Education and Association of American Geographers (1984) *Guidelines for Geographic Education: Elementary and Secondary Schools*. Washington, DC: AAG and NCGE.

GENIP (1999) Website at http://genip.tamu.edu/

Grosvenor, G.M. (1985) 'Geographic ignorance: time for a turnaround', Presidents' Column *National Geographic Magazine*, May 1985.

Grosvenor, G.M. (1995) 'In sight of the tunnel: the renaissance of geography education', *Annals of the Association of American Geographers*, vol. 85, no. 3, pp. 409–20.

Hill, A.D. and laPrairie, L.A. (1989) 'Geography in American education', in Gaile, G.L. and Willmott, C.J. (eds), *Geography in America*. Columbus, OH: Merrill, pp. 1–26.

Joint Committee on Geographic Education (1984) *Guidelines for Geographic Education*. Washington, DC: Association of American Geographers and National Council for Geographic Education.

Lanegran, D. (1989) 'Co-ordinator's column', *The Geography Connection*, Minnesota Alliance for Geographic Education, vol. 4, no. 2, pp. 1–8.

Libbee, M. and Stoltman, J.P. (1994) 'Geography within the social studies curriculum', in Natoli, S.J. (ed.), *Strengthening Geography in the Social Studies*. National Council for the Social Studies.

Mayo, W.L. (1965) *The Development and Status of Secondary School Geography in the United States and Canada*. Ann Arbor, MI: University Publishers.

National Geography Standards Project (1994) *Geography for Life: National Geography Standards*. Washington, DC: National Geographic.

Natoli, S.J. (1994) 'Guidelines for geographic education and the fundamental themes of geography', in Bednarz, R.S. and Petersen, J.F (eds), *A Decade of Reform in Geographic Education: Inventory and Prospect*. Indiana, PA: National Council for Geographic Education, pp. 13–22.

Stoltman, J. (1986) 'Geographical education and society: changing perspectives on school geography in the United States of America', in Hernado, A. (ed.), *Geographical Education and Society: Abstracts and Papers*. Sitges: Commission on Geographical Education, International Geographical Union.

Stoltman, J.P. (1989) 'Geography in the secondary schools 1945–1990', *National Association of Secondary School Principals Bulletin*, vol. 73, no. 521, pp. 9–13.

Stoltman, J.P. (1997) 'Geography curriculum and instruction research since 1950 in the United States', in Boehm, R.G. and Petersen, J.F. (eds), *The First Assessment*. San Marcos, TX: Grosvenor Center for Geographic Education, pp. 131–70.

Stoltman, J.P., Wardley, S. and Pavan, K. (1999) 'Launching geographic education into the 21st century: the view from the United States', *Cahiers de Géographie du Québec*, vol. 43, no. 120, pp. 413–35.

Chapter 21

Towards a new professionalism

Nicola Bright with David Leat

INTRODUCTION

There are few educational settings in the world that are not now subject to tremendous forces of change. There is only sufficient space here to list the causes of this change: new technologies; the need for a more flexible workforce; international educational comparisons; and new forms of accountability for schools and teachers. A common reaction of governments facing such challenges is to impose curricula from above, often with an emphasis on a very basic curriculum. Later changes may involve a broadening to encompass problem-solving approaches.

Yet the overwhelming evidence is that curriculum change is extremely difficult to enact (Cuban, 1993; Leat, 1999). Ford et al. (1998), reviewing the evidence of the impact of the National Curriculum in England and Wales, point to the marginal effects on changing teaching processes, despite official documentation that required enquiry and problem-solving. Accounts of professional development experiences in such contexts make depressing reading, as teachers begin to feel that they are technicians rather than professionals (Helsby and Knight, 1997). Internationally the desire to identify foolproof methods of raising attainment have generated the school effectiveness research movement. However, from inside the movement has come the realisation that correlations of school characteristics and attainment only produce generalisations that are too blunt to inform teachers' actions (Hill, 1998). School improvement, as a movement, offers a more developmental approach but has yet to develop a significant track record.

In such circumstances there is the need for some new perspectives for professional development, which, where appropriate, hand back more control to the profession. Control can be taken to mean both choice over the exact nature of change and tools to understand, monitor and adjust the impact of change.

THE RESEARCH SETTING

The research followed the implementation of thinking skills strategies into the geography curriculum at a highly selective girls' independent school in south-west London. The research took place during the school year 1998/9 and although the department was very receptive to developing teaching and learning styles, circumstances dictated that the changes did not radically disturb schemes of work. This work fitted in well with the school aims, and was supported in principle by many staff, particularly senior management. The school under research is ranked as one of the top 30 schools in the country in terms of achievement (The Times League Table, 1998) so the attraction of the approach for high achievers was to provide appropriate challenge.

The publication *Thinking Through Geography* (Leat, 1998) is a result of action research collaboration between teachers and university staff in the North-East of England. This group is known as the Thinking Through Geography (TTG) Group. The book includes eight infusion strategies tried in the classroom. It includes background information on the strategies and ideas for developing materials, together with the exemplar materials used. The package looked exciting, and as the department had used and liked the Kobe earthquake 'mystery' developed by the TTG Group (SCAA, 1996), it was agreed to try out some more activities with a view to finding out more about them and their effects.

In summary then, reasons for the research being relevant at this school included the school's interest in thinking skills strategies as a way of maintaining and developing both the students' potential and its own position in the national league tables. The high national profile of these strategies made them interesting to investigate at this school, where developments based on a sound pedagogical basis have credence. Strong departmental support enabled the strategies to be effectively implemented and analysed, and was seen to be building on the current good practice. It was possible to change the approach to the curriculum, if not the content of the schemes of work, and thus the research could be seen to be part of ongoing curriculum development. This also took the reflective practitioner concept one stage further, being a departmental initiative that involved collaborative teaching. It was also able to inform future practice.

THE RESEARCH AIMS

The aim of the study was to follow the implementation and development of thinking skills strategies into the curriculum in one geography department, focusing upon the use of a new methodology and the consequences for the members of the department and the students. A further aim was to look at the effect of the research process upon the researcher, and the implications that this has for professional development. It was not seeking to prove that using these strategies increased achievement, but was designed to throw light upon this area of research. To summarise, the study aimed to investigate the process by which teachers learn about the use of strategies designed to promote thinking through geography. The nature of the study dictated the methodology used. The study was also evolutionary by nature. As the study evolved, different ideas emerged as to the best methods to be used next. It was felt that an action research methodology was the right approach for this topic with these constraints. Qualitative, action research methodology was also a new method of working for the researcher.

ACTION RESEARCH

Fien (1992) links the development of action research to the view that teachers do not regard educational research highly. They see much educational research as being artificial and irrelevant to the classroom, mainly due to the fact that university researchers have a different view of the teaching process and the classroom than teachers. Action research is a reaction to these views and attempts to make research for improving teaching useful and valued by teachers.

Cohen and Manion (1998) specify some of the crucial characteristics as follows:

> Action research is small-scale intervention in the functioning of the real world and a close examination of the effects of such intervention . . . we may further identify other tangible features: . . . it is concerned with diagnosing a problem in a specific context and attempting to solve it in that context; it is usually (though not inevitably) collaborative – teams of researchers and practitioners work together on a project; it is participatory – team members themselves take part directly or indirectly in implementing the research; and it is self-evaluative – modifications are continuously evaluated within the ongoing situation, the ultimate objective being to improve practice in some way or other.
>
> (p. 186)

This methodology appeared to be highly appropriate for our purposes. The research was small-scale, had the particular context of the geography department at the school, was collaborative (two of the department working together), participatory (the researcher was part of the research) and self-evaluative (we reviewed each stage together and this influenced the next stage).

The research was planned with the department in three phases. This follows a model of research based on cycles of planning, acting, observing and reflecting (McNiff, 1988). Each phase is located within a cycle, being the 'acting' part of that cycle. Elliott (1991) developed a more complex version where the reflection could lead to the revision of the initial idea being studied.

ISSUES ASSOCIATED WITH ACTION RESEARCH

While action research feeds the results of research directly into practice and so makes a difference, the involvement of the practitioner limits its scope and scale (Denscombe, 1998). It is also difficult to make generalisations on the basis of the results as they are case-specific and not necessarily representative. It is also difficult to control research variables as the research is part of everyday practice not outside it, and is constrained by workplace permission and ethics. Furthermore, it usually involves an extra burden of work for the practitioners at the early stages before the benefits are seen. Denscombe (1998) argues that the 'researcher is unlikely to be detached and impartial in approach to the research', as the researcher has a vested interest in the findings. According to Elliott (1991) 'the fundamental aim of action research is to improve practice rather than to produce knowledge'. Although the primary motivation for this work was to improve practice we will return in the conclusion to issues of whether action research can produce knowledge.

MODEL OF TEACHER BELIEFS, KNOWLEDGE AND PRACTICES

We believe that the complexity of the effect of research on the professional development of those involved can be illuminated by the model of teacher beliefs, knowledge and practices developed during research into the effectiveness of primary numeracy teachers (Askew et al., 1997). The model describes the complexity of the interplay between teachers' practices, beliefs and pedagogic knowledge, and here the model has been applied to geography by replacing the words numerate and numeracy, with geographical and geography (see Figure 21.1).

The main assumption of the model is that practice in the classroom is the major factor influencing learning outcomes, as the interaction between teacher and pupil is the most significant influence that a teacher has on pupil learning. Interacting with teacher practices are a set of beliefs about what it is to be good at geography, how pupils learn to be good geographers, and how best to teach geography. Also influencing practice is teacher's pedagogic content knowledge, or geographical subject knowledge, knowledge of pupils and knowledge of teaching approaches. Furthermore pupils' responses to changes in teachers' practices can influence whether the changes are reinforced or discouraged. The model shows that the relationships are not unidirectional and the strength of the relationship may vary.

Thus the implementation of a curriculum development will clearly affect practice, and by implication both beliefs and knowledge may change as a result of pupil response to teacher practices, and as a direct result of critical reflection upon practice. It is the critical nature of this reflection that is important. In this research critical reflection was attempted through the analysis of questionnaires, interview and teacher

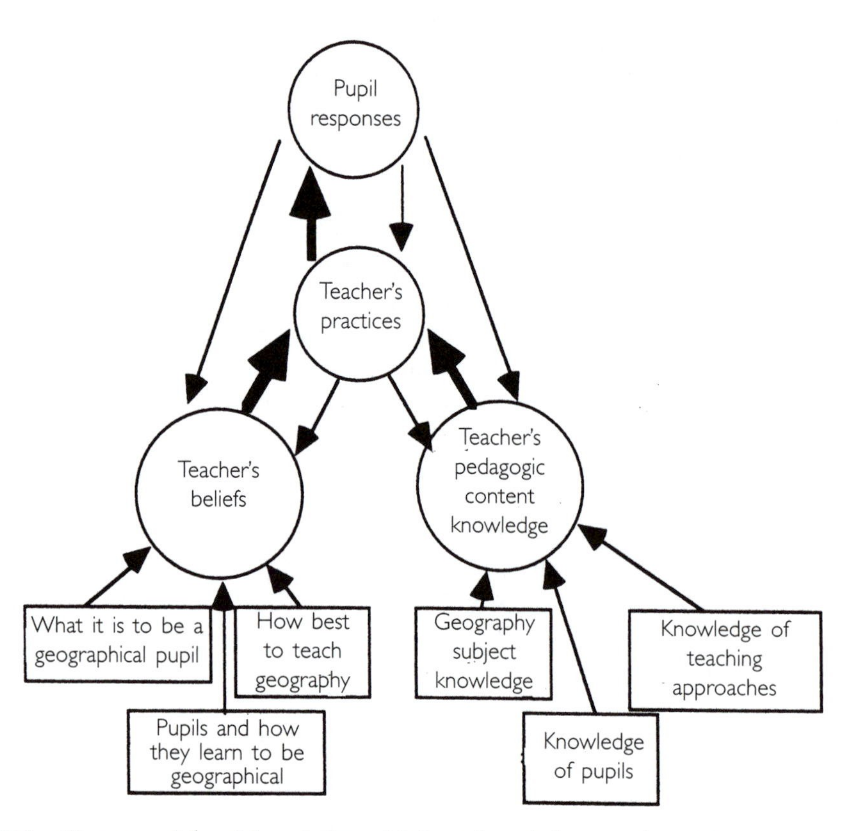

Figure 21.1 Diagram of the elaborated model (based on Askew et al., 1997).

participant observation. The experiences described below are intended to illustrate the effects of the research on the participants in relation to some of the aspects of the model. Through this process we would wish to argue that knowledge of the model can assist action researchers in two ways. Firstly, it can direct their attention to the relationships between components in the model which can be researched. Secondly, the model can prepare teachers for their emotional and cognitive responses the ecology of the situation generates.

EXPERIENCES

Example 1 – Debriefing

The first example illustrates how our knowledge of teaching approaches was altered firstly through our own practices, and also as a result of our analysis of pupil responses.

The research was planned in three phases. A characteristic of thinking skills activities is the debrief, in which the students are encouraged to think about their own thinking (metacognition), and transfer their reasoning to new situations (Leat and Kinninment, 2000). In terms of the model, action for change was initiated by learning something about debriefing through reading and discussing Adey and Shayer (1994) and *Thinking Through Geography* (Leat, 1998). The two staff involved changed their classroom practice by experimenting with debriefing. As this was an innovation in practice with the taught classes, pupil response was inevitable. In turn our practice and knowledge base for teaching adjusted as we reflected on our experiences. At the end of Phase I, staff concerns were related to the difficulties of including everyone into the debrief and of creating the right climate for an effective debrief to take place. As a result some potential debrief prompt questions were devised and applied to Phase II. It is not realistic to map this process meticulously onto the model, but it will be evident that there was an ongoing interaction between our knowledge, our practice and pupil response. Our experience was positive but we could see problems which we attempted to solve, thus increasing our professional expertise. It is worth pointing out that change will often lead to adverse responses from pupils, who are creatures of habit, and it is so easy to return to the normal routine at the first hint of resistance.

Staff perception of this next phase was very positive. We felt that the whole activity, but in particular the debrief, went better than Phase I. We were unsure whether this was due to the suitability of this particular mystery activity, to the improvement in our debrief skills or to an increased confidence in all of the participants, but the responses from the students were encouraging. The students had most to say about the debrief, and were all positive:

> 'The debrief helped me understand it best.'
> 'It removed muddle.'
> 'I didn't really understand the situation at first – after the discussion [debrief] I understood it.'
> 'Our ideas weren't going anywhere at the beginning, we didn't know where to start – discussion finally sorted them.'
> '[Before the debrief] we didn't have much – it helped.'

These comments help us to see the value that the students placed on whole class discussion in resolving their cognitive conflict, once they had the opportunity to resolve part of the problem in their groups. Not one student said that they had the best possible answer by themselves before the class discussion, everyone gained something from it.

We had also decided that we would start the discussion by using the group that had in our opinion the weakest explanation. We determined this by listening to the groups as we circulated during the lesson. We were very careful not to interrupt (Leat, 1998).

'Starting with the weak group and building helped to include everyone.' (staff comment)

We had therefore begun to address one of the concerns we identified in Phase I concerning the involvement of everyone in the discussion. Here again it is possible to see the interaction between our growing understanding, our practice and pupils' evident engagement.

Example 2 – The 'tree' idea

The second example relates to how an individual pupil response was responsible for a change in our pedagogic content knowledge which in turn affected our practice in subsequent phases. Thus our knowledge of teaching approaches developed through the involvement in the research process, without which we would have missed the opportunity.

When interviewed, one student expressed her group's organisation of statements involved in the activity as a tree.

'Our ideas were like a tree with lots of little branches.'

We (the staff) thought about this idea, in which the trunk was the main idea, the branches were the groups of ideas and the leaves were the smaller parts of each group of ideas, the ideas becoming more complex. This student was, fortunately, in the first group that did this activity, and we were able to build this idea into our instructions for the completion of the tasks for the other groups. This worked particularly well, as other students commented.

'It was helpful when you said something about a tree and all the leaves and the other ones.'

We continued to use this idea with other classes, and it appeared to be an effective stimulus for some. For example, we tackled the SCAA (1996) Kobe exercise with Year 10, who had never completed an activity like this before. Not only has this comment affected instructions to pupils in this activity (our practice), it has also contributed to our understanding generally of how causation can be understood.

CONCLUSIONS

Evaluating what was learned in the classroom is difficult. Most of the evaluation was through discussion. Professional development can be seen as the acquiring of new skills, new knowledge and new understanding. Some development can be measured against set criteria, but much cannot as it is based upon feelings and intuition. We both felt that involvement in this curriculum development had changed us, although in the first instance we were less able to clearly articulate how. We felt that perhaps we had added another 'tool' to our kit for the classroom, as although we felt that a change of style was hard work, we have still kept doing things that we were doing before, and haven't completely changed. Indeed it was felt important that we retained what was good in our repertoire, and as such considered that while this curriculum development was valuable, it should just be considered as a tool to use from a complete range.

However, upon thinking more deeply about our learning, it could be argued that we have developed a deeper understanding of the pedagogy behind this work, of the contexts in which it is applied and on the learning outcomes of the students. We understand the different strategies that we have used better, and can discuss their benefits and drawbacks within the context of the theory underpinning these ideas. We can see situations in which these strategies would be appropriate to use, and have begun to devise our own. We can identify students who understand what they are doing far more easily, and can articulate how others are not quite matching this performance. Thus it could be argued that our professional development has been extensive as a result of this work, although we found it difficult to see initially.

We discussed the idea of the 'expert' needing to become a 'novice', and were able to identify with this notion (Leat, 1996).

> 'Normal lessons are safer . . . [with the Thinking Skills activities] you feel more out of control, you don't know what's coming next.'
> 'You feel slightly more out of control.'

This last statement was linked to a discussion about the uncertain direction that the debrief can take. However, this feeling has decreased with the continued use of these activities. It was felt that different skills were needed to keep the tasks going, and that these were developing with practice. Therefore, despite these uncertainties, my colleague wants to retain these activities within next year's scheme of work, and she thinks that this has been a positive experience.

> 'I will do them again!'

We believe that the process of researching has been an important part of our professional development. This was more than simply being a reflective practitioner. The systematic use of methods made us look more critically at the work we were doing at each stage, so that learning from the findings could be applied to new contexts in the next phase. It could be argued that this action research was a form of experiential learning and as such was a powerful form of professional development. We have outlined some of the ways in which our practice and knowledge has changed. It is much harder to be precise about changes in beliefs. More time needs to elapse in order to gain a firmer purchase on this aspect, but we can state that we are not the same teachers that started this research.

This links with Hargreaves' (1994) ideas regarding a 'new professionalism' emerging in teaching, where an increasing debate between teachers is developing, and more collaborative working relationships are being established. Barth's (1990) notion of successful schools as 'learning communities' also can be linked, in which the students benefit from a whole school 'culture' of learning, and the continuous cycle of professional development is more highly valued. Certainly the students were intrigued by the idea that their teachers were learning too!

The idea of continual learning is essential to the profession in our view as we agree with the statement that 'to learn is part of what being a teacher implies' (Rynne and Lambert, 1997). Perhaps, then, research (as learning) should become an essential task for the teacher and should be an important element of teacher training? Lambert (1996) argues that more student teachers should be involved in 'research and development' projects, thus teachers in contact with student teachers will become increasingly involved in this work. However, that this should become an obligatory part of a teacher's repertoire is arguable. Perhaps instead it could be seen as an alternative route for progression for teachers wishing to remain in the classroom. Much valuable work remains to be done in the classroom possibly through videotaping and analysis of debriefing, or peer observation and discussion. It would also be very valuable to be part of a wider local group discussing these approaches and pooling our knowledge in a professional community. So, for example, prompt questions may be found useful by other 'novices'. The prompt questions could also be developed further – perhaps different sets of questions could be developed for the different techniques used, as we felt that different debrief skills were required for different activities. These would not be exclusive, but could help teachers new to these techniques to develop their debriefing skills with some confidence.

Finally, we would like to return to the role of action research. It has been argued that teachers do not have a high regard for educational research, but action research is seen as limited to improving a teacher's or group of teachers' practice rather than producing knowledge (Elliott, 1991). We see a much more substantial role for action research. Firstly, it is our experience that teachers find the results of some action research very compelling, because it can inform action. Watkins and Mortimore (1999), from a higher education perspective, have suggested that the role of research is not to provide solutions. Such a view will do little to build productive partnerships between schools and researchers. Secondly, teachers working together can overcome some of the limitations associated with validity and sample sizes. Action research conducted by communities of teachers can provide generalisable conclusions and add considerably to the professionalism of teachers.

REFERENCES

Adey, P. and Shayer, M. (1994) *Really Raising Standards: Cognitive Intervention and Academic Achievement*. London and New York: Routledge.

Askew, M., Rhodes, V., Brown, M. and Wiliam, D. (1997) *Effective Teachers of Numeracy*. London: King's College.

Barth, R.S. (1990) 'A personal vision of a good school', *Phi Delta Kappa*, March, pp. 512–16.

Bright, N. (1999) 'The implementation of a curricular development: thinking skills in geography', unpublished MA Dissertation. University of London Institute of Education.

Cohen, L. and Manion, L. (1998) *Research Methods in Education*, 4th edn. London and New York: Routledge.

Cuban, L. (1993) 'Computers meet classroom – classroom wins', *Teachers College Record*, vol. 95, pp. 185–210.

Denscombe, M. (1998) *The Good Research Guide*. Buckingham: Open University Press.

Elliott, J. (1991) *Action Research for Educational Change*. Buckingham: Open University Press.

Fien (1992) 'What kind of research for what kind of teaching? Towards research in Geography Education as a critical social science', in Hill, D. (ed.), *International Perspectives on Geography Education*. Skokie, IL: Rand McNally, pp. 265–75.

Ford, K., Clark, J., Leat, D. and Miller, J. (1998) *An Analysis of Research into the Impact of the National Curriculum and the Implications for Teachers and Schools*. London: Schools Curriculum and Assessment Authority.

Hargreaves, D.H. (1994) 'The synthesis of professional and institutional development', *Teaching and Teacher Education*, vol. 10, no. 4, pp. 423–5.

Helsby, G. and Knight, P. (1997) 'Continuing professional development and the National Curriculum', in Helsby, G. and McCulloch, G. (eds), *Teachers and the National Curriculum*. London: Cassell.

Hill, P. (1998) 'Research-driven school reform', *School Effectiveness and School Improvement*, vol. 9, pp. 419–36.

Lambert, D. (1996) 'Understanding and improving school geography: the training of beginning teachers', in Williams, M. (ed.), *Understanding Geographical and Environmental Education: The Role of Research*. London and New York: Cassell Education.

Leat, D. (1996) 'Raising attainment in geography: prospects and problems', in Williams, M. (ed.), *Understanding Geographical and Environmental Education: The Role of Research*. London and New York: Cassell Education.

Leat, D. (ed.) (1998) *Thinking Through Geography*. Cambridge: Chris Kington Publications.

Leat, D. (1999) 'Rolling the stone uphill: teacher development and the implementation of Thinking Skills programmes', *Oxford Review of Education*, vol. 25, pp. 387–403

Leat, D. and Kinninment, D. (2000) 'Learn to debrief', in Binns, T. and Fisher, C. (eds), *Issues in Teaching Geography*. London: Routledge.

McNiff, J. (1988) *Action Research: Principles and Practice*. London: Macmillan Education.

Rynne, E. and Lambert, D. (1997) 'The continual mismatch between undergraduate experiences and the teaching demands of the geography classroom: experiences of pre-service secondary geography teachers', *Journal of Geography in Higher Education*, vol. 21, no. 1, pp. 65–77.

SCAA (1996) *Key Stage 3 Optional Tests and Tasks: Geography Unit 2*. London: SCAA.

Watkins, C. and Mortimore, P. (1999) 'Pedagogy: what do we know?', in Mortimore, P. (ed.), *Understanding Pedagogy and its Impact on Learning*. London: Paul Chapman.

Chapter 22

The secondary/tertiary interface

Shaun Brown and Maggie Smith

INTRODUCTION

> A chasm has developed between those who teach at school and those who teach in universities.
>
> (Professor A.S. Goudie, 1993)

The chasm, which Goudie spoke of in his 1993 guest editorial in *Geography*, has a clearly defined history grounded in the movement to make educational institutions more accountable and more transparent. To consider the current impacts of the divide between school and university geography, and the possible routes open for its resolution, the divide must be set in its historical context.

Figure 22.1 charts the key developments in both school and academic geography. It is apparent from the outset that school and university geography have rarely been similar in the last 40 years, but it will be argued that until recently they were still closely linked to each other through an intergenerational transfer of ideas, flowing from universities into schools through the students who became teachers. If one studies the diagram chronologically, it begins in the early 1960s with a major transition for academic geography. The quantitative revolution was affirmed by the Madingley Lectures in 1963 and swept aside the ageing regional paradigm which had previously dominated. The models and system structures developed in the previous 50 years were embraced as geography set out to study and explain the world scientifically, and to raise its academic standing by rigorously evaluating geographical patterns and processes. It was during this phase that academic geography separated along thematic lines, as a result of particular specialities and differing forms of investigation. It was not until the early 1970s that the regional paradigm was overtaken in schools. But with the introduction of key texts, like Chorley and Haggett's *Frontiers in Geographical Teaching* (1965) and Everson and Fitzgerald's *Settlement Patterns* (1969), physical and human models were introduced to school teachers as a way of explaining the world around them.

In the early 1970s there were two new developments. In academia the Behaviourist and Humanist paradigms put renewed emphasis on human geography and used the theories developed in social studies to examine geographical phenomena in a more qualitative manner. In schools there was a pedagogical shift away from didactic teaching methods. Sponsored by the Schools Council, projects like GYSL and the 14–18

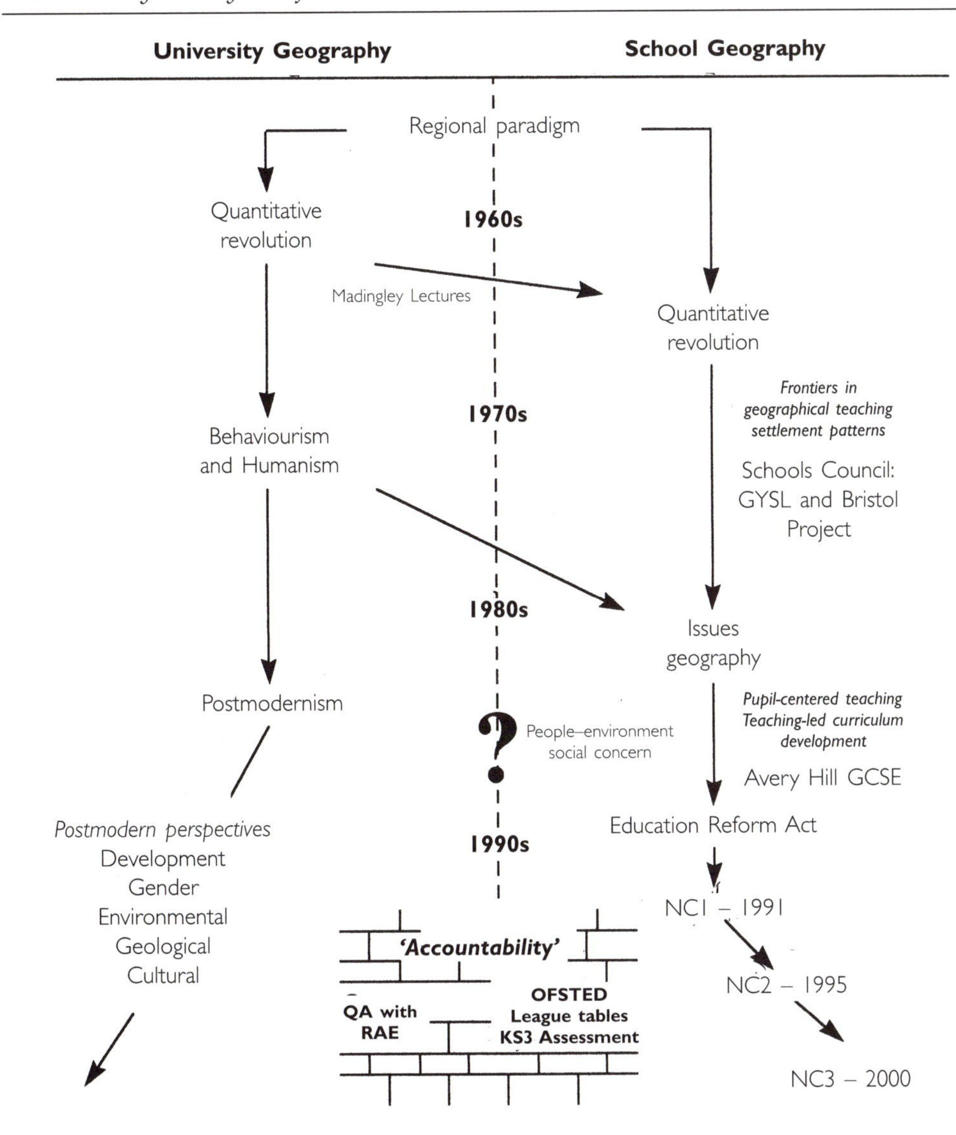

Figure 22.1 The history of the divide between school and university.

Bristol Project led the way in the development of a more pupil-centred curriculum. Behaviourist and Humanist ideas were introduced into school geography curricula in the mid-1980s where there was now much greater emphasis on teaching the geography of issues of social concern and some physical geography began to take a 'people–environment' perspective. With the numbers remaining in school beyond the age of 16 burgeoning, geography was able to unite its pedagogical progress with the study of contemporary issues and develop increasingly relevant and accessible curricula. This led to syllabuses such as the Avery Hill GCSE.

David Harvey's book *The Condition of Postmodernity* (1989) underlined a recent paradigm shift in academic geography. In the postmodern era academic geography has emphasised the uniqueness of space and the close interrelationship between the micro-scale and the global scale. Traditional themes have been viewed with much more focused perspectives, and thus cultural, historical, gender and environmental studies have come increasingly to the forefront alongside the traditional economic and political viewpoints. Due to its sharper focus of study, academic geography has begun to forge much closer links with other academic disciplines where its increasingly specialised geographical perspectives are more constructively utilised. In schools the Education Reform Act in 1988 heralded a decade of upheaval. The most significant of the changes has been the introduction and ongoing redevelopment of the National Curriculum for Key Stages 1, 2 and 3. Despite its revisions, the National Curriculum in many ways has provided a full stop to the development of school geography, particularly since its predetermined and singularly school-biased rationale has now been fed through into the guidelines for the New A-level and the revision of GCSE for 2001.

From its instigation in 1988 the National Curriculum presented a clear conception of geography which was by design intrinsically inward-looking. The rationale for the content selected in the original National Curriculum meant that academic geography was abandoned in favour of a clearly school-based subject. This school basis has led each consequent revision to focus increasingly on making its teaching and its assessment more acceptable to a generation of teachers who were both perturbed and perplexed by its original conception. While these changes were essential, there have only been two token additions, of 'global citizenship' and 'sustainability', to the content of the curriculum, despite all the developments in academic geography during the last decade. However, these additions do not represent evolving content, since no open route exists to actually link the National Curriculum with academia. Instead they represent what now stands in for evolution: first, new content which holds with current political agendas, and second, 'new geography = new news' whereby the newspaper, with all its tendency to bias and misrepresentation, and the 'Discovery Channel' documentary have become the digest with which new curriculum content is informed.

Although the National Curriculum 2000 does not directly instil KS3 geography with a thematic basis as was paramount in earlier incarnations, the thematic framework remains within the units laid out in the forthcoming 24-unit KS3 Scheme of Work, which is soon to be published by QCA. This retention of a thematic framework enables a perspective of the divide to be gained through the eyes of PGCE students. The bar chart in Figure 22.2 resulted from a questionnaire survey of 52 PGCE students (Brown, 1999). They were asked to write down ten topics studied at university and ten taught in school, and then indicate if they perceived them to be in any way related. Interestingly the topic lists, which were in no way intended to be similar, bore a remarkable resemblance to each other, and in Figure 22.2 it is evident that some of the National Curriculum themes were still perceived to be related to the topics studied by university geographers. However, the majority of themes were perceived to be linked by less than 50 per cent of the students, which does suggest that the majority of university students could not relate their academic learning to the majority of the National Curriculum they were teaching.

The 1990s has been the decade of the divide. However, it has not been brought about just by academic geography's pursuit of the postmodern paradigm or the introduction of the National Curriculum. In themselves they would not be enough to cement the

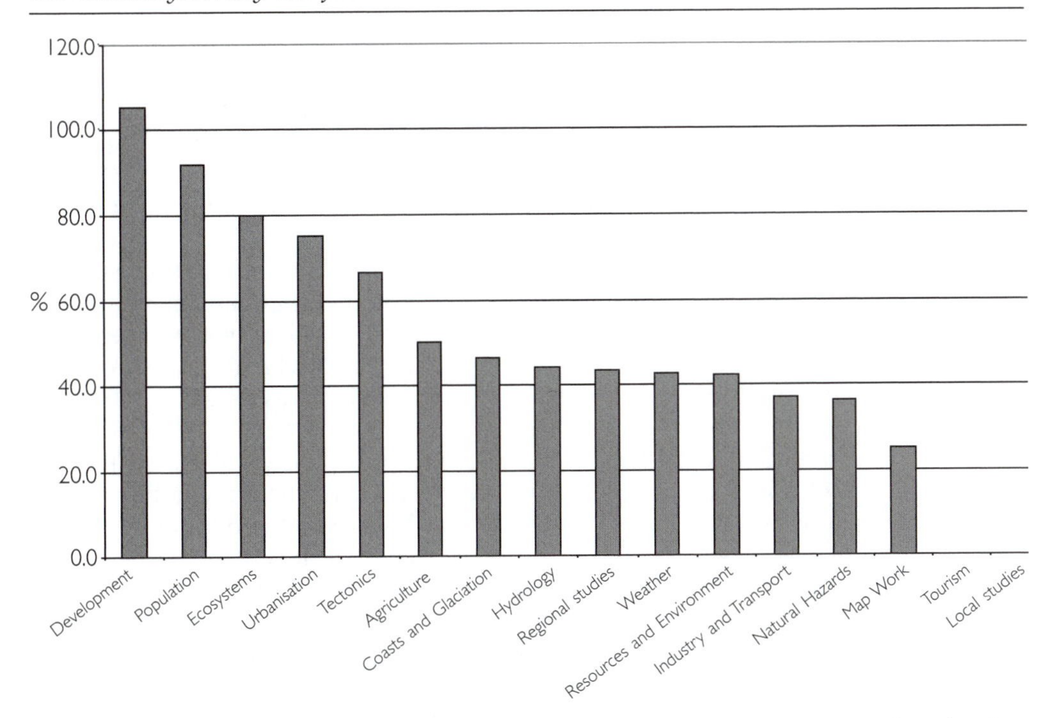

Figure 22.2 Percentage of school topics taught by PGCE students perceived to be related to university topics they studied.

division. The divide may be considered as a wall which has arguably been constructed brick by brick by the government's insensitive pursuit of 'accountability and transparency' in the educational establishment. A series of initiatives has been introduced into both universities and schools which have reformed their institutional structures in such a way as to force them apart. Although accountability and transparency undoubtedly permeate every present-day institutional structure, and often to the greater good, it is the ill-conceived nature of the changes to schools and universities which has constructed the divide rather than it being an overarching intention. In universities the most significant change has been the introduction of the quality assurance (QA) programme, including the subject review and, most notably, the research assessment exercise (RAE), while in schools it has been the OFSTED inspection system and the annual publication of league tables. The parallel introduction of these changes, intended to make both schools and universities more transparently accountable, has forced them to become increasingly preoccupied with their own standing. University departments are narrowly assessed against each other for the allocation of higher education resources, while schools are forced to compete for pupils – and consequently capitation funding – on the basis of OFSTED reports and league table standing. Put simply it has built a wall between the geographers in schools and universities, while depriving them of the resources to see it, let alone cross it.

As we enter the twenty-first century school geography is now fossilised in a form which has been shaped by three uncoordinated influences. This form may be thought of as comprising distinct layers of permafrost, or perhaps as an ill-conceived angel cake. In the first place it contains the thematic framework and content derived from academic geography of the 1950s–1970s which still permeates many textbooks and syllabuses, comprising approaches using systems and models to explain people–environment relationships. On top of this lies the pupil-centred pedagogy of enquiry learning developed through the School's Council Projects of the 1980s and lately transferred to some university courses, and finally we come to the institutional developments of the 1990s which have directed the energies of teachers towards assessment and accountability. This rationale has been clearly evident in each stage of the National Curriculum development and is being continued through new initiatives such as the KS1, 2 and 3 Schemes of Work. In their proposed form the Schemes of Work could be further tools to aid the deconstruction of teaching and assessment, further increasing teachers' accountability when they are assessed in OFSTED inspections.

To conclude this introduction it is useful to return to the diagram with which we began. Figure 22.1 leads us to the point in the late 1990s when school geography turned in upon itself and university geography looked out towards other disciplines, where it could carve out specialist niches which would be valued positively by the RAE. Both institutions are being hemmed in by the constraints of their respective accountability programmes. What is clearly evident is that prior to this period there was a flow of ideas which allowed geography to progress as a whole body. It is important to note that the arrows crossing the diagram do not just represent the transfer of ideas, but they also represent the movements of people. There was roughly a ten-year lag between university and school developments. Crudely this could be accounted for in terms of three years as an undergraduate, one year on a PGCE course and 3–6 years as a main scale teacher. After this period a generation of teachers, influenced by the paradigm prevalent in their undergraduate study, would be in a position to positively influence the content of the geography being taught in schools.

The 1990s is the decade of a lost generation: 'the postmodern geographers', who as a result of the resource constraints and enforced introspection have not been able to influence school geography in the same way as their quantitative and humanist colleagues. In the following sections we will consider how the divide is now reinforcing fossilisation, making the subject increasingly vulnerable in schools and ultimately affecting recruitment at every level. However, while these consequences are explored it is vital to remember this lost generation of geography teachers, and consider the consequences for the generation which follows them into an enclosed school environment in which geography has no recent history of change, or any capacity to make the vital links back to academia.

THE EFFECTS OF THE DIVIDE

It would seem clear that one major effect of the sequence of events described above is the 'fossilisation' of geography as taught in schools. Geography in schools moves forward as the result of stimuli from two sources – first from universities, and second from teachers in the schools. University geography pushes forward the frontiers of the geography subject content – evolving new paradigms, setting out new concepts and taking geography into new fields – while in the schools, teachers look creatively at how the subject is taught, devising new approaches and finding new techniques and emphases for enhancing pupils' knowledge, understanding, skills and values.

In both cases these stimuli recently seem to have been stifled. Changes to the funding and management of higher education in the 1990s, particularly the introduction of quality assurance procedures and notably the research assessment exercises (RAE), have reduced the incentive for academics to write school textbooks or write for journals aimed at the school market since these gain no credit under the terms of the RAE. Jenkins (1995) notes that it is geographers in the highly rated research departments in particular that are not getting involved in, or are being withdrawn from, writing student textbooks, so cutting off a valuable source of new geographical thinking from school geography. A survey by Smith in 1995 revealed that 93 per cent of university tutors interviewed made no personal input into A-level examining, writing A-level textbooks or school curriculum development, although 41 per cent said they would like to be involved in these ways were it not for the constraints of time and the RAE. Kent (1997) notes the lack of involvement of higher education geographers in the 'process' of formulating the national curriculum – arguably resulting in the 'bland and conservative final product'.

In schools, pressures such as the implementation of the National Curriculum and its periodic revisions, OFSTED inspections and planning for the raising of levels of achievement in the key stage tests at GCSE and A-level have tended to push thinking about new curriculum developments lower down on the list of priorities for teachers. Time to find out about new cutting-edge developments in the subject is restricted and teachers are finding it difficult to think about creative pedagogical advances.

The effect of these introspective developments in both higher education and in schools is significant. As Rawling (1996) said: 'The school subject has become decoupled from its academic base.' Schools cannot now be certain that there will be quality textbooks and learning materials written by university geographers who are developing new approaches in the discipline, and the effect of this is likely to be the stagnation of the content of the subject in the school curriculum – an event particularly serious for geography which is a subject that is essentially dynamic in nature.

That teachers in schools already feel the effects of the reduced flow of new ideas and information from universities into their schools is already apparent. A survey of readers of the journal *Geography*, carried out by the editor, Derek Spooner, in 1994, found that one of the most frequent comments was a request for university lecturers to provide 'many more articles on mainstream "A" level topics, and particularly to support teachers with material relevant to new demands' (Spooner, 1995). An informal survey conducted among teachers by both present authors revealed a similar situation – 80 per cent of geography teachers questioned noted difficulties in keeping up to date with geography subject knowledge. The knock-on effects are not hard to predict – if geography loses its base as a subject that deals with contemporary changes in the world, then its attraction as a school subject at GCSE and A-level may diminish, and this in turn may lead to a reduction in the numbers of students wishing to follow courses in geography in higher education.

Following this argument through, it would seem logical to predict that a similar trend would then start to affect the number of geography graduates applying for Initial Teacher Training (ITT) courses. Recent figures seem to bear this out with the total number of applicants to geography secondary PGCE courses falling from 1279 in 1997 to 905 in 1999 (unpublished guideline figure, GTTR Annual Statistical Reports).

The latest figures available (February 2000) indicate a continued decline, with a drop in applications to geography PGCE courses of 19.63 per cent compared to the same time in 1999 (source: GTTR) – a trend that is mirrored in other subject areas on PGCE courses.

The effects of such a continued drop are worrying. The development of geography as a school subject is stimulated at least in part by a strong supply of graduates with new ideas. The subject will become vulnerable if it stands still – it may appear to be less relevant in a world of rapidly changing technology. In the longer term the diminution of 'new blood' into the subject could result in the lowering of geography's ability to compete in the curriculum market with other subjects – both existing established subjects such as history, and with new more vocational subjects such as leisure and tourism. This competition can be seen already in some schools in terms of falling numbers for GCSE and A-level geography courses.

Marsden (1997) notes a further complication. The nature of geography courses in higher education is varied; they often reflect research specialisms rather than being planned as an integrated whole (possibly another effect of the RAE). This means that new entrants to the profession are coming in with widely diverse views of what geography is, and many find it difficult to reconcile their own views with 'geography' as set out in the school curriculum. This predicament is not helped by the present nature of PGCE courses which are regulated by the Teacher Training Agency (TTA). The standards which, since 1998 (DfEE, 4/98), must be met by all beginning teachers, have an apparent emphasis on ensuring sound subject knowledge – but this knowledge is of a traditional variety and certainly does not provide any encouragement to incorporate new content within the discipline.

WHAT CAN BE DONE

Despite this rather gloomy outlook there are nevertheless a number of initiatives that have been set up with the aim of counteracting the present divergence between school and academic geography. Some of these are examined below in the hope that they might provide food for thought on possible strategies for remedying this situation.

Geographical Alliances: potential based on the North American model?

The formation of Geographical Alliances is a trend that has gathered momentum in the USA in the last twenty years. The cause of the concern that led to these being established was the marked decline in the place of geography in the school curriculum in the USA between the 1960s and 1980s, despite the setting up during that time of influential projects such as the American High School Geography Project. Geography in American schools often formed part of a social studies course and was frequently taught by non-specialist teachers. This slippage of status had a knock-on effect for geography at university level. By the early 1980s many prestigious universities had closed their geography departments – and indeed geography was not represented at department level by any of the Ivy League universities. For those university geography courses that remained, the virtual disappearance of 'geography' from the school curriculum was found to have a number of significant impacts:

- Courses had to start from a lower base level – teaching skills and knowledge that would previously have been taught in schools.
- Pupils in schools had a poor understanding of what geography was like as an individual discipline – with a resulting detrimental effect on recruitment as students were less happy to opt for unfamiliar subject areas.
- The status of geography as an academic discipline was lowered.

In the 1980s there was considerable interest in the USA in revitalising school geography. In 1988, for instance, the Geographic Education National Implementation Programme (GENIP), in which the National Geographic Society and the Association of American Geographers were major players, was set up. The National Geographic Society was also a keen supporter, active promoter and funder of state geographic alliances – an idea that has taken off in the USA so that now more than thirty exist. The example of the Arizona Geographic Alliance set up in 1994 will serve as example of how the schemes work.

The Arizona Geographic Alliance involves close cooperation between university geographers, the National Geographic Society and K–12 teachers, all working towards the goal of improving the quality of geographical education. Part of the success of the Arizona Geographic Alliance is undoubtably due to the employment of two coordinators whose role is to maintain the links between geographers in the various education sectors, to establish links with the state Department of Education, and to lobby politicians. The annual Alliance programme provides for the training of a group of teachers who then act as teacher-counsellors, spreading information and ideas within their schools by organising conferences and workshops, and preparing resources. The result is that 'geography teaching is expanding in quality and content and . . . is a benefit to all . . . teachers, geography departments and children' (Conneaux, 1998).

Could such a model work in the UK? At an exploratory meeting initiated by Ashley Kent in London in 1999, and involving geographers working at all levels of education in the south-east of England, the possibility of taking the idea further was discussed. Ashley Kent noted that we already have existing professional support networks in the RGS/IBG and GA, and we have strong university geography sectors and regional elements of the GA and RGS/IBG that could act as bases for alliance-type activities. It would seem that the climate is right for a closer look at the development of this sort of action in Britain.

Action by professional organisations

The two major professional organisations for geography in England – the Geographical Association (GA) and the RGS/IBG (Royal Geographical Society with the Institute of British Geographers) – have both had long-standing interests in the secondary/tertiary interface in geography education. In 1977, Professor Wise, in his presidential address to the GA, expressed the divide as a 'conceptual gap' between university and school geography. This, according to Kirby and Lambert (1978), could be attributed to a delay in the diffusion of ideas from universities to schools. But even as early as 1960, concerns were being expressed at the GA annual conference about the lack of communication and continuity across the 'divide'. A committee was set up, chaired by Professor Honeybone, and its report in 1962 recommended that the GA should promote closer contact and discussion between the two sides. The response to this was the formation of a GA Standing Committee on Sixth Form and University Geography which acted as a forum for investigating a number of interface issues until it was disbanded in the mid-1980s.

In 1986 the GA established a section committee – the Secondary–Tertiary Interface Section Committee (STISC) – to deal specifically with matters relating to the interface. The committee was charged with continuing to develop increased contact and understanding between geography educators in secondary and higher education. In the six years that it operated it provided short courses to develop curriculum materials, linked university and school geography departments through conferences and fieldwork programmes, and set up a research initiative into attitudes of final year undergraduates towards teaching as a career. Many GA branches are still benefiting from the activities initiated during this period of activity even though the committee was disbanded in 1992.

Its successor was a working party on school–higher education links, set up in 1996 and chaired by Derek Spooner. The group put forward seven recommendations for forging closer links across the divide, as summarised in Table 22.1.

Table 22.1 Priorities identified in final action plan of the GA School–Higher Education Links Working Party, 1998

Priority 1	Influence assessment methods and curriculum change (especially at A/AS-level) in geography (especially important in human geography).
Priority 2	Raise the number of students taking geography at school and HE.
Priority 3	Raise recruitment to PGCE geography.
Priority 4	Sell and promote geography as a discipline.
Priority 5	Develop dialogue involving both sides of the interface over the need for liaison.
Priority 6	Develop GA publications reflecting current research/teaching in HE, progress in subject.
Priority 7	Promote geography as a discipline alongside pedagogy.

In his summary, Spooner noted that progress was clearly uneven, especially in relation to Priorities 1 and 2, and he commented on the decline in numbers of academic geographers who were members of the Association. He concluded that it was '... difficult to see this situation changing much in the near future, which makes the building of good links between the Association and university geography departments all the more important' (Spooner, 1999).

The RGS/IBG worked with the GA on interface issues through a joint committee on higher education in the 1980s, and in 1986 held a joint symposium on geography in the education system. This revealed a consensus on both sides of the divide not only for greater communication between geographers at different phases within the education system, but also for a reassessment of the nature of geography and a dissemination of the results to the wider community.

In 1994, the newly formed Council of British Geography (COBRIG) held a seminar in Oxford entitled 'New Perspectives for Geography in Schools and Higher Education' at which the problems resulting from the increasing specialisation of geography courses in higher education, the pressures of the RAE in limiting the ability of university teachers to write for the school market and the pressures of relentless change in the school curriculum were acknowledged and discussed. Suggested ways forward included courses and conferences and enhanced accreditation of INSET qualifications, amongst others, as detailed in the publication *Geography into the Twenty-first Century* (Rawling and Daugherty, 1996) that emerged from the seminar. The biennial seminars have continued (the latest conference took place in Swansea in July 2000) and they have maintained 'communication across the divide' as one of their ongoing themes. Perhaps the increasingly widespread use of information and communications technology will make links easier and quicker to establish.

It is clear therefore that there exists a consensus among geographers at all levels within the professional organisations for the subject that there should be action to forge links across the divide and that geography needs to have a raised profile in order to maintain its position in education and society. Marsden (1997) noted the signs that university geographers and geography teachers are on 'converging tracks'. Initiatives are being set up, notably the Geo Visions Project set up in 1998, to consider the role of geography in the education of young people in the twenty-first century, but the effect of external influences such as the RAE and National Curriculum still exert formidable constraints that make positive action difficult to organise.

A changing role for geography educators?

If there are acknowledged constraints working to reduce the avenues of communication between teachers of geography in schools and academic geographers, then perhaps there is an increasingly important role for the providers of Initial Teacher Training (ITT) in geography in occupying the positions, formerly taken by academic geographers, of feeding information both from universities to schools and from schools to universities. This is not a new idea. Harvey, writing in 1972, noted the problem of diffusion of geographical knowledge and suggested that geography educators were in a good position to 'grapple with the problem in all of its complexity'.

Geography educationalists 'straddle' the divide – they work within a higher education environment and can access the work of colleagues in academic geography departments more easily than schools can, but at the same time they work in partnership with both experienced and beginning teachers. They see at first hand the problems created by the divide – such as the diversity of concepts of the nature of geography being brought into ITT by newly recruited students.

A small-scale survey among geography educators (Smith, 1996) revealed a common desire to move forward in this area. It would seem, however, that keeping up to date with the geography subject content has given way to curriculum planning in ITT courses, and, of course, geography educationalists work under the same RAE constraints as academic geographers. Marsden (1997), for instance, notes the decrease in contributions from geography educators to the journals *Teaching Geography* and *Primary Geography*.

Perhaps a way forward is via the accreditation route – geography educators already have involvement in In-Service Training (INSET) and Continuing Professional Development (CPD) such as MA and MEd courses. This could provide opportunities for including new developments in geography – such as the updating modules provided by some American universities (Daugherty and Rawling, 1996), thus narrowing a perceived gap between geography as taught in schools, geography as taught on geography education courses and geography as taught in academic geography departments.

CONCLUSIONS

In conclusion there are two key questions to ask. The first is 'Is the divide worth closing?' and the second, if it is worth making the effort to cross the wall, is 'What should the starting point be?'. In answer to the first question we believe that the long-term survival of the subject is at stake if school and university geography is not a united body. The existence of any subject is a numbers game, particularly if we are not just content to be in 'existence' but rather desire to be a vital and flourishing subject. In its most basic form any optional subject is dependent upon the through-flow of students from compulsory study in Key Stages 1, 2 and 3, through the optional school levels and onto higher education, and back into the classroom as teachers. At every optional stage there is naturally a high drop-off rate – down to 50 per cent at GCSE, to 6 per cent at A-level, with only 1 per cent of the original cohort remaining by the university stage (DfEE data, 1995–98). The total number, and significantly the quality of that cohort, who carry on through is largely dependent upon the subject retaining its standing and maximising the number of students who successfully transfer across each interface.

If the significance of student flow is accepted, the evidence below suggests that we should be very worried about geography's survival, as there currently appears to be a decrease at every level. The percentage of students opting for GCSE and A-level courses is falling year after year. For GCSE the cohort opting for geography has fallen from 51.5 per cent in 1995 to 41.8 per cent in 1999 (DfEE data, 1995–99). This is a decrease of almost 2 per cent per year. The trend for A-level geography is similar, falling from 6.5 per cent of total students to 5.7 per cent in the last five years (DfEE data, 1995–99), nearly 0.2 per cent per year.

However, the increase in the student population over the last five years masks the reality of the decline. Figures 22.3 and 22.4 illustrate the potential number of students being lost from the GCSE and A-level option groups when the annual change in the student population is taken into account. The reality is that in the last five years 40 000 potential GCSE and 5000 A-level geographers have been lost. These potential students are the pupils who should have opted for geography had the numbers changed in line with the overall student population.

These decreases will become all the more significant as each year progresses, since the proportional decline at each level will be compounded through the system as fewer students are available to make the transfer across each interface. This is now beginning to feed through to the university level, and one senior academic has noted an alarming 6 per cent drop in applications to university geography courses. Alongside this many PGCE courses are struggling to recruit despite geography's 'shortage status', with last year's applications down by 20 per cent (GTTR data, 1998). It was noted earlier that we have already lost the input from one generation of geographers into the content of school geography, and so we could be staring at the loss of the next one.

We must acknowledge the future threat in store for geography, and begin to address the issue while there is still time. We think there are two principles on which the huge effort to overcome the divide must be grounded: first, the validity of the subject as a coherent whole, and second, the inclusion of all practitioners in the discourse which will take the subject forward. The crisis in geography caused by the threat to omit it from the first National Curriculum in 1986 led Bailey and Binns to produce 'A Case

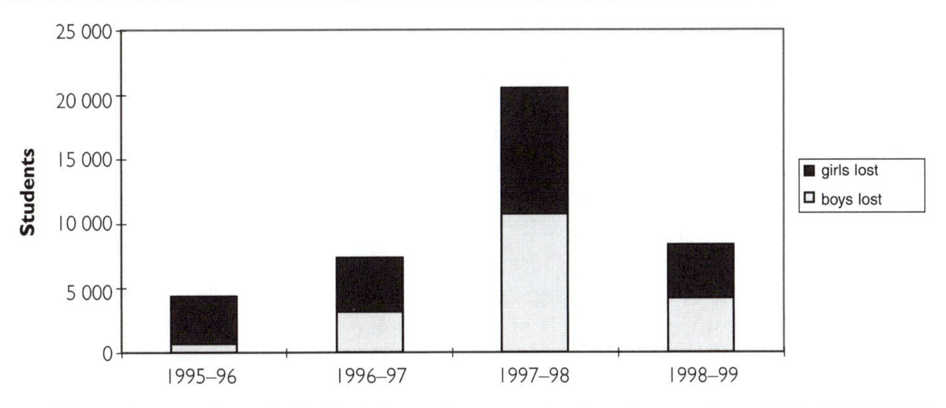

Figure 22.3 The number of GCSE students lost or gained each year from 1995–99 (DFEE data, 1995–98 – 1999 not definitive.

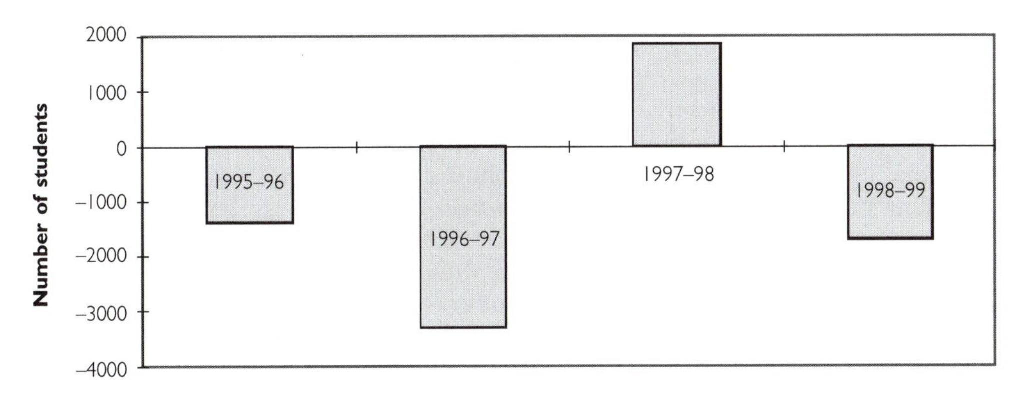

Figure 22.4 Total number of A-level students lost or gained each year from 1995–99 (DFEE data, 1995–98 – 1999 not definitive.

for Geography' as a repost to the seven questions posed by Keith Joseph to the GA. Since this attempt to give geography a clear rationale in schools it has become increasingly defined by its curriculum utility rather than its wider value. To give the subject an overarching validity we must return to the process begun by Bailey and Binns and create a clear rationale for geography which will enable all of its sections to be united. Only if the increasingly disparate sectors of the subject can identify a common cause will they be willing and able to make the effort required to implement the strategies necessary for integration to succeed across the key interfaces. Only the development of such a commonality could justify the application of the required time and resources.

The exact form of this rationale is not our place to define. It must emerge from a common dialogue between all of the participating groups, including teachers, academics, teacher educators and the geographical associations. However, whatever form it takes it must acknowledge the complexity and dynamic nature of contemporary geography, while making use of the most current perspectives from which to view the past, the present and the future.

To identify an inclusive rationale for the subject, the contribution which each group makes must be equally valued from the outset of the discourse. Teachers of geography are the key to supplying students to university, since it remains a largely non-vocational subject and universities will struggle to attract undergraduates who have not previously had a positive and rewarding experience of the subject. Teachers know how the subject should be delivered successfully in a classroom. Academics review the geography of the present and generate the geography of the future. At the same time they also provide the students who will choose to progress and become teachers, taking their academic experience into the classroom. PGCE students personify the divide as they endeavour to make the transition from academia into schools.

The questionnaire study of PGCE students at the Institute of Education London conducted by Brown (1999) provides a very positive outlook on the divide. Of the sample group over 70 per cent of students perceived previous academic experience of geography to be the most positively formative factor influencing their current teaching of geography. This was against factors including present school teaching and their own experience of geography as school students.

To develop a rationale for geography in the twenty-first century all of the groups must be accepted on their own terms and within the boundaries which the current educational policies and directives put upon them. Central to the development of such a rationale, and to the continual evolution of a coherent body of geography is translation, in both a literal and a metaphorical sense. The work of academic geographers must be translated into a form which is accessible to both teachers and consequently students; at the same time routes for this translation must be developed so that the knowledge and understanding can actually be passed across the divide. As they sit on the divide it is perhaps teacher educators and the geographical associations who are best placed to provide the modes and forums for translation to take place. Perhaps now is the time to unite key geographical bodies. COBRIG, the RGS/IBG and the GA have long lamented the existence of the divide and attempted separately to build links across it. However, many well considered initiatives have not progressed, since as independent bodies they have taken discrete agendas to separate forums. Further, with responsibility to their distinct membership groups, it is difficult to justify the allocation of resources towards initiatives which apparently extend beyond the bounds of particular associations. United, in whatever form, the professional bodies could develop coordinated strategies, hold inclusive forums to negotiate the future of geography, and justify the direction of pooled resources towards activities which might close the gap between geography in schools and universities.

If the crisis facing geography is to be resolved, it is paramount that the power to develop its future should not be held by those for whom the subject is just a minor product within a large portfolio of text books, TV programmes and examination entries, or those with an increasingly utilitarian approach to curriculum construction. Ultimately, it must be for each of the groups above, for whom geography has a more ethereal value, to regain control of their subject and direct its future.

REFERENCES

Brown (1999) 'PGCE students experience of the secondary/tertiary interface', MA submission.
Conneaux, M. (1998) 'The Arizona Geographic Alliance', *AAG Newsletter*, vol. 33, no. 4.
Daugherty, R. and Rawling, E. (1996) 'New perspectives for geography: an agenda for action',

in Rawling, E. and Daugherty, R. (eds), *Geography into the Twenty-First Century*. Chichester: John Wiley & Sons, pp. 359–77.

GTTR (1997) Annual Statistical Report.

GTTR (1998) Annual Statistical Report.

Harvey, D. (1972) 'The role of theory', in Graves, N. (ed.), *New Movements in the Study and Teaching of Geography*. London: Temple Smith, pp. 29–41.

Harvey, D. (1989) The Condition of Postmodernity: An Enquiry into the Origins of Cultural Change. Oxford: Blackwell.

Jenkins, A. (1995) 'The impact of research assessment exercises on teaching in selected geography departments in England and Wales', *Geography*, vol. 80, no. 4, pp. 367–74.

Kent, A. and Smith, M. (1997) 'Links between geography in schools and higher education', in Powell, A. (ed.), *Handbook of Post-16 Geography*. Sheffield: Geographical Association.

Kirby, A. and Lambert, D. (1978) 'Geography at school and university: is the gap between them growing?', *Papers on Education in Geography*. University of Reading.

Marsden, B. (1997) 'On taking the geography out of geographical education', *Geography*, vol. 82, no. 3, pp. 241–52.

Rawling, E. (1996) 'School geography: some key issues for higher education', *Journal of Geography in Higher Education*, vol. 20, no. 3, p. 305.

Rawling, E. and Daugherty, R. (1996) *Geography into the Twenty-first Century*. Chichester: John Wiley & Sons.

Smith, M. (1996) 'The secondary–tertiary interface in geography education', unpublished MA dissertation. University of London Institute of Education.

Spooner, D. (1995) 'Editorial: facelifts and formulae', *Geography*, vol, 80, no. 3, pp. 201–2.

Spooner, D. (1999) 'Progress report on the 1998 Action Plan of the School Higher Education Links Working Party'. Geographical Association (unpublished)

Chapter 23

Cultural studies go to school

John Morgan

In 1994, Nick Tate, Chief Executive of the SCAA, wrote:

> A key role of a national curriculum should be the explicit reinforcement of a common culture: pupils first and foremost should be introduced to the history of the part of the world where they live, its literary heritage and main religious traditions. They should be taught these things with the sensitivity a more diverse society demands; they should be taught other things too; but the culture and traditions of Britain should be at the core. Seen in this light, the central role of British history, Christianity and the English literary heritage are axiomatic.
>
> (Tate, 1994, p. 11)

Throughout the 1980s and 1990s, statements such as these have added an important element to educational debate, linked as they are to a broader struggle to restore a 'British' culture to a central place in national life (Ball, 1994). While English and History have been the most obvious sites of struggle over questions of culture, other subjects have not escaped this call to teach for a 'common culture'. Indeed, in a later address to the Geographical Association, Tate called for geography teachers to teach for an explicitly 'British geography'. These debates are never free from wider political questions, and Ken Jones (1999) has pointed out that Tate is a 'neoconservative' concerned to hang on to notions of 'nation' and 'culture' in the face of destabilising economic and political forces. In this chapter I argue that, far from being marginal to these wider questions of culture and identity, geography as a school subject is closely linked to ideals of value and culture. The heightened concern with questions of culture is reflected in the recent publication of the National Advisory Committee on Creative and Cultural Education's (NACCCE, 1999) report to the UK government entitled *All Our Futures: Creativity, Culture and Education*. The report notes that schools have a complex task: 'We expect education to prepare young people for the world of work and for economic independence; to enable them to live constructively in responsible communities; and to enable them to live in a tolerant, culturally diverse and rapidly changing society' (p. 18).

The report notes a number of 'social challenges' linked to the task of living in such a culturally diverse society:

> There have been profound changes in the food we eat, in how we speak and dress, and in how we see ourselves in relation to other countries and communities. Many British families have links across several continents. Many young people now live in a complex web of

> interacting cultures and sub-cultures of families, gender, peer groups, ideological convictions, political communities and of ethnic and local traditions. They also live in a global culture which is driven by the interplay of commercial interests, the creative energies of young people themselves, and the enveloping influence of information technologies. Information and communication technologies and the mass media – films, television, newspapers and magazines – form a torrent of ideas, images and lifestyles which compete for young people's attention and sense of identity.
>
> (p. 22)

The report calls for the development of creative and cultural education that can enable young people to cope with the personal challenges of living in a rapidly changing society. The report states four central roles for 'cultural education':

- to enable young people to recognise, explore and understand their own cultural assumptions and values;
- to enable young people to embrace and understand cultural diversity by bringing them into contact with the attitudes, values and traditions of other cultures;
- to encourage a historical perspective by relating contemporary values to the processes and events that have shaped them;
- to enable young people to understand the evolutionary nature of culture and the processes and potential for change.

The report stresses that all curriculum subjects have the potential to contribute to an expanded creative and cultural education and, in relation to the humanities, argues that subjects such as geography can 'broaden' and 'deepen' young people's understanding of the world around them, enlarge their knowledge of what they share with other people, and develop a 'critical awareness of the society and times in which they live' (p. 69).

While these calls for a 'cultural education' are in many ways uncontroversial and come within the generally agreed aims of geography education, in this chapter I want to argue that questions of culture in the school curriculum are not straightforward. In particular, I argue that the status of the knowledge brought to the classroom by young people is particularly problematic for geography teachers. I want to develop an argument for rethinking our understanding of the school geography curriculum through a discussion of its relationship with a broad and multidisciplinary approach offered by 'cultural studies'. In what follows I discuss the way in which teaching about 'culture' has developed in schools and show how these ideas are linked to dominant approaches to school geography. In relation to the purpose of this part of the book, which has as its title 'Research and Geography Teaching', this chapter is an attempt to show the value of undertaking a contextual reading of the recent history of geography education. Just as my other chapter in this collection sought to demonstrate the value of placing the work of geography teachers in a wider context, this chapter seeks to offer an alternative reading of recent trends in education in order to open up new vistas, or prise open new meanings and possibilities for geography teaching.

AGAINST POPULAR CULTURE

In order to develop the argument, we need to first consider the development of English. English in the school curriculum grew out of the radical changes in the economic and social formations of the early Industrial Revolution. The emergence of English as an academic subject in the school curriculum was linked with the growth of urban society in the nineteenth century which disturbed the moral fabric of the existing social order. English literature was seen as a means of unifying the nation and providing a form of moral training. Literary men such as John Ruskin and Matthew Arnold supported the study of literature in what they regarded as a period of cultural crisis. Matthew Arnold believed that culture must morally and aesthetically constitute the 'best' of human creativity. This was an unashamedly elitist conception that was unequivocal in its contempt for 'mass' or popular culture. The 1921 Newbolt Report consolidated the role of English in the school curriculum. The role envisaged for English in the report was to act as the basis for national unity and as a source of spiritual comfort for those whose good faith had been battered in the Great War. English was to be offered as the key instrument for educating the emotions of the 'masses' so that as individuals they may be raised spiritually while at the same time remain excluded from political and economic power and decision-making. It was in this context that the most influential current in school English developed. Claims for the centrality of English literature were realised in the work of F.R. Leavis and his followers at Cambridge in the 1930s and 1940s. Leavis and Thompson's (1948) *Culture and Environment* warned of the perceived threat to civilisation posed by mass media and popular culture, and called upon teachers to act to resist the effects of the mass media. For Leavis, English teaching was the guarantee of the moral and spiritual health both of the individual and the nation. It played a conservative role, providing active opposition to forces that were seen to be undermining that national culture. English was thus the first line of defence against the ravages of an increasingly commercial and industrial society. Buckingham and Sefton-Green (1994) note that this 'broadly defensive' approach to popular culture still has considerable influence among English teachers. The important point here is that this Leavisite approach to culture necessarily relied on the idea that the 'masses' were unable to read in the desired manner. The classical humanism espoused by Leavis and his followers reflected the tastes of an elite class.

Sinfield (1985) argues that the period after 1945 has been characterised by the gradual but inevitable erosion of the power base of classical humanism in education. He attributes this to the emergence of a 'left culturalism' in the context of postwar reconstruction. By the late 1950s and 1960s the working-class academic began to speak for himself (*sic*). Three important figures are associated with the founding of cultural studies: Richard Hoggart, Raymond Williams and E.P. Thompson. Their work was focused on working-class cultures 'from within'. They adopted a 'culturalist' perspective in that they saw the emergence of a subjective class consciousness based in the material conditions of working-class life. These writers reclaimed an authentic voice for the working-class and refused to see these as inferior and devoid of value. This literature has influenced recent generations of English teachers. For his part, Raymond Williams was concerned to develop a more expansive and inclusive notion of quality than simply a concern with academic standards. Thus schools should allow children to use and critique the media, and recognise the ideological force in advertising. Williams thought that English teaching should incorporate a range of communication forms needed in everyday life as a defence against an elitist pedagogy. Much of Williams' curriculum has become a standard part of the routines of everyday teaching: the media and popular culture are classroom resources, and English teaching lays great stress on the ordinariness of everyday communication needs. Similarly, the recognition and validation of a specifically working-class culture had the effect of encouraging the rejection of the idea of working-class cultural inferiority.

Despite these changes, education has remained quite resistant to recognising and validating other forms of experience. The development of a distinctive phase of 'youth culture' was attributed to the mass society and the mass media, but was also a product of the education system which it was seen to be undermining. Education created a gap between childhood and work and the growth of teenage subcultures was in part the product of young people's attempts to come to terms with the conditions they found themselves in. The question revolved around how these developments were to find expression in the education system. Hall and Whannell's (1964) *The Popular Arts* was an attempt to read popular cultural texts in the same way as literature might be read, and the NUT conference in the same year focused on the impact of the media and questions of discrimination or how to provide young people with the tools to make judgements about the culture they consume.

In response to these developments, a looser and more expansive notion of culture has come to be adopted by English teachers in the postwar period (Jones, 1996). Classrooms have been opened to television, films, advertisements, comics and so on, all part of the 'informal' knowledge children bring with them to school. These have been variously called 'Transitional English' (Moore, 1999) or the 'London School' (Green, 1995), and although there are important tensions within these movements they have in common their willingness to work with children's experiences, are concerned with cultural change and are willing to accept elements of social and cultural criticism (Jones, 1999).

GEOGRAPHY AND CULTURE

The concerns of school English and questions of 'culture' may seem tangential to the work of geography teachers. However, I want to show that we can trace a connection between them. For a start, school geography was born in the same moment as English, in a period of intense 'time–space compression' when older certainties were being swept aside. In many ways geography shared the same concerns about the 'masses' and the popular pleasures they engaged in. In the postwar period, classical humanism formed the dominant idea of education. This approach held that it is

> the task of the guardian class, including the teachers, to initiate the young into the mysteries of knowledge and the ways in which knowledge confers various kinds of social power on those who possess it . . . classical humanism has been associated with clear and firm discipline, high attainment in examinations, continuity between past and present, the cohesiveness and orderly development of institutions.
>
> (Skilbeck and Harris, 1976)

In the development of school geography, Halford Mackinder was perhaps the main proponent of the classical humanist approach in geography with his concern that it should elevate the minds of the masses so that they might rise above such base pleasures (O Tuathail, 1996). It is tempting to speculate that the challenge faced by geographers has been to convince others that geographers' attempts to make sense of a place, a region or a landscape were something more than impressions. This led to a concern to write in detached and 'objective' styles and ignore popular culture, since it is seen as far removed from the concerns of the 'educated' and 'cultivated' mind. Even within the work of humanistic geographers, which has perhaps been more open to the study of 'culture', there has been a marked reluctance to move beyond 'serious' topics and texts and a tendency to dismiss popular cultural landscapes. Warren (1993) notes the neglect of the landscapes of cultural consumption by cultural geographers: 'The most sustained commentary on the everyday has resolutely dismissed it as dangerously mindless "mass culture"' (p. 175).

Humanistic geography has much in common with the conservative tradition of 'culture and society', focusing on the symbolism and meaning found in literature and art. Burgess and Gold (1985) note that from the record of published work about literature, geographers 'emerge as being profoundly elitist in their interests, with a derogatory view of the "mass" media and thus its "mass" audience'. Relph (1976) classified place experiences on a scale ranging from the deepest authentic to the shallowest inauthentic (examples of which included Disneyland and the Mediterranean coast). Gregory (1994) notes that: 'There is on occasion more than a hint of Leavis's rasping elitism in the conservative canon of humanistic geography' (p. 84).

The disdain for 'mass' or popular culture is also evident in the work of radical geography, which has been much influenced by the Frankfurt School of critical theory which tended to regard popular culture as promoting 'false consciousness'. Thus Harvey (1989) and Soja (1989) note the tendency for 'theme park' experiences in the contemporary city, and Sack (1992) condemns the consumer world as immoral.

While geographers have, until recently (see below), tended to ignore the importance of popular culture, schools have not been immune from the types of pressures that have influenced the direction of English in schools. Sinfield (1985) notes that, during the 1960s, four factors were responsible for drawing attention to the curriculum: government pressure for more and better scientists, the anticipated raising of the school leaving age to 16, the amalgamation of grammar and secondary modern schools into comprehensives and the demand for greater student participation. These factors served to problematise dominant forms of school geography. Their overall effect was to promote rival student cultures and challenge geography to address the needs of a larger group of students.

The period between 1945 and 1960 was one of continued growth of educational spending. In the 1960s governments held the conviction that the British economy, in order to compete on a world scale, needed a greater degree of state intervention in economic planning and a thorough overhaul of the social infrastructure of the country. One aspect of this overhaul was the expansion of further and higher education, which required the incorporation of children previously excluded from academic qualifications. These objectives lay behind the growth of comprehensive education.

Although the motives for this expansion in educational provision were primarily economic, designed to maximise the potential of previously untapped human resources, the policies to achieve greater equality of opportunity were primarily cultural. The main agency of curriculum development was the Schools Council. It was a major institution, free from direct control. Both the Schools Council and the major educational reports of the time had a bias towards moral and cultural questions, which they related to individual development. The Newsom Report of 1963 was concerned with those pupils who were 'average and below average' who made up 'Half Our Future'. The point about these major reforms was that they were framed in culturalist terms, which means that they were about changing the cultural values and assumptions of young people in schools. What this meant in practice was that schools sought to find ways to deal with the cultures of young people. In geography this was aided by the various Schools Council Projects, the growth of alternative types of examination systems, and various strategies for progressive teaching which involved different approaches to language, oracy and writing that paralleled the development of the 'New English'. In many cases this involved an engagement with teachers in English and the humanities and led to the study of social issues in the curriculum.

These developments in geography education were linked to wider cultural changes including the growth of feminism, multiculturalism and the growth of youth subcultures. These cultural changes required that teachers develop more inclusive ways of recognising the experiences of young people. As I have suggested in this section, this process has involved arguments and debates about what should constitute geographical education. Indeed, the development of a national curriculum from the late 1980s that harks back to 'traditional' approaches to geography teaching can be interpreted as a response to these processes of cultural change. Such 'curriculum fundamentalism' (Ball, 1994) has quite successfully defined and defended the boundaries of the traditional discipline, excluding other types of geographical knowledge. It is interesting to reflect that there has been an increase in the number of students at British universities studying courses that involve the study of popular culture, and the expanding fields of social and cultural geography are part of this trend. It is perhaps here that the underlying processes of cultural change are most clearly expressed in geography education. In the next section, I discuss some of the research in this area before going on to discuss its implications for geography teaching in school contexts.

THE 'CULTURAL TURN'

In recent years work in the so-called 'new cultural geography' (see Jackson, this volume) has drawn upon the interdisciplinary field of cultural studies. One of the earliest attempts to illustrate the relevance of cultural studies for geography was Burgess and Gold's (1985) edited collection *Geography, the Media and Popular Culture*. The tone of their approach is reflected in the following comment:

> The media have been on the periphery of geographical inquiry for too long. The very ordinariness of television, radio, newspapers, fiction, film and pop music perhaps masks their importance as part of people's geography 'threaded into the fabric of daily life with deep taproots into the well-springs of popular consciousness'
>
> (p. 1)

Burgess and Gold were concerned that 'elite' or dominant forms of culture have been overvalued in geography at the expense of 'popular' or subordinate forms of culture. This theme is taken up in Cosgrove and Jackson's (1987) agenda-setting article on 'New directions in cultural geography'. They cite studies of 'mugging', gender, racism and youth subcultures as relevant to a revised cultural geography that recognises the importance of the strategies of resistance used by subordinate groups to contest the hegemony of powerful groups. These themes are developed in Jackson's (1989) *Maps of Meaning* which develops the idea of cultural politics – defined as the 'domain in which meanings are constructed and negotiated, where relations of dominance and subordination are defined and contested'. Examples of such studies can be found in Anderson and Gale's (1992) *Inventing Places*. The essays in this collection are diverse, ranging from studies of the elite landscapes of corporate culture and high-class residential developments, through the ways in which assumptions about gender relations are encoded in shopping malls and urban space, through to the media coverage of the environmental impacts of economic developments.

The concern that geographers have ignored popular culture in their studies is acknowledged in the recent collection of essays edited by Tracey Skelton and Gill Valentine (1998) entitled *Cool Places: Geographies of Youth Cultures*. The collection seeks to explore the 'diversity in young people's lives in order to place youth on the geographical map and to demonstrate youth's relevance to a range of geographical debates'. The chapters focus on different aspects of young people's identities including gender, ethnicity, disability and sexuality. Throughout there is a concern with the everyday and the popular, including television and the use of computers, and everyday spaces such as the home, school, workplaces, streets and clubs. The book represents a significant contribution to popular geographical studies and challenges geography educators to incorporate such perspectives into our teaching and research.

Perspectives from cultural geography and cultural studies offer geography educators new ways of thinking about their work. Cultural studies is an interdisciplinary, transdisciplinary field that involves the analysis of lived experience of various groups and individuals in late twentieth-century societies. It highlights culture as a living process that shapes the way we live, view ourselves and understand the world around us. Cultural studies is characterised by a variety of approaches. The importance of cultural studies for geography education is expressed in the notion of 'cultural pedagogy', which refers to the idea that education takes place in a variety of social sites including but not limited to schooling. Thus libraries, TV, movies, newspapers, magazines, toys, advertisements, video games, books, sports and so on are all involved in the process of identity formation and its production and legitimation of knowledge. There is much potential for developing forms of critical or 'deconstructive' media literacy in geography education, a wealth of geographical research exists which provides models for teachers to develop approaches, and there is an established body of theory in media education that has so far been largely ignored by geography educators. Examples include the contributions in Burgess and Gold (1985), the essays in Clarke's (1997) *The Cinematic City* and Jackson's (1991) work on advertising and masculinity. In addition, there has been little critical discussion of the implications of 'virtual geographies' linked to the new communications technologies (Crang et al., 1999).

A final example is Bell and Valentine's (1997) *Consuming Geographies*. They note that the 'cultural turn' has brought identity politics and issues of consumption to the fore in geography, and use the example of food as a way of demonstrating the importance of space and place in identity formation (the subtitle of the book is 'We Are Where We Eat'). *Consuming Geographies* can be seen as a geographical contribution to cultural studies. Bell and Valentine consider a range of scales from the body to the global, and show how these get tangled up with issues of race, ethnicity, sexuality, age, gender and class. They draw on an eclectic mix of academic and popular texts, cartoons, television and films as well as the voices of interviewees scattered throughout the text.

These new approaches to cultural geography, by focusing on a plurality of cultures and cultural politics, allow cultural forms to be located in their socio-historical context. They are concerned with the relationships between the economy, state, society, culture and everyday life, but reject the high and low culture distinction, arguing that cultural forms such as film, television and popular music are worthy of study. In short, the study of youth and other cultures is on the agenda of cultural geographers. These are new kinds of geographies that offer potentially exciting opportunities for school geography, yet so far they have been little discussed. In the next section, I discuss the types of pedagogies that might be needed to develop a geographical education that draws upon this work.

TOWARDS A NEW EDUCATION

In this chapter I have sought to locate school geography on the shifting terrain of 'cultural education'. I have suggested that, while school English has, in the postwar period, responded to cultural changes in order to incorporate the experiences of young people, such changes have, to date, been limited in school geography. Consequently, the school geography curriculum remains strongly classified and framed. However, in this concluding section I want to suggest that geography can play its part in what Moore (1999) has called the 'New Education'. New Education has been influenced by perspectives from cultural studies and postmodernism. Green (1995) suggests that such an education is characterised by 'its commitment to notions of process, experience and pleasure; its fluid and dynamic sense of disciplinary and other social boundaries; and generally its attitude to concepts of difference and marginality' (p. 402). What this might mean can be glimpsed in David Buckingham and Julian Sefton-Green's (1994) *Cultural Studies Goes to School,* which is an attempt to import some of the ideas and methods of cultural studies into schools. This involves a broadening of the concerns of English, which is traditionally too concerned with the written word, and challenges the dominant model of media education, which is concerned to 'demystify' texts through producing oppositional readings. In their approach, the focus is much more on the socially situated readings of popular cultural texts made by young people (see also Buckingham, 1998). Moore (1999, p. 121) outlines a number of activities that are features of the New Education including: prioritising issues and contexts in textual study; linguistic and cultural pluralism; deconstructive activities in the study and production of a wide range of media texts; and group discussion and joint decision-making in text production. Moore argues that such practices are being taken up by radical teachers in a range of subjects and contribute to 'what could become the New Curriculum'. This suggests that geography teachers could draw upon cultural studies of the type described in the previous section to contribute to the New Education. Such a geography education would:

- start from the lived experiences of young people – this means that there is a recognition of how our geographical imaginations are being shaped by a range of stimuli;
- be concerned to examine the 'texts' that young people use to construct their identities. In doing so it pays attention to the meanings as encoded in these texts and the meanings that people produce from them;
- be deconstructive in that it seeks to prise open new meanings and provide resources for the construction of new identities.

Finally, I discuss how geography teachers might begin to develop this approach through the use of a popular media text – *The Full Monty*.

THE FULL MONTY

This chapter has suggested that the gap between the formal cultures of the geography classroom and the informal cultures of young people is increasingly blurred. It is simply impossible to close the classroom door on popular culture, since its images, products and ways of reading and speaking all influence what happens in geography classrooms. Indeed, part of my argument here is that the looser, more open ways in which young people relate to and use popular culture contradict the tighter more closed models of geography education, where teachers know and students must submit to the authority of the text. For example, while geography lessons are one of the spaces where young people learn about the economy, about notions of work and the changing nature of employment on places and regions, popular culture also provides knowledge of these issues. The 'New Education' discussed in this chapter suggests that geography teachers need to make such popular cultural texts the object of classroom study.

The Full Monty is about the aftermath of the closure of the steelworks in Sheffield. The film starts with a promotional film from 1970 which names Sheffield as the steel city, a city with night clubs, a city on the move, located at the centre of Britain's industrial north, with 90 000 men employed in steel production. The film then deploys a classic pedagogical trick, the before-and-after scene, as the present-day steelyard is derelict, rusted and abandoned, except for two redundant steelworkers 'liberating' a girder.

The film explores issues of gender politics in a post-industrial context, and the common feature of all the male characters is that they are experiencing a 'crisis of identity' following their redundancy. This crisis of masculinity is manifested in a variety of ways: the redundancy of fathers, the infantilisation of unemployed men and sexual impotency. The central characters have lost their work and as such their foundational identities. This is symbolised in the film by the advance of women into 'men's space'. Thus the working men's club is appropriated by women for the Chippendales event, a point stressed by the fact that women even use men's toilets.

There are significant opportunities for geography teaching here. Most notably, there are themes about the gendered nature of work, the separation of the private and public spheres, and the gendered use of space that could usefully be explored (see McDowell, 1999). The organisation of many places around such a set of gendered relations could be discussed. The film is also a commentary on changing economic activities. The types of work shown in *The Full Monty* reflect wider patterns of employment in Britain, where nearly half the workforce is female, mostly in casualised and low-paid forms of white-collar work. In the film, places of active employment are supermarkets, where women serve and men act as security guards, and female dominated factory work, which men (predictably) avoid at all costs. The film tends to focus on gender relations, with the effect that questions of class are downplayed. The geography teacher may want to raise questions about the 'invisible' forces that are shaping such places as Sheffield. The film makes use of the metaphors of 'stripping' in relation to the stripped nature of the landscapes of industrialisation, and in the fact that the craft-skills of the men are no longer needed (as one of the characters says 'like skateboards'), who are stripped of their identities. In order to regain their identities, they learn to 'strip', in the process becoming commodities (again, the gendered role reversal is notable, in that this time the male strippers are the ones who are watched, subject to display, rather than the traditional female stripper). Indeed, this notion, that in order to regain their identities men must repackage themselves as 'commodities' comes close to the role envisaged for workers in post-Fordist capitalism: workers must be flexible, adaptable, enterprising and skilled at packaging themselves for the demands of the market.

Claire Monk (2000) suggests that the film offers male audiences a 'symbolic, if inevitably problematic, solution' to the problems of male unemployment. She argues that the film expresses the problems of the post-industrial male in a 'feminised' society as problems of gender, rather than economic, realities. Indeed, Monk worries about the misogyny of this 'solution', especially when the working-class community whose passing is being mourned is defined as a community of *men*. Indeed, the position of women in the film is open to question. While there are some key women characters – such as Gaz's wife Mandy, portrayed negatively as a social climber, expressed geographically in her move to the suburbs and socially in her relationship with a rather priggish, middle-class man – others are marginal to the narrative. Nonetheless, the film enjoyed great popularity among female viewers, possibly because of the extent to which traditional gender roles are reversed.

All these issues can be explored in geography lessons, and I have hinted at the type of geographical literature that might be used to support such work. The question revolves around the way in which geography teachers might develop a cultural pedagogy to make use of a film such as *The Full Monty*. Such a pedagogy is always discursive. It revolves around discussions about the meanings of the text, drawing out its meanings and making them speak to the reader. In developing such a pedagogy it is less important to provide 'correct' interpretations about a text than to achieve a critical position on it. There is no inherent meaning in the text itself, but films are read socially.

Finally, though, the question remains of how far the types of approaches associated with the 'New Education' can be developed in school geography classrooms. Over the last decade, curriculum and assessment systems have limited the space for geography teachers to develop student-centred approaches, and a conservative version of geography has been installed as constituting the 'core' curriculum. The tiering of exams and the renewed focus on setting and selection make it difficult to imagine classrooms as places where a wide range of student experiences can be brought together.

REFERENCES

Anderson, K. and Gale, F. (eds) (1992) *Inventing Places: Studies in Cultural Geography*. Melbourne: Longman.

Ball, S. (1994) *Education Reform: A Critical and Post-structural Approach*. London: Routledge.

Bell, D. and Valentine, G. (1997) *Consuming Geographies: We Are Where We Eat*. London: Routledge.

Buckingham, D. (ed.) (1998) *Teaching Popular Culture: Beyond Radical Pedagogy*. London: UCL Press.

Buckingham, D. and Sefton-Green, J. (1994) *Cultural Studies Goes to School*. London: Taylor & Francis.

Burgess, J. and Gold, J. (1985) *Geography, the Media, and Popular Culture*. Beckenham: Croom Helm

Clarke, D. (1997) *The Cinematic City*. London: Routledge.

Cosgrove, D. and Jackson, P. (1987) 'New directions in cultural geography', *Area*, vol. 19, pp. 95–101.

Crang, M., Crang, P. and May, J. (eds) (1999) *Virtual Geographies*. London: Routledge.

Green, B. (1995) 'Post-curriculum possibilities: English teaching, cultural politics, and the postmodern turn', *Journal of Curriculum Studies*. vol. 27, pp. 391–409.

Gregory, D. (1994) *Geographical Imaginations*. Oxford: Basil Blackwell.

Hall, S. and Whannell, P. (1964) *The Popular Arts*. London: Hutchinson.

Harvey, D. (1989) *The Condition of Postmodernity*. Oxford: Blackwell.

Jackson, P. (1989) *Maps of Meaning*. London: Unwin Hyman

Jackson, P. (1991) 'Black male: advertising and the cultural politics of masculinity', *Gender, Place and Culture*, vol. 1, pp. 49–59.

Jones, K. (ed.) (1996) *Education after the Conservatives*. London: Trentham Books.

Jones, K. (with Franks, A.) (1999) 'English', in Hill, D. and Cole, M. (eds), *Promoting Equality in the Secondary School*. London: Cassell, pp. 31–56.

Leavis, F.R. and Thompson, D. (1948) *Culture and Environment*. London: Chatto & Windus.

McDowell, L. (1999) *Gender, Identity and Place*. Cambridge: Polity Press.

Monk, C. (2000) 'Men in the 90s', in R. Murphy (ed.), *British Cinema of the 90s*. London: British Film Institute.

Moore, A. (1999) 'English, fetishism and the demand for change: towards a post-modern agenda for the school curriculum', in Edwards, G. and Kelly, A. (eds), *Experience and Education: Towards an Alternative National Curriculum*. London: Paul Chapman.

National Advisory Committee on Creative and Cultural Education (1999) *All Our Futures: Creativity, Culture and Education*. London: DfEE.

O Tuathail, G. (1996) *Critical Geopolitics*. London: Routledge.

Relph, E. (1976) *Place and Placelessness*. London: Pion.

Sack, R. (1992) *Place, Modernity and the Consumer's World*. Baltimore, MD: Johns Hopkins University Press.

Sinfield, A. (1985) 'Give an account of Shakespeare and education, showing why you think they are effective and what you have appreciated about them. Support your comments with precise references', in Dollimore, J. and Sinfield, A. (eds), *Political Shakespeare: New Essays in Cultural Materialism*. Manchester: Manchester University Press, pp. 134–57.

Skelton, T. and Valentine, G. (1998) *Cool Places: Geographies of Youth Cultures*. London: Routledge.

Skilbeck, M. and Harris, A. (1976) *Culture, Ideology and Knowledge*. Milton Keynes: Open University Press.

Soja, E. (1989) *Postmodern Geographies*. London: Verso.

Tate, N. (1994) 'Off the fence on common culture', *Times Educational Supplement*, 29 July p. 11.

Warren, S. (1993) '"This heaven gives me migraines": the problems and promises of landscapes and leisure', in Duncan, J. and Ley, D. (eds), *Place/Culture/Representation*. London: Routledge, pp. 173–86.

Chapter 24

The role of research in supporting teaching and learning

Margaret Roberts

INTRODUCTION

During the last decade, the role of educational research in the UK has been the subject of considerable debate. Discussion has centred on issues such as: priorities for educational research; how 'user groups' of research should be involved; the extent to which research should lead to 'applied outcomes'; and the 'relevance' of research (Rudduck and McIntyre, 1998). Underpinning this debate is the notion accepted by most educational researchers that there should be some sort of connection between educational research on the one hand and the policy and practice of education on the other. How this connection is conceptualised varies, however, particularly in relation to teaching. Hargreaves has argued that teaching should be a 'research-based' profession and that it should be 'evidence-based' (Hargreaves, 1998). These phrases suggest a direct relationship between applied research and application in the classroom. Hannon (1998), however, sees the role of research somewhat differently when he states, 'Teachers do not use research as a cookbook but as a resource in constructing their view of what is worth aiming for and likely ways to get it' (p. 151).

The general debate about educational research has raised questions that are important for geographical education. What is worth researching? Can research provide evidence for a basis for teaching geography? How can it help teachers to construct their views of what is worth aiming for? These questions provide a context for this chapter which sets out to explore the role of research in supporting the teaching and learning of geography in schools. The approach I have adopted is different from others who have written about geography education research. Other approaches have given emphasis to what has been researched and how. Foskett and Marsden (1998) have compiled a useful bibliography, categorising what has been written on geographical and environmental education into themes. Williams (1996) and Slater (1996) were both concerned with how research into geographical education has been carried out and have illustrated different 'approaches', 'methods' and 'ideologies' with examples. The starting point for these writers was the research itself.

I have approached the question about the role of research in supporting teaching and learning from the other end of the research/practice debate. I want to focus more on the 'actors' involved in the process of teaching and learning, the teachers and the learners, and the contexts within which the teaching and learning of geography takes place.

A MODEL OF THE TEACHING AND LEARNING SITUATION.

I have represented the teaching and learning situation diagrammatically in the model shown in Figure 24.1 on which I have identified three components of the teaching and learning situation in schools: learners, teachers and the context. They are represented by three overlapping circles, A, B and C. I have used the term 'learner' to mean the children, pupils or students learning geography, although I recognise that the teacher is also a learner in the classroom. I have used the term 'teacher' to mean the adult in the teaching and learning situation although I recognise that pupils can teach their peers. By the 'context' I mean everything in the school and organised by the school which can support learning. Together, these three overlapping inner circles represent the world of formal school education. They are situated on the diagram in the wider context of the world outside the school. I have labelled this outer circle, marked H, as 'culture' by which I mean the complex processes through which groups and individuals make sense of their world. Within the cultural circle I have identified four interrelated aspects of culture as being particularly relevant to the teaching and learning of geography: experience, cultural change, policy and values. I have drawn the boundaries between the inner circles and the wider context as broken lines, to emphasise the fact that the formal world of schooling and the cultural context are not distinct. Much learning takes place beyond the confines of formal schooling and this is significant to what takes place in school.

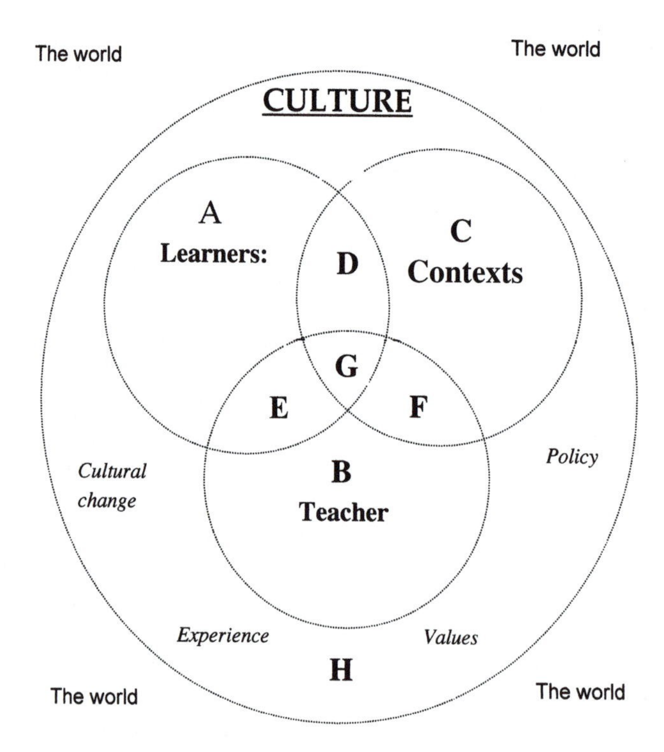

Figure 24.1 A model of the teaching and learning situations: actors and contexts (see text for discussion of A–H).

Beyond the circle representing the cultural context I have placed the 'real world'. This is the world that is mediated to us through culture experienced individually and in groups. The 'real' world that geographers investigate in schools is mediated particularly through what is currently accepted as appropriate for geographical education, influenced to some extent by what constitutes and has constituted 'geography' in higher education, and by national and school policies.

MAPPING GEOGRAPHY EDUCATION RESEARCH ONTO THE MODEL

I would now like to use this model to explore how research in geographical education can support the teaching and learning of geography in schools. For each section, marked A–H on the model, I will discuss the type of research that can be mapped into the section, giving examples.

A Learners

The research I have mapped into section A is concerned with how learners construct their own meanings of the world, i.e. how they make sense of what they know and experience. Researchers have investigated children's understanding of concepts in physical geography, for example the greenhouse effect, ozone depletion and acid rain (Dove, 1996). Others have researched children's understandings of place, e.g. Matthews (1992). Robertson (2000) has investigated the affective rather than the cognitive domain in her study of the hopes and visions young people expressed for an area in which they carried out a land-use survey of England and Wales in 1987.

The research mapped into this sector is underpinned by a constructivist theory of learning. According to this theory, which is currently widely accepted, knowledge is not 'out there' for learners to receive. It has to be actively constructed by the learner and made sense of in terms of existing ways of thinking. Sometimes, the prior concepts of learners gained from experience in the wider context can be a barrier to learning in school. Research into learners' prior conceptions can inform the teacher of the potential difficulties of teaching specific geographical concepts and can suggest ways of tackling them. It is important for teachers to know individual starting points so that they can cater for different needs.

Research in this sector generates a particular way of thinking about teaching and learning. Such a view can inform and transform curriculum development and practice, as Driver (1994) has shown in relation to the science curriculum.

In geography there has been more research into children's ideas of concepts in physical geography than in human geography. There has been more research on the cognitive domain than on the affective domain.

B Teachers

The research I have mapped into this section recognises that teachers, in the same way as learners, bring prior conceptions to the teaching and learning situation. They bring geography subject knowledge, constructed during their own schooling, during different higher education courses and through continuing professional study of the subject. They also bring pedagogic knowledge, knowledge of how they understand and practice teaching geography, and this is influenced by their own experiences as a teacher and as a learner. Examples of research on teachers include work on their perceptions of environmental education (Corney, 1997) and on their interpretations of the geography National Curriculum (Roberts, 1995). Investigating teacher perspectives was a major part of the research by Parsons (1988) on the implementation of the Schools Council Geography for the Young School Leaver Project.

Research in this sector increases knowledge and understanding of different ways of conceptualising the subject, ways of teaching it and different ways of interpreting policy. It indicates how influential teachers' prior conceptions can be on the way they work in the classroom. This research can enhance professional understanding by raising important questions about taken for granted views and practices that are taken for granted. It can probe the values underpinning practice.

C The school context and resources.

Research in category C focuses on resources as objects of research in themselves. Most of the geography education research that can be mapped into this section is related to textbooks. There have been many studies of geography textbooks investigating, for example, changes (Marsden, 1988) and bias (Hicks, 1980).

Most of the research in this area seems to be concerned with making teachers and publishers more aware of how textbooks represent the world. Lester and Slater (1996), however, researched and constructed a text on South Africa designed to make the learner aware of different representations in text. I would suggest that the role of research into resources is of growing significance for two reasons. First, developments in geography in higher education emphasise different views and representations of the world. One authoritative text cannot represent it. Second, the increasing availability of a large amount of information through the Internet gives access to far more viewpoints and voices than are available in schools. Future research into resources needs to take account of new perspectives in geography in higher education and the easy access of learners to knowledge not controlled by a teacher. It needs to investigate how learners can be made aware of issues of representation for themselves and how they can be supported to help them make sense of different viewpoints and voices.

D Learners using resources

Research in section D, at the interface of learners and resources, is investigating the learners' use and understanding of resources. Research in this section is dominated by research into learners' understanding of maps. Examples of research into map use include the use by young children of maps in their physical environment (Spencer et al., 1989) and children's understanding of thematic maps in atlases (Wiegand, 1996).

There has been some research on other resources used in geographical education. Blades and Spencer (1987) have studied young children's understanding of aerial photographs. As part of research into thinking skills, Leat and Nichols (1999) have investigated how secondary school pupils manipulate and make sense of text in 'mysteries' activities in geography.

Research in this section is important because the teaching and learning of geography at the beginning of the twenty-first century in the UK is very dependent on the use of resources. Geography examinations at GCSE and A-Level present data which candidates are expected to use and interpret. The geography National Curriculum for England requires that pupils learn to use both primary and secondary sources of data.

Yet, with the exception of research into understanding of maps, there is relatively little research into how learners use and make sense of data in the resources presented to them.

E Teacher/learner interactions

Research in this overlapping section of the model focuses on ways in which teachers and learners interact with each other. This interaction involves the use of language, spoken or written. Much of the research into classroom talk in geography lessons has been carried out as part of research into language across the curriculum, (Mercer, 1995). Carter's research (1991) was specifically focused on geography and contributed to the National Oracy Project.

Teachers and learners also interact through written work. Again, much of the research has been carried out across the curriculum and has referred to geographical examples. This work has focused on, for example, how learners interpret what teachers expect from written work (Sheeran and Barnes, 1991) and how pupils responded to written activities set up by teachers to explore audience-centred writing in geography (Butt, 1993).

Research in this area is crucially important because language is the medium through which most learning takes place in geography. What learners learn, how they learn and what they think is important to learn are strongly influenced by written and spoken dialogues between teacher and learner and between learner and learner. Research into this area can probe familiar habitual classroom practices. It helps us to see them differently and to understand them more fully. It can indicate what helps and what hinders learning. Research can suggest strategies for teachers to use to promote learning

F Teachers and the resources they use

Little research has been carried out on the way teachers use different resources and the thinking underpinning such different use. An example which could be included in this section is Job's (1996) investigation of how teachers thought about the use of the environment. He revealed the different ideologies underpinning practice, and produced a framework that helps clarify understanding.

G Learners, teachers and resources

Research in this sector, at the overlapping centre of the model, is concerned with teachers, learners and resources, when all three elements are present in the research. It includes curriculum development research, research on assessment and research into classroom practices.

The geography curriculum development projects of the 1970s and 1980s were all developed through research.

Research that focuses on the whole process of assessment can also be mapped into this sector. Daugherty (1996) provides a useful overview of research on assessment, in which he comments that 'the professional discourse about assessment has only infrequently been informed by research studies seeking to gather evidence from empirical investigation' (p. 242). This would suggest that policy decisions that have a profound affect on teaching and learning are made at national and school level without the benefit of evidence from research. It seems vitally important at a time when so much importance is placed on the results of summative assessments that more is understood about how different forms of assessment help and/or hinder learning. It is also important to know how the official assessment structures influence the teaching and learning of geography. Such research should inform policy which in turn influences teaching and learning.

Classroom research that takes place in a 'real-life' rather than experimental setting, with a teacher, a class of learners and resources, can be mapped into this section. Some of this work is on a small scale, for example, Rickinson (1999) has investigated the teaching and learning of people–environment issues in the classroom. An example of developmental research in this area is Leat's (Leat and Nichols, 1999) work with teachers in their classrooms in the North East of England. The focus of this work is on 'thinking skills', and the work has included development and research of resources, close observation and recording of classroom practices and interviews with teachers and learners. Much of the research is carried out by the teachers as action researchers with the aim of changing and improving teaching and learning in their own classrooms. Action research has the potential to improve understanding of classroom processes, to change and improve classroom practices, to improve the quality of learning and to promote professional development.

H The wider context

I have selected three aspects of the cultural context to examine the role of research in this sector: cultural change, policy and values.

Research on the history of geographical education provides an overview of changes in teaching and learning practices and of underpinning rationales. Research into the history of geographical education helps us understand the present. It reveals that what has been accepted as good practice in teaching and learning is subject to change and is therefore open to question. Furthermore, accounts of geographical education in the past help to ensure that valuable lessons learnt from the curriculum research and development projects of the 1970s and 1980s are not lost.

The teaching and learning of geography in England and Wales is taking place in the context of nationally produced policy frameworks. Research into policy asks critical questions about how policy has been constructed (Rawling, 1992), about its underpinning ideologies (Lambert, 1994) and about its reconstruction by teachers in schools (Roberts, 1995). As policy undoubtedly influences the teaching and learning of geography in schools, it is essential that critical questions continue to be asked about policy. Policy research does not have a direct impact but it does have a role in informing future policy decisions, with possible profound effects on the teaching and learning of geography.

All the research into geographical education mentioned so far is underpinned by views about the purposes of geographical education. What sort of geography and what sort of educational practices are valued in the research and why? Whose interests do they serve? It is important that these bigger questions about what is valued and why are not ignored in research directly focused on teaching and learning. In this section I would include research which maps other research into different ideologies, revealing underpinning values (e.g. Slater, 1996). The role of this research, like the other research referred to in this section, is more diffuse, but has the power to change the way we think about teaching and learning.

CONCLUSIONS

I would now like to return to the questions raised at the beginning of this chapter: What is worth researching? What evidence is provided by research to support the teaching and learning of geography? Can it help teachers construct their views on what is worth aiming for?

The model in Figure 24.1 has provided a framework for revealing areas of attention and neglect in geography education research. There is undoubtedly scope for more sustained detailed research in every sector of the model, including areas which have received most attention such as textbook research and children's understanding of maps. I would, however, highlight some areas of neglect:

- children's prior understanding of concepts in human geography;
- resources other than textbooks, with attention to the implications of accessibility of new and varied sources of data;
- learners' uses and understanding of resources other than maps;
- processes of teaching and learning in real-life classroom situations.

There is also a need for research that investigates issues through a range of scales, from the individual learner to the social and cultural context, and from national policy to how it impacts on learning in the classroom.

Some geography education research provides evidence that would seem to be of direct relevance to teaching and learning in the classroom. For example, research on misunderstandings of geographical concepts, on how children understand maps, how writing frames can support learning, and curriculum development projects all provide ideas and strategies to improve teaching and learning. Action research, involving classroom teachers, has direct implications for improving practice.

However, the application of the 'evidence' from research entails more than copying the strategies that others have developed. It often demands significant changes in thinking about teaching and learning. Educational research aimed at increasing knowledge and understanding of the processes of teaching, learning and assessment can lead to insights that can be profoundly influential.

I would not value research that has the potential to be applied directly to teaching and learning more than I would value research which is more diffuse in its influence. The role of research in supporting teaching and learning in geography is greater than providing information on what works in the classroom. It also has a role in challenging assumptions, in identifying underpinning values and in asking critical questions about purposes. Research into geographical education can help us see things differently and freshly. It can empower teachers to construct their own understandings, to clarify their own values and to have professional confidence to make changes in classroom practices.

REFERENCES

Blades, M. and Spencer, C. (1987) 'Young children's recognition of environmental features from aerial photographs and maps', *Environmental Education and Information*, vol. 6, no. 3, pp.

189–98.

Butt, G. (1993) 'The effects of audience-centred teaching on children's writing in geography', *International Research in Geographical and Environmental Education (IRGEE)*, vol. 2, no. 1, pp. 11–25.

Carter, R. (1991) *Talking about Geography: The Work of Geography Teachers*. Sheffield: Geographical Association.

Corney, G. (1997) 'Conceptions of environmental education', in Slater, F., Lambert, D. and Lines, D. (eds), *Education, Environment and Economy: Reporting Research in a New Academic Grouping*, (Bedford Way Papers). London: University of London Institute of Education, pp. 37–56.

Daugherty, R. (1996) 'Assessment in geographical education', in Williams, M. (ed.), *Understanding Geographical and Environmental Education: The Role of Research.*, London: Cassell.

Dove, J. (1996) 'Student misconceptions on the greenhouse effect, ozone layer depletion and acid rain', *Environmental Education Research*, vol. 2, no. 1, pp. 89–100.

Driver, R. (1994) *Making Sense of Secondary Science: Research into Children's Ideas*. London: Routledge.

Foskett, N. and Marsden, B. (eds) (1998) *A Bibliography of Geographical Education 1970–1997*. Sheffield: Geographical Association.

Hannon, P. (1998) 'An ecological perspective on educational research', in Rudduck, R. and McIntyre, D. (eds), *Challenges for Educational Research*, London: Paul Chapman.

Hargreaves, D. (1998) 'A new partnership of stakeholders and a national strategy of research in education', in Rudduck, J. and McIntyre, D. (eds), *Challenges for Educational Research*. London: Paul Chapman, pp. 114–36.

Hicks, D. (1980) 'Bias in books', *World Studies Journal*, vol. 1, no. 3, pp. 14–22.

Job, D. (1996) 'Geography and environmental education: an exploration of perspectives and strategies', in Kent, A., Lambert, D., Naish, M. and Slater, F. (eds), *Geography in Education: Viewpoints on Teaching and Learning*. Cambridge: Cambridge University Press, pp. 22–49.

Lambert, D. (1994) 'Geography in the National Curriculum: a cultural analysis', in Walford, R. and Machon, P. (eds), *Challenging Times: Implementing the National Curriculum in Geography*. Cambridge: Cambridge Publishing Services, pp. 88–94.

Leat, D. and Nichols, A. (1999) *Mysteries Make You Think*. Sheffield: Geographical Association.

Lester, A. and Slater, F. (1996) 'Reader, text, metadiscourse and argument', in van der Schee, J., Schoenmaker, G., Trimp, H. and van Westrhenen, H. (eds), *Innovation in Geographical Education*. Utrecht/Amsterdam: Centrum voor Educatieve Geografie Vrije Universiteit, pp. 115–25.

Marsden, W. (1988) 'Continuity and change in geography textbooks: perspectives from the 1930s to the 1960s', *Geography*, vol. 73, no. 4, pp. 327–43.

Matthews, M.H. (1992) *Making Sense of Place: Children's Understanding of Large-Scale Environments*. Hemel Hempstead: Harvester Wheatsheaf.

Mercer, N. (1995) *The Guided Construction of Knowledge: Talk amongst Teachers and Learners*. Clevedon: Multilingual Matters.

Parsons, C. (1988) *The Curriculum Change Game: A Longitudinal Study of the Schools Council GYSL Project*. London: Falmer Press.

Rawling, E. (1992) 'The making of a national geography curriculum', *Geography*, vol. 77, no. 4, pp. 292–309.

Rickinson, M. (1999) 'People–environment issues in the geography classroom: towards an understanding of students' experiences', *International Research in Geographical and Environmental Education (IRGEE)*, vol. 8, no. 2.

Roberts, M. (1995) 'Interpretations of the geography national curriculum: a common curriculum for all?', *Journal of Curriculum Studies*, vol. 27, no. 2, pp. 187–205.

Robertson, M. (2000) 'Young people speak about the landscape', *Geography*, vol. 85, no. 1, pp. 24–36.

Rudduck, J. and McIntyre D. (eds) (1998) *Challenges for Educational Research*. London: Paul

Chapman.

Sheeran, Y. and Barnes, D. (1991) *School Writing*. Milton Keynes: Open University Press.

Slater, F. (1996) 'Illustrating research in geographical education', in Kent, A. et al. (eds), *Geography in Education: Viewpoints on Teaching and Learning*. Cambridge: Cambridge University Press, pp. 291–320.

Spencer, C., Blades, M. and Morsley, K. (1989) *The Child in the Physical Environment*. Chichester: John Wiley.

Wiegand, P. (1996) 'A constructivist approach to children's understanding of thematic maps', in van der Schee, J., Schoenmaker, G. et al. (eds), *Innovation in Geographical Education*. Utrecht/Amsterdam: Centrum voor Educatieve Geografie Vrije Universiteit, pp. 57–65.

Williams, M. (ed.) (1996) *Understanding Geographical and Environmental Education: The Role of Research*. London: Cassell.

Index